Mrs Anne Clarke

The Ideal Cookery Book

Mrs Anne Clarke

The Ideal Cookery Book

ISBN/EAN: 9783744786454

Printed in Europe, USA, Canada, Australia, Japan

Cover: Foto ©Andreas Hilbeck / pixelio.de

More available books at **www.hansebooks.com**

MRS. CLARKE'S
COOKERY BOOK.

THE QUEEN OF HOME.

THE LATEST AND THE BEST.

The Ideal Cookery Book

ECONOMY, WEALTH AND COMFORT IN THE HOUSEHOLD.

1,349

New, Useful and Unique Recipes

—— IN ——

Cookery and all Departments of Housekeeping.

By MRS. ANNE CLARKE,

ASSISTED BY SOME OF THE MOST SUCCESSFUL HOUSEKEEPERS AND HOME-MAKERS IN THE UNITED STATES, CANADA, FRANCE, GERMANY AND GREAT BRITAIN.

CHICAGO:
F. J. SCHULTE & COMPANY,
Publishers.

PREFACE.

As a general rule, I do not believe in prefaces, but feeling bound to submit to the time-honored custom, I am free to confess that, had I known the labor necessary to produce a *first-class* "COOKERY BOOK," I should hardly have had the resolution to commence it. However, I have done my utmost to make it useful and acceptable. The recipes have been most carefully compiled, and valuable assistance has been rendered me by friends in France, Germany, Great Britain and Canada, as well as in the United States, to all of whom I render my most sincere thanks. I also desire to record my grateful appreciation of the immense success my "COOKERY BOOK" has met with. The number of orders already received for it convinces me that I have supplied a real want, and that my book will help my sisters to lighten their toil and gladden the hearts of their families.

ANNE CLARKE.

CONTENTS.

	PAGE
PREFACE	5
INTRODUCTORY OBSERVATIONS	9
SOUPS	17
FISH	31
POULTRY AND GAME	49
MEATS:	
Beef	62
Pork	71
Veal	76
Mutton	84
CURRIES	93
GRAVIES	99
SAUCES	102
STOCKS	112
VEGETABLES	114
SALADS	137
PICKLES	143
EGGS	147
KETCHUPS	156
FORCEMEATS	161
BREAD AND CAKES	164
PASTRY AND PUDDINGS	198

CONTENTS.

Sweet Dishes	240
Dessert	248
Colorings for Confectionery	253
Ices and Creams	255
Preserves	268
Canned Fruits, &c.	279
Jellies	284
Milk, Butter and Cheese	294
Beverages	305
Wines and Brandies	318
Sick Room Cookery	327
The Doctor	342
What to Name the Baby	375
Index	387

INTRODUCTORY OBSERVATIONS.

"The number of inhabitants who may be supported in any country upon its internal produce depends about as much upon the state of the Art of Cookery as upon that of Agriculture; but if Cookery be of so much importance, it certainly deserves to be studied with the greatest of care. Cookery and Agriculture are arts of civilized nations. Savages understand neither of them."—*Count Rumford's Works*, Vol. 1.

The importance of the Art of Cookery is very great; indeed, from the richest to the poorest the selection and preparation of food often becomes the chief object in life. The rich man's table is luxuriously spread; no amount of money is spared in procuring the rarest delicacies of the season. Art and Nature alike contribute to his necessities. The less wealthy have, indeed, fewer resources, yet these may be greatly increased by the knowledge of what may be called trifling details and refinement in the art of cookery, which depend much more on the *manner* of doing a thing than on the cost attending it. To cook well, therefore, is immensely more important to the middle and working classes than to the rich, for they who live by the "sweat of their brow," whether mentally or physically, must have the requisite strength to support their labor. Even to the poor, whose very life depends upon the produce of the hard earned dollar, cookery is of the greatest importance. Every wife, mother, or sister should be a good plain cook. If she has servants she can direct them, and if not, so much the more must depend upon herself. To such we venture to give a few general hints. An old saying (to be found in one of the earliest cookery books): "First catch your hare, etc." has more significance than is generally supposed. To catch your hare well, you must spend your income judiciously. This is the chief thing. In our artificial state of society, every income, to keep up appearances, has at least half as much more to do than it can afford. In the selection of provisions, the *best* is generally the *cheapest*. Half a pound of good meat is more nutritious than three times the amount of inferior. As to vegetables buy them fresh. Above all, where an income is small, and there are many to feed, be careful that all the nourishment is retained in the food that is purchased. This is to be effected by careful cooking. Cleanliness is an imperative condition. Let all cooking utensils be clean and in order. Uncleanliness produces disorder, and disorder confusion. Time and money are thus wasted, dinner spoiled, and all goes wrong. In the cooking of meat by any process whatever, remember, above all, to cook the juices *in it*, not *out* of it.

BOILING.

In boiling, put the meat if fresh into cold water, or, if salt, into luke-warm. Simmer it very gently until done. It is a general rule to allow a quarter of an hour to every pound of meat; but in this, as in everything else, judgment must be used according to the bone and shape of the joint, and according to the taste of the eaters. All kinds of meat, fish, flesh, and fowl, should be boiled very slowly, and the scum taken off just as boiling commences. If meats are allowed to boil too fast they toughen, all their juices are extracted, and only the fleshy fibre, without sweetness, is left; if they boil too long they are reduced to a jelly, and their nourishing properties are transferred to the water in which they are boiled. Nothing is more difficult than to boil meat exactly as it should be; close attention and good judgment are indispensable.

ROASTING.

In roasting meat the gravy may be retained in it by pricking the joint all over with a fork and rubbing in pepper and salt. Mutton and beef may be underdone, veal and pork must be well cooked. Young meat generally requires more cooking than old; thus lamb and veal must be more done than mutton and beef. In frosty weather meat will require a little more time for cooking. All joints for roasting will improve by hanging a day or so before cooking.

BROILING.

Broiling is the most nutritious method of cooking mutton and pork chops, or beef and rump steaks, kidneys (which should never be cut open before cooking), etc. Have the gridiron clean, and put over a clear fire; put the meat on it; "keep it turned often." This last is a common direction in books but the reason why is never stated; it is to keep the gravy in the meat. By letting the one side of a steak be well done before turning, you will see the red gravy settled on the top of the steak, and so the meat is hard and spoiled. This is cooking the gravy out of, instead of keeping it in, the meat to nourish the consumer. Never stick the fork in the meaty part; you will lose gravy if you do. Be sure to turn often, and generally the chop or steak is done if it feels firm to the fork; if not done, it will be soft and flabby. It is economical to broil well. Many a very little piece of meat, nicely broiled, with gravy in it, well seasoned with pepper and salt, a very little butter on it, and served up quite hot, will make a better and more nourshing meal than four times the amount of badly-cooked in the frying pan.

FRYING.

Although very bad for chops or steaks, the frying pan is indispensable for some things, such as veal cutlets, lamb chops (sometimes), fish, pancakes, etc. Most meats and fish are usually fried with egg and bread crumbs. The frying pan must be kept clean. This is very essential, as the dirt that sticks to the pan absorbs the fat, prevents the meat browning, and turns it a nasty black color. Have a clear brisk fire, as the quicker meat is fried the tenderer it is. According to what is to be fried, put little or much fat in the pan, fish and pancakes require a considerable quantity. The fat must always *boil* before putting the meat into it; if not, it coddles. For veal cutlets a little butter is best and most economical, as it helps to make the gravy; but even this expense may be dispensed with, if incompatible with the income of the family, and yet the cutlets be well cooked. Most have a few slices of bacon with either cutlets or liver; the fat from this, if the bacon be not rank, will do very nicely; and if the meat be well flavored and fried quickly, and some nice gravy made to it, few persons would know the difference. Some like thickened and some plain gravy to these fried meats; some a large quantity, others very little; all these must be accommodated. To make these gravies, have ready a little burnt sugar to brown with; empty the pan of the fat, if it be, as is most likely, too rank to use; put some warm water, as much as you wish to make, in the pan; mix very smoothly sufficient flour and water to thicken it to taste; into this put as much butter as you like to use (a little will do, more will make it richer); pepper and salt it sufficiently; stir it very smoothly into the pan, while the water is only warm; stir it well until it boils, and brown it with the burnt sugar to your taste. This will be a cheap and very nice gravy for all fried meats; and where meat is short, children are very fond of such over potatoes, haricot beans, or even bread in their plates; and not being too rich or greasy it will not disagree with them. Care must be taken after the gravy is boiled not to let it boil fast for any length of time, as all *thickened* gravies, hashes, etc., boil away very fast and dry up; neither must it stand still in the pan; a whitish scum then settles on the top and spoils the appearance of it. On the plainest and humblest dinner table, dishes may as well look inviting. N. B.—For all frying purposes be particular that the pan is thoroughly hot before using.

SOUPS.

1. **CROWDIE, or SCOTCH SOUP.**—Ingredients—2 gallons of liquor from meat, ½ pint of oatmeal, 2 onions, salt and pepper.

Any kind of liquor, either salt of fresh; remove all fat from it, and put in a stewpan. Mix the oatmeal with a ¼ of a pint of the liquor, into a smooth paste; chop the onions as finely as possible, and put them into the paste, add salt and pepper to taste. Allow the liquor to boil before stirring in the paste, boil twenty minutes, stirring occasionally to prevent it getting lumpy. N.B.—Salt to be omitted if salt liquor is used.

2. **MACARONI SOUP.**—Ingredients—5 cts. worth of bones, 1 tablespoonful of salt and peppercorns, 1 good sized turnip and 4 leeks, 2 carrots, 4 onions, 2 cloves, 1 blade of mace, 1 bunch of herbs, i. e. marjoram, thyme, lemon-thyme and parsley, ¼ lb. of macaroni.

Time required about 2½ hours. Break up the bones and put them into a stewpan with cold water enough to cover them and one quart more. When on the point of boiling put in a tablespoonful of salt to help the scum to rise, then take the turnip, peel it and cut it in quarters; then take two carrots, wash and scrape them; take also 4 leeks, wash and shred them up finely; now take 4 onions, peel them and stick 2 cloves into them; then skim the soup well and put in the vegetables, add a blade of mace and a teaspoonful of peppercorns, then allow soup to simmer gently for 2½ hours, then take ¼ lb. of macaroni, wash and put in a stewpan with plenty of cold water and a little salt. Allow it to boil until tender, then strain off the water and pour some cold water on, to wash the macaroni again; then cut in small pieces and it is ready for the soup. When the soup is ready for use strain it over the macaroni.

3. **MILK SOUP.**—Ingredients—4 potatoes, 2 leeks or onions, 2 oz. of butter, pepper, ¼ oz. of salt, 1 pint of milk, 3 tablespoonfuls of tapioca.

Put 2 qts. of water into a stewpan, then take 4 potatoes, peel and cut in quarters, take also 2 leeks, wash well in cold water and cut them up; when the water boils put in potatoes and leeks, then add the butter, salt, and pepper to taste. Allow it to boil to a mash, then strain the soup through a cullender, **working the vegetables through also**; return the pulp and the soup to the stewpan, add one pint of milk to it and boil; when boiling, sprinkle in by degrees tapioca, stirring all the time; then let it boil for 15 minutes gently.

4. **TAPIOCA SOUP.**—Ingredients—1 pint of white stock, 1 oz. of tapioca, yolks of 2 eggs, 2 tablespoonfuls of cream or milk, pepper and salt.

Put stock on to boil, then stir in gradually the tapioca, and allow it to simmer until quite clear, then to the yolks of the eggs add the cream or milk and stir with wooden spoon, strain into basin. Take stock from the fire to cool a little, add by degrees three tablespoonfuls of it to the liaison, stirring well all the time. Then mix all together, stir well, and add pepper and salt to taste. Warm before serving, but do not boil.

5. **SPRING VEGETABLE SOUP.**—Ingredients—2 lbs. of the shin of beef, 2 lbs. of knuckle of veal, a little salt, 2 young carrots, 1 turnip, 1 leek, ½ head of celery, 1 cauliflower, 1 gill of peas, ¼ of saltspoonful of carbonate of soda.

Cut the meat from the bone—do not use the fat; break the bones in halves, do not use the marrow. Put the meat and bones into a stock pot with five pints of cold water, a teaspoonful of salt will assist the scum to rise, boil quickly and remove scum as it rises, then simmer gently five hours. Cut carrots and turnips in slices, the head of celery and leek wash well and cut in squares, put the cauliflower in sprigs after washing. One hour before serving add vegetables; the sprigs of cauliflower can be put in fifteen minutes before serving. Put one gill of peas, a teaspoonful of salt, a quarter of a saltspoonful of soda into boiling water and boil fifteen minutes, then put peas in tureen and pour soup over them.

6. **GOOD GRAVY SOUP.**—Ingredients—1 lb. of beef, 1 lb. of veal, 1 lb. of mutton, 6 quarts of water, 1 crust of bread, 1 carrot, 1 onion, a little summer savory, 4 cloves, pepper, and a blade of mace.

Cut the meat in small pieces and put into the water, with the crust of bread toasted very crisp. Peel the carrot and onion, and, with a little summer savory, pepper, four cloves, and a blade of mace, put in the stew-pan. Cover it and let it stew slowly until the liquor is reduced to three qts. Then strain it, take off the fat, and serve with sippets of toast.

7. **SCOTCH MUTTON BROTH.**—Ingredients—2 qts. of water, neck of mutton, 4 or 5 carrots, 4 or 5 turnips, 3 onions, 4 large spoonfuls of Scotch barley, salt to taste, some chopped parsley.

Soak a neck of mutton in water for an hour; cut off the scrag, and put it into a stew-pot with two quarts of water. As soon as it boils skim it well, and then simmer it an hour and a half; then take the best end of the mutton, cut it into pieces (two bones in each), take some of the fat off, and put as many as you think proper; skim the moment the fresh meat boils up, and every quarter of an hour afterwards. Have ready four or five carrots, the same number of turnips, and three onions, all cut, but not small, and put them in soon enough to get quite tender; add four large spoonfuls of Scotch barley, first wetted with cold water. The meat should stew three hours. Salt to taste, and serve all together. Twenty minutes before serving put in some chopped parsley. It is an excellent winter dish.

8. **A ROAST BEEF AND BOILED TURKEY SOUP.**—Ingredients—Bones of a turkey and beef, 2 or 3 carrots, 2 or 3 onions, 2 or 3 turnips, ½ doz. cloves, pepper, salt, and tomatoes, 2 tablespoonfuls of flour, some bread.

Take the liquor that the turkey is boiled in, and the bones of the turkey and beef; put them into a soup-pot with two or three carrots, turnips, and onions, half a dozen cloves, pepper, salt, and tomatoes, if you have any; boil it four hours, then strain all out. Put the soup back into the pot, mix two tablespoonfuls of flour into a little cold water; stir it into the soup; give it one boil. Cut some bread dice form, lay it in the bottom of the tureen, pour the soup on to it, and color with a little soy.

9. **VEAL OR LAMB SOUP.**—Ingredients—Knuckle of veal, 2 onions, 5 or 6 turnips, some sweet marjoram, salt and cayenne pepper, flour, 6 or 8 potatoes, a few dumplings, 1 tablespoonful of burnt sugar.

Take a knuckle of veal crack the bone, wash, and put it on to boil in more than sufficient water to cover it. After boiling some time, pare, cut, and wash two onions, five or six turnips, and put in with the meat. When this has boiled one hour, add some sweet marjoram, rubbed fine, with salt and cayenne pepper to taste. Then take flour, which mix with cold water to the consistency of cream, and add to the soup while boiling. Care must be taken not to make it too thick. Then pare and cut into small pieces six or eight potatoes, which add about half an hour before being served; and about ten minutes before sending to table put in a few dumplings. As veal makes a white soup, the color is much improved by adding a tablespoonful of burnt sugar. This soup may be thickened with rice, if preferable.

10. **FRENCH SOUP.**—Ingredients—1 sheep's head, 3 qts. of water, 1 bunch of sweet herbs, 1 teacupful of pearl barley, 6 onions, 1 turnip, 1 carrot, few cloves, wineglass of white wine, mushroom catsup, butter and flour.

Take one sheep's head, remove the brains, and steep it as

before. Put it into a saucepan with three quarts of water, one teacupful of pearl barley, six onions, one turnip, one carrot, a bunch of sweet herbs, and a few cloves. Let it simmer gently for about five hours, then remove the head; strain and rub the vegetables through a sieve, or leave them whole, according to taste. Let it stand all night, and when cold take off every particle of fat; cut up the meat from the head into small pieces, and warm it up in the soup. Season to taste, add a wineglassful of white wine, a little mushroom ketchup, and thicken with butter and flour. This will be found very little inferior to mock turtle soup.

11. **GREEK SOUP.**—Ingredients—4 lbs. of lean beef, 1 lb. of lean mutton, 1 lb. of veal, 4 oz. of lean ham, 4 carrots, 4 onions, 1 head of celery, a little soy, a few allspice and a few coriander seeds, some pepper and salt, 10 quarts of water.

Cut up the beef, mutton, and veal into small pieces, and throw into a stewpan with ten quarts of cold water; add a little salt, and then place on the stove to boil; take off the scum, add a little cold water, and take off the second scum; then cut up the carrots, onions, and celery and throw in the pot; add a little more salt, a few allspice, and coriander seeds; let it simmer six hours, color the soup with a little soy, and strain it through a fine cloth; take off any fat that may be on the soup with a sheet of paper; before sending to table boil the soup, and place in the tureen a little fried lean ham cut into small pieces.

12. **GIBLET SOUP.**—Ingredients—3 sets of ducks' giblets, 2lbs. of beef, some bones, shank bones of two legs of mutton, 3 onions, some herbs, pepper and salt, carrots, 3 quarts of water, ¼ pint of cream, 1 oz. of butter, 1 spoonful of flour.

Thoroughly clean three sets of ducks' giblets, cut them in pieces, and stew with two lbs. of beef, some bones, the shank bones of two legs of mutton, three small onions, some herbs, pepper and salt to taste, and carrots, for three hours in three quarts of water. Strain and skim, add one quarter pint of cream mixed with one ounce of butter kneaded with a spoonful of flour and serve with the giblets. (Only the gizzard should be cut.)

13. **CALF'S HEAD SOUP.**—Ingredients—7 lbs. of shin of beef, a little lean ham, 5 qts. of water, 1 oz. of salt, savory herbs, 1 onion, some celery, 3 carrots, 2 turnips, a little mace, 8 or 10 cloves, some peppercorns, ½ calf's head, 8 oz. of fine rice flour, ¼ teaspoonful of cayenne, some pounded mace, 2 glasses of sherry, some forcemeat.

Stew seven lbs. of shin of beef with a little lean ham in five quarts of water till reduced one-half, adding, when boiling, one ounce of salt, savoury herbs, one onion, some celery, three carrots, two turnips, a little mace, eight or ten cloves, some peppercorns. It should gently boil seven hours and then be set aside for use. In this stock stew half a boned calf's head, rolled and tied with a string, half an hour; let it cool in the liquor, strain and skim and heat five pints in a large saucepan with the flesh of the head cut into dice; use all the skin and tongue but only part of the flesh. Simmer till quite tender, stirring in eight oz. of fine rice flour, one quarter teaspoonful of cayenne, pounded mace, and some more broth or water if thicker than batter. Boil ten minutes, add two glasses of sherry, and serve the soup with fried forcemeat.

14. **MULLAGATAWNY SOUP.**—Ingredients—Some good butter, 3 or 4 large onions, limbs of a rabbit or fowl, 5½ pints of boiling stock, 2 tablespoonfuls of currie powder, and 3 of browned flour, a little cold stock and meat, part of a pickled mango, some carefully boiled rice, the juice of a lemon.

Slice and fry in some good butter three or four large onions; put them in a saucepan with a little butter, and brown in it the limbs of a rabbit or fowl well floured. Add one quart of good boiling stock, and stew gently one hour. Pass the stock and onions through a strainer, add one and a half pints more stock, put it in a clean pan, and when boiling add two tablespoonsful of currie powder mixed with three of browned flour, a little cold stock and meat, and simmer 20 minutes. Part of a pickled mango cut into shreds is often served with the soup, and some like the taste of freshly grated cocoa nut, but it is by no means generally admired. Send to table with carefully boiled rice. The juice of a lemon added before serving is an improvement.

15. **OYSTER SOUP A LA REINE.**—Ingredients—2 or 3 doz. small oysters, some pale veal stock, 2 qts. of stock, mace, cayenne, 1 pt. boiling cream.

Two or three dozen small oysters to each pint of soup should be prepared. Take the beards and simmer them separately in a little very pale veal stock thirty minutes. Heat two quarts of the stock, flavor with mace and cayenne, and add the strained stock from the oyster beards. Simmer the fish in their own liquor, add to it the soup and one pint of boiling cream. Put the oysters in a tureen, pour over the soup, and serve. If not thick enough thicken with arrowroot or butter mixed with flour.

16. **CHICKEN SOUP** (Brown).—Ingredients—One or two fowls, a bunch of herbs, 1 carrot, 1 onion, 2 oz. lean ham, 2 oz. of butter, pepper and salt, 2 quarts of good stock, and a little roux, a few allspice, a little grated nutmeg and mace.

Cut up the carrot and onion, and fry in 2 oz. of good butter a nice light brown, add the ham and fowls cut up small, taking care to break up the bones with a chopper, add the stock, and boil until the fowl is cooked to rags; thicken with a little roux, add the allspice and mace and a little grated nutmeg, color with a little soy, add seasoning to taste. Serve with the soup some plain boiled rice.

17. **BEEF GRAVY SOUP.**—Ingredients—Some beef water, 2 oz. of salt to every gal. of water, 4 turnips, 2 carrots, some celery, 4 young leeks, 6 cloves, 1 onion, ½ teaspoonful of peppercorns, some savory herbs.

Various parts of beef are used for this; if the meat, after the soup is made, is to be sent to the table, rump steak or the best parts of the leg are generally used, but if soup alone is wanted, part of the shin with a pound from the neck will do very well. Pour cold water on the beef in the soup pot and heat the soup slowly, the slower the better, letting it simmer beside the fire, strain it carefully, adding a little cold water now and then, put in two oz. of salt for every gallon of water, skim again, and put in four turnips, two carrots, some celery, four young leeks, six cloves stuck into an onion, half a teaspoonful of peppercorns, and some savory herbs; let the soup boil gently for six hours; strain.

18. **RICE-FLOUR SOUP.**—Ingredients—A little cold broth, 8 oz. of fine rice-flour, 2 qts. of fast boiling broth, mace, cayenne and salt, 2 dessert spoonfuls of currie powder, juice of ½ a lemon.

Mix to a smooth batter, with a little cold broth, eight oz. of fine rice flour, and pour it into a couple of quarts of fast boiling broth or gravy soup. Add to it a seasoning of mace and cayenne, with a little salt if needful. It will require but ten minutes boiling. Two dessert spoonfuls of currie powder, and the strained juice of half a moderate sized lemon, will greatly improve this soup; it may also be converted into a good common white soup (if it be made of real stock) by the addition of three quarters of a pint of thick cream to the rice.

19. **MILK SOUP WITH VERMICELLI.**—Ingredients—Salt, 5 pints of boiling milk, 5 oz. of fresh vermicelli.

Throw a small quantity of salt into five pints of boiling milk, and then drop lightly into it five oz. of good fresh vermicelli; keep the milk stirred as this is added, to prevent its gathering into lumps, and continue to stir it very frequently from fifteen to twenty minutes, or until it is perfectly tender. The addition of a little pounded sugar and powdered cinnamon makes this a very palatable dish. For soup of this description, rice, semolina, sago, cocoa-nut, sago and maccaroni, may all be used, but they will be required in rather smaller proportions to the milk.

20. **GREEN PEA SOUP.**—Ingredients—4 lbs. of beef, ½ pk. of green peas, 1 gal. of water, ½ cup of rice-flour, salt, pepper and chopped parsley.

Four lbs. beef, cut into small pieces, half a peck of green peas, one gallon water, half a cup of rice-flour, salt, pepper and chopped parsley; boil the empty pods of the peas in the water one hour before putting in the beef. Strain them out, add the beef, and boil slowly for an hour and a half longer. Half an hour before serving, add the shelled peas, and twenty minutes later, the rice-flour, with salt, pepper and parsley. After adding the rice-flour, stir frequently, to prevent scorching. Strain into a hot tureen.

21. **CELERY SOUP.**—Ingredients—The white part of three heads of celery, half a lb. of rice, 1 onion, 1 quart of stock, 2 quarts of milk, pepper and salt, and a little roux.

Cut up the celery and onions very small, boil them in the stock until quite tender, add the milk and the rice, and boil together until quite a pulp, add pepper and salt and a little roux, strain through a fine hair sieve or metal strainer, and boil a few minutes, taking care it does not burn. Serve some small croutons of fried bread with it.

22. **TOMATO SOUP.**—Ingredients—4 lbs. of tomatoes, 2 onions, 1 carrot, 2 quarts of stock or broth, pepper and salt, a little roux, 2 oz. of fresh butter.

Cut up the onions and carrot, place them in a stewpan with the butter, and lightly fry them. Take the seeds out of the tomatoes, then put them in the stewpan with the fried onions and carrot, add the stock, pepper and salt, and let them boil for one hour, occasionally stirring them: add a little roux to thicken the soup, and strain through a fine hair sieve. Serve the soup very hot, and send to table with it some small pieces of fried bread, sprinkled with chopped parsley.

23. **WHITE SOUP.**—Ingredients—6 oz. of sweet almonds, 6 oz. of the breast of roasted chicken, 3 oz. of white bread, some veal stock, 1 pint of thick cream.

Pound six oz. of sweet almonds, six oz. of the breast of roasted chicken, and three oz. of white bread soaked in veal stock and squeezed dry. Beat all to a paste and pour over it two quarts of boiling veal stock, strain through a hair sieve, add one pint of thick cream, and serve as soon as it is on the point of boiling.

24. **APPLE SOUP.**—Ingredients—12 large fresh apples, 2 spoonfuls of sugar or syrup, ½ lb of raisins or apples, 1 spoonful of potato meal.

Dry well twelve large fresh apples, cut them in quarters, and put them into a pan with boiling water. When the soup has a strong taste of apples, strain it through a hair sieve, and add more water, until there are about nine pints ; add two good spoonfuls of sugar or syrup, half a pound of well-washed and picked raisins, or apples pared and cut in pieces, which must be boiled until soft. The soup is to be thickened with a good spoonful of potato-meal, dissolved in a little water. It is best cold.

25. **SOUP A LA DAUPHINE**.—Ingredients—Six pounds of lean beef, 4 carrots, 2 turnips, 4 onions, 1 head of celery, 4 oz. of lean ham, pepper and salt, a little soy, 2 bay leaves, a bunch of herbs, a few allspice, 2 blades of mace, 5 quarts of water.

Cut up the onions, carrots, turnips, and celery into small pieces, and lay in the bottom of a large stewpan ; cut up the six lbs. of lean beef, and lay on the top of the vegetables, sprinkle a little salt over it, and cook over the fire (taking care it does not burn) for two hours, add five quarts of water, and bring it to the boil ; take off the fat and scum, add a little more cold water, and throw in two blades of mace, two bay leaves, a bunch of herbs, four oz. of lean ham cut up very fine, and a few allspice, color a light brown with a little soy, and simmer for five hours, and then strain through a fine cloth, and with a sheet of paper take off any floating fat; boil again, and before serving throw in the soup some green taragon leaves and a little chervil.

26. **JULIENNE SOUP**.—Ingredients—1 carrot, 1 turnip, 1 stick of celery, 3 parsnips, 2 or 3 cabbage leaves, butter, 1 lettuce, 1 handful of sorrel and chervil, stock, salt and pepper.

Cut in very small slices a carrot, a turnip, a stick of celery, three parsnips, and two or three cabbage leaves, put them in a saucepan with butter and give them a nice color, shaking the saucepan to prevent them from sticking to the bottom, then add a lettuce and a handful of sorrel and chervil torn in small pieces, moisten these with stock and leave them on the fire for a few minutes, then boil up, add the whole of the stock and boil gently for three hours ; season with salt and pepper.

27. **MULLAGATAWNY**.—Ingredients—1 chicken or rabbit, butter, flour, 2 qts. of veal stock, salt, white pepper, curry powder, cayenne pepper and salt, 1 large spoonful of rice, ½ pint of cream.

Stew a chicken or a rabbit in a little butter until tender, and when done wash in warm water. Put a little butter and flour in another stewpan, stir for five minutes, then add two quarts of good veal stock in which you have boiled carrots, turnips, celery and onions ; the stock being also flavored with salt and white pepper, and carefully skimmed and strained. Boil for fifteen minutes, then add the chicken or rabbit cut in small pieces, flavor with curry powder, cayenne pepper and salt, put in a large spoonful of rice, and boil until the rice is tender. Skim carefully, and before serving stir in half a pint of cream. The quantity of curry powder must depend upon taste; two tablespoonfuls will probably be sufficient for this quantity of soup.

28. **SPANISH SOUP** (1).—Ingredients—1½ lbs. of mutton or veal, 1½ lbs. of garbanzos or chick peas, 1 slice of lean raw ham, remnants of game or poultry, a little bacon, salt, vegetables.

Throw one lb. and a half of either mutton or veal in a vessel, with water (the Spaniards use a pipkin, called in the vernacular a "marmite,"), one lb. and a half of "garbanzos," or chick peas, one good slice of lean raw ham, and any *debris* (no matter how small) of game or poultry. Cook gently with the lid on, skim, and add a little bacon cut small, and as much salt as necessary; cook for another half-hour, then pour off the broth slowly, to be used afterwards for the soup and sauce; add as much vegetable as you please, thoroughly well washed, and cook over a clear fire until done. About five minutes before the Olla is ready, it is *de rigueur* in Madrid kitchens to throw in a piece of "chorizo" (black pudding). Serve the meat separately on one dish, the vegetables on another, and in a third the sauce for the whole, either of the following being appropriate.

TOMATO.—Cook three or four large juicy tomatoes until quite tender, and pass them through a sieve. Add some of the broth, some vinegar and salt, to the purée.

PARSLEY.—Pound some young parsley and bread crumbs in a mortar. Moisten with the broth, add vinegar and salt to taste.

These sauces should properly be served in a small silver or china bowl, surrounded by vegetables. For the tomato, spring and summer vegetables, and for the parsley sauce, those of autumn and winter are customarily used, with the rigorous exclusion, in both cases, of cabbage.

A Cocido compounded of the above ingredients, without the auxiliary black pudding or vegetables, the Spaniards call a "Puchero," de los enfermas.

29. **SPANISH SOUP** (2).—Ingredients—1 clove of garlic, 7 well-dried beans or almonds, olive oil and water, vinegar and salt, breadcrumbs.

The second soup, Ajo blanco, or white garlic soup, is more intricate in its manufacture, though compounded of as quaint and unlikely materials. It is extensively eaten in Andalusia To be completely varacious, I must of necessity commence with that formidable brother to our harmless, necessary little onion—big garlic. Pound one clove of garlic and seven well-dried beans, or better still, almonds, in a small spice mortar to a smooth paste. Moisten this paste with olive oil, drop by drop, then water by degrees, so as to thoroughly incorporate and amalgamate the whole. Add until it is sufficiently wet to soak some bread, which must be added later on, pouring in some vinegar and a little salt. Then put in the bread crumbs, size of half an almond, and allow it to soak. A final mixing of the bowl, and this quaint and perfectly national dish awaits your consumption.

30. **SPANISH SOUP** (3).—Ingredients—Chives, cucumber, some water, 1 pinch of salt, some lemon juice, some oil, crumbled bread, chopped marjoram.

Put some chopped chives and cucumber cut up in the shape of dice into a large salad bowl, add a small quantity of water, a pinch of salt, lemon juice and oil. Throw in some crumbled bread, which must be able to float. Finally sprinkle some fine chopped marjoram over the whole, and your "gaspacho" is ready.

31. **ALMOND SOUP.**—Ingredients—Some sweet almonds, pounded white sugar, pounded cinnamon, bread.

This is the usual dish for a Christmas supper, and is eaten hot. It is of almost Arcadian simplicity. Throw some sweet almonds in boiling water to get rid of the husk, skin and pound them in a mortar with some *lukewarm* water, adding by degrees pounded white sugar and pounded cinnamon; turn it out on a plate or dish, which must be able to stand the fire, previously lining the bottom with fingers of bread powdered with cinnamon. Thoroughly heat these ingredients over a clear fire and serve.

32. **BARLEY SOUP (CREME D'ORGE).**—Ingredients—½ pint of pearl barley, 1 qt. of white stock, the yolk of 1 egg, 1 gill of cream, ½ pat of fresh butter, bread.

Boil half a pint of pearl barley in a quart of white stock till it is reduced to a pulp, pass it through a hair sieve, and add to it as much well-flavored white stock as will give a purée of the consistency of cream; put the soup on the fire, when it boils stir into it, off the fire, the yolk of an egg beaten up with a gill of cream; add half a pat of fresh butter, and serve with small dice of bread fried in butter.

33. **LOBSTER SOUP (BISQUE).**—Ingredients—1 lobster, butter, pepper, salt, and grated nutmeg, breadcrumbs, stock, 1 tablespoonful of flour, bread.

Pick out all the meat from a lobster, pound it in a mortar with an equal quantity of butter until a fine orange-colored pulp is obtained; to this add pepper, salt, and grated nutmeg to taste. Take as much bread crumbs as there is lobster pulp, soak them in stock, then melt a piece of butter in a saucepan, amalgamate with it a heaped tablespoonful of flour; mix the lobster pulp with the bread crumbs, and put them into the saucepan with the butter and flour, stir well, and add more stock until a purée is obtained, rather thinner in consistency than the soup should be. Put the saucepan on the fire, stirring the contents until they thicken and boil; draw it then on one side, and carefully skim off superfluous fat, then strain the soup through a hair sieve, make it boiling hot, and serve with small dice of bread fried in butter.

34. **SOUP MADE FROM BONES.**—Ingredients—Bones of any freshly roasted meat, remnants of any poultry or game, fresh livers, gizzards, necks, combs of any poultry, 1 slice of lean ham, salt, 1 onion, 1 turnip, 1 leek, 1 head of celery, 4 carrots, 3 tomatoes, ¼ of bay leaf, 3 or 4 cloves, 6 peppercorns, 3 allspice, 1 bunch of parsley and chervil, tapioca, sago, vermecelli or semolina.

Have the bones of any freshly roasted meat—beef, veal, pork, venison, mutton or lamb—broken up into largish pieces. the four first sorts may be mixed with advantage, while mutton and lamb are better alone. Add the carcases or remaining limbs of any roast poultry—ducks, fowls, pigeons, geese, turkey or game, and the fresh livers, gizzards, necks, and combs of any poultry you happen to be going to cook the same day, and a slice of lean ham if you have it. Put all these together in an earthen soup pan that will stand the fire and will hold one-third more cold water than you require for your soup to allow for the loss in boiling; fill with water, and place on a brisk fire till it boils. Then add salt (less quantity if there be ham in the soup), one large onion, one large turnip, one large leek, one head of celery, four large carrots, three sliced tomatoes, a quarter of a bay leaf, three or four cloves stuck into a carrot or turnip, six whole peppercorns, and as much more ground as is liked, three allspice whole, and, finally, a good-sized bunch of parsley and chervil tied together. We find a piece of calf's liver and a fresh young cabbage an improvement, but this is a matter of taste. When boiling skim thoroughly, and take the pot off the fire, placing it quite at the edge so as merely to simmer gently—or, as the French call it, to *smile*—for six hours at least. The great art in making this sort of simple broth is never to let the fire go down too much, nor to allow the soup to boil too fast, so as not to require filling up with other water to replace what has been consumed—or, rather, wasted by rapid ebullition. Half an hour before you require your soup take it off the fire and strain through a cullender, then through a fine sieve, and put it on a brisk fire. When quite boiling add tapioca, sago, vermicelli, or semolina, scattering it lightly, and allowing one tablespoonful to each person. Rice may also be used, but it requires a full half hour, and consumes more broth. We use this broth as a foundation to every kind of vegetables purées.

35. HARE SOUP.—Ingredients—1 hare (newly killed), 1 lb. of lean beef, 1 slice of ham, 1 carrot, 2 onions, some herbs, roll crumbs, salt, pepper, 3 qts. water, ¼ bottle port, the liver of the animal.

For this purpose, if possible, a young newly-killed animal should be used; in cleaning and skinning it preserve the blood and liver; cut it in pieces and put it in a saucepan with one pound of lean beef, a slice of ham, a carrot, two onions, some herbs, the crumb of two rolls, some salt, pepper, and three quarts of water; let it boil gently for eight hours; add quarter of a bottle of port; chop the liver and mix it with the blood, and put the mixture into the saucepan, stirring well for a little while, then remove the pieces of hare, bone them and cut them in small pieces, pass the soup through a hair sieve and then put back the pieces of hare before serving.

36. OXTAIL SOUP (Clear).—Ingredients—1 oxtail, 4 carrots, 4 onions, 2 turnips, 1 bunch of herbs, little allspice, 1 head of celery, 2 qts. of good stock, a little soy, 2 glasses of sherry, pepper, salt, ½ lb. of lean beef.

Cut up the oxtail into small pieces, well blanch them in salt and water, boil them in water, throw into cold water. Cut up the vegetables into small pieces (taking care to save some of the best pieces for boiling to go in the soup to table), throw them into a stewpan with the herbs, allspice, soy, pepper and salt, put the oxtail on the top, cover with the gravy, and cook until the tail is quite tender. When cooked, take out the tail, and cut up half a pound of lean beef quite fine and throw in the gravy, let it boil a few minutes, and strain through a cloth, add the pieces of tail and some pieces of carrot and turnip cooked as follows: Boil the vegetables in water, with a little sugar, salt, and a small piece of butter. Serve very hot.

37. OXTAIL SOUP (Thick).—Ingredients—1 oxtail, 6 carrots, 4 onions, 4 turnips, allspice, 1 head of celery, 1 qt. of water, 1 qt. of stock, a pinch of pepper, sugar and salt, a little sherry, some roux.

Cut up the oxtail into small pieces, throw them into cold water with a little salt, bring them to the boil, and throw them into clean cold water. Cut up the vegetables into a stewpan, place the oxtail on the top, cover with the water and stock, let it simmer until the oxtail is quite tender, take out the pieces of tail, add the roux to the gravy, also the sugar and the seasoning. Boil well together, strain through a fine hair sieve, taking care to pass the vegetable pulp through, add the sherry, drop in the pieces of tail, and bring to the boil. Let it stand on the side of the stove until wanted.

38. **MOCK TURTLE SOUP.**—Ingredients—A knuckle of veal, 2 cow's heels, 2 onions, a few cloves, a little allspice, mace and sweet herbs, 2½ qts. of water, 1 tablespoonful of sugar, 2 tablespoonfuls of walnut, 1 of mushroom catsup, 1 tablespoonful of lemon juice, forcemeat balls.

Put into a large pan or jar a knuckle of veal, two well-cleaned cow-heels, two onions, a few cloves, a little allspice, mace, and some sweet herbs; cover all with two and a half quarts of water, and set it in a hot oven for three hours. Then remove it, and when cold take off the fat very nicely, take away the bones and coarse parts, and when required, put the remainder on the fire to warm, with a tablespoonful of moist sugar, two of walnut, and one of mushroom catsup; add to these ingredients the jelly of the meat. When it is quite hot put in the forcemeat balls, and add a teaspoonful of lemon juice.

39. **MOCK TURTLE SOUP.**—Ingredients—½ a calf's head, ¼ lb. of butter, ¼ lb. of lean ham, two tablespoonfuls of minced parsley, a little minced lemon thyme, a little sweet marjoram and basil, two onions, a few chopped mushrooms, 2 shallots, 2 tablespoonfuls of flour, 1½ doz. forcemeat balls about the size of a nutmeg; cayenne and salt, to suit your taste; the juice of one lemon, and 1 Seville orange, 1 dessertspoonful of pounded sugar, 3 quarts of best stock.

Proceed as in Recipe No. 38.

40. **ONION SOUP.**—Ingredients—Water that has boiled a leg or neck of mutton, 1 shank bone, 6 onions, 4 carrots, 2 turnips, salt to taste.

Into the water that has boiled a leg or neck of mutton put the carrots and turnips, shank bone, and simmer two hours, then strain it on six onions, first sliced and fried a light brown, simmer three hours, skim carefully, and serve. Put into it a little roll or fried bread.

41. **ALMOND SOUP.**—Ingredients—4 lbs. of lean beef or veal, a few vegetables as for stock, 1 oz of vermicelli, 4 blades of mace, 6 cloves, ½ lb. sweet almonds, the yolks of 4 eggs, 1 gill of cream, 3 qts. of water.

Boil the beef or veal, vegetables, and spices gently in the water that will cover them, till the gravy is very strong, and the meat very tender; then strain off the gravy, and set it on the fire with the specified quantity of vermicelli to 2 quarts. Let boil till sufficiently cooked. Have ready the almonds, blanched and pounded very fine; the yolks of the eggs boiled hard; mixing the almonds, whilst pounding, with a little of the soup, lest the latter should grow oily. Pound them to a pulp and keep adding to them, by degrees, a little soup, until they are thoroughly mixed together. Let the soup be cool when mixing, and do it perfectly smooth. Strain it, set it on the fire, stir well and serve hot; just before taking it up add the cream.

42. **EEL SOUP.**—Ingredients—3 lbs. of eels, 1 onion, 1 oz. of butter, 3 blades of mace, 1 bunch of sweet herbs, ¼ oz. of peppercorns, salt, 2 tablespoonfuls of flour, ¼ pt. cream, 2 qts. water.

Wash the eels, cut them into thin slices and put them in the stew-pan with the butter; let them simmer for a few minutes, then pour the water to them, and add the onion cut in small slices, the herbs, mace and seasoning. Simmer till the eels are tender, but do not break the fish. Remove them carefully, mix flour smoothly to a batter with the cream, bring it to a boil, pour over the eels, and serve.

43. **TOMATO SOUP.**—Ingredients—8 middling sized tomatoes, 1 bundle of sweet herbs, 1 clove of garlic, 1 onion stuck with 3 or 4 cloves, a little allspice, whole pepper, salt to taste, 1 qt. of stock, 2 eggs.

Take tomatoes, cut them in two, and removing the pips of watery substance, put them in a saucepan, with a bundle of sweet herbs, a clove of garlic, an onion stuck with three or four cloves, some allspice, whole pepper, and salt to taste. Place the saucepan on a gentle fire, stirring contents occasionally. When the tomatoes are thoroughly done, turn them out on a hair sieve, remove the onion, garlic, and sweet herbs; remove also the moisture which will drip from the tomatoes; then work them through the sieve until nothing remains on the top but the skins. Have a quart of plain stock boiling hot, stir the tomato pulp into it, and, removing the saucepan from the fire, stir in two eggs, beaten up with a little cold water and strained. Serve over small dice of bread fried in butter.

44. **ASPARAGUS SOUP.**—Ingredients—25 heads of asparagus, 1 qt. of stock, 1 tablespoonful of flour, 1 oz. of butter, sugar, pepper and salt; some spinach greening, 1 pat of fresh butter or 1 gill of cream, small dice of bread.

Take twenty-five heads of asparagus, put them in a saucepan with a quart of stock, free from fat, let them boil till quite done; remove the asparagus, pound it in a mortar, then pass it through a sieve; mix a tablespoonful of flour and one ounce of butter in a saucepan on the fire, add a little sugar, pepper and salt, quantity sufficient for the asparagus pulp, and the stock in which the asparagus was originally boiled; let the whole come to a boil, then put in a little spinach greening, and lastly a pat of fresh butter, or stir in a gill of cream. Serve over small dice of bread fried in butter.

FISH.

OBSERVATIONS ON DRESSING FISH.

If the fishmonger does not clean it, fish is seldom very nicely done, but those in great towns wash it beyond what is necessary for cleaning, and so by much washing diminish the flavor. If to be boiled, some salt and a little vinegar should be put in the water to give firmness; but cod, whiting, and haddock are far better if salted and kept a day: and if not very hot weather they will be better kept two days. Those who know how to purchase fish, may by taking more than they want for one day, often get it cheaper; and such kinds as will pot or pickle, or keep by being sprinkled with salt, and hung up, or being fried will serve for stewing the next day, may then be bought with advantage. Fresh water fish have often a muddy smell and taste, to take off which soak it in strong salt and water after it is nicely cleaned, then dry and dress it. The fish must be put in the water while cold and set to do very gently, or the outside will break before the inner part is done. Crimp fish should be put into boiling water, and when it boils up put a little cold water in, to check extreme heat, and simmer it a few minutes. Small fish nicely fried, covered with egg and crumbs, make a dish far more elegant than if served plain. Great attention should be paid to the garnishing of fish, use plenty of horse-radish, parsley and lemon. If fish is to be fried or broiled it must be wrapped in a clean cloth after it is well cleaned. When perfectly dry, wet with an egg (if for frying) and sprinkle the finest bread crumbs over it, then, with a large quantity of lard or dripping boiling hot, plunge the fish into it and fry a light brown; it can then be laid on blotting paper to receive any grease. Butter gives a bad color, oil fries the finest color for those who will allow for the expense. Garnish with raw or fried parsley, which must be thus done: when washed and picked throw it again into clean water; when the lard or dripping boils, throw the parsley into it immediately from the water and instantly it will be green and crisp, and must be taken up with a slice. If fish is to be broiled, it must be seasoned, flavored and put on a gridiron that is very clean, which when hot should be rubbed with a piece of suet to prevent the fish from sticking. It must be broiled on a very clear fire and not too near or it may be scorched.

45. COD'S HEAD AND SHOULDERS (to Boil).—Ingredients —1 cod's head and shoulders, salt water, 1 glass of vinegar, horseradish.

Wash and tie it up, and dry with a cloth. Salt the water, and put in a glass of vinegar. When boiling, take off the scum; put the fish in, and keep it boiling very briskly about half an hour. Parboil the milt and roe, cut in thin slices, fry, and serve them. Garnish with horse-radish; for sauce, oysters, eggs, or drawn butter.

46. COD'S HEAD AND SHOULDERS.—Ingredients—1 bunch parsley, 1 lemon, horseradish, milt, roe and liver.

Tie it up, and put on the fire in cold water which will completely cover it; throw a handful of salt into it. Great care must be taken to serve it without the smallest speck of black or scum. Garnish with a large quantity of double parsley, lemon, horseradish, and the milt, roe and liver, and fried smelts if approved. If with smelts, be careful that no water hangs about the fish; or the beauty of the smelts will be taken off, as well as their flavor. Serve with plenty of oyster or shrimp sauce, and anchovy and butter. It will eat much finer by having a little salt rubbed down the bone, and along the thick part, even if to be eaten the same day.

Though it is important to buy fresh codfish, it is not quite so well to cook it immediately, as, when freshly caught, it is apt to be watery; but when rubbed with salt and kept a day or two, it acquires the firmness and creaminess so much prized. Cod is better crimped than when cooked whole, the operation of boiling being more successfully performed under these conditions. The fish may be partially crimped by scoring it at equal distances, without absolutely cutting it through into slices; but the effect of the operation is always to improve the fish. When thoroughly cleaned the cod should be scored or sliced at regular intervals of about one and a half or two inches, then washed clean in spring-water, and laid in a pan of spring-water in which a handful of salt has been allowed to dissolve. After about two hours' soaking in this brine, the fish may be washed and set to drain. Some people boil the cod whole; but a large head and shoulders contain all the fish that is proper to help, the thinner parts being overdone and tasteless, before the thick are ready. But the whole fish may be purchased at times more reasonably; and the lower half, if sprinkled and hung up, will be in high perfection in one or two days. Or it may be made salter, and served with egg-sauce, potatoes and parsnips.

47. SALT COD.—Ingredients—Cod, vinegar (1 glass), parsnips, cream, butter, flour.

Soak and clean the piece you mean to dress, then lay it all night in water, with a glass of vinegar. Boil it enough, then break it into flakes on the dish; pour over it parsnips boiled, beaten in a mortar, and then boiled up with cream and a large piece of butter rubbed with a little flour. It may be served as above with egg sauce instead of the parsnip, and the root sent up whole; or the fish may be boiled and sent up without flaking, and sauces as above.

48. CURRIE OF COD.—Ingredients—Salt and cayenne, cod, onions, white gravy, currie powder, butter, flour, 3 or 4 spoonsful of cream.

Should be made of sliced cod, that has been either crimped or sprinkled a day to make it firm. Fry it of a fine brown with onion; and stew it with a good white gravy, a little currie powder, a piece of butter and flour, three or four spoonfuls of rich cream, salt, and cayenne, if the powder be not hot enough.

49. CODS' ROES.—Ingredients—1 or more cod's roes, 1½ oz. of butter, 2 eggs, 1 teaspoonful of salt, 1 pinch of cayenne pepper, 1 grate of nutmeg, 1 dessertspoonful of tomato or Mogul sauce or vinegar.

Boil one or more cod's roes, according to size, till quite set and nearly done. Take them out of the water, and when cold cut them into slices three-quarters of an inch thick. Now put into a small stewpan one and a half oz. of butter; when made liquid over the fire, take it off and stir into it the yolks of two eggs, a small teaspoonful of salt, a pinch of cayenne pepper, a grate of nutmeg, and a dessert-spoonful of tomato or Mogul sauce, or the vinegar from any good pickle. Mix all well together, and stir it over the fire for two or three minutes to thicken. Dip the slices of cod's roe in this sauce to take up as much as they will, lay them in a dish, pour over them any of the sauce that may be left, put the dish into the oven for ten minutes, and send to table very hot.

50. COD-FISH CAKES.—Ingredients—1 salt codfish, potatoes, milk, butter.

Take salt cod-fish, or cold fresh fish, boiled; mince it fine with potatoes, moistened with a little milk, having a piece of butter in it. Mould into biscuit-sized cakes, and fry them to a light brown in butter or lard. They should be fried to the same color on both sides.

51. CRIMPED COD AND OYSTER SAUCE.—Ingredients—
Cod and salt water.

Cut into two-inch slices the best part of a fresh cod, boil them twenty to twenty-five minutes in boiling salted water; serve on a napkin with the sauce in a tureen.

52. COD STAKES (with Mock Oyster Sauce).—Ingredients
1 tail of cod or head and shoulders, salt, and breadcrumbs.

The most economical way of having cod steaks is to order either the tail of a good-sized cod or a cod's head and shoulders, so cut that there is sufficient to take off some steaks, and what remains comes in for luncheon or the children's dinner the following day. Sprinkle the cod with salt, and fry, either with or without bread crumbs, a golden brown.

53. CODFISH BALLS.—Ingredients—Equal quantities of potatoes and boiled codfish, 1 oz. of butter, 1 egg.

Take equal quantities of mashed potatoes and boiled codfish minced fine; to each half-pound allow one ounce of butter and a well-beaten egg; mix thoroughly. Press into balls between two spoons; drop into hot lard, and fry till brown.

54. SALT SALMON (to Souse).—Ingredients—1 salt salmon, cayenne, whole allspice, a little mace, cold vinegar.

Take a salt salmon, wash and cover it with plenty of clean water. Let it soak twenty-four hours, but be careful to change the water several times. Then scale it, cut it into four parts, wash, clean, and put on to boil. When half done change the water; and when tender, drain it, put it in a stone pan, sprinkle some cayenne, whole allspice, a few cloves, and a little mace over each piece; cover with cold vinegar. This makes a nice relish for tea.

55. SALMON (to Broil).—Ingredients—Salmon, pepper, salt.

Cut slices an inch thick, and season with pepper and salt; lay each slice in half a sheet of white paper well buttered, twist the ends of the paper, and broil the slices over a slow fire six or eight minutes. Serve in the paper with anchovy sauce.

56. SALMON (to Pot).—Ingredients—Salmon, a little mace, 6 cloves, 6 whole peppers, butter.

Take a large piece, scale and wipe, but do not wash it; salt very well, let it lie till the salt is melted and drained from it, then season with beaten mace, cloves, and whole pepper; lay in a few bay leaves, put it close into a pan, cover it over with butter, and bake it; when well done, drain it from the gravy, put it into the pots to keep, and when cold, cover it with clarified butter. In this manner you may do any firm fish.

57. SALMON (to Dry).—Ingredients—Salt, 3 or 4 oz. of saltpetre, 2 oz. of bay salt, 2 oz. coarse sugar.

Cut the fish down, take out the inside and roe. Rub the whole with common salt after scaling it; let it hang for 24 hours to drain. Pound three or four ounces of salt-petre, according to the size of the fish, two ounces of bay-salt, and two ounces of coarse sugar; rub these, when mixed well, into the salmon, and lay it on a large dish or tray two days, then rub it well with common salt, and in 24 hours more it will be fit to dry; wipe it well after draining. Hang it either in a wood chimney or in a dry place; keeping it open with two small sticks. Dried salmon is eaten broiled in paper, and only just warmed through; egg-sauce and mashed potatoes with it; or it may be boiled, especially the piece next the head.

58. SALMON (Dried).—Ingredients—Flakes of salmon, 2 eggs, 1 pint cream, 2 or 3 oz. butter, 1 teaspoonful of flour, mashed potatoes.

Pull some into flakes; have ready some eggs boiled hard, and chopped large; put both into half a pint of thin cream, and two or three ounces of butter rubbed with a teaspoonful of flour; skim it and stir till boiling hot; make a wall of mashed potatoes round the inner edge of a dish, and pour the above into it.

59. SALMON (Fried, with Anchovy Sauce).—Ingredients—Some thin slices from the tail end of a salmon, anchovy sauce, flour, bread-crumbs, eggs, water, a little roux, a little cayenne pepper, lard.

Scrape the scales off the tail end of a salmon, cut in thin slices, dip them in flour, then in two eggs whisked up with a tablespoonful of water, and a tablespoonful of anchovy sauce, then dip them in bread crumbs, and fry in boiling lard for eight or ten minutes; dish them up on a napkin in a nice heap, and sprinkle a little chopped parsley over them, and serve in a sauceboat some sauce.

60. SALMON (Dressed. Italian Sauce).—Ingredients—two slices, about 3 inches thick, of good salmon, 2 onions, 1 carrot, 1 shalot, 2 gherkins, a few preserved mushrooms and a few capers, 3 oz. of butter, a little chopped parsley, 1 tablespoonful of anchovy sauce, and a pint of good stock, and a little roux.

Cut up two onions and one carrot into thin slices, and lay them in the bottom of a baking dish with a little pepper and salt and one oz. of butter; lay the slices of salmon on the top of the vegetables, cover them with buttered paper, and bake for thirty-five minutes in a warm oven; when cooked, serve with sauce made as follows: Cut up one shalot very fine, and lightly fry in two oz. of butter, throw in a little chopped parsley, two gherkins chopped fine, and a few capers and mushrooms cut up very fine, and one pint of good stock, a little roux to thicken, and one tablespoonful of anchovy sauce and a little pepper; boil these ingredients together for thirty minutes, lift the salmon carefully on to a dish (taking care no onion or carrot hang to it), pour the boiling sauce over it, and serve very hot.

61. **FRESH SALMON (to Boil).**—Ingredients—Fresh salmon, salt, water.

This fish needs more boiling, in more water, than any other fish. It is not wholesome unless thoroughly done. Make the water quite salt; boil, skim, then put in the salmon. Continue to skim. For each half pound allow fifteen minutes. Lobster, egg, or drawn butter for sauce.

62. **WHITINGS (Fried).**—Ingredients—Whitings, egg, bread-crumbs.

Dip them in egg and bread-crumbs and fry a clear golden brown. Serve on a napkin, with shrimp or lobster sauce in a tureen.

63. **LOBSTERS (to Boil).**—Ingredients—Lobsters, salt water, salad oil.

The heaviest are best. Put them alive into a kettle of salted boiling water, and let them boil from half an hour to three quarters, according to size. Then wipe them, and rub the shell with a little salad oil: this will give them a clear red color. Crack the large claws without mashing them, and with a sharp knife split the body and tail from end to end.

64. **LOBSTERS (Potted).**—Ingredients—Lobsters, **mace,** white pepper, nutmeg and salt, butter.

Half boil them, pick out the meat, cut it into small pieces, season with mace, white pepper, nutmeg and salt, press close into a pot, and cover with butter, bake half an hour; put the spawn in. When cold, take the lobster out, and put it into the pots with a little of the butter. Beat the other butter in a mortar with some of the spawn; then mix that colored butter with as much as will be sufficient to cover the pots, and strain it. Cayenne may be added if approved.

65. **LOBSTERS (Potted as at Queen's Hotel).**—Ingredients— Lobster, mace, nutmeg, white pepper, salt, 1 or 2 cloves, butter, bay leaves.

Take out the meat as whole as you can; split the tail and remove the gut; if the inside be not watery, add that. Season with **mace, nutmeg,** white pepper, **salt,** and a clove or two in the finest powder. Lay a little fine butter at the bottom of a pan, and the lobster smooth over it, with bay leaves between, cover it with butter, and bake gently. When done, pour the whole on the bottom of a sieve; and with a fork lay the pieces into potting-pots, some of each sort, with the seasoning about it. When cold, pour clarified butter over, but not hot. It will be good next day; or if highly seasoned, and thick covered with butter, will keep some time. Potted lobster may be used cold, or as a fricassee, with cream sauce: and then it looks very nicely, and eats excellently, especially if there is spawn.

66. **LOBSTER (to Dress).**—Ingredients—1 lobster, salt, cayenne, mustard, salad oil, and vinegar.

After mincing it very fine, add salt, cayenne, mustard, salad oil, and vinegar, to taste; mix these well together.

67. **LOBSTER CROQUETTES.**—Ingredients—1 lobster, pepper, salt, spices, cayenne, a piece of butter, 1 tablespoonful of flour, 1 bunch of parsley, fish stock, 2 eggs, breadcrumbs,

Mince the flesh of a lobster to the size of small dice, season with pepper, salt, spices, and as much cayenne as will rest on the point of a trussing needle. Melt a piece of butter in a saucepan, mix with it a tablespoonful of flour, then the lobster, and some chopped parsley; moisten with a little fish stock until the mixture looks like minced veal; then stir into it off the fire a couple of yolks of eggs, and put it by to get cold. When nearly so, shape it into the form of corks, egg them, and roll them in baked breadcrumbs. After the lapse of an hour, egg and breadcrumb them again, taking care to preserve the shape. After a little time fry them a light colour in hot lard.

68. **LOBSTER CROQUETTES.**—Ingredients—lobster, pepper, salt, powdered mace, bread crumbs, 2 tablespoonfuls of butter, egg, biscuit, parsley.

To the meat of a well-boiled lobster, chopped fine, add pepper, salt, and powdered mace. Mix with this one quarter as much bread-crumbs, well rubbed, as you have meat; make into pointed balls, with two tablespoonfuls of butter melted. Roll these in beaten egg, then in biscuit powdered fine, and fry in butter or very nice sweet lard. Serve dry and hot, and garnish with crisped parsley. This is a delicious supper dish or entrée.

69. **FISH PÂTÉ.**—Ingredients—1lb. of cold fish, ½lb. of butter, 4oz. of bread crumbs, 1 whole egg, 3 yolks, 2lbs. of fresh fish, anchovy, sliced truffles, oil, pepper, salt, and spices, 1 glass of rum or Madeira.

The following is a French receipt for making a fish pâté. Take 1 lb. of any cold fish you may have left, such as pike, whiting, etc., quite free from bones and skin; pound it in a mortar adding half-pound of butter and four ounces of bread-crumbs soaked in milk and dried on the fire; season with salt and pepper, and then pound the whole till well mixed, adding a whole egg, and the yolks of three more. Take two pounds of fresh tunny fish, remove the skin and cut it into slices about one inch thick and three long, placing on each a thin strip of anchovy and some sliced truffles; let these soak for some hours in oil seasoned with pepper, salt, and different spices. Place in a pie dish a layer two inches thick of the pounded fish, then above this half the slices of tunny; repeat these two layers, and at the top put another layer of pounded fish, and above this a thin layer of butter. Then put on the crust, glazing it with the yolk of an egg, cook for three or four hours, according to the size of the pie, pouring in when done a glass of rum or Madeira through the hole in the crust. Serve cold. The pounded fish and bread crumbs will make very nice fish cakes, mixed with beaten-up egg, and fried in oil or butter.

70. **CRAB (Hot)**.—Ingredients—1 good sized crab, pepper, salt, bread crumbs, milk, cream, or oiled butter, parsley.

For this, one good-sized crab, or three or four small ones, may be used. The meat must be picked from the claws and the soft inside from the body; season with pepper and salt, add a small quantity of breadcrumbs, and moisten with milk, or, better still, a few spoonfuls of cream or oiled butter. When well mixed, put it into the large shell, strewing fresh breadcrumbs over the top, and sprinkling some oiled butter over these; let it remain in the oven just long enough to get hot through and to be a nice golden-brown colour. It should be served very hot on a napkin garnished with parsley.

71. **CRABS (Boiled)**.—Ingredients—Crabs, salt water, sweet oil.

Boil them in salt and water twenty minutes; take them out, break off the claws, wipe the crabs, throw away the small claws, and crack the large ones and send to table. Rub a little sweet oil on the shells.

72. **CRAB (Mock Dressed)**.—Ingredients—1 tin of lobster, bread crumbs, 4 eggs, 2 tablespoonfuls of cream and 1 of liquid essence of shrimps, 1 dessertspoonful of made mustard, cayenne, white pepper, vinegar, salt, 1 tablespoon of Parmesan.

Drain the liquid from a tin of fresh lobster, and divide the flesh into small flakes with a couple of forks. Should there be any coral amongst it set it aside for garnish. Boil four *new laid* eggs for three minutes (the whites must be like curd). Scoop the whites and yolks from the shell and mix them together in a basin with two tablespoonfuls each of thick cream and the liquid from the lobster. Add a tablespoonful of grated

Parmesan, a tablespoonful of essence of shrimps, a dessert-spoonful of made mustard, cayenne, white pepper, vinegar, and salt to taste. Stir in the lobster flakes and mix all well together. One large, or two or three small, crab shells must be kept ready for this. Fill them with the above, cover the opening with fine breadcrumbs, and sprinkle it with the coral, or, failing that, a few slices of red capsicums. If a hot dish is preferred, place the basin containing the lobster, etc., in a saucepan of boiling water, and stir until it is hot enough, then put it into the shells, cover with the breadcrumbs and little pieces of butter. Brown these with a hot salamander, sprinkle with the coral and serve quickly. Omit the vinegar for this, or use very little. This is an excellent imitation of dressed crab, and makes a very useful luncheon or supper dish to those who live far from a fish market.

73. **SOFT CRABS**.—Ingredients—Crabs, salt, cayenne, butter.

Take off the claws, wash, wipe, and open them; and, after removing the spongy part and sand-bag, season in and outside with salt and cayenne. Then close them, and fry in fresh butter a light brown. Send to table hot.

74. **OYSTERS** (Stewed).—Ingredients—oysters, a piece of mace, some lemon peel, a few white peppers, cream, butter, and flour.

Open and separate the liquor from them, then wash them from the grit; strain the liquor, and put with the oysters a piece of mace and lemon-peel, and a few white peppers. Simmer them very gently, and put some cream, and a litle flour and butter. Serve with sippets.

75. **OYSTERS** (Boiled).

Let the shells be nicely cleaned first, and serve in them, to eat with cold butter.

76. **OYSTERS** (Scalloped).—Ingredients—crumbs of bread, pepper, salt, nutmeg, a piece of butter.

Put them with crumbs of bread, pepper, salt, nutmeg, and a piece of butter, into scallop-shells or saucers, and bake in oven, or better still before the fire in a Dutch oven.

77. **OYSTERS** (Broiled).—Ingredients—Large, fat oysters, salt, cayenne pepper, biscuit dust or flour, butter.

Choose large, fat oysters; wipe them very dry; sprinkle salt and cayenne pepper upon them, and broil upon one of the small gridirons sold for that purpose. You can dredge the oyster with biscuit-dust or flour, if you wish to have it brown; and some fancy the juices are better kept in this way; others dislike the crust thus formed. Butter the gridiron well, and let your fire be hot and clear. If the oysters drip, withdraw the gridiron for a moment, until the smoke clears away. Broil quickly and dish hot, putting a tiny piece of butter, not larger than a pea, upon each oyster.

78. **OYSTERS (Fried, to garnish boiled Fish).**—Ingredients —flour, milk, eggs, seasoning, nutmeg, bread crumbs.

Make a batter of flour, milk, and eggs, season it a very little, dip the oysters into it, and fry them a fine yellow-brown. A little nutmeg should be put into the seasoning, and a few crumbs of bread into the flour.

79. **OYSTERS (Stewed).**—Ingredients—Liquor from 2 qts. of oysters, 1 teacupful of hot water, salt, pepper, 2 tablespoonsful of butter, 1 cupful of milk.

Drain the liquor from two quarts of firm, plump oysters; mix with it a small teacupful of hot water, add a little salt and pepper, and set over the fire in a saucepan. Let it boil up once, put in the oysters, let them boil for five minutes or less —not more. When they "ruffle," add two tablespoonsful of butter. The instant it is melted and well stirred in, put in a large cupful of boiling milk, and take the saucepan from the fire. Serve with oyster or cream biscuits, as soon as possible. Oysters become tough and tasteless when cooked too much or left to stand too long after they are withdrawn from the fire.

80. **OYSTER SAUSAGES.**—Ingredients—1 doz. large oysters, ½ lb. rump steak, a little seasoning of herbs, pepper and salt.

Chop all fine, and roll them into the form of sausages.

81. **ANGELS ON HORSEBACK.**—Ingredients—Oysters, bacon.

Trim the beards from as many oysters as may be required, wrap each in a very thin shaving of fat, streaky bacon (cold boiled bacon is the best); run them one after the other on to a silver skewer, and hold them over a toast in front of a clear fire until the bacon is slightly crisp; serve on the toast immediately.

82. **CREAM OYSTERS ON THE HALF-SHELL.**—Ingredients—Hot water (1 cup), 1 cup of cream, 1 cup of milk, a little salt, 2 tablespoonsful of butter, white pepper, 2 tablespoonsful of arrowroot, rice flour, or corn starch, cold milk.

Pour into your inner saucepan a cup of hot water, another of milk, and one of cream, with a little salt. Set into a kettle of hot water until it boils, then stir in two tablespoonsful of butter and a little salt, with white pepper. Take from the fire, and add two heaped tablespoonsful of arrowroot, rice flour, or corn starch, moistened with cold milk. By this time your shells should be washed and buttered, and a fine oyster laid within each. Of course, it is *selon les regles* to use oyster shells for this purpose; but you will find scollop-shells more roomy and manageable, because more regular in shape. Range these closely in a large baking-pan, propping them with clean pebbles or fragments of shell, if they do not seem inclined to retain their contents. Stir the cream *very* hard, and fill up each shell with a spoon, taking care not to spill any in the pan. Bake five or six minutes in a hot oven after the shells become warm. Serve on the shell. Some substitute oyster liquor for the water in the mixture, and use all milk instead of cream.

83. **OYSTER PATTIES.**—Ingredients—Oysters, paste.

Make a rich paste, roll it out half an inch thick, then turn a teacup down on the paste, and, with the point of a sharp penknife, mark the paste lightly round the edge of the cup. Then, with the point of the knife, make a circle about half an inch from the edge; cut this circle half way through. Place them on tins, and bake in a quick oven. Remove the centre, and fill with oysters, seasoned and warmed over the fire.

84. **SHAD AND HERRING (to Pot).**—Ingredients—A shad, salt, cayenne, allspice, cloves, 1 stick of cinnamon, cider vinegar.

Clean the shad, take off the head, tail, and all the fins; then cut it in pieces, wash and wipe it dry. Season each piece well with salt and cayenne. Lay them in layers in a stone jar; place between each layer some allspice, cloves, and stick of cinnamon. Cover with good cider vinegar; tie thick paper over the jar; place them in a moderate oven for three or four hours.

85. **RED HERRINGS (to Dress).** — Ingredients — Herrings, small beer, butter.

Choose those that are large and moist, cut them open, and pour some boiling small beer over them to soak half an hour; drain them dry; make them hot through before the fire, then rub some cold butter over them and serve. Egg-sauce, or buttered eggs and mashed potatoes, should be sent up with them.

86. **BAKED HERRINGS OR SPRATS.**—Ingredients—Herrings, allspice, salt, black pepper, 1 onion and a few bay leaves, vinegar.

Wash and drain without wiping them; season with allspice in fine powder, salt, and a few whole cloves; lay them in a pan with plenty of black pepper, an onion, and a few bay-leaves. Add half vinegar and half small beer, enough to cover them. Put paper over the pan, and bake in a slow oven. If you like, throw saltpetre over them the night before, to make them look **red**. **Gut, but do not open them.**

87. BLOATER TOAST.—Ingredients—2 or 3 bloaters, butter, hot buttered toast, black pepper.

When bloaters are in season, split open two or three, rub them over with fresh butter, and make them hot through in the frying pan; serve them on fingers of hot buttered toast, with a slight sprinkling of black pepper over each. The heads and tails should be removed before cooking.

88. PERCH AND TENCH.

Put them into cold water, boil them carefully and serve with melted butter and soy. Perch is a most delicate fish. They may be either fried or stewed, but in stewing they do not preserve so good a flavor.

89. TROUT AND GRAYLING (to Fry.)

Scale, gut, and wash well; then dry them, and lay them separately on a board before the fire, after dusting some flour over them. Fry them of a fine color with fresh dripping; serve with crimp parsley, and plain butter. Perch and tench may be done the same way.

90. TROUT a-la-GENEVOISE.—Ingredients—pepper, salt, a few cloves, crust of French bread, bunch of parsley and thyme, flour, butter.

Clean the fish very well; put it upon your stew-pan, adding half Champagne and half Moselle, or Rhenish, or sherry wine. Season it with pepper, salt, an onion, a few cloves stuck in it, and a small bunch of parsley and thyme; put in it a crust of French bread; set it on a quick fire. When the fish is done take the bread out, bruise it, and then thicken the sauce; add flour and a little butter, and let it boil up. See that your sauce is of a proper thickness. Lay your fish on the dish, and pour the sauce over it. Serve it with sliced lemon and fried bread.

91. PERCH AND TROUT (to Broil).

Split them down the back, notch them two or three times across, and broil over a clear fire; turn them frequently, and baste with well-salted butter and powered thyme.

92. MACKEREL.

Boil, and serve with butter and fennel.

To broil them, split, and sprinkle with herbs, pepper, and salt; or stuff with the same, crumbs, and chopped fennel.

Potted: clean, season, and bake them in a pan with spice, bay-leaves and some butter; when cold, lay them in a potting-pot, and cover with butter.

Pickled: boil them, then boil some of the liquor, a few peppers, bay-leaves, and some vinegar; when cold, pour it over them.

93. **MACKEREL** (Pickled, **called Caveach**).—Ingredients—Six mackerel, 1 oz. of pepper, 2 nutmegs, a little mace, 4 cloves, 1 handful of salt.

Clean and divide them; then cut each side into three, or leaving them undivided, cut each fish into five or six pieces. To six large mackerel, take near an ounce of pepper, two nutmegs, a little mace, four cloves, and a handful of salt, all in the finest powder; mix, and making holes in each piece of fish, thrust the seasoning into them, rub each piece with some of it; then fry them brown in oil: let them stand till cold, then put them into a stone-jar, and cover with vinegar; if to keep long, pour oil on the top. Thus done, they may be preserved for months.

94. **MACKEREL** (Scalloped).—Ingredients—Mackerel, ½ pint of shrimps, milk, cornflour, soy, walnut, mushroom catchup, essence of anchovies, grated lemon peel, nutmeg, cayenne, white pepper, salt, lemon juice, bread crumbs, capers, vinegar.

Boil as many mackerel as you require, and, while they are still hot, remove from them all bones and skin and divide the flesh into small flakes, shell half a pint of shrimps (for two mackerel), and mix them with the fish; simmer the shells and mackerel trimmings for twenty minutes, with just sufficient water to cover them. Strain the liquid into a fresh saucepan, and add to it enough new milk to make your quantity of sauce. Thicken this to the consistency of thick cream with corn flour, and flavor it delicately with essence of anchovies, soy, walnut and mushroom catchup, grated lemon peel and nutmeg, cayenne, white pepper, and salt if required; stir to this sufficient lemon juice to give an agreeable acid, and mix well with the fish. Put this mixture into china or silver scallop shells, or on a flat dish, and cover thickly with fine breadcrumbs; moisten these slightly with liquid butter and brown in a quick oven or before a clear fire. Scald a few capers in their own vinegar, and just before serving the scallop drain and sprinkle them over it. The remains of any cold fish may be served like this with great advantage: also tinned salmon, etc. Cod, fresh haddock, and soles are best flavored with oysters instead of shrimps.

95. **MULLET** (**Baked**).—Ingredients—1 mullet, pepper and salt, eschalots and mushrooms, 1 wineglassful of sherry.

Scale and trim the fish, and put it into a frying pan, season with pepper and salt, cover with chopped eschalots and mushroom, moisten with a wineglass of sherry, and bake it over a slow fire for twenty minutes, if a medium-sized fish; keep well basting in the liquor, and turn now and then; dish up very carefully. Make a sauce with half a glass of sherry, a teaspoonful of chopped parsley, with twelve drops of anchovy sauce.

Reduce the gravy to one-half by boiling, strain into the sauce, and pour over the fish.

96. RED MULLET (called the Sea-Woodcock).

Clean, but leave the inside, fold in oiled paper, and gently bake in a small dish. Make a sauce of the liquor that comes from the fish, with a piece of butter, a little flour, a little essence of anchovy, and a glass of sherry. Give it a boil; and serve in a boat, and the fish in the paper cases.

97. MULLET WITH TOMATOES.—Ingredients—½ doz. red mullet, pepper, salt, and chopped parsley, 5 or 6 tablespoonsful of tomato sauce.

Butter a baking dish plentifully, lay on it side by side half a dozen red mullet, sprinkle them with pepper, salt, and chopped parsley, then add about five or six tablespoonsful of tomato sauce, cover the whole with a sheet of well-oiled paper, and bake for about half an hour.

98. SOLES.

If boiled, they must be served with great care to look perfectly white, and should be well covered with parsley. If fried, dip in egg, and cover them with fine crumbs of bread; set on a frying-pan that is just large enough, and put into it a large quantity of fresh lard or dripping, boil it, and immediately slip the fish into it; do them of a fine brown. Soles that have been fried eat very well cold with oil, vinegar, salt and mustard.

99. SOLES.—Ingredients—2 or 3 soles, salt.

Take two or three soles, divide them from the back-bone, and take off the head, fins, and tail. Sprinkle the inside with salt, roll them up tightly from the tail end upwards, and fasten with small skewers. If large or middling, put half a fish in each roll.

100. FILLETS OF SOLES A L'INDIENNE.—Ingredients— 3 soles filleted, 1 pint of good stock, a little roux, the juice of 2 lemons, pepper and salt, a little chopped parsley, and a little hot Indian pickle.

Wash the fillets in cold water, dry them with a clean cloth, and sprinkle some chopped parsley and pepper and salt over them, and roll like corks; place them in a tin baking dish with a little butter, and squeeze the juice of two lemons over them, and bake them in a hot oven for ten minutes, and dish them in a circle, and pour over them a sauce made as follows: One pint of good stock thickened with a little flour, reduce to half a pint, occasionally stirring to prevent its burning; add a tittle pepper and salt and a little vinegar, and about eight pieces of Indian pickle chopped fine.

101. SOLES.—Ingredients—Butter, 1 teaspoonful of chopped onions, 1 wineglass of white wine, 4 teaspoonsful of stock, 2 oz. of fine breadcrumbs, parsley, salt, pepper, 2 oz. of butter, juice of 1 lemon.

Put in a tin dish a little butter to grease it, add a small teaspoonful of finely chopped onions and a wineglassful of white wine. Then put the sole in the pan, add four tablespoonsful of stock, and sprinkle 2 oz. of fine bread-crumbs over it, and some parsley finely chopped. Add a little salt and pepper, and cover the dish with 2 oz. of butter, stuck over in small pieces. Add the juice of a lemon. Put the dish in a slow oven or on a slow fire for half an hour, and serve it on the dish in which it has been cooked.

102. SOLES AU GRATIN.—Ingredients—Soles, a little stock, 1 lemon, a little anchovy, pepper and salt, bread-crumbs, a small piece of butter, and a little vinegar.

Place a sole in an oval tin baking-dish, lay on the top a piece of butter, and round it the juice of half a lemon and a little anchovy sauce, a tea-spoonful of vinegar and a little pepper, and then bake it for 15 minutes in a hot oven; when nearly cooked sprinkle some bread-crumbs over it, and color the top with a salamander. Serve in the tin it was baked in with a little chopped parsley on the top.

103. STURGEON (to Roast).

Put it on a lark-spit, then tie it on a large spit; baste it constantly with butter; and serve with a good gravy, an anchovy, a squeeze of Seville orange or lemon, and a glass of sherry.

104. STURGEON (Fresh).—Ingredients—Sturgeon, egg, bread-crumbs, parsley, pepper, salt.

Cut slices, rub egg over them, then sprinkle with crumbs of bread, parsley, pepper, salt: fold them in paper, and broil gently. Sauce; butter, anchovy, and soy.

105. TURBOT EN MAYONNAISE.—Ingredients—Some fillets of turbot, oil, tarragon vinegar, salt and pepper, eggs, cucumbers, anchovies, tarragon leaves, beets, capers, aspic jelly.

Cut some fillets of cooked turbot into moderate-sized round or oblong pieces, carefully taking off the skin and extracting all bones. Place these pieces of fish into a bowl, with a dressing made of oil, tarragon vinegar, salt and pepper As soon as the fish is well-flavored with this seasoning, arrange the pieces round a dish like a crown. Place a circle of chopped hard-boiled eggs, tiny pickled cucumbers, anchovies, tarragon leaves, beetroot, and capers round the dish, and then arrange a wall of aspic jelly round the edge of the dish. Fill up the centre of the crown of fish with good mayonnaise sauce.

106. TURBOT (Fillet of. with Dutch Sauce).—Ingredients— 2 fillets of turbot, ¼lb. of butter, 1 egg, a little flour, half a pint of milk, a little vinegar, some horse-radish, pepper, and salt.

Place the fillets of turbot cut up in nice-sized pieces in a baking-dish, sprinkle some pepper and salt over them and about two oz. of butter, and bake for half an hour in a hot oven, cover them with a piece of buttered paper if the oven is two fierce ; when cooked send to table with a sauce made as follows : Place the milk in a stew-pan with a little pepper and salt, a little scraped horse-radish, and a wine-glassful of vinegar, boil them well together, knead two oz. of butter in flour, stir it in the boiling milk, and well mix it in, then add one egg, and just bring to the boil, stirring all the time, add more seasoning if required, and serve very hot.

107. TURBOT AU GRATIN (a nice Dish for Luncheon)—Ingredients—cold cooked turbot, anchovy sauce, a little stock, cayenne pepper, 2 oz. of butter, a little flour, and some bread crumbs.

Place a piece of butter, about two oz., in a stewpan and melt it on the fire, add a little flour, then a little anchovy sauce and a little cayenne pepper, stir these well together and then drop in the sauce any cold turbot you may have left from dinner the evening before, place some of the turbot out of the sauce in large pattie pans, and cover it with bread-crumbs and bake it in a hot oven; if the top does not get brown enough heat a salamander, and finish off that way. Serve the pattie pans up on a napkin or paper.

108. SMELTS (to Fry). — Ingredients — Smelts, egg, bread crumbs, lard.

They should not be washed more than is necessary to clean them. Dry them in a cloth, then lightly flour them, but shake it off. Dip them into plenty of egg, then into bread crumbs, grated fine, and plunge them into a good pan of *boiling* lard ; let them continue gently boiling, and a few minutes will make them a bright yellow-brown. Take care not to take off the light roughness of the crumbs, or their beauty will be lost.

109. EEL PIE.—Ingredients—1 or 2 eels, seasoning, gravy, gelatine.

Cut up one or two eels, and stew gently until tender in a little good brown gravy, seasoned to taste, when done enough, strain the gravy through muslin, add gelatine and pour over the fish. A few sprigs of parsley placed about the mould will much improve the appearance.

110. **EELS (to Boil).**—Ingredients—Eels, salt water.

Clean, cut off the heads, and dry them. Joint them into suitable lengths, or coil them on your fish plate; boil them in salted water. Use drawn butter and parsley for sauce.

111. **WHITEBAIT.**—Ingredients—Whitebait, flour, lard, salt.

Drain the fish from the water, lay it on a cloth, sprinkle flour on it, double up the cloth, and shake it about from side to side until the fish is well covered with flour. Transfer it to a frying basket; shake it gently to get rid of the superfluous flour. Have a panful of boiling lard, try it with a small piece of bread; if the fat hisses sharply, and the bread colors at once, the fat is hot enough; plunge the basket into it, and never cease shaking until the whitebait is cooked (two or three minutes). Turn the fish out on a napkin in front of the fire, and sprinkle it freely with salt at the time of serving. It is a good plan, when practicable, to have two pans of boiling fat, and when the whitebait has been cooked in the one, to take it out, drain it, and plunge it for a second or two in the other pan, the fat in which should be boiling hot.

112. **HADDOCK WITH TOMATOES.**—Ingredients—1 dried haddock, 1 onion, 1 oz. butter, 1 ripe tomato, pepper, parsley.

Soak a dried haddock in plenty of cold water for half a day, drain off the water and replace it with boiling water; when the haddock has been in this for two hours, take it out, carefully remove all the bones and skin, and break the meat into flakes; slice a moderate sized onion, put it into a saucepan with one ounce of butter; as soon as the onion is soft, add one ripe tomato, cut into slices; after a couple of minutes add the flesh of the haddock, a sprinkling of pepper and some finely minced parsley; shake the saucepan on the fire, until the contents are thoroughly heated, then draw it aside, to be kept warm till the time for serving.

113. **FISH CROQUETTES.**—Ingredients—Remnants of turbot, brill, haddock, or salmon, butter, pinch of flour, some milk, pepper, salt, nutmeg, parsley.

Take some remnants of boiled turbot, brill, haddock, or salmon, pick out the flesh carefully, and mince it, not too finely; melt a piece of butter in a saucepan, add a small pinch of flour and some hot milk; stir on the fire until the mixture thickens then put in pepper, salt, and a little grated nutmeg, together with some finely-chopped parsley, and, lastly, the minced fish. As soon as the whole is quite hot, turn it out on a dish to get cold, then fashion and finish the croquettes as in the first recipe.

114. HALIBUT (Boiled).—Ingredients—Halibut, salted water.

Allow the fish to lie in cold salt water for an hour. Wipe dry in a clean cloth and score the skin, then put into the fish kettle with cold salted water sufficient to cover it. Let it come slowly to the boil, and allow from half to three-quarters of an hour for a piece weighing four or five lbs. When ready drain, and serve with egg sauce.

115. HALIBUT (Baked).—Ingredients—Halibut, a little butter, salt and water, a tablespoonful of walnut catchup, a dessert spoonful of Worcestershire sauce, the juice of a lemon, a little brown flour.

A piece of halibut weighing five or six lbs, lay in salt and water for two hrs. Wipe in a clean cloth and score the skin. Have the oven tolerably hot, and bake about an hour. Melt a little butter in hot water and baste the fish occasionally. It should be of a fine brown color. Any gravy that is in the dripping pan mix with a little boiling water, then stir in the walnut catchup and Worcestershire sauce, the juice of the lemon, and thicken with the brown flour (the flour should be mixed with a little cold water previously), give one boil and serve in sauce-boat.

116. HALIBUT STEAK.—Ingredients—2 eggs, some brittle crackers, oil or lard, salt.

Wash. Wipe the steaks in a clean cloth and sprinkle with a little salt. Dip them into beaten egg, then into crushed crackers (pound the crackers until they are as fine as powder), and fry in boiling oil or lard.

117. STUFFING for PIKE, HADDOCK and SMALL COD.—Ingredients—equal parts of fat bacon and beef suet, some fresh butter, parsley, thyme, savory, 1 onion, a few leaves of marjoram, 1 or 2 anchovies, salt, pepper, 1 nutmeg, crumbs and egg.

Take equal parts of fat bacon, beef-suet, and fresh butter, some parsley, thyme, and savory; a little onion, and a few leaves of scented marjoram shred fine; an anchovy or two; a little salt and nutmeg, and some pepper. Oysters will be an improvement with or without anchovies; add crumbs, and an egg to bind.

POULTRY AND GAME.

OBSERVATIONS.

The following is translated from a German cookery book:—

"In Vienna, especially in the hotels, young chickens are killed immediately before they are wanted, plucked and cleaned as quickly as possible before the flesh becomes cold, otherwise it would be tough. They are cut up into joints and sprinkled with salt; each piece must then be dipped into flour, and then into egg and grated bread crumbs, and fried immediately; or they may be dipped first into butter, and then into bread crumbs mixed with a little flour. This method admits of no delay in performance if the whole flavor of the meat is to be preserved and the gravy kept in; but in private houses the chickens are generally allowed to hang a day or two, to ensure their being tender."

In choosing ducks, be careful to secure those with plump bellies and thick and yellowish feet; and to ensure them being tender, it is advisable to let them hang a day or two.

In choosing turkeys, the hen turkey is preferable for boiling, on account of their whiteness and tenderness.

Partridges in perfection will have dark colored bills and yellowish legs; the time they should be kept entirely depends upon the taste of those for whom they are intended, as what some people would consider delicious, to others would be disgusting and offensive. Young hares may be known by their smooth and sharp claws, and the cleft in the lip not much spread. It is preferable to hang without being paunched, but should it be previously emptied, wipe the inside every day and sprinkle over it a little ginger and pepper.

Rabbits when young have smooth and sharp claws.

In selecting a goose, choose one with a clean white skin, plump breast and yellow feet. Charcoal is considered as an admirable prevention for decomposition.

118. CHICKEN PATTIES.—Ingredients—Cold chicken, milk, cornflour, pepper, salt and butter, puff paste.

Mince cold chicken, and stir it into a white sauce, made of milk thickened with cornflour and flavored with pepper, salt and butter; line small patty pans with puff paste, bake first, then fill with the mixture, and set in a hot oven for a few minutes to brown.

119. FOWL (to Boil).

For boiling, choose those that are not black-legged. Pick them nicely, singe, wash and truss them. Flour them, and put them into boiling water. Serve with parsley and butter; oyster, lemon, liver, or celery sauce.

120. FOWLS (Roast).—Ingredients—Butter, flour, gravy, lemon juice, sausages, bacon.

Fowls require constant attention in dredging and basting, and the last ten minutes let butter rolled in flour be stuck over them in little bits, and allowed to melt without basting. The gravy for fowls should always be thickened, and slightly flavored with lemon-juice. Sausages or rolled bacon should be served on the same dish, and white mashed potatoes should always be handed with poultry.

121. CHICKEN CUTLETS (with Rice).—Ingredients—A teacupful of rice, some good stock, 1 onion, salt and pepper, some cold ham and chicken, egg, bread-crumbs.

Boil a teacupful of rice in some good stock, and pound it in a mortar with an onion that has been cooked in butter, with salt and pepper. Pound separately in equal portions cold ham and chicken, form this into cutlets; cover them with egg and bread-crumbs and fry. Serve with a sharp sauce.

122. CHICKEN A LA JARDINIERE.—Ingredients—2 young chickens, butter, 1 onion, some savory herbs, salt and sufficient water, carrots, turnips, onions, beef stock, mushrooms, 2 cabbages, some heads of asparagus, pepper, sugar.

Take two young chickens and put them in a saucepan with some butter, a large onion chopped up, some savory herbs, some salt and sufficient water; the chickens should be dropped in the mixture when it is boiling, and left in the saucepan until the liquid is reduced by half; cut up in good shapes some carrots and turnips, some whole onions skinned and blanched, and put them in a saucepan with some butter, some beef stock, some mushrooms, two very young cabbages and some heads of asparagus; season with salt, pepper, and a little sugar; cook very gently, and fifteen minutes before serving add a piece of butter kneaded with flour. Serve with the vegetables well arranged round the dish.

123. **CHICKEN RISSOLES.**—Ingredients—Some remnants of fowl, ham and tongue, butter, a pinch of flour, white pepper, salt, nutmeg, parsley, eggs, a few drops of lemon-juice. flour, water, 3 pinches of sugar.

Mince very finely some remnants of fowls, free from skin, add an equal quantity of ham or tongue, as well as a small quantity of truffles, all finely minced; toss the whole in a saucepan with a piece of butter, mixed with a pinch of flour; add white pepper, salt, and nutmeg to taste, as well as a little minced parsley; stir in off the fire the yolks of one or two eggs beaten up with a few drops of lemon-juice, and lay the mixture on a plate to cool. Make a paste with some flour, a little water, two eggs, a pinch of salt, and two or three of sugar; roll it out to the thickness of a penny piece, stamp it out in round pieces three inches in diameter; put a piece of the above mince on each, then fold them up, fastening the edges by moistening them with water. Trim the rissoles neatly with a fluted cutter, dip each one in beaten-up egg, and fry a golden color in hot lard.

124. **CHICKEN (Jollied).**—Ingredients—A chicken, 1 oz. of butter, pepper and salt, ½ packet of gelatine.

Boil the chicken as in recipe 119 until the water is reduced to a pint; pick the meat from the bones in fair sized pieces, removing all gristle, skin, and bone. Skim the fat from the liquor, add an ounce of butter, a little pepper and salt, and half a packet of gelatine. Put the cut-up chicken into a mould, wet with cold water; when the gelatine has dissolved pour the liquor hot over the chicken. Turn out when cold.

125. **CHICKEN LOAF.**—Ingredients—A chicken, 2 oz. of butter, pepper, salt, egg.

Boil a chicken in as little water as possible until the meat can easily be picked from the bones; cut it up finely, then put it back into the saucepan with two ounces of butter, and a seasoning of pepper and salt. Grease a square china mould and cover the bottom with slices of hard-boiled egg; pour in the chicken, place a weight on it, and set aside to cool, when it will turn out.

126. **CHICKEN CROQUETTES.**—Ingredients—Breast of a roast fowl, tongues, truffles, butter, flour, stock, parsley, pepper, salt, nutmeg, eggs, lemon-juice, parsley.

Take of the breast of a roast fowl two parts, of boiled tongue one part, and of truffles one part; mince all these very finely, and mix them together. Melt a piece of butter in a saucepan, stir a little flour into it, then put in the above mixture, and moisten with a small quantity of stock; add some finely minced parsley, pepper, salt, and nutmeg to taste. Stir it on the fire for a few minutes, then stir in, off the fire, the yolks of one or two eggs beaten up with the juice of a lemon and strained. Spread out this mince (which should be pretty stiff) on a marble slab, and when it is nearly cold fashion it into small portions in the shape of balls or of corks. Dip each in a beaten-up egg, and then roll it in very fine baked bread-crumbs; repeat this operation after the lapse of an hour, and after a similar interval fry the croquettes in hot lard to a golden color. Serve on a napkin, with plenty of fried parsley.

127. **CHICKENS (to Pull).**

Take off the skin; and pull the flesh off the bone of a cold fowl, in as large pieces as you can: dredge it with flour, and fry it of a nice brown in butter. Drain the butter from it; and then simmer the flesh in a good gravy well-seasoned, and thickened with a little flour and butter. Add the juice of half a lemon.

128. **CHICKENS (to Pull).**

Cut off the legs, and the whole back of a dressed chicken; if under-done the better. Pull all the white part into little flakes free from skin; toss it up with a little cream thickened with a piece of butter mixed with flour, half a blade of mace in powder, white pepper, salt, and a squeeze of lemon. Cut off the neck end of the chicken; and broil the back and sidesmen in one piece, and the two legs seasoned. Put the hash in the middle, with the back on it; and the two legs at the end.

129. **GALANTINE OF FOWL.**—Ingredients—1 fowl, 1 lb. of veal, ½ lb. of fat bacon, spice and sweet herbs, pepper, salt, ½ lb. of boiled tongue, ½ doz. truffles, 1 calf's foot, 2 or 3 onions, 2 carrots, 1 clove of garlic, 1 bundle of sweet herbs, cloves, whole pepper, mace.

Take a fowl, bone and trim it; take one lb. of veal, and half a pound of fat bacon, pound together in a mortar, season with powdered spice and sweet herbs, pepper and salt to taste, then pass the mixture through a wire sieve. Cut half a pound of boiled tongue in pieces about an inch square, cut half-a-dozen truffles each into three or four pieces, lay the prepared fowl, skin downwards, on the table, sprinkle with pepper, salt, and powdered spices; lay the pounded meat, the truffles, and the tongue on it, then roll up neatly as a roly-poly pudding, and tie it up in a cloth (tightly); put all the trimmings of the fowl into a saucepan, large enough to hold the galantine; add a calf's foot cut in pieces, the trimmings of the bacon (mind they are perfectly sweet), two or three onions, two carrots, cut in pieces, a clove of garlic, a bundle of sweet herbs, cloves, whole pepper, mace, and salt, according to taste ; fill up with such a quantity of water (cold) as will leave room for the galantine to be put in, set the saucepan on the fire to boil for two hours, strain, and when the liquor boils put in the galantine, and let it boil two or two and a half hours, then lift it out, and when cold it is ready for eating.

130. **BRAIZED FOWL (with Macaroni).**—Ingredients—A pair of fowls, 2 onions, butter, 2 slices of bacon, 2 carrots, pepper, salt, a bundle of sweet herbs, stock, 1 lb. of ribbon macaroni, 15c. bottle of French tomato sauce, 1 oz. of butter, Parmesan cheese.

Trim a pair of fowls as for boiling, putting a piece of butter and an onion inside each ; lay in a saucepan over two slices of bacon with an onion and two carrots cut in pieces ; add pepper and salt to taste, and a bundle of sweet herbs ; moisten with a little stock, put a piece of buttered paper over the fowls, and set to braize very slowly for an hour, frequently basting with their own liquor. Throw one lb. of ribbon macaroni into fast-boiling salt water ; when done (twenty minutes) drain off the water, put them into a saucepan with the contents of a fifteen cent bottle of French tomato sauce, and one oz. of butter previously melted ; toss on the fire a few minutes, adding plenty of Parmesan cheese. Place the chickens on a dish with the macaroni round them and serve.

131. **BROILED CHICKEN (with Mushrooms).**—Ingredients—1 fowl, liver, gizzard, butter, pepper and salt, stewed mushrooms.

Cut some fowls down the back, truss legs and wings as for boiling, with the liver and gizzard under the wing ; baste them well with butter, sprinkle with pepper and salt, and broil them slowly over a clear fire, turning frequently, and basting well till cooked ; serve with stewed mushrooms.

132. **PUREE OF GAME.**—Ingredients—Carcases of roast game, ½ an onion, 1 carrot, 1 bay leaf, a small piece of celery, 2 cloves, a little piece of mace, some whole pepper, pinch of salt, stock, ½ lb. lean beef.

Take any carcases of roast game, say three snipe or two partridges, cut them up into convenient pieces, and pack them into a saucepan with half an onion, a carrot, and bay leaf, a small piece of celery, a couple of cloves, a little piece of mace, some whole pepper, and a large pinch of salt ; pour in just enough stock to cover the contents ; let the whole boil a couple of hours, strain the liquor and put it by ; take half a pound of lean beef, chop it up and pound it in a mortar with all the flesh that can be picked out of the pieces of game, then pass the whole through a sieve, moistening now and then with some of the liquor. Lastly, heat the purée, correct the flavoring if necessary, stir in a piece of fresh butter the size of a walnut, serve with fried sippets round and poached eggs on the top.

133. **WILD DUCK (Roast).**—Ingredients—Duck, bread-crumbs, carrot, pepper and salt, sage and onions, currant jelly, 1 pinch of cayenne, browned flour.

Before roasting, parboil with a small carrot peeled and put inside. This will absorb the fishy taste. If you have no carrot at hand, an onion will have the same effect, but unless you mean to use onion in the stuffing a carrot is preferable. When parboiled, throw away the carrot or onion, lay in fresh water for half an hour, stuff with bread-crumbs seasoned with pepper, salt, sage, and an onion, and roast till brown and tender, basting half the time with butter and water, then with drippings. Add to the gravy when you have taken up the ducks, one tablespoonful of currant jelly and a pinch of cayenne. Thicken with browned flour and serve in a tureen.

134. **QUAIL PIE.**—Ingredients—Puff paste, salt pork or ham, 6 eggs, butter, pepper, 1 bunch of parsley, juice of 1 lemon.

Clean and dress the birds, loosen the joints, but do not divide them, put on the stove to simmer, while you prepare puff paste. Cover a deep dish with it, then lay in the bottom some shreds of pork or ham, then a layer of hard boiled eggs, a little butter and pepper. Take the birds from the fire, sprinkle with pepper and minced parsley. Squeeze lemon juice upon them, and upon the breasts of the birds a few pieces of butter rolled in flour. Cover with slices of egg, then shred some ham and lay upon this. Pour in a little of the gravy in which the quails were parboiled, and put on the lid. Leave a hole in the middle and bake a little over one hour.

135. **QUAILS (Roasted, with Ham).**

Prepare the birds as you would grouse, but cover the ham or pork with a sheet of paper, having secured the meat with pack thread. Stitch the papers on, and keep well basted with butter and water. Roast three quarters of an hour. Remove papers and meat before dishing, and brown quickly. This is a favorite way of cooking quails.

136. **RABBIT PIE.**—Ingredients—2 rabbits, $\frac{1}{4}$ lb. of fat pork, 4 eggs, pepper, butter, a little powdered mace, a few drops of lemon juice, puff paste.

Cut a pair of rabbits into ten pieces, soak in salt and water half an hour and simmer until half done, in enough water to cover them. Cut a quarter of a pound of pork into slices, and boil four eggs hard. Lay some pieces of pork in the bottom of the dish, the next a layer of rabbit. Upon this spread slices of boiled egg and pepper and butter. Sprinkle, moreover, with a little powdered mace, a few drops of lemon juice upon each piece of meat. Proceed in this manner until the dish is full, the top layer being pork. Pour in water in which the rabbit was boiled; when you have salted it and added a few lumps of butter rolled in flour, cover with puff paste, make a hole in the middle and bake for one hour. Cover with paper if it'should boil too fast.

137. **RABBIT (Stewed).**—Ingredients—1 rabbit, salted water, dripping or butter, flour, six onions.

Cut a rabbit in pieces, wash it in cold water, a little salted. Prepare in a stewpan some flour, and clarified dripping or butter; stir it until it browns. Then put in the pieces of rabbit, and keep stirring and turning, until they are tinged with a little color; then add six onions, peeled, but not cut up. Serve all together in a deep dish.

138. **A GERMAN DISH.**—Ingredients—A tender fowl, salt, pepper, mace, flour, yolk of 1 egg, hot lard, liver, gizzard, parsley.

Quarter a tender fowl, season the pieces with pepper and salt and mace; flour, and then dip them in the beaten-up yolk of an egg; fry a golden color in hot lard; dish them, garnished with the liver and gizzard fried separately, and with fried parsley. Serve either with a salad garnished with hard-boiled eggs or tomato sauce.

139. **GIBLETS (to Stew).**—Ingredients—Salt and pepper, butter, 1 cup of cream, 1 teaspoonful of flour.

Do them as directed for giblet-pie (under the head PIES); season them with salt and pepper, and a very small piece of mace. Before serving give them one boil with a cup of cream, and a piece of butter rubbed in a teaspoonful of flour.

140. **PIGEONS.**

May be dressed in so many ways, that they are very useful. The good flavor of them depends very much on their being cropped and drawn as soon as killed. No other bird requires so much washing. Pigeons left from dinner the day before may be stewed or made into a pie; in either case care must be taken not to overdo them, which will make them stringy. They need only be heated up in gravy, made ready, and forcemeat-balls may be fried and added, instead of putting a stuffing into them. If for a pie, let beef-steaks be stewed in a little water, and put cold under them, and cover each pigeon with a piece of fat bacon, to keep them moist. Season as usual, and put eggs.

141. PIGEONS (to Broil).—Ingredients—Pigeons, pepper and salt, stewed or pickled mushrooms, butter.

After cleaning, split the backs, pepper and salt them, and broil them very nicely; pour over them either stewed or pickled mushrooms in melted butter, and serve as hot as possible.

142. PIGEONS (Roast).

Should be stuffed with parsley, either cut or whole; and seasoned within. Serve with parsley and butter. Peas or asparagus should be dressed to eat with them.

143. TURKEY (to Roast).

The sinews of the legs should be drawn, whichever way it is dressed. The head should be twisted under the wing; and in drawing it, take care not to tear the liver, nor let the gall touch it. Put a stuffing of sausage meat; or, if sausages are to be served in the dish, a bread stuffing. As this makes a large addition to the size of the bird, observe that the heat of the fire is constantly to that part; for the breast is often not done enough. A little strip of paper should be put on the bone to hinder it from scorching while the other parts roast. Baste well and froth it up. Serve with gravy in the dish, and plenty of bread-sauce in a sauce-tureen. Add a few crumbs, and a beaten egg to the stuffing of sausage-meat.

144. ROAST TURKEY.—Ingredients—Plain forcemeat, 1 turkey, bacon, butter, salt, pork sausages, gravy.

Pluck, singe, draw, wipe thoroughly, and truss a fine turkey, stuff it with plain forcemeat, pack it up in some thin slices of fat bacon, and over that a sheet of buttered paper; put in oven, basting frequently with butter. A quarter of an hour before it is done, remove the paper and slices of bacon. Sprinkle with salt just before serving. Garnish with pork sausages, and serve with a tureen of gravy. Time of roasting, two or three hours, according to size.

145. BRAISED TURKEY.—Ingredients—1 turkey, truffle, chestnut stuffing, bacon, 2 carrots, 2 onions, sweet herbs, parsley, bay leaf, 1 clove of garlic, whole pepper and salt, stock, 1 glass of sherry.

Truss the turkey as for boiling; stuff it with truffle and chestnut stuffing. Line the bottom of a braising pan with slices of bacon, lay the turkey on these, and place more slices of bacon on the top of it. Put in two carrots and two onions cut in slices, some sweet herbs, parsley, bay leaf, a clove of garlic and whole pepper and salt to taste; moisten with some stock and a tumblerful of sherry. Lay a round of buttered paper on the top, put on the lid, and braise with a moderate fire for about four hours; then serve with the gravy strained and freed from excess of fat.

146. TRUFFLE AND CHESTNUT STUFFING.—Ingredients—1 lb. fat bacon, 2 shallots, 1 lb. chestnuts, ½ lb. truffles, pepper, salt, spices, thyme, marjoram.

Mince one lb. of fat bacon and a couple of shallots, give them a turn on the fire in a saucepan; then put in one lb. of chestnuts, boiled and peeled, and one-half pound of truffles, both cut up in moderate-sized pieces; add pepper, salt, and spices to taste; also a little powdered thyme and marjoram. Give the mixture another turn or two on the fire, and it is ready.

147. TRUFFLE SAUCE.

Rub a saucepan with a shallot, melt a piece of butter in it, add a very small quantity of flour and the trimmings of the truffles chopped coarsely; moisten with some good stock free from fat, and a little white wine, season with pepper, salt, and the least piece of nutmeg. Let the sauce simmer about ten minutes, and it is ready.

148. TURKEY (Pulled).

Divide the meat of the breast by pulling instead of cutting; then warm it in a spoonful or two of white gravy, and a little cream, grated nutmeg, salt, and a little flour and butter; don't boil it. The leg should be seasoned, scored, and broiled, and put into the dish with the above round it. Cold chicken does as well.

149. GAME (Chaudfroid).—Ingredients—2 birds, a piece of ham or bacon, 1 onion, 1 carrot, 1 oz. of butter, 1 bundle of sweet herbs, spices, pepper and salt; 1 cupful of white wine, 1 pint of stock, butter, flour, 1 cupful of aspic jelly, 2 partridges.

Remove the legs, breast, and wings from two uncooked birds, pound the carcases in a mortar, put them into a saucepan with a piece of ham or bacon chopped up, an onion, a carrot, an ounce of butter, a bundle of sweet herbs, and spices, pepper and salt to taste, put the saucepan on the fire, and when the contents are quite hot add a small cupful of white wine (sherry or marsala), and a few minutes after add rather more than a pint of good ordinary stock; let the whole gently simmer over an hour, then strain, and carefully remove all fat; mix a little butter and flour in a saucepan, and stir them on the fire till the mixture browns, then gradually add the liquor and a cupful of unclarified aspic jelly. If at hand, a cupful of well-made Spanish sauce may be used instead of the thickening of butter and flour. Roast two partridges, and when cold divide them into joints; trim each joint neatly, removing the skin from it;

dip them in the above sauce, made hot for the purpose, and if, when cooled, the pieces of partridges are not well covered over with it, repeat the operation. Arrange the pieces pyramidally on a dish, with a border of chopped-up aspic jelly round them. The wings and breasts cut from the birds used to make the sauce can be served in various ways in the form of fillets, and the legs can also be utilized, either to make a stew, or for the stock pot.

150. **GAME (Aspic).**—Ingredients—Butter, pepper, salt, breasts of a brace of birds, forcemeat.

Cut the breasts of a brace of birds into fillets, cook them in the oven, smothered in butter, in a tin with pepper and salt, and put them between two plates under a weight to get cold. With the rest of the flesh of the birds make a forcemeat as follows: pound it in a mortar with an equal quantity of lean veal; add as much butter as there is game meat, and as much breadcrumbs soaked in stock and squeezed dry; mix the whole thoroughly well in the mortar, then pass the mixture through a sieve; return it to the mortar; work into it one tablespoonful of Spanish sauce or chaudfroid sauce, pepper and salt, a little powdered sweet herbs or spices, then the yolks of two and the white of one egg. Put this composition into a plain buttered mould, steam it for half an hour, and turn it out. When cold cut in slices, and cut the slices into rounds all of a shape; cut all the fillets to the same size; cut also some ready cooked truffles into slices; set some white of egg in a jam pot placed in a saucepan full of boiling water, turn it out, cut it in slices, and from them cut pieces all of a size. Pour a little well-flavored aspic jelly into a mould; when it begins to set arrange the above materials in it, filling up with jelly until the mould is full, and when quite set turn it out.

151. **FORCEMEAT, for Pulled Turkey.**

Take one part of finely-shredded suet and two parts of breadcrumbs, season with pepper, salt, powdered spices, sweet herbs, and finely minced parsley; mix all well together, then add as many eggs as will bind the ingredients together into a stiff paste.

152. **GRAVY, for Pulled Turkey.**

Mince an onion finely, fry it in butter to a dark brown, then add three quarters of a pint of good stock, pepper and salt to taste, a small piece of ham minced small, a sprig of thyme, one of parsley, and a little Worcester sauce; let the whole boil five or ten minutes, put it by till wanted, then strain it into a sauce boat.

153. CHESTNUT SAUCE, for Roast Turkey.

Remove the outer skin from a number of chestnuts (carefully excluding any that may be the least tainted), put them to boil in salted water with a handful of coriander seeds, and a couple of bay leaves. When thoroughly done, remove the outer skin, and pound the chestnuts in a mortar, adding a little stock (free from fat) now and then. When a smooth paste is obtained, fry an onion in butter to a light color, add the chestnut paste and sufficient stock to get the sauce of the desired consistency; add salt and pepper to taste, pass through a hair sieve, and serve.

154. ROAST HAUNCH OF VENISON.—Ingredients—Butter, salt, flour and water.

Trim the joint neatly, wipe it well with a cloth, rub it over with butter, and sprinkle it with salt; then wrap it up in a sheet of buttered kitchen paper. Make a paste with flour and water, roll it out to the thickness of about half an inch, wrap the joint in this, and close up all the openings carefully by wetting the edges of the sheet of paste; lastly, pack up the haunch into a sheet of well buttered paper, put in the oven for about three hours, basting occasionally, then remove the paste and paper coverings, baste the haunch plentifully with butter, and when nearly done dredge some flour over it and some salt. Serve on a hot water dish.

155. BREAST OF VENISON (Stewed).—Ingredients—1 onion, 1 carrot, a bundle of sweet herbs, a few cloves, pepper and salt, common stock, claret, butter, 1 table spoonful of flour, 1 squeeze of lemon.

Remove the bones and skin, roll it up and tie it with a string in the shape of a round of beef, put it into a stewpan with an onion and carrot, sliced, a bundle of sweet herbs, a few cloves and pepper, and salt to taste, add common stock and claret in equal parts, sufficient to come up to the piece of venison, cover up the stewpan and let the contents simmer gently for about three hours, turning the meat occasionally; when done strain as much of the liquor as will be wanted for sauce, into a saucepan containing a piece of butter, previously melted and well mixed with a tablespoonful of flour, stir the sauce on the fire until it thickens, then add a squeeze of lemon; pour it over the meat in a dish and serve.

156. HASHED VENISON.—Ingredients—Some haunch or neck of venison, venison gravy, ½ pt. of claret, stock, 4 challots, 4 cloves, 1 teaspoonful of mushroom catchup, butter, 1 tablespoonful of flour, pepper and salt.

Cut some cold haunch or neck of venison into thin slices, trimming off all outside parts. Put any venison gravy that may be left, the bones and trimmings, half pt. of claret, and as much stock into a saucepan with four challots finely chopped, four cloves, and a teaspoonful of mushroom catchup ; let all this simmer slowly for an hour or two, then strain into a saucepan in which a good piece of butter has been amalgamated with a tablespoonful of flour, add pepper and salt to taste, and when the sauce boils take it off the fire, and let it get cold, then put in it the slices of venison, and let the whole slowly get hot by the side of the fire. It should take a couple of hours. Serve garnished with tippets of bread fried in butter and serve red currant jelly with it.

157. **WILD DUCKS (Stewed).**—Pepper, salt, flour, butter, gravy made of the giblets, necks, and some pieces of veal, 1 challot, 1 bunch of sweet herbs, ½ cup of cream or rich milk in which an egg has been beaten, brown flour, one tablespoonful of wine, juice of half a lemon.

Prepare to parboil for ten minutes. Lay in cold water for half an hour. Cut into joints, pepper, salt and flour them. Fry a light brown in some butter. Put them in a stewpan and cover with gravy made from the giblets, necks, and some pieces of veal. Add a minced challot, bunch of sweet herbs, salt and pepper. Cover and stew for half an hour or until tender, take out the duck, skim the gravy and strain ; add half a cup of cream, or some rich milk in which an egg has been beaten, thicken with brown flour, add one tablespoonful of wine, and the juice of half a lemon beaten in slowly, or the cream may curdle. Boil up and pour over the ducks and serve.

158. **WOODCOCK.**

These birds are very delicious, and may be either roasted or boiled.

MEATS.

OBSERVATIONS ON MEAT.

In purchasing beef secure meat of a deep red color, with the fat mingled with the lean, giving it a mottled appearance. The fat will be firm, and the color resembling grass butter. The smaller the breed, so much sweeter the meat. It will be better for eating if kept a few days. Veal, lamb and pork (being white meat), will not keep more than a day or two.

Beef.—For roasting, the sirloin and rib pieces are the best. The chief object is to prevent the escape of the juices, and if you are roasting in an oven, it is a very good plan to throw a cup of *boiling* water over the meat when first put in the oven. This will prevent the escape of the juices for a while, and will thoroughly warm through the meat.

Mutton.—Choose this by the fineness of its grain, good color, and firm white fat. It is not the better for being young; if of a good breed and well fed, it is better for age; but this only holds with wether-mutton: the flesh of the ewe is paler, and the texture finer. Ram-mutton is very strongly flavored; the flesh is of a deep red, and the fat is spongy.

Lamb.—Observe the neck of a fore-quarter; if the vein is bluish, it is fresh; if it has a green or yellow caste it is stale. In the hind quarter, if there is a faint smell under the kidney, and the knuckle is limp, the meat is stale. If the eyes are sunken, the head is not fresh. Grass-lamb comes in season in April or May, and continues till August. House-Lamb may be had in great towns almost all the year, but is in highest perfection in December and January.

Pork.—Pinch the lean, and if young, it will break. If the rind is tough, thick, and cannot easily be impressed by the finger, it is old. A thin rind is a merit in all pork. When fresh, the flesh will be smooth and cool; if clammy it is tainted. What is called measley pork is very unwholesome, and may be known by the fat being full of kernels, which in good pork is never the case. Pork fed at stillhouses does not answer for curing any way, the fat being spongy. Dairy-fed pork is the best. A sucking pig, to be eaten in perfection, should not be more than three weeks old, and should be dressed the same day it is killed.

Veal.—Veal should be perfectly white; if purchasing the loin, the fat enveloping the kidney should be white and firm. Veal will not keep so long as an older meat, especially in hot or wet weather. Choose small and fat veal. It is in season from March to August.

Tripe.—This requires to be well cooked and nicely served, and then it is both light and nutritious, and can often be eaten by invalids, or persons having a delicate digestion. Choose a nice white piece; wash it well, and put into a stew-pan with sufficient milk and water in equal parts to cover it; let it simmer gently for about half an hour after it has boiled up. Serve with white sauce, omitting the parsley, and garnish the dish with slices of beetroot. Onion sauce may be substituted if preferred, or it may be served simply with a little of the liquor in which it has been cooked poured over it, and some plainly boiled Spanish onions handed round in a vegetable dish.

BEEF.

159. **SPICED BEEF.**—Ingredients—8 or 9 lbs. of beef, fat, ¼ oz. of salt prunella, ¾ oz. of saltpetre, 2 oz. of pounded spices, ½ lb. garlic, ¼ lb. of moist sugar.

Take 8 or 9 lbs. of beef, with a good piece of fat, mix well together ¼ oz. salt prunella, ¾ oz. saltpetre, about two oz. pounded spices—mace, cinnamon, cloves, allspice, nutmeg, ½ lb. garlic chopped very fine, and ¼ lb. moist sugar; rub this mixture well into the beef, and let it remain in the pickle a week, turning and rubbing it every day; tie up the beef, put it into cold water, boil it up slowly, skim well, and simmer for two or three hours; put it under heavy weights. Trim, and serve cold.

160. BEEF-STEAK PUDDING.—Ingredients—½ lb. of flour, 6 oz. of beef suet, 2½ lbs. of rump or beef steak, pepper and salt, 1 doz. oysters, ¼ pint of stock.

Chop the suet finely, and rub it into the flour with your hands, sprinkling a little salt, then mix with water to a smooth paste; roll the paste to the eighth of an inch; line a quart pudding basin with the paste; cut the steak into thin slices, flour them, and season with pepper and salt; put the oysters and the liquor that is with them into a saucepan and bring it to the point of boiling; then remove from the fire, and strain the liquor into a basin; then cut off the beards and the hard parts, leaving only the soft, roll the slices of steak, filling the basin with the meat and oysters; pour in the stock and liquor from the oysters. Cover with paste and boil three hours.

N.B. Be sure the water is boiling before putting the pudding in.

161. FILLETS OF BEEF (with Olives).—Ingredients—A piece of rump steak, pepper, salt, olives, onions, flour, stock, sauce.

Take a piece of rump steak, cut it into slices three-eighths of an inch thick, and trim them into shape. Melt plenty of butter in a baking-tin, lay the fillets of beef in this, and let them stand in a warm place for an hour or so; then sprinkle them with pepper and salt, and fry them in some very hot butter, turning them to let both sides take color. Stone a quantity of olives, and parboil them. Fry some onions a brown color in butter, add a little flour, and, when that is colored, as much stock as you want sauce, pepper, salt, and spices to taste. Let the sauce boil, then strain it, add the olives, and serve when quite hot, with the fillets in a circle round them.

162. GRENADINS OF BEEF.—Ingredients—Rump steak, lard, bacon fat, rich stock or gravy, onions, turnips, butter, flour, milk, pepper, salt, and nutmeg.

Cut some rump steak in slices a little more than half an inch thick, trim them all to the same size in the shape of cutlets, and lard them thickly on one side with fine lardoons of bacon fat. Lay them out, the larded side uppermost, into a flat pan, and put into it as much highly-flavored rich stock or gravy as will come up to the grenadins without covering them. Cover the pan, and place it in the oven to braise gently for an hour. Then remove the cover, baste the grenadins with the gravy, and let them remain uncovered in the oven till the larding has taken color; they are then ready. Take equal quantities of carrots and turnips cut into the shape of olives. Boil all these vegetables in salted water, then melt a piece of butter in a saucepan, add a tablespoonful of flour, stir in sufficient milk to make a sauce, add pepper, salt, and a little grated nutmeg. Put all the vegetables into this sauce, of which there should be just enough to hold them together; toss them gently in it till quite hot. Dress them in the middle of a dish, round them dispose the grenadins in a circle, and, having removed the superfluous fat from their gravy, put this round the grenadins, and serve.

163. **BEEFSTEAK PIE**.—Ingredients—Forcemeat, 2 oz. of fat bacon, 2 oz. of bread-crumbs, parsley, thyme, a small onion, mushrooms, seasoning for forcemeat, salt, pepper and nutmeg, 2 eggs, a tender rumpsteak, shalot, gravy.

Make some forcemeat with two oz. of fat bacon, two oz. of bread-crumbs, a little chopped parsley, thyme, a small onion, and some mushrooms; add seasoning of salt, pepper and nutmeg, pound in a mortar, moistening with the yolks of two eggs. Take a tender rump steak or the under cut of a sirloin of beef, cut it in thin slices, season with salt, pepper, and a little shalot. Roll each slice like a sausage with some forcemeat inside. border a pie dish, put in the beef and forcemeat, fill it up with good gravy, flavored with Harvey sauce. Cover with puff paste; bake in a moderate oven. Make a hole in the top, and add some reduced gravy.

164. **FILLETS OF BEEF (a la Chateaubriand)**.—Ingredients —A piece of sirloin of beef, pepper, salt, oil.

Take a piece of the undercut of the sirloin of beef, trim off the fat neatly, and the skin next to it; cut it across the grain into slices 1½in. thick, sprinkle them with pepper, dip them in oil, and broil over a clear fire, sprinkle with salt, and serve very hot in a dish garnished with potatoes *sautees au beurre*. For potatoes *sautees au beurre* see receipt in " Vegetables."

165. **STEWED BEEF**.—Ingredients—7 or 8 lbs. of fresh silver beef, bacon, pepper, spices and sweet herbs, onions, carrots, bay leaves, salt and pepper, 1 pint of common claret, ½ pint of common stock.

Take a piece of fresh silver of beef (7lb. or 8lb.); with a sharp knife make five or six incisions through it. Cut as many square pieces of bacon, fat and lean, long enough to go right through from one side of the piece of meat to the other. Roll each piece of bacon in a mixture of powdered pepper, spices, and sweet herbs, and insert one into each incision; tie up the meat carefully, line the bottom of a stewpan with slices of fat bacon, put the meat on this with some onions and carrots cut in slices, some sweet herbs, a couple of bay leaves, parsley, whole pepper, and salt to taste; add a pint of common claret, and half that quantity of stock; set the whole to stew gently for some hours, turning the meat occasionally. At the time of serving strain off the gravy, skim it well of fat, remove the string from the meat, pour the gravy over it, and garnish with cauliflower sprouts.

166. **BEEF A-LA-MODE.**—Ingredients—7 or 8 lbs. of the thick shank of beef, a little fat bacon, a teacupful of vinegar, allspice, black pepper and 2 cloves, 1 bunch of savory herbs, a little parsley, 3 carrots, 3 onions, 1 turnip and a head of celery, 1 quart of water, 1 glass of port wine.

Make holes in the beef large enough to put the bacon in; cut the bacon into long slices about an inch thick; dip in vinegar, then in the above seasoning. (The herbs and spices must be finely mixed.) Having filled the holes in the beef with bacon, rub the former over with the remaining seasoning and bind up with tape; slice and fry the onions a light brown; cut the vegetables into small pieces; have ready your stewpan into which put the beef with the vegetables, vinegar and water; simmer *slowly* for five hours. When ready to serve, dish the beef, remove the tape, take off every particle of fat from the gravy, and add the port wine, just let it come to a boil and pour over the meat and serve.

167. **CORN BEEF.**—Ingredients—4 gallons of fresh water, ½ lb. of coarse brown sugar, 2 oz. of saltpetre, 7 lbs. of common salt.

Put four gallons of fresh water, ¼ lb. of coarse brown sugar, 2 oz. saltpetre, 7 lb. of common salt, into a boiler; remove the scum as it rises, and, when well boiled, leave it to get cold. Put in the meat in the pickle, lay a cloth over it, and press the meat down with bricks or any weight.

168. **BEEF CAKE (Cold meat cookery).**—Ingredients—to each pound of cold roast meat allow ¼ lb. of bacon or ham, a little pepper and salt, 1 bunch of minced savoury herbs, 2 eggs.

Take your meat underdone and mince very finely, add the bacon, which must also be well minced; mix together, stir in the herbs and bind with 2 eggs; make into square cakes about ½ inch thick; fry in hot dripping, drain on blotting paper, and serve with gravy poured round.

169. **BEEF (Cold meat cookery).**—Ingredients—about 2 lbs. of cold roast beef, 1 large onion, 1 large carrot, 1 turnip, 1 bunch of savoury herbs, salt and pepper to taste. 4 tablespoonfuls of ale, ½ pint of gravy, a crust of mashed potatoes.

Cut the beef into slices allowing a little fat, put a layer of this at bottom of pie dish, slice vegetables and sprinkle a layer of them upon the meat; pound the herbs, strew a little over the meat with pepper and salt and proceed in this manner, until the ingredients are used; pour in gravy and ale. If this should not be approved, water can be substituted ; cover with crust of mashed potatoes.

NOTE.—Parboil vegetables before adding them to meat, and the liquor in which they are boiled can be used in the place of gravy if there is none at hand.

170. **BUBBLE AND SQUEAK** (Cold meat cookery).—Ingredients—A few thin slices of cold boiled beef, a little butter, small cabbage, 1 sliced onion, pepper and salt to taste.

Fry the beef gently in the butter, place them on a flat dish, and cover with fried greens. Savoys can be used. Boil until tender, press in cullender, mince and then put in frying pan with butter and sliced onion and a little salt and pepper.

171. **BEEF COLLOPS.**—Ingredients—2½ lbs. of rump steak, ¼ lb of butter, 1 pint of gravy or water, salt and pepper, challot minced finely, 1 pickled walnut, a teaspoonful of capers.

Cut thin slices of steak and divide into pieces about two inches long and dredge with flour ; put butter into frying pan and when quite hot add the meat and pour upon them the gravy or water ; allow them to fry for three minutes, add a little more butter, put in seasoning and other ingredients and allow the whole to simmer for ten minutes. Serve on hot dish.

172. **BEEF SAUSAGES.**—Ingredients—To every lb. of suet allow 2 lbs. of lean beef, seasoning to taste, a little mixed spice.

Chop the suet finely, taking care that there is no skin with it, add pepper, salt, and spices ; mix well together, form into flat cakes and fry brown.

173. **ROAST BULLOCK'S HEART.**—Ingredients—1 bullock's heart, ¼ lb. suet, 6 oz. of bread crumbs, ¼ pint of milk, 1 tablespoonful of chopped parsley, 1 dessertspoonful of chopped mixed herbs, ¼ lb. of dripping or butter, 1 pint of gravy or beef-tea. For the sauce—one small onion, a dessertspoonful of flour, salt and pepper, butter the size of an egg, a large spoonful of mushroom catchup.

Wash the heart in salt water, taking care to remove all the blood ; wash in a second water and dry with a clean cloth ; be careful to dry it thoroughly ; chop the suet as finely as possible, mix with some bread-crumbs the suet, parsley, herbs, salt and pepper ; lastly put in the milk, then proceed to fill all the cavities of the heart with the stuffing ; take a piece of paper, grease it well with butter or dripping, place this over the cavities and tie it on tightly with string ; put one oz. of dripping into the pan, and baste the heart occasionally ; when the gravy boils, cut up the onion, sprinkling with pepper and salt, and add to the gravy ; allow it to stew *gently* until about five minutes before the heart is done ; skim occasionally; when done strain the liquor ; into another saucepan put the butter, and allow it to melt a minute or two ; then add the flour and mix smoothly together ; then pour in slowly the liquor, stirring until it boils and thickens. Then dish up, remove paper, and add to the sauce the mushroom catchup. Immediately pour this sauce round the heart and serve.

174. **A POLISH DISH**.—Ingredients—About 2 lbs. of rump steak cut thickly, some bread-crumbs, butter and salt, 1 onion.

Chop the onion as finely as possible ; make deep incisions in the beef, taking care not to go through ; fill the incisions with the bread, etc. ; roll steak, put in stewpan, adding a little butter ; allow to simmer about two and a half hours. Serve with its own gravy thickened and flavored with catchup or sauce.

175. **BEEF OLIVES**.—Ingredients—Some steaks weighing about ¼ lb., a little white pepper and salt, forcemeat made with the fat and lean of veal, a small piece of lean ham or bacon, a bunch of parsley, about ½ lb. of bread-crumbs, 2 eggs.

Cut some steaks, flatten them with a roller, dredge them with a small quantity of white pepper and salt, have some forcemeat made with the fat and lean of veal mixed together, a small piece of lean ham or bacon, parsley, with a few bread-crumbs, all beaten in a mortar and mixed with the egg ; lay a little over each steak, and roll it up tightly, fastening with a skewer ; dip them in the yolk of an egg, then in crumbs of bread, and fry them of a pale brown ; dish them with brown sauce seasoned with cayenne.

176. **BEEFSTEAK** (Stuffed).—Ingredients—About 2 lbs. of beefsteak, about 6 oz. of bread crumbs, savory herbs, needle and thread.

Take the steak an inch thick ; make a stuffing of bread, herbs, etc., and spread it over the steak ; roll it up, and with a needle and coarse thread sew it together. Lay it in an iron pot on one or two wooden skewers, and put in water just sufficient to cover it ; let it stew slowly for two hours ; longer if the beef is tough ; serve it in a dish with the gravy turned over it. To be carved crosswise, in slices, through beef and stuffing.

177. **BEEF OMELET**.—Ingredients—3 lbs. of beefsteak, ¾ of a lb. of suet, salt and pepper, a little sage, 3 eggs, 6 Boston crackers.

Three pounds of beefsteak, three-fourths of a pound of suet, chopped fine ; salt, pepper, and a little sage, three eggs, six Boston crackers rolled ; make into a roll and bake.

178. **BEEF (Braized).**—Ingredients—1 cupful of stale bread, pepper and salt, a tablespoonful of onion, 2 tablespoonfuls of dripping, 1 tablespoonful of flour.

Buy a piece of the flank that gives a strip about three times as long as it is wide, so that it can be rolled up easily. Trim off any tough, outer skin which may seem too hard to cook, wipe the meat all over with a damp towel, and lay it flat on the table with the outside down ; season it highly with salt and pepper ; make a stuffing by soaking a cupful of stale bread in cold water until it is soft, and then squeeze it in a towel to free it from the water; season it highly with salt and pepper, mix with a tablespoonful of onion, and spread it over the beef, then roll up the beef without displacing the stuffing, and tie it tightly with cord ; let two tablespoonfuls of drippings or bacon fat get hot in the bottom of a saucepan just large enough to contain the beef, then brown the beef in the drippings, over a hot fire ; when it is brown dust over it a tablespoonful of flour, turning the beef about until the flour is quite brown, and then cover the meat with boiling water, and season the gravy thus made with pepper and salt ; next put on the cover of the saucepan, and if it does not fit steam-tight, seal it with a thick paste of flour and water, and set it where its contents will cook slowly for three hours. At the expiration of that length of time the meat will probably be tender ; the strings can then be removed, and the beef served with the gravy in which it was cooked.

179. **BEEF (Stewed).**—Ingredients—1 tablespoonful of butter, 2 sliced onions, 12 whole cloves, allspice, ½ teaspoonful of salt, ¼ teaspoonful of black pepper, 1 pint of cold water, 2 or 3 lbs of tender beef, a little flour, a few sprigs of sweet basil.

In a stew-pan place a large tablespoonful of butter, in which fry until quite brown two sliced onions adding, while cooking, twelve whole cloves ; ditto allspice ; half a teaspoonful of salt, and half that quantity of black pepper; take from the fire pour in a pint of cold water, wherein lay two or three pounds of tender lean beef cut in small, thick pieces ; cover closely, and let all stew gently two hours, adding, just before serving, a little flour thickening. A few sprigs of sweet basil is an improvement.

180. **HUNTER'S BEEF.**—Ingredients—To a round of beef that weighs 25 lbs, take 3 ounces of saltpetre, 3 oz of the coarsest sugar, 1 oz. of cloves, 1 nutmeg, ½ an oz. of allspice, 3 handfuls of common salt, all in the finest powder.

The beef should hang two or three days ; then rub the above well into it, and turn and rub it every day for two or three weeks. The bone must be taken out at first. When to be dressed, dip it into cold water, to take off the loose spice, bind it up tightly with tape, and put it in a pan with a teacupful of water at the bottom ; cover the top of the meat with shred suet, and the pan with a brown crust and paper, and bake it five or six hours ; when cold, take off the paste and tape. The meat should be cut with a very sharp knife, to prevent waste.

181. BAKED OX TONGUE.—Ingredients—2 eggs, a few cloves, 6 oz. of bread-crumbs, ¼lb. of butter, ½ pt. of good gravy, a glass of wine, red currant jelly.

Soak the tongue well in lukewarm water for about twelve hours, scrape and trim it, stick it over with cloves (about twenty-four), and boil slowly according to size for two or three hours. Then take it up and brush it over with the yolks of two eggs and sprinkle it with bread-crumbs (6oz.). Next bake it to a good brown, beating it constantly with a quarter of a pound of butter. Put it on a dish, and pour round it half a pint of good gravy with a glass of wine. Serve with red currant jelly.

182. BRAIZED STEAK.—Ingredients—Slices of bacon, steak, an oz. of butter, carrot, turnip, onion, a bay leaf, a blade of mace, small piece of lemon peel, ½ pt. of good brown stock or a teaspoonful of extract of beef.

For this the meat should be well hung and tender, and about an inch in thickness. First cut off all the fat and lay it aside, then lard the steak by drawing tiny slices of bacon through it. Put 1oz. of butter in a frying-pan and fry the steak in this for about a minute, this is to keep in the juices of the meat ; then put into a stewpan two or three small slices of each of the following : carrot, turnip, and onion, together with a bay leaf, a blade of mace, and a small piece of lemon peel ; add half a pint of good brown stock (this is the quantity for about ¾lb. of meat), and stew gently three-quarters of an hour. If no stock is at hand, a teaspoonful of extract of beef dissolved in water will answer the purpose. Before dishing up, cut up about the quarter of a small carrot, ditto turnip, into small strips ; boil them till tender, then drain and place on the steak when serving. The gravy in which the meat is cooked should be carefully strained over it, and for garniture, besides the vegetables already mentioned, it should have the fat, which must be cut into small dice, and fried for the purpose,

183. BIFSTECK SAUTE.—Ingredients—Steak, pepper and flour, butter, cold water, or stock flavored with mushroom catchup, a teacupful of chopped parsley, a dessertspoonful of lemon juice.

Have your steak cut not more than an inch thick, and beat it thoroughly with a meat bat until the fibre is quite divided. Sprinkle it with pepper, and flour it thickly on both sides. Melt butter in a deep frying or sauté pan to thinly cover the bottom of it, and when it is quite hot put in the steak, and just scald it on both sides for a second or two, and then pour in from time to time a little cold water or stock well-flavored with mushroom catchup. The steak will take from twenty to twenty-five minutes to cook, according to whether it is liked with the gravy in it or not, and during that time it must be constantly attended to, turned every two or three seconds, and kept all the time just gently simmering. If all these directions are carefully followed, you will have a steak as tender as it should be when well stewed, with the additional advantages of retaining its own juices and being quickly prepared. For a steak of 2lbs. boil a teacupful of chopped parsley to look quite green, and mix with it quickly ½oz. of butter and a dessertspoonful of lemon juice. Arrange this in little heaps upon the steak, which should be served on a hot water dish. Pour some of the gravy round it, and send the remainder to table in a tureen. This is a useful dish for "parlor cookery," being easily prepared on an ordinary spirit stove. Instead of the parsley, button mushrooms stewed in butter can accompany the steak, which, to vary the flavor, may be first steeped for an hour or two in a marinade of oil and vinegar, flavored with a little French mustard, shalot, vinegar, and allspice: one part vinegar to two of oil should be used, and the steak allowed to lie in it on a flat dish for an equal time for each side. A cutlet from a leg of mutton is very good cooked as above, and fillets from the undercut of a sirloin, are excellent. French fried potatoes, or potatoes mashed and browned are improvements to these dishes. Thick brown oyster or brown soubise sauce may be spread over the steak; and a mutton cutlet looks well and is very nice bordered with tomatoes halved, sprinkled with pepper and salt, and fried in butter, or it may be served with capers scalded with vinegar and sprinkled over it.

184. BEEF TONGUE.

If it has been dried and smoked before it is dressed it should be soaked over night, but if only pickled a few hours will be sufficient. Put it in a pot of cold water over a slow fire for an hour or two before it comes to a boil; then let it simmer gently for from three to four hours, according to its size: ascertain when it is done by probing it with a skewer. Take the skin off, and before serving surround the root with a paper frill.

PORK.

185. LEG OF PORK (to Roast).

Choose a small leg of fine young pork; cut a slit in the knuckle with a sharp knife, and fill the space with sage and onion chopped, a little pepper and salt. When half done, score the skin in slices, but do not cut deeper than the outer rind. Apple sauce and potatoes should be served to eat with it.

186. LEG OF PORK (to Boil).

Salt it eight or ten days: when it is to be dressed, weigh it; let it lie half an hour in cold water to make it white ; allow a quarter of an hour for every pound, and half an hour over, from the time it boils up ; skim it as soon as it boils, and frequently after. Allow water enough. Save some of it to make peas-soup. Some boil it in a very nice cloth, floured, which gives a very delicate look. It should be small and of a fine grain. Serve peas-pudding and turnips with it.

187. LOIN AND NECK OF PORK.

Roast them. Cut the skin of the loin across, at distances of half an inch, with a sharp penknife.

188. SHOULDERS AND BREASTS OF PORK.

Put them into pickle, or salt the shoulders as the leg; when very nice, they may be roasted.

189. NECK OF PORK (Rolled).—Ingredients—Neck of pork, forcemeat of chopped sage, a few bread-crumbs, salt and pepper, 2 or 3 berries of allspice.

Bone it; put a forcemeat of chopped sage, a very few crumbs of bread, salt, pepper, and two or three berries of allspice, over the inside; then roll the meat as tight as you can, and roast it slowly.

190. PORK PIE.—Ingredients—¼ lb. of lard, 1 lb. of pork (leg or loin), seasoning, 1 lb. of flour and an egg, ½ glass of cold water.

Put the lard and water in rather a large saucepan ; place upon the fire and allow to boil (take care it does not boil over, or it will catch fire). Cut the pork into pieces about an inch square ; when the lard and water are quite boiling pour into the middle of the flour and mix with a spoon. When the paste is cool enough knead it well ; it must be rather stiff; cut off a quarter of the paste, and the remainder mould into the shape of a basin, pressing it inside; shape it evenly all round, it should be about the third of an inch in thickness; dip the pieces of pork into cold water, seasoning well with pepper and salt, then place them in the mould of paste as closely as possible. If liked a little chopped sage can be sprinkled over the pork, then take the rest of the paste, roll it, and cut to the size of the top of the mould; taking care to have it the same size as the inside; break an egg, and divide the yolk from the white; with a paste brush dip into the white of egg, and brush the edge of the paste; then place this on the top of the pie, pressing the edges well. Any trimmings of paste that are left, cut into little leaves, dip into the white of egg, and stick them on top of the pie; then wet the pie all over with the yolk of the egg and bake for about two hours.

191. **PIG'S FRY.**—Ingredients—1 lb. of pig's fry, 3 lbs. of potatoes, 1 onion, sage and seasoning.

Put the potatoes into cold water, scrub and wash them well; then place them in a saucepan of cold water and put upon the fire to boil; directly they boil, take them out of the water, peel, and cut them into slices; peel the onion and chop it and two or three sage leaves together; cut the pig's fry into small pieces; grease a dish, and put a layer of the potatoes in the bottom; then sprinkle a little of the sage and onion, pepper and salt, then a layer of the pig's fry; then another sprinkling of the seasoning, and so on until the dish is full, then put in a little water for gravy; the skin usually sent with pig's fry put over the top of the dish; if the skin is not sent, take a piece of whity brown paper and grease it and place upon the dish instead. Bake for about one hour.

192. **PORK (Pickled).**

The quantities proportioned to the middlings of a pretty large hog, the hams and shoulders being cut off.

Mix, and pound fine, four ounces of salt-petre, a pound of coarse sugar, an ounce of sal-prunel, and a little common salt: sprinkle the pork with salt and drain it twenty-four hours; then rub with the above; pack the pieces tight in a small deep tub, filling up the spaces with common salt. Place large pebbles on the pork to prevent it from swimming in the pickle which the salt will produce. If kept from air, it will continue very fine for two years.

193. **PORK (Hashed).**—Ingredients—Some remnants of cold roast pork, pepper and salt to taste, 2 onions, 2 blades of mace, 1 teaspoonful of flour, 1 teaspoonful of vinegar, 2 cloves, ½ pint of gravy.

Take the onions, chop and fry them of a nice brown; then take the pork and cut it into thin slices, seasoning with pepper and salt to taste, and add these to the rest of the above ingredients; stew it for about half an hour gently, and serve with sippets of toasted bread.

194. **PORK CUTLETS.**—Ingredients—Loin of pork, pepper and salt.

Cut the loin into chops, take the bone out, and greater portion of the fat; season with pepper, and place upon a perfectly hot gridiron, and broil for about fifteen minutes. Be particular that they are thoroughly done; dish, sprinkle with a little salt, and serve plain, or with tomato sauce.

195. **SUCKING PIG** (Roast).—Ingredients—pig, 8 oz. of breadcrumbs, 18 sage leaves, pepper and salt, tablespoonful of butter, salad oil to baste with, tablespoonful of lemon juice, ½ pint of gravy.

Stuff the pig with finely grated bread-crumbs, minced sage, pepper and salt, and a tablespoonful of butter. Take care these are well blended. After stuffing the pig, sew up the slit neatly, truss the legs back, to allow the inside to be roasted, put in oven, and directly it is dry have ready some butter tied in a piece of thin cloth, and rub the pig with this in every part. Continue this operation several times while roasting; do not allow the pig to burn in any part. Then take half a pint of gravy, a tablespoonful of lemon juice, and the gravy that flowed from the pig,; pour a little of this over the pig, and the remainder send to table in a tureen. Instead of butter for basting many cooks use salad oil as this makes the crackling crisp. Before dishing cut off the head and part the body down the middle, and lay on the dish back to back. Take care that it is sent to table *very* hot, and serve with apple sauce. It will take about two hours for a small pig to roast.

196. **PIG'S PETTITOES.**—Ingredients—A slice of bacon cut thin, an onion, a blade of mace, 5 peppercorns, 4 sprigs of thyme, 1 pint of gravy, pepper and salt, thickening of butter and flour.

Put the heart, pettitoes and liver, into a saucepan, add the bacon, mace, peppercorns, onion, thyme and gravy; simmer gently for fifteen minutes; take out the head and liver and mince very finely; allow the feet to stew until quite tender, they will take about half an hour, then return to the saucepan the liver, thicken the gravy with a little butter and flour, sprinkle a little pepper and salt, and simmer very gently for five or six minutes, stirring occasionally; when ready to dish split the feet, and arrange them round the mince with sippets of toasted bread, and pour the gravy in the centre.

197. PORK CHEESE.—Ingredients—About 2 lbs. of cold roast pork, a dessertspoonful of chopped-up parsley, 5 sage leaves, pepper and salt, a bunch of savory herbs, 2 blades of mace, a little nutmeg, ½ teaspoonful of minced lemon peel, sufficient gravy to fill the mould.

Cut the pork into pieces, but do not chop; there should be about a quarter of fat to a pound of lean; sprinkle with pepper and salt, pound the spices thoroughly and mince as finely as possible, the parsley, sage, lemon peel and herbs: then mix all this nicely together. Place in mould and fill with gravy. Bake a little over an hour. When perfectly cold turn out.

198. SAUSAGES.—Ingredients—Pork, fat and lean, sage, pepper and salt, a little allspice.

Chop fat and lean of pork together; season with sage, pepper and salt, and you may add two or three berries of allspice; *half fill* hogs' guts that have been soaked and made extremely clean: or the meat may be kept in a very small pan, closely covered; and so rolled and dusted with a very little flour before it is fried. Serve on stewed red cabbage; or mashed potatoes, put in a form, brown with a salamander, and garnish with the above; they must be pricked with a fork before they are dressed, or they will burst.

199. HAM (how to Boil to give it an excellent flavor).—Ingredients—2 heads of celery, 2 turnips, vinegar and water, a large bunch of savory herbs, and 3 onions.

In choosing a ham, be sure that it is perfectly sweet. To ascertain this stick a sharp knife into it near the bone, when the knife is taken out, it will have an agreeable smell if the meat is sweet. If the meat has been hung for a long time, and it is salt and dry, it would be necessary to soak for twenty-four hours, and change the water often. Put the meat in a large pot with sufficient water to cover it; bring it to the boil *gradually*, and carefully take off the scum as it rises; when on the point of boiling add the vegetables and herbs; let it simmer gently until quite tender, then take it out, strip off the skin, cover with bread raspings and put a paper frill round the knuckle. Four hours will be sufficient for a ham weighing ten pounds.

200. HAM (Potted).—Ingredients—2½ lbs. lean ham, ¾ lb. of fat, 1 teaspoonful of pounded mace, a saltspoonful of pounded allspice, ½ nutmeg, clarified butter, pepper.

Take some slices of cold ham, cut them small, mixing the lean and fat in the above proportions; proceed to pound the ham to a fine paste in a mortar; gradually add the seasoning, and take care that all the ingredients are well mixed, press the mixture into pots, cover with the clarified butter and keep it cool.

201. **HAM (Baked).**—Ingredients—Ham, **crust.**

Allow the ham to soak in water for twelve hours; wipe it dry, and trim any rusty places underneath; cover with a common crust, taking care that it is thick enough to keep the gravy in; have the oven at a moderate heat and bake for about four hours; when done, take off crust and skin, cover with raspings, and garnish the knuckle with a paper frill. Very good.

202. **TO GLAZE A HAM.**—Ingredients—An egg, salt, melted butter, a cup of powdered cracker, a little cream.

After the ham is skinned and cold, brush all over with beaten egg; mix the cracker, salt, and melted butter with cream enough to make a thick paste; spread it evenly over the ham and brown in a moderate oven.

203. **TO MAKE LARD.**

Take the inner part of the pig, put into a stone jar, and place in a saucepan of boiling water; allow it to simmer gently, and as it melts, strain carefully from the sediment; put in small jars and keep in a cool place. The fleed makes exceedingly light crust, and is very wholesome.

204. **TRIPE (To Dress).**—Ingredients—Tripe, milk and water, onion sauce.

Cut away the coarsest fat, take equal proportions of milk and water, and boil for three quarters of an hour. Have ready some onion sauce and when ready to dish, smother the tripe with the sauce, and, any that is left, send to table in a tureen.

205. **FRIED TRIPE.**—Ingredients—Salt and water, pepper, flour, lard, a tablespoonful of vinegar.

Scrape the tripe well; cut into squares the size of your hand; boil in salt and water (a tablespoonful of salt to one quart of water) till very tender. The next day cut into smaller pieces, season with salt and pepper, dredge with flour, fry brown on both sides in a pan of hot lard. When done, take it out, pour nearly all the lard out, add a good gill of boiling water, thicken with flour, mixed smooth with a tablespoonful of vinegar; season to taste, and pour hot over the tripe. A nice breakfast dish.

Tripe may be cooked several ways, it can be stewed in gravy with mushrooms, or cut into collops, sprinkled with chopped onion and savoury herbs, and fried a nice brown in clarified butter.

206. **TRIPE (Stewed).**—Ingredients—2 quarts of water, pepper and salt, onions, a piece of butter, 2 tablespoonsful of cream, nutmeg, 2 slices of buttered toast.

See that the tripe is washed very white; cut up in pieces and put them into a stewpan with two quarts of water, and pepper and salt to taste. Let boil until quite tender, which will take about two hours and a half, or perhaps longer; have some white onions boiled until quite tender; then turn them out in a cullender to drain; then mash them, putting them back into your saucepan (which you have previously wiped out) with a piece of butter, two tablespoonsful of cream or milk, a grating of nutmeg and a very little salt; sprinkle in a little flour, set the pan on the fire, keeping it well covered, and give it one boil. Place at the bottom of a dish two slices of buttered toast, cut in pieces, and put the tripe over it.

VEAL.

207. **ROAST VEAL** (Stuffed).—Ingredients—8 oz. of bruised bread-crumbs, 4 oz. of chopped suet, shallot, thyme, marjoram, and winter savory, 2 eggs, salt and pepper.

To eight ounces of bruised crumbs of bread add four ounces of chopped suet, shallot, thyme, marjoram, and winter savory, all chopped fine; two eggs, salt and pepper to season; mix all these ingredients into a firm, compact kind of paste, and use this stuffing to fill a hole or pocket which you will have cut with a knife in some part of the piece of veal, taking care to fasten it in with a skewer. A piece of veal weighing four pounds would require rather more than an hour to cook it thoroughly before a small fire.

208. **VEAL** (Stewed).—Ingredients—2 quarts of water, 1 peeled onion, a few blades of mace, a little salt, ¼ lb. of rice, butter, chopped parsley.

Break the shank bone, wash it clean, and put it into two quarts of water, an onion peeled, a few blades of mace and a little salt; set it over a quick fire, and remove the scum as it rises; wash carefully a quarter of a pound of rice, and when the veal has cooked for about an hour skim it well and throw in the rice; simmer for three quarters of an hour slowly; when done put the meat in a deep dish and the rice around it. Mix a little drawn butter, stir in some chopped parsley, and pour over the veal.

209. **VEAL AND HAM PIE**.—Ingredients—Forcemeat balls, 1 or 2 eggs, ham and veal, mushrooms, gravy, pie crust, jelly, onions, herbs, lemon peel, salt, cayenne, mace, parsley, whites of eggs.

Cut some thin slices off the leg or neck of veal, free them from skin and gristle, lard them well, and season with salt and pepper. Have some eggs boiled hard and some thin slices of ham. Make some forcemeat balls with fat bacon, the trimmings of the veal, chopped onions, parsley, and sweet herbs, grated lemon peel, salt, cayenne, and pounded mace. Pound all in a mortar, and bind with one or two eggs. Line a pie dish with good paste, and fill it with layers (not too close)— first one of ham, then one of veal, of forcemeat balls, of the eggs (cut in halves), and so on ; a few mushrooms may be added ; put in some gravy ; lastly, a layer of thin bacon ; and cover all with tolerably thick crust, glaze. Bake for about four hours in a moderate oven. Make a hole in the top, and insert some good savoury jelly—made with ox or calf's foot, knuckle of veal, and trimming of bacon and ham well flavored with onions, more herbs and lemon peel, and cleared with the whites of egg. Leave till quite cold, then it can be cut with a sharp knife into slices.

210. **VEAL PUDDING**.—Ingredients—A few pieces of salt pork, butter, pepper, salt, parsley, thyme and flour.

Line a pudding mould or tin pail with a rich paste and fill the cavity with bits of veal cut into small pieces ; add a few pieces of salt pork and season to taste with butter, pepper, salt, parsley and thyme, and sufficient boiling water to fill the mould two-thirds full ; dredge with flour and then cover the top with paste, and after placing the cover on firmly tie a cloth closely over the entire mould, and place it in boiling water and allow it to boil an hour or more.

211. **VEAL CAKE**.—Ingredients—Some hard boiled eggs, a layer of ham, tongue or sausage meat, salt, pepper, and nutmeg, a layer of veal.

Have some slices of veal ; put a layer of hard boiled eggs in a dish, then a layer of ham, tongue or sausage meat ; season with salt, pepper, and a little nutmeg ; then a layer of veal—in this way fill up the dish. Bake in the oven with a little water in the dish, keep it covered while baking ; when done put a weight on until cold, then turn it out. A nice dish for breakfast or supper.

212. **VEAL CAKE**.—Ingredients—1 lb. of veal cutlet, ½ lb. of blanched streaky bacon, 3 or 4 eggs, aspic jelly, pepper, salt, herbs, parsley, chervil and shalot, lemon peel.

Take about one lb. of veal cutlet and half lb. of blanched streaky bacon, cut the veal into neat collops, and slice the bacon ; boil three or four eggs hard, and slice them. Have ready some aspic jelly or some reduced, well-flavored, clarified white stock ; put into a plain mould a layer of the aspic jelly, then some slices of the egg, a layer of veal, then one of bacon, sprinkling each layer freely with pepper, salt, and chopped herbs, parsley, chervil, and shalot, and on the layer of veal add a small quantity of grated lemon peel ; repeat till all the ingredients are used up. Fill up the mould with aspic jelly, cover it either with stiff flour-and-water paste or with double paper tied securely on ; bake about an hour in a moderate oven. When cold turn it out, and garnish with sprigs of chervil, watercress, or parsley.

213. **VEAL (Marbled).**—Ingredients—Spice, butter, tongue and veal.

Take some cold roasted veal, season with spice, beat in a mortar ; skin a cold boiled tongue, cut up and pound it to a paste, adding to it nearly its weight of butter; put some of the veal into a pot, and strew in lumps of the pounded tongue ; put in another layer of the veal and then more tongue ; press it down and pour clarified butter on top ; this cuts very prettily like veined marble. White meat of fowls may be used instead of veal.

214. **VEAL SCALLOP.**—Ingredients—Pepper and salt, crackers, milk and gravy from meat, 2 eggs, butter.

Chop some cold roast or stewed veal very fine ; put a layer on the bottom of a pudding dish well buttered ; season with pepper and salt. Next have a layer of finely-powdered crackers ; wet with a little milk or some of the gravy from the meat. Proceed until the dish is full ; spread over all a thick layer of cracker-crumbs, seasoned with salt and wet into a paste with milk and two beaten eggs. Stick pieces of butter all over it, cover closely, and bake half an hour: then remove the cover and bake long enough to brown nicely. Do not get it too dry.

215. **QUENELLES OF VEAL.**— Ingredients — 1 lb. of veal cutlet, a gill of water, salt, butter, nutmeg, flour, 4 eggs, ½ gill of cream.

Remove the skin from one lb. of veal cutlet, and cut it into small pieces. Put into a stewpan a gill of water, a pinch of salt, and a small piece of butter ; when boiling stir in as much flour as will form a paste ; when it is smooth put it away to get cold, then take half the quantity of butter that you have of veal, and half the quantity of paste you have of butter, put the paste into a mortar, pound it well, then add the butter, pound it, then add the veal ; pound well for ten minutes, add one whole egg, three yolks of eggs, salt, pepper, a little grated nutmeg, work well together, pass through a wire sieve, stir in half a gill of cream, shape the quenelles with two tablespoons, place them in a well-buttered sauté-pan, leaving a clear space on one side ; put a good pinch of salt in that space, pour in sufficient boiling water to cover the quenelles, and leave them to poach for ten minutes, then drain them carefully on a cloth ; arrange on a dish.

216. FRICANDEAU OF VEAL.—Ingredients— A fillet or cushion of veal, lard, bacon, carrots, onions, sweet herbs, salt, pepper, spices, stock, spinach.

Neatly trim a nice piece of fillet or cushion of veal, lard it thickly on one side with bacon. Place in a large stewpan a layer of slices of bacon, then some carrots and onions cut in slices, with a bundle of sweet herbs, pepper, salt, and spices to taste; lay the piece of veal in the middle, and moisten with about a pint of stock. Let the meat stew gently for two or three hours, basting the top occasionally. Then strain off the gravy, put it into a small saucepan, skim off superfluous fat, add to it a little butter mixed smooth with a small quantity of flour, and let the gravy reduce nearly to a glaze; pour it over the meat, the top of which should be previously browned with a salamander if necessary, and serve with a border of spinach.

217. ROLLED VEAL—Ingredients—Loin of veal, forcemeat, bacon, bread-crumbs, eggs, lemon peel, sweet herbs, salt, cayenne, pounded mace, fat bacon.

Bone a loin of veal and stuff it with forcemeat made of bacon, bread-crumbs, and eggs, and flavored with lemon peel, sweet herbs, salt, cayenne, and pounded mace. Tie it up, keeping it the shape of a large sausage; lay some slices of fat bacon on it, and stew gently for four hours in well-flavored stock. Let it cool; remove from the stock, and put it under heavy weights. When quite cold, glaze it.

218. COLLARED CALF'S HEAD.—Ingredients—A calf's head, 5 tablespoonsful of parsley, 4 blades of pounded mace, pepper to taste, a grated nutmeg, a few thick slices of ham, the yolks of 5 eggs boiled hard.

Scald the head for ten minutes, then scrape off the hair; divide the head and remove the brains; boil for about two hours, and if tender remove the bones. When this is done, flatten it on the table, sprinkle a thick layer of parsley, likewise of ham, and cut the yolks of the eggs into rings, and place these upon the ham, then season with pounded mace, white pepper, and nutmeg between each layer; roll the head in a cloth, and tie as tightly as possible. Boil for about four hours then remove from the pot; place a heavy weight on the top. Let it remain till cold, then remove the cloth and serve.

219. VEAL SAUSAGES.—Ingredients—Equal quantities of lean veal and fat bacon, a handful of sage, salt, pepper, a few anchovies.

Chop equal quantities of lean veal and fat bacon, a handful of sage, a little salt, pepper, and a few anchovies. Beat all in a mortar; and when used, roll and fry it, and serve with fried sippets, or on stewed vegetables, or on white collops.

220. **VEAL CUTLETS.**—Ingredients—4lbs. of the best end of the neck of veal, ½ teaspoonful of minced thyme, rind of a small lemon, 1 bunch of parsley, 1 tablespoonful of butter, 1 teaspoonful of lemon juice, 1 egg, pepper and salt, bread-crumbs, ½lb. of bacon.

To shape the cutlets, saw off the end of the rib bone, saw off the chine bone also, which lies at the back of the cutlets ; then form the cutlets to a neat shape. Mince thyme, and lemon rind and parsley, as finely as possible ; melt the butter, and add these ingredients to it ; add also the egg, pepper and salt, and beat all up together ; then rub very finely some crumbs of bread ; dip each cutlet into the mixture, then cover with bread-crumbs ; when the gridiron is perfectly warm, arrange the cutlets upon it. Have the fire nice and bright, but do not allow them to cook too fast or the bread-crumbs will burn before the cutlets are cooked through ; allow them to brown nicely on both sides ; about ten minutes will be the time. Serve on a wall of mashed potatoes in a circle ; fill the centre of dish with rolls of bacon and with a nice brown sauce. (See " Sauces.")

For rolls.—Cut some neat slices of bacon, roll them up and run a skewer through each ; place this in the oven for about five minutes, then remove skewer and arrange in centre of the dish.

221. **HARICOT OF VEAL.**—Ingredients—Best end of a small neck, a little brown gravy, 1 pt. of peas, 6 small cucumbers, 2 lettuces, a little broth, a few forcemeat balls.

Take the best end of a small neck ; cut the bones short, but leave it whole ; then put it into a stewpan just covered with brown gravy ; and when it is nearly done, have ready a pint of boiled peas, six cucumbers pared and sliced, and two cabbage-lettuces cut into quarters, all stewed in a little good broth ; put them to the veal, and let them simmer ten minutes. When the veal is in the dish, pour the sauce and vegetables over it, and lay the lettuce with forcemeat balls round it.

222. **HASHED CALF'S HEAD (a la Poulette).**—Ingredients— Calf's head, 2oz. of butter, 2 tablespoonsful of flour, ½ pint of white stock, a few button mushrooms, white pepper, and salt to taste, 2 eggs, juice of a lemon, parsley.

Cut the remnants of a boiled head into uniform pieces the size of half an apple. Melt in a saucepan one or two ounces of butter, according to the quantity of meat to be hashed ; amalgamate with it one or two tablespoonsful of flour, then stir in half a pint, more or less, of white stock. Stir well, then add a few button mushrooms, white pepper and salt to taste, and let the sauce boil for ten minutes. Put the saucepan by the side of the fire, and lay the pieces of calf's head in it; let them get hot slowly, but not boil. Just before serving stir in off the fire the yolks of two eggs, beaten up with the juice of a lemon, and strained; also a small quantity of either tarragon or parsley very finely minced.

223. **MINCED VEAL.**—Ingredients—Some remnants of roast or braized veal, a shallot, a little butter, a little flour, a little stock, a few sprigs of parsley, pepper and salt, nutmeg to taste, a few drops of lemon juice, fried bread, and poached eggs.

Take some remnants of roast or braized veal, trim off all browned parts, and mince it very finely; fry a shallot, chopped small, in plenty of butter; when it is a light straw color add a large pinch of flour and a little stock, then the minced meat, with chopped parsley, pepper, salt, and nutmeg to taste; mix well, add more stock if necessary, and let the mince gradually get hot by the side of the fire; lastly, add a few drops of lemon juice. Serve with sippets of bread fried in butter round, and the poached eggs on the top.

224. **VEAL (Braized Loin of).**—Ingredients—Veal, 2 oz. of butter, 1 carrot, 1 onion, a little parsley, sweet herbs, a leaf or two of basil, a bay leaf, a crust of bread toasted brown, a little flour, and a little stock.

Take about two oz. of butter, one carrot, one onion, a little parsley, sweet herbs, a leaf or two of basil, and a bay leaf; brown a large crust of bread, and put it in a stewpan with the above things, and fry them until they are brown; then flour the meat, and brown it well, putting it back in the saucepan; add a little stock, and baste it in the gravy till done, and keep turning the meat. Simmer four pounds for three or four hours.

225. **HASHED CALF'S HEAD.**—Ingredients—An onion, a slice of fat bacon, an oz. of butter, a tablespoonful of flour, a 15ct. bottle of French tomato sauce, a bay leaf, 2 sprigs of thyme, 1 of marjoram, 3 of parsley, 2 cloves, a doz. peppercorns, salt, cayenne pepper, a little stock, fried sippets of bread.

Mince an onion and a slice of fat bacon, fry them both with an ounce of butter until the onion begins to color, stirring well all the time to avoid any piece of one or the other getting burnt. Stir in a tablespoonful of flour, and a minute afterwards, moisten with a 15c. bottle of French tomato sauce; add a bay leaf two sprigs of thyme, one of marjoram, and three of parsley, two cloves, a dozen peppercorns, salt to taste, and the least possible quantity of cayenne pepper (as much as can be taken up with the end of a trussing needle). Let the sauce boil gently for half an hour; add a little stock to it if necessary, and strain it into a clean saucepan; when quite cold lay the pieces of calf's head into it, and let the whole be warmed very gradually on a slow fire ; the longer it will take to get hot, the better will the dish be. Care should be taken that the pieces of calf's head are well covered with the sauce. Serve garnished with fried sippets of bread.

226. **HASHED CALF'S HEAD.**—Ingredients—1 pint of brown sauce, 1 glass of sherry, a doz. of button mushrooms, the same quantity of pieces of pickled gherkins, a doz truffles, a doz. olives stoned, bread sippets, a little butter and 3 eggs, forcemeat balls.

Take a pint of brown sauce, add to it one glass of sherry, a dozen or more button mushrooms, the same quantity of pieces of pickled gherkins and of truffles cut with a vegetable cutter to the shape of olives, and a dozen olives stoned. Let the sauce come to a boil, then lay in it the remnants of a boiled calf's head cut in uniform and shapely pieces, simmer very slowly for about an hour, and serve garnished with bread sippets fried in butter, and hard-boiled eggs. The tongue, cut in convenient pieces, can also be added to this hash, as well as cocks' combs and forcemeat balls, etc. N.B.—The gherkins, after being cut, should be steeped in cold water for two or three hours.

227. **TRIMBALES OF VEAL.**—Ingredients—Turnip and carrots, salt water, a pinch of sugar, butter, flour, veal suet, boiled onion, pepper, and spices to taste, a little nutmeg, 3 or 4 eggs.

With a column cutter cut out of turnips and the red part of carrots a number of long, round pieces rather less than three-eighths of an inch in diameter. Cut these pieces into slices about one-eighth of an inch thick. Be careful to have all these pieces, which should be like very small counters, of uniform shape. Boil them separately in salted water with a pinch of sugar ; do not let them be overdone, and turn them out on a sieve to drain quite dry. Take a number of cake moulds, butter them thickly, and, using a trussing needle for the purpose, line them with the pieces of carrots and turnips in alternate rows by pressing them gently against the buttered bottom and sides. When they are all done, fill them with the following composition: put half a pint of water into a stewpan, with a pinch of salt and a small piece of butter; when it boils, stir into it enough flour to make a thick paste ; put it by to get cold. Take equal parts of this paste and veal suet, carefully picked ; pound them first separately, then together, in a mortar, with a piece of boiled onion, more or less, according to taste. Pound some lean veal, and of this take as much as there is paste and suet ; work the whole together in a mortar, seasoning the mixture with pepper and salt and spices to taste, one of which should be nutmeg. Pass the whole through a sieve; work in as many whole eggs as will bind the mixture. Place the moulds into a stewpan with hot water, with a piece of paper over them, and steam them for about half an hour. Turn them out very carefully on a dish, and pour under them a sufficient quantity of the following sauce: put into a pint of milk two or three mushrooms, one onion and a carrot cut into pieces, a bunch of sweet herbs, whole pepper and salt to taste, a few cloves, and a little mace; let the whole gently simmer for about an hour. Put an ounce of butter into a saucepan, and mix with it a tablespoonful of flour; then strain the flavored milk into the saucepan, and stir on the fire until it thickens. Finish by stirring in a gill of cream.

228. **GALANTINE OF VEAL.**—Ingredients—A breast of veal, ½ lb. of fat bacon, powdered spice, sweet herbs, pepper and salt, ½ lb. of boiled tongue, ½ doz. truffles, a calf's foot, 2 or 3 onions, 2 carrots, a clove of garlic, a bundle of sweet herbs (thyme, marjoram, parsley and bay leaf), cloves, whole pepper mace and salt.

Take a piece of breast of veal about twelve or fourteen inches long; bone and trim it carefully, removing all gristle and superfluous fat, as well as some of the meat (about one lb.) Take this meat and ½ lb. of fat bacon, pound together in a mortar, season with powdered spice and sweet herbs, pepper and salt to taste; then pass the mixture through a wire sieve; cut ½ lb. of boiled tongue in pieces about one inch square; cut half a dozen truffles each into three or four pieces. Lay the prepared breast of veal skin downwards on the table, sprinkle it with pepper, salt, and powdered spices; lay the pounded meat, the truffles, and the tongue on it, then roll it up neatly as a roly-poly pudding, and tie it up tightly in a cloth. Put all the trimmings and bones into a saucepan large enough to hold the galantine, add a calf's foot cut in pieces, the trimmings of the bacon (mind they are perfectly sweet), two or three onions, and two carrots cut in pieces, a clove of garlic, a bundle of sweet herbs (thyme, marjoram, parsley, and bay leaf), cloves, whole pepper, mace, and salt, in proportions according to taste. Fill up with such a quantity of cold water as will leave room for the galantine to be put in. Set the saucepan on the fire; when the contents boil put in the galantine; let it boil gently without interruption from two to two and a half hours; then lift it out, put it on a plate, and when it has cooled a little take off the cloth, tie it up afresh, and lay it between two dishes with a moderate weight upon it, to remain till cold. Care must be taken in this last operation that the "seam" of the galantine be made to come undermost. When quite cold undo the cloth, glaze the galantine, and garnish with savoury jelly made from the liquor in which it was boiled.

MUTTON.

MUTTON CUTLETS.

This is an entrée always ready to hand, but it must be carefully and neatly prepared. A dish of well-dressed mutton cutlets is truly "a dish to put before a king;" whereas greasy, fat, gristly lumps of meat, called for the nonce cutlets, offend the taste of the least fastidious. The first thing to attend to is the cutting and trimming of the cutlets neatly. Take a piece of the best end of the neck of mutton, saw off the bones short, remove gristle and fat, cut the cutlets about one-third of an inch in thickness, shape and trim them neatly, beat them with a cutlet bat dipped in water, and then proceed to cook them by any of the following recipes:

229. Pepper, salt, and broil them over a brisk fire, serve them with mashed or *sautees* potatoes in the centre of the dish.

230. Season as above, and before broiling dip them in oil or oiled butter. Serve with

231. SOUBISE SAUCE.

Peel and blanch four onions, cool them in water, drain and put them in a stewpan with sufficient water or white stock to cover them, add some cayenne, bay leaf, a little mace, a small piece of ham or bacon; keep the lid closely shut and simmer gently until tender; take them out, drain them thoroughly, press through a sieve or tammy cloth, add half pint of béchamel sauce made thus: put in a stewpan a little parsley, one clove, a small piece of bay leaf, sweet herbs, and one pint of white stock freed from fat; when boiled long enough to extract the flavor of the herbs, etc., strain it, boil up quickly, till reduced to half the quantity; mix a tablespoonful of arrowroot with half pint of milk or cream, pour on the reduced stock and simmer for ten minutes.

232. Boil them as in recipe 231, and serve with a *puree* of vegetables—haricot beans or celery—in the centre of the dish, or with chestnut sauce.

233. PUREE OF HARICOT BEANS.

Soak one pint of beans for twelve hours at least, put them with three quarts of stock, an onion stuck with cloves, a carrot, half a head of celery, one-quarter pound of bacon, some parsley, thyme, and bay leaf; simmer till quite tender, drain, strain the broth, pass the *puree* through a sieve, moistening with the broth, add pepper, salt, and it is ready for use.

234. PUREE OF CELERY.

Clean, cut into small pieces the white part of three or four heads of celery. Stew them, till quite tender, in white stock, season with pepper, salt, and mace. Pass them through a sieve, put them into a saucepan with a small piece of butter, add a little cream ; mix well and serve.

235. CHESTNUT SAUCE.

Remove the outer shell from some fine chestnuts, scald them in boiling water, and remove the inner skin. Stew them in good white stock till quite tender, drain, and while hot press them through a sieve. Put the pulp into a saucepan, add a small piece of butter, a little sugar, pepper, and salt. Stir over the fire till quite hot, but do not let it boil, and serve.

236. Prepare and season the cutlets as in recipe 233, dip them into the beaten-up yolk of an egg, or into oiled butter. Strew over them some plain (or better still, baked) bread crumbs, some finely minced parsley, and shalot ; broil and serve with Italian sauce.

237. ITALIAN SAUCE.

Put a slice of ham, two tablespoonsful of finely chopped mushrooms, and an onion (also chopped) into a stewpan with one gill of oil ; when the onion is well colored add three quarters of a pint of reduced gravy, a wineglass of white wine or vinegar, a spoonful of chopped parsley, pepper, salt, and a few slices of lemon ; simmer for half an hour, skim, remove the ham and slices of lemon, and serve hot.

238. Cut the cutlets about three-quarters of an inch thick, trim as before, and flatten with the cutlet bat, beat up the yolk of an egg, and mix with it chopped herbs—parsley, thyme, marjoram—some grated bread, nutmeg, salt, and pepper. Cover the cutlets with this, and put each one into a well-buttered paper, broil over a clear fire on both sides, remove the paper, and serve with

239. MUSHROOM SAUCE.

Remove the stalks and gritty part from half a pint of mushrooms ; wash, drain, and put them into half a pint of well-flavored gravy, simmer them till quite tender, drain them, and keep them hot. Melt one oz. of butter in a saucepan, add to it one oz. of flour, stir over the fire till brown; pour in the gravy, stirring till it boils. Arrange the mushrooms in the centre of the dish, the cutlets round them, and pour the sauce over.

240. Dip them in oiled butter, sprinkle them with bread crumbs and grated parmesan cheese, then dip them in beaten yolk of egg, put another layer of bread-crumbs and grated par-

mesan cheese; fry in boiling lard till of a gold color, and serve with

241. TOMATO SAUCE.

Mix in a saucepan one half oz. of butter and one half oz. of flour, add by degrees a small bottle of *conserve de tomates* and a small quantity of stock, boil it up, and serve.

242. Cutlets may be fried in hot butter, lard, or clarified dripping, after having been simply floured, or dipped in egg, melted butter, or oil, then bread-crumbed, etc., as in recipes 237 and 239. Can be served with plain gravy, with the *purees* of vegetables, or with any of the above sauces and garnishes.

243. Cut (not too thin) and trim some cutlets. Prepare some vegetables—carrots, turnips, celery, and potatoes—cut them all one size and shape, toss them in butter (each vegetable separately) till nearly done; add to the butter a thickening of flour. When colored add about one pint of stock, free from grease, two tablespoonsful of *conserve de tomates*, a faggot of herbs, pepper, salt; put in the cutlets, stew them gently, when nearly done add the vegetables, simmer them together till quite tender, remove the faggot, and serve with the gravy and the vegetables. (The vegetables may be stewed with the cutlets, but in that case the turnips and potatoes must be put in after the carrots.)

244. Cut them rather thick, lard and put them in a braizing pan, with enough good gravy to cover them; add an onion stuck with cloves, a sliced carrot, a faggot of herbs; braize till quite tender. Remove them from the gravy, strain, then reduce it, and skim well. When cold trim the cutlets carefully, simmer them till hot in the reduced gravy. Have ready a block of bread (pyramid shape); fry it in butter, put it in the centre of the dish, the cutlets round it (the gravy in the dish), and garnish with carrots and turnips (cut up small, and previously tossed in butter) arranged alternately between the cutlets. Instead of the block of bread, and garnish of carrots and turnips, they may be served with any *puree* of vegetable, with tomatoes, etc., according to the season.

245. **CHARTREUSE OF MUTTON.**—Ingredients—Some cold boiled vegetables of any kind and cut into various shapes, cold mashed potatoes; for the sauce, 2 oz. of butter, a little flour, stock flavored with mushroom or vegetables.

Butter the inside of a straight-sided tin mould. Take some cold boiled vegetables of different kinds, and cut them into small slices of various shapes—squares, circles, triangles, etc. —then arrange them in a mosaic pattern on the inside of the mould, to which the butter will make them adhere. The vegetables may be carrots, turnips, beetroot, Jerusalem artichokes, and Brussels sprouts in the winter, and in summer carrots, turnips, asparagus points, French beans, and peas. The great thing is to contrast the colors well, and make a really pretty mosaic. Then, in order to keep the vegetables in their places, spread over them a layer of cold mashed potatoes about 1½ in. thick. Now make a thick white sauce as follows : Put two ounces of butter into a stewpan, and thicken it slowly with sifted flour (taking care not to color the flour) ; then add some strong stock flavored with mushrooms or vegetables, and the cold mutton cut into small slices about ½ in. thick and 2 in. square. Stew gently for half an hour. In the meantime let the mould be put in the oven until the vegetables and mashed potatoes are heated through ; then pour into it the sauce and meat, and, placing a dish on the top of the mould, turn out the chartreuse. This is a very pretty dish ; but care must be taken not to break the shape in turning it out of the mould, and, also a great deal depends on the taste with which the vegetables are arranged.

246. **CROQUETTES OF MUTTON.**—Ingredients—Some cold minced mutton with a few oysters or mushrooms, some highly flavored strong stock, a little roux, a little butter, a little sifted flour (baked), yolk of an egg, bread crumbs, spinach.

Croquettes to be good should be of a golden brown color, not at all greasy, crisp on the outside, and quite soft inside. To make them like this, follow the recipe here given ; Mince very finely some cold mutton with a few oysters or a few mushrooms; take some strong stock well flavored with vegetables and highly seasoned, put it in a stewpan, and thicken it with roux (*i. e.*, butter melted over a slow fire, well skimmed, thickened to a stiff paste with baked sifted flour, and left to cool before use). Let the stock simmer, and stir in the roux, taking care to stir always in the same direction ; when a nice and tolerably thick sauce has been made, add the minced mutton, etc., to it, and let the mince warm through, stirring it gently round as it does so ; then put it on a dish, and leave it to cool for some hours. When it is quite cold it should form a jelly-like paste, just consistent enough to make soft balls. These balls should be of the shape and size of a large egg. Dip them twice over, first in the yolk of an egg and then in grated bread-crumbs, then fry them in boiling fat. The boiling fat should cover them entirely ; they must be put into it one at a time very carefully and gently, and taken out with equal care to prevent the risk of breaking them. It is for this reason that it is necessary to egg and bread-crumb them twice over. Arrange them round a dish with boiled peas, French beans, or spinach, piled up in the centre.

247. CORNETTES DE MOUTON.—Ingredients—Some cold mutton with oysters or mushrooms, some puff paste, the yolk of an egg, vermicelli.

Mince some cold mutton with either oysters or mushrooms very finely, as for croquettes. Make a thick sauce in the same way as that described in the preceding recipe, add the mince to it, and leave it to cool in precisely the same manner as if for croquettes. Then make some puff paste, roll it out very thin—almost as thin as a wafer—cut it into pieces, and wrap up in them lumps of the prepared mince about the size of a walnut, making small triangular patties. Brush these patties over with the yolk of an egg. Dip them in uncooked vermicelli, which will adhere to the egg and paste, and bake them in the oven till the vermicelli is of a pale golden brown color. Serve them up dry on a folded napkin. These cornettes should be quite soft inside, and melt in the mouth when eaten.

248. MOUTON A L'ITALIENNE.—Ingredients—Slices of underdone leg of mutton, buttered white paper, macaroni. For the sauce—a little strong stock, roux to thicken, juice of a lemon, mushroom catchup to taste, cayenne pepper, and ½ glass of claret.

Cut some slices of underdone leg of mutton about half an inch thick. Wrap them each in a piece of buttered white paper, and broil them over a clear fire. Then remove the papers as quickly as possible, and put the meat in the centre of dish, arranging round it a wall of hot boiled macaroni. Pour over it a sauce made as follows, and serve very hot. THE SAUCE: Take some strong stock, thicken with brown roux and flavor the sauce with lemon juice, mushroom catchup, cayenne pepper, and half a glass of claret. All these receipts for doing up cold mutton were given to me by a first-rate French cook, and, if followed carefully by a cook who has some taste and discretion in seasoning, will be found to be very good.

249. HARICOT MUTTON.—Ingredients—Scrag of mutton, a little flour, 2 small onions, 1 bunch of savory herbs, 3 cloves, pepper and salt, 1 blade of mace, 2 small carrots, 1 turnip, a little sugar.

Cut the meat into shapely pieces and fry a nice color; sprinkle them with a little flour, pepper and salt. Put all into a stewpan, just cover with boiling water, then put in your onion stuck with three cloves, the herbs and mace. Allow this to boil *very* gently till the meat is tender; take off any fat there may be. Cut up the turnip and carrots (if cut with vegetable cutter they will look nicer); fry them in a little sugar to color them; add these to the meat and allow to simmer for fifteen or twenty minutes. When ready to serve, take out the onion and bunch of herbs.

250. MUTTON PUDDING.—Ingredients—2 lbs. of the chump end of the loin, weighed after being boned; suet crust (proportions—6 oz. of suet to each lb. of flour), 1 tablespoonful of minced onion, pepper and salt.

Cut the meat into thin slices, sprinkling with pepper and salt. For the suet crust use the above proportions of flour and suet, mixing with a little salt and pepper, milk or water, to the proper consistency. Line your dish with the crust, lay in the meat, *nearly* fill the dish with water; add the minced onion and cover with the crust.

251. LAMB (Epigrammes of).—Ingredients—Breast of lamb, some onions, carrots, celery, whole pepper, salt, cloves, parsley and sweet herbs; 2 eggs, ½ lb. of bread-crumbs, lard.

Braise a piece of breast of lamb in a stewpan with a little water and some onions, carrots, celery, whole pepper, salt, cloves, parsley, and sweet herbs to taste. When sufficiently cooked to allow it, pull out all the bones, and put the breast between two dishes with a heavy weight on it. The breast being quite cold and flat, cut it out into small cutlets; egg and breadcrumb them, then fry them a nice color in lard, and serve with a purée of peas in the centre of the dish.

252. PUREE OF PEAS (to serve with the above).—Ingredients—1 pt. of green peas, a little salt, 1 slice of onion, a sprig of parsley and a few leaves of mint; a little stock and a small piece of fresh butter.

Boil one pint of green peas in water, with salt, a slice of onion, a sprig of parsley, and a few leaves of mint. When cooked, drain off the water, and pass them through a hair sieve. Moisten the purée to a proper consistency with some good stock, perfectly free from fat; work it well in a saucepan on the fire with a piece of fresh butter until it is quite hot, and serve.

253. MUTTON (Boned Leg of, Stuffed).—Ingredients—A leg weighing 7 or 8 pounds, 2 shalots, forcemeat.

Make forcemeat, to which add the minced shalots. Get the butcher to take the bone from the mutton, as he can do it without spoiling the skin; if very fat, cut off some of it. Fill up the hole with the forcemeat, then sew it up to prevent it falling out, tie up neatly and roast about 2½ hours or a little longer. When ready to serve, remove the string and serve with a good gravy.

254. LAMB (Stewed).—Ingredients—A breast of lamb, 1 tablespoonful of salt, 1 qt. of canned peas, 1 tablespoonful of wheat flour, 3 tablespoonsful of butter, pepper to taste.

Cut the scrag, or breast of lamb, in pieces and put in a stewpan with water enough to cover it. Cover the stewpan closely and let it simmer or stew for fifteen or twenty minutes; take off the scum, then add a tablespoonful of salt and a quart of canned peas; cover the stewpan and let them stew for half an hour; work a small tablespoonful of wheat flour with three tablespoonsful of butter, and stir it into the stew: add pepper to taste; let it simmer together for ten minutes.

255. LAMB CHOPS.—Ingredients—A little butter, a little water, enough potatoes to fill a small dish, 1 teacupful of cream.

Lamb chops are excellent cooked this way: Put them in a frying-pan with a very little water, so little that it will boil away by the time the meat is tender; then put in lumps of butter with the meat and let it brown slowly; there will be a brown, crisp surface, with a fine flavor. Serve for breakfast with potatoes cooked thus: Choose small ones and let them boil till they are tender; drain off the water, and pour over them, while still in the kettle, at least one teacupful of cream; mash them smooth in this.

256. LAMBS' TAILS.—Ingredients—A few slices of bacon, 8 onions and carrots, 1 clove of garlic, 1 sprig of thyme, 1 bay leaf, 1 bunch of parsley, a little salt, a few cloves, a little whole pepper, 1 glass of sherry, 1 pint of stock or water, a puree of spinach or sorrel.

Trim the tails. Place some slices of bacon in a saucepan, over them a layer of onions and carrots sliced, then the tails; then a clove of garlic, a sprig of thyme, a bay leaf, and some parsley tied up in a bundle, salt to taste, a few cloves, and some whole pepper. Place the saucepan over the fire for ten minutes, then add a glass of sherry and about a pint of stock, or water, and let the whole simmer gently for two or three hours. Take out the tails, strain the liquor; let it reduce almost to a glaze, put back the tails in it to get warm, and serve with a puree of spinach or sorrel.

257. SHOULDER OF MUTTON (Boiled with Oysters).—Ingredients—A little pepper, a piece of mace, about 2 dozen oysters, a little water, an onion, a few peppercorns, about ½ pint of good gravy, a tablespoonful of flour and butter.

Hang it some days, then salt it well for two days; bone it, and sprinkle it with pepper and a piece of mace pounded: lay some oysters over it, and roll the meat up tight and tie it. Stew it in a small quantity of water, with an onion and a few peppercorns, till quite tender. Have ready a little good gravy, and some oysters stewed in it: thicken this with flour and butter, and pour over the mutton, when the tape is taken off. The stewpan should be kept covered.

258. SWEETBREADS.

Half boil them, and stew them in a white gravy: add cream, flour, butter, nutmeg, salt, and white pepper. Or do them in brown sauce seasoned. Or parboil them, and then cover them with crumbs, herbs, and seasoning, and brown them in a Dutch-oven. Serve with butter, and mushroom-catchup or gravy. N. B.—If there is no oven at hand, they may be toasted before the fire upon a toasting fork.

259. SWEETBREADS (Roasted).

Parboil two large ones when cold, lard them with bacon, and roast them in a Dutch-oven. For sauce, plain butter, and mushroom-catchup.

260. SWEETBREAD (Ragout).

Cut them about the size of a walnut, wash and dry them, and fry them of a fine brown; pour to them a good gravy seasoned with salt, pepper, allspice, and either mushrooms or mushroom catchup: strain, and thicken with butter and a little flour. You may add truffles and mushrooms.

261. SWEETBREADS (Larded).—Ingredients—A couple of sweetbreads, a few slips of bacon, onions, carrots, sweet herbs, pepper, salt, spice to taste, a small quantity of rich stock.

Trim a couple of sweetbreads, soak them half an hour in tepid water, then parboil them for a few minutes, and lay them in cold water; when quite cold take them out, dry them, and lard them thickly with fine strips of bacon. Put a slice of fat bacon in a stewpan with some onions, carrots, a bunch of sweet herbs, pepper, salt, and spices to taste, and a small quantity of rich stock; lay the sweetbreads on this, and let them gently stew till quite done, basting the top occasionally with the liquor. When cooked, strain the liquor, skim off superfluous fat, reduce it almost to a glaze, brown the larded side of the sweetbreads with a salamander, and serve with sauce over them.

262. SWEETBREAD (Lamb's).—Ingredients—Sweetbreads, a ladleful of broth, pepper and salt, a bunch of onions, a blade of mace, butter and flour, 2 or 3 eggs, some cream, parsley, nutmeg, asparagus-tops.

Blanch them, and put them a little while into cold water, Then put them into a stewpan with a ladleful of broth, some pepper and salt, a small bunch of small onions, and a blade of mace; stir in a piece of butter and flour, and stew half an hour. Have ready two or three eggs well beaten in cream, with a little minced parsley, and a few grates of nutmeg. Put in some boiled asparagus-tops to the other things. Don't let it boil after the cream is in: but make it hot, and stir it well all the while. Take great care it does not curdle.

263. KIDNEYS (a la Brochette).

Plunge some mutton kidneys in boiling water; open them down the centre, but do not separate them; peel and pass a skewer across them to keep them open, pepper, salt, and dip them into melted butter, broil them over a clear fire on both sides, doing the cut side first; remove the skewers, have ready some maître d'hotel butter, viz., butter beaten up with chopped parsley, salt, pepper, and a little lemon juice. Put a small piece in the hollow of each kidney, and serve very hot.

264. KIDNEYS (Fried).

After plunging in boiling water cut them in thin slices, and fry in hot butter; add pepper, salt, and toss them for a few minutes in rich brown gravy.

265. KIDNEYS (Grilled).

Prepare them as above, cut each kidney in half, and dip them in egg beaten up with salt and pepper; breadcrumb them, dip them in melted butter, breadcrumb them again, then grill before a slow fire; serve with *piquante* sauce.

266. KIDNEYS (with Macaroni).

Cook two ounces of macaroni, broken into convenient pieces, in boiling water; skin two or three mutton kidneys, remove the fat, and cut them into thin slices; season with salt, cayenne, and finely-minced herbs; fry them on both sides in butter, then stew them in half a pint of gravy, well flavored with fresh tomatoes or with *conserve de tomates* and a little basil, dish with a layer of the macaroni over them, the gravy poured over; add pepper, salt, and some grated Parmesan cheese; brown with salamander.

267. KIDNEY TOAST.—Ingredients—Some kidneys, butter, cayenne, salt, mustard, yolks of 2 eggs, sippets of thin toast.

Partially cook some kidneys in butter; remove the skin and any hard parts, and pound the remainder to a paste, with the butter, in a marble mortar. Season with nutmeg, cayenne, salt, and a little mustard, and mix with it the yolks of two or more eggs, according to the quantity of paste; spread this on sippets of thin toast. Cover the bottom of a dish with the liquid butter; lay on this the toasts, brown them in a brisk oven and serve quickly.

268. KIDNEYS (A L'Indienne).—Ingredients—Kidneys, good curry powder, yolk of egg, croutons, chutnee sauce, thick brown gravy, tomato sauce.

Prepare kidneys as above, season the paste with some good curry powder, and mix with beaten yolks of egg. Fry lightly some round croûtons, spread them with the paste, and set them in a brisk oven to brown. Serve with chutnee sauce poured round them. For the sauce, mince finely some good chutnee and mix it with some rich thick brown gravy, flavored with tomato sauce. Beef or pork kidneys can be used for these toasts, but mutton or veal is better. If veal, cook them with some of their own fat instead of butter.

CURRIES.

OBSERVATIONS ON CURRIES.

Most people, more especially old Anglo-Indians, have a liking for a really good curry; but how very rarely it is to be obtained in America, unless at the house of some one who has passed a good many years in India. The dish miscalled a curry is frequently set before people, but too often as far as possible removed from the real and appetising *plat* which a good Indian cook will send to table. The meat is tough, has most likely been boiled instead of gently simmered, the sauce, or thick gravy, is hot enough in all conscience, but it tastes only of curry powder of an inferior kind; the rice is a sloppy mess, and the result is a fiery leathery sort of indigestible hash, instead of a sweet, acid, highly but agreeably flavored, perfectly cooked and digestible dish, fit to set before a prince. It is said, however, that, even in India, the art of curry-making is declining, that the cunning secrets of curry powder and curry paste mixing are, to a certain extent, lost, from the fact that curry is no longer so fashionable as it once was, and is much more rarely seen on the table. The mere cooking of a curry is not the difficult part of it, though that requires to be understood. Any cook, of whatever nationality, who has really mastered the art of stewing properly, that is very gently and slowly, can cook a curry; the real difficulties lie in procuring good curry powder or curry paste.

269. **CURRIED OYSTERS.**—Ingredients—50 large oysters, a lump of fresh butter, a small onion, a tablespoonful of curry powder, broth, or hot water, $\frac{1}{2}$ a cocoanut, $\frac{1}{2}$ a sour apple, flour, salt, $\frac{1}{2}$ a vegetable marrow, a tomato, the juice of $\frac{1}{2}$ a lemon.

Take the oysters with their liquor, in a basin. Slice the onion and fry in butter until of a rich brown, put in large stewpan, then add a little more butter and the curry powder; mix well with a wooden spoon. Add gradually broth or hot water, nearly filling the stewpan. Allow the whole to boil.

Grate the cocoanut, chop the apple, and add these to the other ingredients. Allow to simmer until the cocoanut is very tender. Make a thickening of flour and water (about a cupful); sprinkle a little salt in it. Put this in the stewpan also and allow it to boil five minutes. Having boiled the vegetable marrow until tender, cut into pieces, put this with the tomato the oysters, their liquor, and milk of cocoanut to the former ingredients. Allow to stew for a few minutes and lastly put in the juice of the lemon. As soon as the oysters are done, serve with a corresponding dish of rice. The curry must be kept well-stirred.

270. **CURRY POWDER.**—Ingredients—1 lb. pale turmeric seed, ¼ lb. of cumin seed, ¼ lb. of black pepper, ½ lb. of coriander seed, 2 oz. of cayenne pepper, ¼ lb. Jamaica ginger, 10 ozs. of caraway seed, ¼ oz. of cardamines.

Take care to purchase these ingredients of a first-class druggist. Additional heat can be obtained by those who like very hot curries, if red Chili powder be added to the above ingredients, according to taste. Mix together all these ingredients well powdered, and place before the fire or in the sun, stirring occasionally. Keep in well corked bottles. N. B. —This will be found very good.

271. **INDIAN CURRY.**—Ingredients— 2 large tablespoonsful of curry powder, a dessert spoonful of salt, the same of black pepper, 4 onions, ¼ lb. of butter, 1½ lbs. of meat, ½ pint of milk, lemon juice or Chili vinegar.

Two large tablespoonsful of curry powder, a dessert spoonful of salt, the same of black pepper. Fry and chop very fine four onions, then moisten the curry powder with water, and put it in a stewpan, with all the above ingredients, and a quarter of a pound of butter. Let it stew for twenty minutes, stirring all the time to prevent burning, then add one and a half pounds of cold or fresh meat, or any fowl or rabbit, cut into short thick pieces, without fat, add half a pint of milk or good stock to make the curry thick. Boil all up at once, and let it stew gently for three or four hours. When ready add lemon juice or Chili vinegar.

272. **CURRIED RABBIT.**—Ingredients—1 rabbit, ¼ lb. of butter, 1 apple, 2 onions, 2 tablespoonsful of curry powder, ¼ of a pint of cream, 1 pint of stock, 1 lemon, a salt spoonful of salt.

Melt the butter over the fire, peel and chop the onions as finely as possible, then put them into the melted butter to fry a light brown. After the rabbit has been properly prepared for cooking, wash well and dry in a cloth, cut in pieces of equal size. After straining the butter from the onions, return the former to the stewpan, put in pieces of rabbit, and allow to fry for ten or fifteen minutes, turning occasionally. Peel and core the apple, and chop as finely as possible. When the meat is done add to it two tablespoonsful of curry powder, the salt, stirring for five minutes, then add the fried onion, chopped apple and a pint of good stock. Allow to simmer for two hours, at the end of the time add the cream, squeeze the juice from the lemon into the stewpan. It is then ready to serve.

N. B.—Veal or chicken can be used, if preferred.

273. **CURRY OF MUTTON.**—Ingredients—Mutton, 1 onion, butter the size of an egg, curry powder, a little salt, a cup of cream.

Slice a medium-sized onion, and put it with a large lump of butter in a saucepan; let it cook slowly for five minutes. Cut the mutton in neat pieces; sprinkle curry powder over them, also a litttle salt, and just before putting in the saucepan pour a part of a cup of sweet cream over them. Let this all simmer gently for half an hour, so that the ingredients will become thoroughly mixed.

274. **A DRY MALAY CURRY.**—Ingredients—A cauliflower, 2 onions, a sour apple, a pint of shrimps, slices of cold mutton, 2 ozs. of butter, a large tablespoonful of curry powder, a lemon, a small teaspoonful of salt.

Pick a cauliflower into small pieces and well wash them; chop two onions and one sour apple, pick a pint of fresh boiled shrimps, cut some slices of cold mutton about half an inch thick, knead two ounces of butter with a large tablespoonful of curry powder, and a small teaspoonful of salt. Put the butter, onions and apple into a stewpan, and fry till brown, then add the cauliflower and shrimps. Shake the saucepan frequently, and let it simmer for an hour and a half, adding the slices of mutton towards the end of the time, that they may be heated through. Finally, add the juice of a lemon. Place the slices of mutton round the dish with the cauliflower, &c., in the middle. Serve very hot, with a separate dish of boiled rice.

275. **CURRIED LOBSTER.**—Ingredients—Lobster, cream, rice.

Take the flesh of a lobster (or a tin of lobster does very well for this dish), make curry gravy with plenty of cream; pour into a saucepan with the lobster, warm it just to boiling point; serve with rice round.

277. **A TURKISH DISH.**—Ingredients—6 oz. of East India rice, a pint of water, 1 oz. of butter, salt, pepper, ½ pint of broth.

Wash well six ounces of East India rice, and boil it in a pint of water for eight or ten minutes at the most, throw into a cullender, that it may thoroughly drain. Then place it in a stewpan with an ounce of butter, salt and pepper to taste, stirring well, and adding by degrees about half a pint of good fowl broth. After about fifteen minutes or so it should be properly done, turning out with the grains separately. It is to be served perfectly hot. The foregoing is a true pillau, but additions may be made of portions of the meat of the fowl, or of any other animal matter, of a little curry powder, of chutnee, fried onions, or mushrooms.

278. **BOILED RICE FOR CURRY.**—Ingredients—Rice, lemon.

Put the rice on the stove in cold water, and allow it to come to a boil for a minute or two. Strain, dry and put in stewpan without lid at the back of the stove, to allow the steam to evaporate; shake into dish very hot; a few drops of lemon juice put in directly after it boils will make the grains separate better.

279. **CURRIED EGGS.**—Ingredients—6 eggs, 2 onions, butter, a tablespoonful of curry powder, 1 pint of broth, a cup of cream, arrowroot.

Slice the onions and fry in butter a light brown, add curry powder, and mix with the broth, allowing to simmer till tender; then put in cream, and thicken with arrowroot; simmer for five minutes, then add 6 hard boiled eggs, cut in slices.

280. **CURRIED BEEF.**—Ingredients—Beef, 2 oz. of butter, 2 onions, a tablespoonful of curry powder, ¼ pint of milk, lemon juice.

Slice the onions and fry in butter a light brown, mix well with the curry powder, adding the beef, cut into small pieces about an inch square, pour in milk and allow to simmer for thirty minutes, stirring frequently; when done add lemon juice. It greatly improves the dish to build a wall of mashed potatoes or boiled rice round it.

281. **CURRY.**—Ingredients—Scraps of cold meat, 1 apple, 1 onion, 2 oz. of clarified dripping, 1 dessertspoonful of curry powder, salt.

Put the dripping into a stewpan on the fire to heat, chop the onion as finely as possible, and when the dripping is hot put in the onion to brown (do not allow it to burn), cut the meat into small pieces, peel and core the apple, and chop finely. When the onion is brown strain it off and put the dripping back into the saucepan, put pieces of meat into the saucepan and brown them both sides; add the curry powder, apple and a little salt; pour in half pint of cold water, and return the browned onion to the saucepan, stir until it boils, then move to the back of the stove and allow to simmer half an hour. When done take it out and place on a hot dish, and pour the sauce over it.

282. CURRIED TRIPE.—Ingredients—1 lb. of tripe, ¼ lb. of Patna rice, 1 onion, flour, sugar, and curry powder.

Put the tripe into a saucepan of cold water, and let it boil up; immediately it boils, take it out of the water (this is called blanching). After this operation, scrape with a knife to thoroughly cleanse it. Cut up into small pieces, and lay in a saucepan, pouring sufficient cold water to cover the tripe. Peel the onion and cut it partially through. Add this to the tripe. Put the saucepan on the fire, and bring to a boil, then remove to the back of the stove, and allow to simmer for 2½ hours. Then dish the tripe. Into a small saucepan put one oz. of flour, a dessertspoonful of curry powder and a half oz. of dripping, and mix well with a wooden spoon. Make into a stiff paste with cold water. Add half pt. of the liquor in which the tripe was boiled. Put on the fire, and stir the mixture until it thickens (take care there are no lumps). To this ad l a quarter of a teaspoonful of brown sugar and salt according to taste. Then put on one side to get cool. Cut into shreds the onion that was boiled with the tripe, and add it to the sauce. As soon as the sauce is a little cool put in the tripe, and let it warm through. Heat a dish and pour the tripe and sauce upon it; keep it in the centre of the dish. Wash the rice and put it in a saucepanful of boiling water. Add a saltspoonful of salt. Allow to boil for 15 or 20 minutes. When done strain and pour cold water upon it. Return the rice to the empty saucepan, stand on back of stove to dry the rice. When perfectly dry arrange it on the dish round the tripe.

283. POTATO CURRY (1).—Ingredients—One onion, potatoes, butter, 1 pt. of stock, a tablespoonful of curry powder, a little milk from a cocoanut, a tomato, a small vegetable marrow, lemon juice, rice.

Cut an onion into thin slices; wash, pare, and slice some good sound potatoes, fry slightly in butter, and then simmer them slowly for some hours in one pint of stock, in which one tablespoonful of curry powder has been mixed. add a little milk from the cocoanut—when procurable, a tomato, a small vegetable marrow boiled and sliced; simmer all together a few minutes longer, add a dash of lemon juice, and serve garnished with thin strips of fried onion, and with boiled rice in a separate dish.

284. POTATO CURRY (2).—Ingredients—Cold potatoes, onion, salt and pepper, curry powder to taste, egg, and bread crumbs, gravy.

Mash cold potatoes with minced onion, salt, pepper, and curry powder to taste; form into small balls with egg and bread crumbs, fry crisp, serve with rich gravy flavored with curry powder.

285. **POTATO CURRY** (3).—Ingredients—Raw potatoes, onions, butter, curry powder, a little stock, cream, lemon juice.

Fry some sliced raw potatoes and onions slightly in butter with a little curry powder, then simmer until done in a very little stock, add some cream, butter, and lemon juice before serving.

286. (**POTATO CURRY** (4).—Ingredients—Curry powder, mashed potatoes, milk.

Put a good pinch of curry powder in mashed potatoes, allowing rather more butter and milk than usual. This last is a delicious accompaniment to cutlets.

287. **CURRY (Dry)**.—Ingredients—A few onions, $\frac{1}{4}$ lb. of butter, 1$\frac{1}{2}$ lbs. of steak, a little flour and curry powder, salt to taste, juice of 1 lemon.

Slice up a good-sized onion, and fry it a golden color in a quarter of a pound of butter; cut up one and a half pounds of fresh steak into pieces the size of dice. Dredge them well with flour and curry powder, add a little salt, and squeeze the juice of a lemon over them, then fry them lightly in the butter in which the onions had been previously cooked. Add all together, and stew gently in a saucepan for a quarter of an hour.

GRAVIES.

GENERAL DIRECTIONS RESPECTING GRAVIES.

Gravy may be made quite as good of the skirts of beef, and the kidney, as of any other meat, prepared in the same way.

An ox-kidney, or milt, makes good gravy, cut all to pieces, and prepared as other meat; and so will the shank end of mutton that has been dressed, if much be not wanted.

The shank-bones of mutton are a great improvement to the richness of gravy; but first soak them well, and scour them clean.

Parragon gives the flavor of French cookery, and in high gravies is a great improvement; but it should be added only a short time before serving.

288. **A GOOD BEEF GRAVY (for Poultry or Game).**—Ingredients—½ lb. of lean beef, ½ a pint of cold water, 1 small onion, a saltspoonful of salt, a little pepper, a tablespoonful of mushroom catchup or Harvey's sauce, ½ a teaspoonful of arrowroot.

Cut the beef into small pieces and put it and the water into a stewpan. Add the onion and seasoning, and simmer gently for three hours. A short time before it is required, mix the arrowroot with a little cold water, pour into the gravy, while stirring, add the Harvey's sauce and allow it just to come to the boil. Strain into a tureen and serve very hot.

289. **SAVORY GRAVY (Thick).**—Ingredients — 1 onion, butter, a tablespoonful of flour, ½ pint of broth or stock, pepper and salt, a small quantity of Worcester sauce.

Mince one onion fine, fry it in butter to a dark brown, and stir in a tablespoonful of flour. After one minute add half a pint of broth or stock, pepper and salt, and a very small quantity of Worcester sauce.

290. **GRAVY FOR ROAST MEAT.**—Ingredients—Gravy, salt.

Put a kitchen dish with a sprinkling of salt in it beneath the meat about twenty minutes before it is removed from the oven.

Then remove, baste the meat, and pour the gravy oe the dish intended for serving the joint upon.

291. **GRAVY FOR VENISON.**—Ingredients—Remnants of venison, 4 mutton shank bones, a little salt, 2 glasses of water, 1 dessertspoonful of walnut catchup.

Brown the venison over a clear fire, and put this with the shank bones and water into a stewpan and allow it to boil very gently for about two hours. Strain and add the catchup and a sprinkling of salt. Serve very hot.

292. **STRONG FISH GRAVY.**—Ingredients—2 or 3 eels, crust of toasted bread, 2 blades of mace, some whole pepper, sweet herbs, a piece of lemon peel, an anchovy, a teaspoonful of horse radish.

Skin two or three eels, and wash them very clean; cut them into small pieces, and put them into a saucepan. Cover them with water, and add a little crust of bread toasted brown, two blades of mace, some whole pepper, sweet herbs, a piece of lemon peel, an anchovy or two, and a teaspoonful or two of horse-radish. Cover close, and simmer; add a piece of butter and flour, and boil with the above.

293. **PLAIN GRAVY.**—Ingredients—An onion, a little butter, ¾ pint of stock, pepper and salt, a small piece of lean ham or bacon, a dessertspoonful of Worcester sauce, a sprig of parsley and thyme.

Mince an onion finely, fry it in butter to a dark brown color, then add three-quarters of a pint of stock, pepper and salt to taste, a small piece of lean ham or bacon minced small, a little Worcester sauce, a sprig of thyme and one of parsley. Let it boil five or ten minutes, put it by till wanted, and strain it before serving.

294. **GRAVY FOR HASHES.**—Ingredients—Remanants and bones of the joint intended for hashing, a pinch of salt and pepper, ¼ teaspoonful of whole allspice, a bunch of savory herbs, a saltspoonful of celery salt or ½ a head of celery, an onion, a small piece of butter, a little corn flour, and boiling water.

Put the bones (having previously chopped them), with the remnants of meat, salt, pepper, spice, herbs and celery into a stewpan. Cover with boiling water and allow it to simmer for two hours. Cut up the onion in neat slices and fry in butter a pale brown. Then mix slowly with the gravy from bones. Boil fifteen minutes, strain, then return to stewpan, flavor with catchup or any flavoring that may be preferred. Thicken with butter and flour and just allow it to come to the boil. Serve very hot.

295. **GRAVY FOR A FOWL** (when there is no meat to make it from).—Ingredients—The feet, liver, gizzards and neck of the fowl, a little browned bread, a slice of onion, a sprig of parsley and thyme, some pepper and salt, a teaspoonful of mushroom catchup, a little flour and butter.

Wash the feet nicely, and cut them and the neck small; simmer them with a little bread browned, a slice of onion, a sprig of parsley and thyme, some pepper and salt, and the liver and gizzards, in a quarter of a pint of water, till half wasted. Take out the liver, bruise it, and strain the liquor to it. Then thicken it with flour and butter, and add a teaspoonful of mushroom catchup, and it will be very good.

296. **VEAL GRAVY.**—Ingredients—Bones, any cold remnants of veal, 1½ pints of water, an onion, a saltspoonful of minced lemon peel, a little salt, a blade of mace, a few drops of the juice of the lemon, butter and flour.

Place all the ingredients (excepting the lemon juice and flour) into a stewpan and allow them to simmer for one hour. Strain into a basin. Add a thickening of butter and flour mixed with a little water, also the lemon juice. Give one boil and serve very hot. Flavor with tomato sauce or catchup.

297. **COLORING FOR SOUPS OR GRAVIES.**

Put four ounces of lump sugar, a gill of water, and half an ounce of the finest butter into a small tosser, and set it over a gentle fire. Stir it with a wooden spoon, till of a bright brown. Then add half a pint of water; boil, skim, and when cold, bottle and cork it close. Add to soup or gravy as much of this as will give a proper color.

SAUCES.

OBSERVATIONS ON SAUCES.

The appearance and preparation of sauces are of the highest importance. Brown sauces should not be as thick as white ones, and both should possess a decided character, so that whether sweet or sharp, plain or savory, they would bear out their names. Care is also to be taken that they blend and harmonize with the various dishes they are to accompany.

298. **WHITE SAUCE.**—Ingredients—1 pint of milk, 2 or 3 mushrooms, 1 onion, 1 carrot, 1 bundle of sweet herbs, whole pepper and salt to taste, a few cloves, a little mace, 1 oz. of butter, and 1 gill of cream.

Put into one pint of milk two or three mushrooms, an onion and a carrot cut into pieces, a bundle of sweet herbs, whole pepper and salt to taste, a few cloves, and a little mace; let the whole gently simmer for about an hour, put an ounce of butter into a saucepan, and stir on the fire until it thickens. Finish by stirring in a gill of cream.

299. **WHITE SAUCE (Voloute)**—Ingredients—A fowl, 1 lb. of lean veal 1 onion, 5 oz. of butter, white stock, a carrot, a bundle of sweet herbs, some whole pepper, a pinch of sugar, 2 oz. of flour.

Take a fowl, cut up into small joints, and one pound of lean veal cut into small dice, put both into a saucepan with an onion sliced, an ounce of butter, and a cupful of white stock; keep tossing on the fire for half an hour, taking care that none of the contents take color; then add as much white stock as will well cover them, together with a carrot cut into small pieces, a bundle of sweet herbs, some whole pepper, and a pinch of sugar, and let the whole gently simmer for a couple of hours or more. Melt quarter pound of fresh butter in a saucepan, and amalgamate two ounces of flour with it without letting the mixture take any color; strain the above liquor gradually into it; set the saucepan at the edge of the fire to simmer for an hour and a half, skimming the contents carefully from time to time. Lastly, turn out the sauce into a basin, keeping it stirred till wanted, or cold. This sauce will keep several days in a good larder, but it must be warmed up every day.

300. WHITE SAUCE (Suprême).—Ingredients—A punnet of fresh mushroom, some truffle trimmings, ½ pint of white stock, a little more than a pint of velonté, 1 tablespoonful of cream, and a small pat of fresh butter.

Boil a punnet of fresh mushroom and some truffle trimmings in half a pint of white stock for a quarter of an hour; strain the liquor, and add to it rather more than a pint of velonté, let the whole simmer for about twenty minutes, skimming occasionally. At the time of serving stir in one tablespoonful of cream and a small pat of butter.

301. WHITE SAUCE (Allemande).

Proceed as for supréme, adding a little grated nutmeg to the stock in which the mushrooms were boiled. Finish the sauce by stirring into it, off the fire, the yolks of two eggs beaten up with a little cold stock and strained.

302. LIVER SAUCE.—Ingredients—Livers of any kind of poultry, butter, flour, minced shallots, gravy stock, a small pinch of sweet herbs, and pepper, spices, and salt to taste, a glass of port wine, juice of ½ a lemon.

Take the livers of any kind of poultry, rabbits, or hares; scald them and mince them finely. Melt a piece of butter in a saucepan, add a little flour to it and a small quantity of minced shallots. Let the whole fry for a minute or two, then add gravy stock in sufficient quantity to make a sauce, and a small pinch of powdered sweet herbs and pepper, spices and salt to taste. Put in the minced livers and a glass of port wine. Let the sauce boil for twenty minutes, and at the time of serving add a small piece of fresh butter and the juice of half a lemon.

303. FENNEL SAUCE.—Ingredients—Fennel, 3 oz. of butter, rather more than a tablespoonful of flour, pepper and salt to taste, yolks of 2 eggs, juice of 1 lemon.

Blanch a small quantity in boiling salted water, take it out, dry it in a cloth, and chop it finely; melt three oz. of fresh butter, add rather more than a tablespoonful of flour, mix well, and put in pepper and salt to taste, and about a pint of hot water; stir on the fire till the sauce thickens, then stir in the yolks of two eggs beaten up with the juice of a lemon and strained. Add plenty of the chopped fennel, and serve.

304. SHRIMP SAUCE.—Ingredients—½ pt. of shrimps, juice of half a lemon, butter, a dust of cayenne.

Take half a pint of shrimps, pick out all the meat from the tails, pound the rest in a mortar with the juice of half a lemon and a piece of butter; pass the whole through a sieve. Make a pint of melted butter, put the meat from the tails into it, add a dust of cayenne, and when the sauce boils stir into it the shrimp butter that has come through the sieve, with or without a tablespoonful of cream.

305. **WINE SAUCE.**—Ingredients—1 tablespoonful of potato flour, 3 gills of sherry, yolks of 4 eggs, some powdered white sugar, cinnamon, lemon peel.

Mix a tablespoonful of potato flour with a gill of sherry; beat up another gill of sherry with the yolks of four eggs; mix the two together, add powdered white sugar, powdered cinnamon, grated lemon peel to taste, and a third gill of sherry. Put the whole in a saucepan, and keep stirring on the fire till the sauce thickens, when it is ready.

306. **MANGO CHUTNEY SAUCE (Bengal Recipe).**—Ingredients—¼lb. of garlic, 1½ lbs. of brown sugar, ¾lb. of salt, 2 bottles of the best vinegar, ¼lb. of onions, ¼lb. of dried chilies, ¾lb of mustard seed, ¾lb. of stoned raisins, 2½ doz. large unripe sour apples, ¾lb. of powdered ginger.

Reduce the sugar to a syrup. Pound the onions, garlic and ginger finely in a mortar; wash the mustard seed in cold vinegar, and allow to dry in the sun; peel, core and slice the apples, then boil them in a bottle and a half of vinegar. When this has been done, and the apples are quite cool, put them into a good sized pan, and mix the whole of the remaining ingredients (as well as the other half bottle of vinegar) *gradually*. Stir well until all are thoroughly mixed, and then put into bottles until wanted. Tie wet bladder over the bottles after they have been corked. This is a delicious chutney and has been well tried and proved.

307. **EGG SAUCE.**

Boil the eggs hard and cut them into small pieces; then put them to melted butter.

308. **GOVERNOR'S SAUCE (A Canadian Recipe).**—Ingredients—1 peck of green tomatoes, a cupful of salt, vinegar, 6 green or red chilies, a teacupful of brown sugar, 1 of scraped horse radish, a tablespoonful each of cloves and allspice, a teaspoonful each of red and white pepper, 4 large onions.

Slice a peck of green tomatoes, sprinkle them with a cupful of salt, and let them stand a night; in the morning pour off the liquor, and put them into a saucepan with vinegar enough to cover them. Add six green or red chilies, four large onions chopped fine, a teacupful of brown sugar, one of scraped horseradish, a tablespoonful each of cloves and allspice, and a teaspoonful each of red and white pepper. Let it simmer till soft, put into jars and keep it air-tight.

309. CAULIFLOWER SAUCE.—Ingredients—Two small cauliflowers, 1½ oz. of butter, 1 tablespoonful of flour, ½ pint of boiling water, pepper and salt to taste, yolks of 2 eggs, juice of a lemon.

Boil two small cauliflowers; when done, pick them out into sprigs and arrange them, head downwards, in a pudding basin, which must have been made quite hot; press them in gently, then turn them out dexterously on a dish, and pour over them the following sauce, boiling hot: Melt one and a half ounces of butter in a saucepan, mix with it a tablespoonful of flour, and then add half a pint of boiling water; stir till it thickens; add salt and white pepper to taste; then take the saucepan off the fire, and stir in the yolks of two eggs beaten up with the juice of a lemon and strained.

310. MUSHROOM SAUCE.—Ingredients—A punnet of mushrooms, 3 shallots, 2 or 3 sprigs of parsley, gravy stock, pepper and salt to taste, a small piece of butter, flour.

Pick clean a punnet of mushrooms, put them into a saucepan with three shallots chopped up, and two or three sprigs of parsley, cover up with gravy stock, add pepper and salt to taste, and let the whole boil for a couple of hours. Strain the liquor, passing the mushrooms, etc., through a hair sieve. Melt a piece of butter in a saucepan, add a little flour, mix well, then add the above.

311. DUTCH SAUCE.—Ingredients—3 tablespoonsful of vinegar, 1 lb. of butter, yolks of 2 eggs, pepper and salt to taste.

Put three tablespoonsful of vinegar in a saucepan, and reduce it on the fire to one-third; add a quarter of a pound of butter and the yolks of two eggs. Place the saucepan on a slow fire, stir the contents continuously, and as fast as the butter melts add more, until one pound is used. If the sauce becomes too thick at any time during the process, add a tablespoonful of cold water and continue stirring. Then put in pepper and salt to taste, and take great care not to let the sauce boil. When it is made—that is, when all the butter is used and the sauce is of the proper thickness—put the saucepan containing it into another filled with warm (not boiling) water until the time of serving.

312. PIQUANTE SAUCE (without Eggs).

(1) Melt one oz. of butter, and add gradually two tablespoonsful of white wine vinegar, a shalot and a litle parsley chopped very fine, pepper and salt; stir over the fire till it boils. (2) Chop up some herbs—thyme parsley, tarragon, chervil, and a chalot (about a tablespoonful in all)—and put them into a saucepan with one and a half gills of vinegar; reduce to one gill; add half pint of broth, strain, thicken with a roux of half oz. of butter

and half oz. of flour; boil up the sauce, stirring all the time, add a few chopped herbs, pepper and salt, and serve. (3) The following is taken from "Round the Table:" "Fry some slices of chalots, or onions, till they assume a light brown color (taking care by frequent stirring that they do not get burnt or done too much); add a small piece of garlic, some sweet herbs, and a mixture of equal parts of vinegar and water (or of vinegar and broth), strain and let the whole boil, then stir this mixture into a saucepan containing butter and flour, as for prepared plain melted butter; add pepper, salt, some minced parsley, and chopped gherkins.

313. **ANCHOVY SAUCE**.—Ingredients—About ½ oz. of butter, yolk of 1 fresh egg, 1 teaspoonful of anchovy sauce, cayenne pepper and salt to taste, squares of freshly browned toast.

Heat a dinner-plate until it will melt half an ounce of butter placed on it; take the yolk of a fresh egg, beat it with a fork into the butter, add a teaspoonful of anchovy sauce, cayenne pepper and salt to taste. Have ready some freshly-browned squares of toast, dip them into the mixture, covering both sides, and serve at once.

314. **GRILL SAUCE**.—Ingredients—1 gill of good gravy, 1 tablespoonful of mushroom catchup, 1 of French mustard, a few chopped capers, a little grated lemon peel, butter, flour, a few drops of lemon juice.

Take one gill of good gravy, mix with it one tablespoonful of mushroom catchup, one of French mustard, a few chopped capers, a little grated lemon peel; add a thickening of butter and flour and a few drops of lemon juice, simmer till quite hot, and pour over the grill, and serve. Legs of chicken and game may be treated in the same way, but in making the sauce substitute a tablespoonful of chutney for the chopped capers, and instead of lemon juice add a small quantity of Chili vinegar.

315. **MINT SAUCE**.—Ingredients—A quantity of mint leaves, equal quantities of wine-vinegar and water, and a small portion of sugar.

Chop as finely as possible a quantity of mint leaves previously washed; add to these sufficient wine-vinegar and water, in equal parts, to float them, and a small quantity of powdered sugar. Let the sauce stand for an hour before serving.

316. **SWEET SAUCE**—Ingredients—1 tablespoonful of flour, 4 tablespoonsful of water, ½ pint of boiling water, sugar or treacle to taste, 1 oz. of butter, 1 tablespoonful of lemon juice.

Mix a tablespoonful of flour quite smooth in four tablespoonsful of water, then stir into it half a pint of boiling water, sugar or treacle to taste; stir over the fire until the sauce boils, when, if allowed, an ounce of butter may be added, with a tablespoonful of lemon juice. When sweetened with sugar, a little nutmeg or ground cinnamon may be used instead of lemon juice, if preferred. A tablespoonful of raspberry jam or any fruit syrup may be used to flavor the sauce, and is generally much liked.

317. **REMOULADE SAUCE**—Ingredients—Chervil, chives, capers, parsley, cress, and a little shalot, a little French mustard, the yolks of two raw eggs, pepper and salt, olive oil, a little Chili vinegar.

Chop some chervil, chives, capers, parsley, cress, and a little shalot; pound them in a mortar, add a little French mustard, the yolks of two raw eggs, season with pepper and salt; add, drop by drop, good olive oil, in the proportion of two tablespoonsful to each egg: beat up the mixture, and when quite smooth add a little chili vinegar.

318. **HORSE RADISH SAUCE.**

One teaspoonful of made mustard, one tablespoonful of vinegar, three tablespoonsful of cream, a little salt, as much horse radish grated as will make it as thick as cream.

319. **MAYONNAISE SAUCE.**—Ingredients—The yolks of 4 eggs, a teaspoonful of salt, salad oil, tarragon vinegar, white pepper.

Carefully strain the yolks of four eggs into a basin, place it in a cool place, or, if necessary, on ice; add a teaspoonful of salt, mix well; then proceed to pour in, a few drops at a time, some salad oil, without ceasing to stir the mixture. When one spoonful of oil is well incorporated with the yolks of the eggs, put in, in the same manner, a teaspoonful of tarragon vinegar; keep on adding oil and vinegar in these proportions until the sauce becomes of the consistency of very thick cream; then add white pepper to taste, and more salt if necessary.

320. **POOR MAN'S SAUCE.**—Ingredients—A good sized onion, butter, ½ pint of common stock or water, a little vinegar, a little minced parsley, pepper and salt to taste, a tablespoonful of flour.

Mince a good-sized onion, not too finely, put it into a saucepan with a piece of butter equal to it in bulk. Fry till the onion assumes a light brown color, add half a pint of common stock or water and a small quantity of vinegar, pepper and salt to taste, and some minced parsley; then stir the sauce into another saucepan, in which a tablespoonful of flour and a small piece of butter have been mixed, over the fire. Let the sauce boil up, and it is ready.

321. BROWN SAUCE (Genevoise).—Ingredients — 1 onion, small piece of garlic, 1 oz of butter, a tumblerful of claret, a bunch of sweet herbs, whole pepper, 2 tumblersful of gravy stock, a tablespoonful of flour, the flesh of 2 or 3 anchovies.

Put into a saucepan one onion finely minced, a small piece of garlic, and one ounce of butter; when the onion begins to color add a tumblerful of claret, a faggot of sweet herbs, and some whole pepper. Let the whole boil fifteen minutes, strain and add two tumblersful of gravy stock. Melt an ounce of butter in a saucepan, add a tablespoonful of flour; when it begins to color add the sauce, stir it, and skim it well, as it gently simmers, for five or ten minutes. Take the flesh of two or three anchovies, pound it in a mortar with half an ounce of butter, pass the whole through a fine sieve, and stir it into the sauce at the last moment.

322. A CHEAP BROWN SAUCE.—Ingredients—1 pint of brown stock, 1½ oz. of flour, 2 oz. butter, 4 mushrooms, salt and pepper.

Put the butter into a stewpan and put it on the fire to melt; wash the mushrooms in cold water, cut off the stalks and peel them; when the butter is melted stir in the flour and mix to a smooth paste; then add the stock and mushrooms, and stir the sauce smoothly until it boils and thickens; then remove the stewpan to the back of the stove, and let it simmer gently for eight or ten minutes; season with pepper and salt; be careful to skim off the butter as it rises to the top of the sauce. Should the sauce be not brown enough, a teaspoonful of caramel might be stirred into it; strain and serve.

323. CRANBERRY SAUCE.—Ingredients—1 qt. of ripe cranberries, granulated sugar, a teacupful of water.

Wash the berries, and carefully pick them, then put them into a stewpan with the above quantity of water; allow them to stew very slowly, stirring occasionally. They require about an hour and a half to cook; when done sweeten with sugar, put into a mould, and when cold it is ready to serve.

324. PEACH SAUCE.—Ingredients—Peaches, water, sugar.

Take a quart of dried peaches and soak in water four hours, wash them, drain, and put in saucepan with enough water to cover them; when they break in pieces, pulp them, and sweeten to taste with white sugar.

325. PLUM PUDDING SAUCE.—Ingredients—1 glass brandy, 1 glass Maderia, 2 oz. butter, pounded sugar to taste.

Put the sugar into a basin with part of the brandy and butter, stand this in front of the stove until warm, and the butter and sugar are melted; then add the Maderia and remainder of brandy. Pour over pudding, or serve in a sauce boat.

326. **ONION SAUCE (Brown).**—Ingredients—2 oz. of butter, rather more than ½ a pint of rich gravy, 6 large onions, pepper and salt to taste.

Put into your stewpan, the onions, sliced, fry them of a light brown color, with the two ounces of butter; keep them stirred well to prevent them turning black; as soon as they are of a nice color, pour over the gravy, and simmer gently until tender; skim off all fat, add seasoning and rub the whole through a sieve; then put in a saucepan and when it boils, serve. If a high flavor is wanted a small quantity of port wine or mushroom catchup may be added.

327. **ROUX (Brown, a thickening for soups and gravies).**—Ingredients—6 oz. of butter, 9 oz. of flour.

Melt the butter slowly over the fire, and dredge in *very slowly* the flour, stirring all the time, and when it turns a light brown color it is done, and can be put aside into a jar ready for use. It will keep good for some time.

328. **ROUX (White, for thickening white sauces).**

Proceed as in last receipt, but do not keep it on the fire so long, and take care not to let it color.

329. **SAUCE HOLLANDAIS.**—Ingredients—About ½ a teacupful of vinegar, bruised peppercorns, bay leaves, salt, 5 or 6 eggs, water, a small handful of the best flour, butter, ¼ pt. of whipped cream.

Put about half a teacupful of vinegar into a saucepan with some bruised peppercorns, bay leaves, and salt. Set the saucepan on the fire to simmer till the vinegar is almost dried up. Then beat the yolks of five or six eggs into it, beat them up a little and for economy a little water may be added, and a small handful of the best flour. Continue to stir with a whisk, adding a lump of butter about two inches square. Put it to simmer on the fire, watching it and stirring all the time, but not letting it boil. After six or ten minutes remove it, and place it in a bain Marie. Then add in small lumps the best part of a pound of butter, stirring well. Put it back on the fire, but it must not boil. Strain this through a tammy. Stir in about a quarter of a pint of whipped cream.

330. **TOMATO SAUCE.**—Ingredients—10 lb. ripe tomatoes, 1 pint best brown vinegar, 2 oz. salt, ½ oz. cloves, 1 oz. allspice, ½ lb. white sugar, 1 oz. garlic, ½ oz. black pepper, ½ oz. cayenne pepper.

Wipe the tomatoes clean, and boil or bake till soft; then strain and rub through a sieve that will retain the seeds and skins. Boil the juice for an hour, then add the above ingredients (all the spices must be ground). Boil all together for a sufficient time, which may be known by the absence of any watery particle, and by the whole becoming a smooth mass; five hours will generally suffice. Bottle without straining into perfectly dry bottles, and cork securely when cold. The garlic must be peeled. The proportions of spice may be varied according to taste.

331. **TARTARE SAUCE**.—Ingredients—Yolk of 1 egg, 1 pinch of salt, a small pinch of pepper, 4 oz. of oil, vinegar, 1 tablespoonful of dry mustard, ½ oz. of shalots, ½ oz. of gherkins, 1 tablespoonful of ravigote (chervil, tarragon, and burnet chopped), 1 teaspoonful of Chili vinegar, or one small pinch of cayenne pepper.

Put in a small basin the yolk of one egg well freed from white, one pinch of salt, and a small pinch of pepper; stir with a wooden spoon, and pour in (by drops at first, then by teaspoonfuls) about four ounces of oil, being careful to mix the oil well before adding any more; at every eighth teaspoonful of oil add one teaspoonful of vinegar, till all the oil is used; then add one tablespoonful of dry mustard, three shalots (say ½ ounce) chopped fine and well washed, six gherkins (say ½ ounce) also chopped fine, one tablespoonful of ravigote (chervil, tarragon, and burnet, chopped), one teaspoonful of Chili vinegar, or one small pinch of cayenne pepper; mix all together.

332. **OYSTER SAUCE**.—Ingredients—Oysters, butter, a little flour, milk, blade of mace, bay leaf, pepper and salt to taste, a little cayenne, a few drops of lemon juice.

Parboil the oysters in their own liquor, beard them, and reserve all the liquor. Melt a piece of butter in a saucepan, add a little flour, the oyster liquor, and enough milk to make as much sauce as is wanted. Put in a blade of mace and a bay leaf tied together, pepper and salt to taste, and the least bit of cayenne. Let the sauce boil, add the oysters, and as soon as they are quite hot remove the mace and bay leaf, stir in a few drops of lemon juice, and serve.

333. **WORCESTER SAUCE**.—Ingredients—Two tablespoonsful Indian soy, two ditto walnut catchup, one dessertspoonful of salt, one teaspoonful cayenne pepper, one nutmeg (sliced thin), one dozen cloves, ½ oz. root ginger pounded, a little lemon peel, a small head of garlic divided into cloves, one pint vinegar, 3 oz. lump sugar.

Dissolve the sugar in a little of the vinegar over the fire, add the other ingredients; put all into a wide-necked bottle. It should stand for a month before using, and is better if shaken every day. At the end of the month pour off clear into bottles. It is well to make a quart or three pints at a time.

334. **BREAD SAUCE (to serve with Poultry or Game).**—Ingredients—giblets, ¼ lb. of stale bread, an onion, 10 whole peppers, a blade of mace, a little salt, 2 tablespoonsful of cream, a pint of water.

Put the giblets into a pint of water, add the onion, pepper, mace, salt. Allow it to simmer for an hour, then strain the liquor over the bread crumbs. Cover the stewpan and let it stand on the stove for an hour (do not allow it to boil), then beat the sauce up with a fork until it is nice and smooth. Allow it to boil five minutes, stirring well until it is thick, then add cream and serve hot.

335. **SWEET SAUCE FOR VENISON.**—Ingredients—a glass of port wine, about half a tumbler of red currant jelly.

Put the above ingredients into a stewpan and allow them to melt slowly, do not boil. When melted it is ready to serve.

336. **CAPER SAUCE.**—Ingredients—2 oz. of butter, a tablespoonful of flour, a pint of boiling stock, pepper and salt, Worcester sauce, capers.

Put two oz. of butter and a tablespoonful of flour into a saucepan; stir the mixture on the fire until it acquires a brown color; add rather less than a pint of boiling stock, free from fat; season with pepper, salt, and a little Worcester sauce. When the sauce boils throw in plenty of capers; let it boil once more, and it is ready.

STOCKS.

337. COMMON STOCK.

Take all the bones of joints, etc., that are available, carcases and bones of poultry and game (not high), chop them all into convenient pieces and put them into a saucepan together with any scraps of meat, cooked or uncooked, resulting from remnants, the trimming of cutlets, etc. Add a couple of carrots, one onion, a bunch of parsley, one bay leaf, a small sprig of thyme, and one of marjoram ; salt to taste, a small quantity of white pepper and allspice mixed, and two or three cloves. Fill the saucepan with cold water until it covers the contents by one inch, and set it on the fire to boil slowly for about four hours ; strain the liquor through a cloth into a basin and when cold, the cake of fat on the top being removed, the stock will be fit for use.

338. GRAVY STOCK.

Place a layer of slices of onion in a saucepan holding a gallon, over this a layer of fat bacon, and over all about two pounds of shin of beef chopped in small pieces ; one pint of common stock or even water, being poured on the whole, set the saucepan on the fire for one hour, until the liquor is almost evaporated—what is called reduced to a "glaze"—then add sufficient cold common stock or cold water to cover contents of the saucepan, and two or three carrots cut in slices, one leek, a head of celery (when in season), or some celery seed, a handful of parsley, half a clove of garlic, a sprig of marjoram and one of thyme, a bay leaf, four or five cloves, white pepper and salt to taste. After boiling for about three hours strain off the liqour, and, being absolutely freed from fat, it is ready for use.

339. VEAL STOCK.

Toss a couple of onions, sliced, and one pound of lean veal cut in pieces in a saucepan with some butter until they assume a light color, then add half a pound of ham chopped up small, and moisten with a pint of common stock cold and perfectly free from fat. Let the liquor reduce almost to a "glaze"— then add two quarts of cold common stock, a knuckle of veal, or two calves' feet, a couple of carrots, head of celery, parsley, bay leaf, thyme, mace, pepper and salt, all in due proportion. After boiling two or three hours strain free from fat and it is ready.

340. WHITE STOCK.

Put a knuckle of veal, or two calves' feet, together with an old fowl or a rabbit, and a piece of ham about half pound, all cut up in small pieces, into a saucepan with sufficient water to cover the contents; the stock should be carefully skimmed as it gradually becomes heated, then put in two carrots, a head of celery, two onions and a bunch of parsley, together with two bay leaves, a sprig of thyme, mace, cloves, pepper and salt to taste, and leave the whole to boil from three to four hours, when it should be strained and freed from fat.

341. FISH STOCK.

Take a couple of pounds of any kind of fish, such as flounders, small eels, or the trimmings of soles that have been filleted; pack them into a saucepan, with a head of parsley, including the root, a head of celery, two blades of mace, a few cloves, some white pepper and salt to taste, and a bay leaf. Put in as much cold water as will cover the contents of the saucepan, set it to simmer gently for a couple of hours, then strain off the liquor, and it is ready.

VEGETABLES.

OBSERVATIONS.

Take care to purchase them perfectly fresh, as this is their chief value and excellence. The middle-sized are preferable to the larger or smaller; they are more tender, juicy, and are better flavored. Peas and potatoes are seldom worth eating before midsummer. Salads, greens, roots, when first gathered are firm and have a fragrant freshness.

Vegetables should be carefully cleaned from insects, and nicely washed. Boil them in plenty of water, and drain them the moment they are done enough. If overboiled, they lose their beauty and crispness. Bad cooks sometimes dress them with meat, which is wrong, except carrots with boiling beef.

To boil vegetables green, be sure the water boils when you put them in. Make them boil very fast. Don't cover, but watch them; and if the water has not slackened, you may be sure they are done when they begin to sink. Then take them out immediately or the color will change. Hard water, especially if chalybeate, spoils the color of such vegetables as should be green.

To boil them green in hard water, put a teaspoonful of salt of wormwood into the water when it boils, before the vegetables are put in.

---

342. VEGETABLE MARROW (to Boil or Stew).

This excellent vegetable may be boiled as asparagus. When boiled, divide it lengthways into two, and serve it upon a toast accompanied by melted butter; or when nearly boiled, divide it as above, and stew gently in gravy like cucumbers. Care should be taken to choose young ones not exceeding six inches in length.

343. SPINACH.

Carefully wash and pick. When that is done, throw it into a saucepan that will just hold it, sprinkle it with a little salt, and cover close. The pan must be set on the fire, and well shaken. When done, beat the spinach well with a small piece of butter; it must come to table pretty dry, and looks well if pressed into a tin mould in the form of a large leaf, which is sold at the tinshops. A spoonful of cream is an improvement.

344. SPINACH.—Ingredients—Spinach, butter, pepper and salt, boiled eggs.

Wash and pick your spinach very carefully; drop into boiling water and cook fifteen minutes. Drain thoroughly through a cullender, then chop quite fine. Return to the stove, add one tablespoonful of butter, pepper and salt to taste; put in a vegetable dish and garnish with hard-boiled eggs.

345. POTATOES (to Boil).

Put them on the fire, without paring them, in cold water; let them half boil, then throw in some salt and a pint of cold water, and allow to boil again until almost done. Pour off the water and put a clean cloth over them, and then the saucepan cover, and set them by the fire to steam till ready. Many persons prefer steamers. Potatoes look best when the skin is peeled, not cut. Do new potatoes the same, but be careful they are taken off in time, or they will be watery. Before dressing, rub off the skin with a cloth, salt, and then wash.

346. POTATOES (to Broil).

Parboil, then slice and broil them. Or parboil and then set them on the gridiron over a very slow fire, and when thoroughly done send them up with their skins on. This last way is practised in many Irish families.

347. POTATOES (to Roast).

Half boil, take off the thin peel, and roast them of a beautiful brown.

348. POTATOES (to Fry).

Take the skin off raw potatoes, slice and fry them, either in butter or thin batter.

349. POTATOES (to Mash).

Boil the potatoes, peel them, and break them to paste; then to two pounds of them add a quarter of a pint of milk, a little salt, and two ounces of butter, and stir it all well over the fire. Either serve them in this manner, or place them on the dish in a form, and then brown the top with a salamander, or in scallops.

350. POTATOES (Stuffed).—Ingredients—5 medium-sized potatoes, ½ oz. of butter, 1 tablespoonful of grated cheese, pepper, salt, and the yolk of 1 egg.

For these take five of medium size, bake in their skins, and when done cut off a small slice from one end, scoop out the inside, and rub through a wire sieve. Add to it half an ounce of butter, one tablespoonful of grated cheese, pepper, salt, and the yolk of an egg. Mix well, refill the skins, fit on the slices which were cut off, and put into the oven again for ten minutes before serving.

351. **LYONNAISE POTATOES.**—Ingredients—A lump of butter, a small onion, cold boiled potatoes, a little parsley.

Into a saucepan put a large lump of butter and a small onion finely chopped, and when the onion is fried to an amber color, throw in slices of cold boiled potatoes, which must be thoroughly stirred until they are turning brown : at this moment put in a spoonful of finely chopped parsley, and as soon as it is cooked drain through a cullender, so that the potatoes retain the moisture of the butter and many particles of parsley.

352. **SARATOGA POTATOES.**—Ingredients—Potatoes, boiling lard and salt.

Peel, and slice on a slaw-cutter into cold water, wash thoroughly and drain ; spread between the folds of a clean cloth, rub and pat until dry. Fry a few at a time in boiling lard, salt as you take them out. Saratoga potatoes are often eaten cold. They can be prepared three or four hours before needed, and if kept in a warm place they will be crisp and nice.

353. **BERMUDA POTATOES (fried).**—Ingredients—2 oz. of butter, parsley, salt and pepper, a cup of milk, tablespoonful of flour.

Slice the potatoes and put them into boiling water ; cook until tender ; remove and put them into a saucepan with two ounces of butter, chopped parsley, salt and pepper and a cup of milk ; cook all together and thicken with a tablespoonful of flour stirred in cold water.

354. **POTATOES (Sautees au Beurre).**—Ingredients—Butter, salt.

Cut with a vegetable cutter into small balls about the size of a marble ; put them in a stewpan with plenty of butter and a good sprinkling of salt ; keep the saucepan covered, and shake it occasionally until they are quite done, which will be in about an hour.

355. **POTATOES (Stewed).**—Ingredients—Milk, 1 pint, a tablespoonful of flour.

Peel and cut into small uniform pieces as many potatoes as may be needed. Have ready enough boiling water (slightly salted) to cover them ; boil until done. Skim them out of the water into a dish and pour milk gravy over them (made of a pint of boiled milk, into which has been stirred a tablespoonful of flour previously dissolved in a little cold milk). Cold boiled potatoes can be served in the same way.

356. **POTATO BALLS.**—Ingredients—4 large potatoes, 2 tablespoonsful of butter, a pinch of salt, a little pepper, 1 tablespoonful of cream, 2 eggs, boiling lard.

Four large mealy potatoes, cold ; mash them in a pan with two tablespoonsfuls of melted butter, a pinch of salt, a little pepper, one tablespoonful of cream and the beaten yolk of one egg ; rub it together for about five minutes, or until very smooth ; shape the mixture into balls about the size of a walnut or small rolls, dip them into an egg well beaten and then into the finest sifted bread crumbs ; fry them in boiling lard.

357. **POTATOES (Escalloped).**—Ingredients—Cream, a large piece of butter, a little salt.

Having boiled, beat them fine in a bowl, with cream, and a large piece of butter, and a little salt. Put them into escallop shells, make them smooth on the top, score with a knife, and lay thin slices of butter on the tops of them. Then put them into an oven to brown.

358. **POTATO CHIPS.**—Ingredients—Boiling lard and salt.

Peel a raw potato as apples are peeled, let the parings be as nearly as possible the same thickness, and let them be as long as possible. Dry them thoroughly in a cloth, put them in the frying basket, and plunge it into boiling hot lard. When the chips are a golden color drain them well in front of the fire, sprinkle fine salt over them.

359. **POTATO CAKE.**—Ingredients—Potatoes, flour and lard.

Take cold mashed potatoes, and form into flat cakes, flour and fry in lard until they are a golden brown.

360. **SWEET POTATOES (Roast).**

Wash, wipe, and roast. Serve in their jackets.

361. **SWEET POTATOES (Boiled).**

Wash them, plunge into cold water, (no salt) boil till tender, drain, and put to dry for five minutes. Peel before serving.

362. **SWEET POTATOES (Fried).**—Ingredients—lard or dripping.

Take cold boiled potatoes, slice and fry in dripping or lard until of a golden brown.

363. **CABBAGE (Boiled).**—Ingredients—To half a gallon of water a tablespoonful of salt, and a small piece of soda.

Pick off the outside leaves, cut off as much of the stalk as possible, cut across the end of the stalk twice. Wash well in cold water, drain and plunge into boiling water, in which the above proportions of salt and soda have been added; boil without cover. Take up directly after they are done, drain, dish and serve.

364. **CABBAGE (a la Cauliflower).**—Ingredients—Butter, salt, ½ a cup of cream.

Cut the cabbage fine as for slaw; put it into a stewpan, cover with water and keep closely covered; when tender, drain off the water; put in a small piece of butter with a little salt, one half a cup of cream, or one cup of milk. Leave on the stove a few minutes before serving.

365. **FARCI (or Stuffed Cabbage).**—Ingredients—Veal stuffing, slices of sausage meat, gravy.

Cook the cabbage in salt and water sufficiently to open the leaves, and insert between them layers of ordinary veal stuffing, slices of sausage meat, then tie it securely round with thread to prevent the meat falling out. Replace in the stewpan, and cook briskly at first, then simmer till completely tender; serve in the same manner as ragout—that is to say, with a little gravy poured over the whole. In winter roast chestnuts hidden in the centre are sometimes added, when it is termed "Chou en surprise."

366. **EN RAGOUT.**—Ingredients—Clarified fat, small pieces of bacon or ham, pepper and salt, a little stock or water.

Soak a fresh fair-sized cabbage for ten minutes in strong salt and water, then take it out and drain carefully; put some clarified fat into a clean stewpan, and some small pieces of bacon or ham; lay half the cabbage on the top (either whole-leaved or cut up into large pieces, whichever is preferable), some more fat, and pepper and salt to taste, remembering that the bacon or ham will add to the saltness; place the other half of the cabbage on the top, and pour in a little stock (water can be used in default of stock, but the latter is by far the best), just enough to cover the ingredients. Cook briskly at first, then withdraw to the side, and keep it simmering for a considerable time. When it is thoroughly done, pour off the liquid, and set aside. Place the cabbage in the centre of a heated dish, as much raised as possible, and, having skimmed off the fat from the liquor, pour it over the vegetable, and serve.

376. **À LA CRÊME.**—Ingredients—1 oz. of butter, salt, white pepper, spoonful of flour, ¼ pt. of cream, fried croutons.

For this entrée, which is very delicate if carefully prepared, it is necessary to choose a cabbage as firm and white as possible. Throw the vegetable into boiling water with some salt, and boil till it is almost done, but not quite tender; take it out, and drain it thoroughly from all moisture; then cut it up lengthwise into several pieces; melt about an ounce of butter in a stewpan; the quantity of butter must be regulated by the size of the cabbage; sufficient must be used to make a rich sauce. Add salt, white pepper to avoid any discoloration, and a spoonful of flour; then put in the cream, according to desire, in any case not less than a quarter of a pint. Lay in the pieces of cabbage, and finish cooking in the sauce until perfectly tender. Arrange symmetrically on the dish, and place some fried croûtons round.

368. **CHOU ROUGE EN QUARTIERS**.—Ingredients—1 or 2 well grown red cabbages, clarified butter, pepper and salt, bacon, stock, Espagnole or brown sauce.

Take one or two well-grown red cabbages, according to the size required for your dish; cut each vegetable into four quarters lengthways, and throw them into boiling water for one quarter of an hour; then take them out carefully and drain well. Put some clarified fat into a stewpan, and lay in the quarters of cabbage; season with pepper and salt, and cover completely with slices of bacon, cut very thin, and moisten with stock. When done, take them out carefully, and press each quarter into a shape—either a round, heart, diamond, or in the form of cutlets, which is always a successful shape. Arrange artistically on a heated dish, and pour over the whole some Espagnole or brown sauce.

369. AUX POMMES.—Ingredients—1 red cabbage, 3 or 4 moderate sized apples, butter, salt, pepper, walnut, 3 or 4 cloves, 1 dessert spoonful of vinegar, the same quantity of red currant jelly, flour for thickening sauce.

Put a red cabbage into a saucepan, having previously washed it well; just cover it with water; peel, halve, and core three or four moderate-sized apples, and add them to the cabbage with a piece of butter about the size of a walnut, salt, pepper, and three or four cloves. Cook very gently over a slow fire for three hours. When ready to be served, add one dessert spoonful of vinegar, the same quantity of red currant jelly, and sufficient flour to thicken the sauce. Pour over and send to table.

371. **MARINE**.—Ingredients—A large red cabbage, pepper, salt, wine-glass of white wine vinegar, and the same quantity of water, 1 oz. of butter, brown gravy.

Take a large red cabbage and cut it into four pieces, first taking away the outside leaves and hard piece of stem; then take each piece separately and mince it in strips as fine as vermicelli, commencing at the head of the piece, and finishing at the stem end. Throw it all into boiling salt and water for ten minutes, drain, and place in a terrine or low-rimmed earthen jar. Season with pepper and salt, pour on a wine glassful of white wine vinegar, and the same quantity of water; leave it for fully three hours, then press it well to extract the juice; melt one ounce of butter in a stewpan, add the cabbage, and pour on some brown gravy. Cook very gently, indeed, until the vegetable is thoroughly done. There is a pleasant acid flavor about this entrèe, which should be eaten after any rich fish, such as salmon, shad, or eels.

370. **RED CABBAGE** (to Stew).—Ingredients—a small red cabbage, pepper, salt, butter, 2 or 3 spoonfuls of vinegar.

Slice a small, or half a large red cabbage, wash and put it into a saucepan with pepper, salt, no water but what hangs about it, with a piece of butter. Stew till quite tender; and when going to serve, add two or three spoonfuls of vinegar, and give one boil over the fire. Serve it for cold meat, or with sausages on it.

372. **TOMATOES** (Stewed). — Ingredients — Tomatoes, gravy, cream and arrowroot.

Arrange them in a single layer and pour over them as much gravy as will cover half their height. Stew very gently until the under sides are done, then turn and finish them; thicken the gravy with cream and arrowroot and serve it round them; the tomatoes may have some forcemeat put in the centre of each.

373. **TOMATOES** (Baked).—Ingredients—half a dozen tomatoes, bread-crumbs, pepper and salt, butter.

Cut half a dozen tomatoes in halves, remove the pips, and fill the insides with a mixture of bread-crumbs, pepper, and salt in due proportions; place a small piece of butter on each half tomato, and lay them close together in a well buttered tin; bake in a slow oven about half an hour, and serve. They may be eaten hot or cold.

374. **TOMATOES** (Stuffed).—Ingredients — Tomatoes, shallot, butter, 2 parts bread-crumbs, 1 part ham, parsley, sweet herbs, pepper and salt to taste, toast.

Dip some tomatoes in hot water, peel them, cut them in half, and remove the pips; rub a baking sheet with shallot, butter it well, and lay the tomatoes in it, filling each half with the following composition: Two parts bread-crumbs, one part ham finely minced, and, according to taste, parsley and sweet herbs also finely minced, and pepper and salt. Put a small piece of butter on each half tomato, and bake them a quarter of an hour; have ready some round pieces of buttered toast, on each of these put a half tomato, and serve.

375. **TOMATOES (with Macaroni)** (1).—Ingredients — Small quantity of tomatoes, butter, pepper, salt, a bay leaf and some thyme, a few spoonfuls of either stock or gravy, macaroni.

Take a quantity of tomatoes, cut them up, and remove from each the pips and watery substance it contains; put them into a saucepan with a small piece of butter, pepper, salt, a bay leaf, and some thyme; add a few spoonfuls of either stock or gravy; keep stirring on the fire until they are reduced to a pulp, pass them through a hair sieve, and dress the macaroni with this sauce and plenty of Parmesan cheese freshly grated.

376. **TOMATOES (with Macaroni)** (2).—Ingredients—Tomatoes, clove of garlic, a few sprigs of thyme, marjoram, basil, parsley, whole pepper, salt to taste, and macaroni.

Cut up a quantity of tomatoes, put them into a saucepan containing a little water, with a clove of garlic and a few sprigs of thyme, marjoram, basil, and parsley, with whole pepper and salt to taste. When quite done turn them out on a hair sieve and throw away the water that drains from them, then pass them through the sieve; warm the pulp thus obtained in a saucepan with a piece of butter, and use this sauce to dress the macaroni, as above.

377. **TOMATO PIE**.—Ingredients—Cold mutton or pork, a few slices of potatoes, onions, tomatoes, crust, stock or water.

Cold pork or mutton, a few slices of potatoes and onions, cover with sliced tomatoes, add a little stock or water, make a short crust and bake.

378. **TOMATOES (au Gratin)**.—Ingredients—Tomatoes, garlic, butter, two parts bread-crumbs, one part mushrooms, parsley, pepper and salt.

Dip the tomatoes in hot water, and peel them; cut them in half, and remove the pips; rub a baking tin with garlic, butter it, lay the tomatoes in side by side, and fill one half with the following composition: Two parts bread-crumbs, one part mushrooms finely minced, a little parsley chopped fine; pepper and salt to taste; put a small piece of butter on each. Bake for ten or fifteen minutes, and serve.

379. **TOMATO FRITTERS**.—Ingredients—1 quart of stewed tomatoes, 1 egg, 1 small teaspoonful of soda, flour, lard.

Use one quart of stewed tomatoes, one egg, one small teaspoonful of soda; stir in flour enough to make a batter like that for griddle cakes. Have some lard, very hot, on the stove; drop the batter in, a spoonful at a time, and fry.

380. **TOMATOES (Broiled).**—Ingredients—Some large, fresh tomatoes, butter, pepper, and salt, a small portion of sugar, an eggspoonful of made mustard.

In buying tomatoes for broiling, be careful to select large and fresh ones. Do not pare them. Slice in pieces about half an inch thick, and broil them for a few minutes upon a gridiron; while they are broiling prepare some hot butter in a cup, seasoning with pepper, salt, an eggspoonful of made mustard, and a little sugar; when the tomatoes are finished dip each piece into this, and then dish (the dish must be hot). If any of the seasoning remains, heat to the point of boiling and pour over the dish; serve immediately. This is a very nice dish if cooked well.

381. **TOMATOES (Raw).**

Pare them with a sharp knife, slice them neatly and place on a dish; sprinkle with pepper and salt, and pour over a little vinegar. Place this in the refrigerator until it is needed.

NOTE: This dish will be much improved by stirring a piece of ice about in the dressing before pouring over the tomatoes.

382. **BEET ROOTS.**

Beet roots make a very pleasant addition to winter salad, of which they may agreeably form a full half, instead of being only used to ornament it. This root is cooling, and very wholesome.

It is extremely good boiled, and sliced with a small quantity of onion; or stewed with whole onions, large or small, as follows:—

Boil the beet tender with the skin on, slice it into a stewpan with a little broth, and a spoonful of vinegar; simmer till the gravy is tinged with the color, then put it into a small dish, and make a round of the button onions, first boiled till tender, take off the skin just before serving, and mind they are quite hot and clear.

Or roast three large onions, and peel off the outer skins till they look clear, and serve the beet-root stewed round them.

If the beet root is in the least broken before dressed, it parts with its color, and looks ill.

383. **ONIONS (Boiled).**

Skin them thoroughly. Put them to boil; when they have boiled a few minutes, pour off the water and add clean cold water, and then set them to boil again. Pour this away and add more cold water, when they may boil till done. This will make them white and clear, and very mild in flavor. After they are done, pour off all the water, and dress with a little **cream, salt,** and pepper to taste.

384. **SPANISH ONIONS (a la Grecque).**—Ingredients—Onions, butter, salt, pepper.

Peel off the very outer skins, cut off the pointed ends like a cigar, put them in a deep dish, and put a piece of butter and a little salt and pepper on the place where the point has been cut off, cover them with a plate or dish, and let them bake for not less than three hours. They will throw out a delicious gravy.

385. **SPANISH ONIONS (Baked).**—Ingredients—4 or 5 Spanish onions, butter, salt and water.

Salt a saucepanful of boiling water slightly, put the onions into this, leaving the skins on, and let them boil sharply for about an hour. When they are done, take them out, wipe them, and cover each in a piece of brown paper, bake in the oven for two hours. Add butter, pepper, and salt to taste, and serve in their skins.

386. **SPANISH ONIONS (Stewed).**—Ingredients—5 or 6 medium-sized Spanish onions, 1 pint of broth or gravy.

In paring the onions be careful not to cut off too much of the tops and ends. Put them into a large saucepan (avoid placing one on top of the other). Add the broth or gravy, and allow it to simmer gently until the onions are quite tender, then dish them, pour the gravy over them, and serve quickly.

387. **ONIONS (Burnt, for Gravies).**—Ingredients—Half lb. of onions, 1 glass of water, 8 oz. of moist sugar, ¾ pt. of vinegar.

Peel and mince the onion finely, and put into an iron stewpan, and add the water; allow to boil seven minutes. Then put in the sugar, and allow to simmer until the mixture is nearly black and begins to smoke. Have ready the vinegar boiling hot, and strain the liquor slowly into it, stirring with a wooden spoon until it is thoroughly mixed; set aside to cool, when ready, bottle for use.

388. **ONIONS** (Stuffed). — Ingredients — Very large Spanish onions, cold fat pork or bacon, bread-crumbs, pepper, salt, mace, 10 spoonfuls of cream or milk, a well-beaten egg, butter, juice of half a lemon, browned flour, milk.

Wash and skin very large Spanish onions. Lay in cold water an hour. Parboil in boiling water half an hour. Drain, and while hot extract their hearts, taking care not to break the outside layers. Chop the inside thus obtained very fine, with a little cold fat pork or bacon. Add bread-crumbs, pepper, salt, mace, and wet with a spoonful or two of cream (or milk in default of cream). Bind with a well-beaten egg, and work into a smooth paste. Stuff the onions with this; put into a dripping pan with a very little hot water, and simmer in the oven for an hour, basting often with butter melted. When done, take the onions up carefully, and arrange the open ends upwards in a vegetable dish. Add to the gravy in the dripping pan the juice of half a lemon, four tablespoonfuls of cream or milk, and a little browned flour wet with cold milk. Boil up once, and pour over the onions.

389. MUSHROOMS.

The cook should be well acquainted with the different sorts of things called by this name by ignorant people, as the deaths of many persons have been caused by carelessly using the poisonous kinds. The eatable mushrooms first appear very small and of a round form on a very small stalk. They grow very fast, and the upper part and stalk are white. As the size increases, the under part gradually opens and shows a fringy fur of a very fine salmon color which continues more or less till the mushroom has been picked, when it turns to a brown. The skin can be more easily peeled from the real mushroom than the poisonous kind. A good test is to sprinkle a little salt on the spongy part or gills of the sample to be tried; if they turn black they are wholesome, if yellow they are poisonous. Give the salt a little time to act, before you decide as to their quality.

390. Do. (Stewed).—Ingredients—Mushrooms, salt, butter and browned flour.

Gather those that have red gills; cut off that part of the stem which grew in the earth; wash, and take the skin from the top; put them in a stew-pan, with some salt; stew them till tender; thicken with a spoonful of butter and browned flour.

391. Do. (Broiled).—Ingredients—Mushrooms, salt, pepper, butter.

Prepare them as directed for stewing. Broil them on a griddle; and when done, sprinkle salt and pepper on the gills, and put a little butter on them.

392. Do. (Baked).—Ingredients—18 or 20 mushroom-flaps, pepper and butter to taste.

Pare the top and cut off part of the stalk, wipe them carefully with a piece of flannel or cloth and a little fine salt. Then put them into a baking dish and put a piece of butter on each mushroom. Sprinkle with pepper to taste and bake for twenty minutes or half an hour. When done serve on a hot dish with the gravy poured over the mushrooms.

393. Do. (a la Creme).—Ingredients—Mushrooms, butter, salt, nutmeg, a bunch of herbs, yolk of one egg, some good cream.

Cut the mushrooms in pieces, and toss them over a brisk fire in butter seasoned with salt, a very little nutmeg, and a bunch of herbs. When they are done enough, and the butter nearly all wasted away, take out the herbs, add the yolk of an egg beaten up in some good cream; make very hot and serve.

394. MUSHROOMS (Ragout of).—Ingredients—Mushrooms, melted lard or butter, salt, pepper, minced parsley, broth, a spoonful of cullis, a squeeze of lemon juice.

Skin and cut the mushrooms in slices, toss them in melted lard or butter, seasoned with salt, pepper, and minced parsley; moisten with broth and a spoonful of cullis. Just before serving add a squeeze of lemon juice.

395. Do. (Essence of).—Ingredients—Mushrooms, salt.

Sprinkle a little salt over flap or button mushrooms. Allow them to stand three hours. Mash them, and the following day strain off the liquor that will flow from them. Put in stewpan, and boil till it is reduced one half. It will not keep very long, but it is a delicate relish.

396. Do. (Powder).—Ingredients—Half a peck of large mushrooms, 2 teaspoonfuls of white pepper, one quarter oz. of pounded mace, 2 onions, a dozen cloves.

Pare and wipe the mushrooms, be careful that no grit or dirt adheres to them; remove the black fur; put into stewpan without water; add ingredients and shake over a clear fire, till the liquor is evaporated. Under no consideration allow them to burn. Place upon tins, and dry in a slow oven. Then proceed to pound it into a fine powder. Have ready some *perfectly dry* small bottles, and put the powder in them. Cork and seal and keep in a dry place. This is a splendid substitute for mushrooms, when they are not in season.

397. PARSNIPS.

Boil, mash, season with butter, pepper and salt, make into little cakes; roll in flour and brown in hot lard. They are very nice cooked in this manner.

398. Do. (American Fashion).

Scrape and boil some parsnips, then cut each lengthwise in four, and fry them very brown, and dish in pairs. There is no vegetable so nourishing as parsnip, and when done in this way is very nutritious.

399. Do. (Buttered).—Ingredients—Parsnips, butter, pepper, salt, chopped parsley.

Boil the parsnips tender and scrape; slice lengthwise. Put three tablespoonfuls of butter into a saucepan, with pepper, salt, and a little chopped parsley. When heated put in the parsnips. Shake and turn until mixture boils, then lay the parsnips in order upon a dish, and pour the butter over them and serve.

400. **PARSNIPS (Mashed).**—Ingredients—Parsnips, 3 dessert spoonfuls of cream, butter the size of an egg, pepper, salt.

Boil and scrape the parsnips. Mash with potato beetle, remove the fibres, add the above ingredients, place in saucepan, heat to boiling, and serve in the form of a mound on a hot dish.

401. Do. **(Fried).**—Ingredients—Parsnips, flour, dripping, pepper.

Boil until tender, scrape and cut into pieces (lengthwise), dip in flour and fry in boiling dripping, browning both sides. Drian, first on sieve, then on blotting paper, pepper to taste, and serve very hot.

402. Do. **(Fricassed).**—Ingredients—Parsnips, milk, white sauce, 2 spoonfuls of broth, a piece of mace, 1 half cupful of cream, butter, flour, pepper and salt.

Scrape them; boil in milk till they are soft; then cut them lengthwise into pieces two or three inches long, and simmer in a white sauce, made of two spoonfuls of broth, a piece of mace, one-half cupful of cream, a piece of butter, and some flour, pepper and salt.

403. **CUCUMBERS (to Dress).**—Ingredients—Half a teacupful of vinegar, 3 tablespoonfuls of salad oil, pepper and salt.

Pare and cut the cucumber into slices as thin as a wafer (it is better to commence at the thick end). Place in a glass dish; sprinkle with salt and pepper, and pour over the above proportions of oil and vinegar. This is a nice accompaniment to boiled salmon, and is useful in concocting a salad. It is also an excellent garnish for lobster salad.

404. Do. **(Stewed).**—Ingredients—3 large cucumbers, a little butter, half a pint of brown gravy, a little flour.

Cut the cucumbers lengthwise, removing the seeds. Have the pieces a convenient size for the dish they are served in. Plunge them into boiling water with a little salt. Allow it to simmer for five minutes. Put the gravy into another saucepan, and when the cucumbers are done, remove from the water and place in the gravy, and allow to boil until they are tender. If there should be a bitter taste, add a teaspoonful of granulated sugar. Dish carefully, skim the sauce, and pour over the cucumbers.

405. Do. **(Fried).**—Ingredients—Two nice cucumbers, pepper and salt, oil or butter.

Pare cucumbers, cut into slices, press the slices upon a dry clean cloth; dredge with flour; have ready a pan of boiling oil or butter, put the slices into it, and keep turning them until they are brown; remove them from pan and lay upon a sieve to drain. Serve on a hot dish.

406. **CUCUMBER (a la Maitre d'Hotel).**—Ingredients—A nice straight cucumber, boiling water, a little salt, piece of butter size of an egg, bunch of parsley, some small onions, pepper.

Peel a nice, straight cucumber, and cut it in four pieces lengthways; scoop out all the seeds, and then cut it up again into small long pieces about a finger length; throw these into a saucepan of boiling water and some salt. When they bend under the touch they are done, and must be taken out and very carefully drained in a sieve; then put them into a stewpan, with a good sized piece of butter, some finely chopped parsley, some onions, and salt and pepper to taste. The cucumber will not, however, require much salt, as the acid itself renders it salt tasting. Toss the pieces of vegetables well over a brisk fire until thoroughly heated through, and serve on a very hot dish.

407. **Do. (Fircis).**—Ingredients—Cucumber, meat stuffing, a bunch of herbs, and some good stock, a little corn flour, butter the size of an egg.

Cut of the tail ends of a short, thickly made cucumber, and scoop out the seeds with the end of a spoon, or marrow-spoon is best, then peel it very thinly; prepare a good meat stuffing, or even fish can be used as a forcemeat for a change, and fill the cucumber with it, replacing the ends originally cut off with the aid of little wooden skewers. Wrap round the vegetable with a thin linen cloth, and put it into a stewpan with a bouquet of herbs and some good stock. Simmer over a clear fire until done, then reduce the liquid, thickening it with flour (a little cornflour is preferable) and butter. Serve in the gravy thus made.

408. **Do. (a la Poulette).**—Ingredients—Butter the size of an egg rolled in flour, slices of cucumber, a little cream or stock, 2 eggs, a few drops of vinegar.

Put some floured butter (butter rolled in flour) into a stewpan, with slices of cucumber dressed as for à la maitre d'hotel; moisten with some good cream, or stock in default of cream. Toss the cucumber until well heated through, then take it off the fire, and add two yolks of eggs, and a few drops (to taste) of vinegar.

409. **Do. (Frits).**

Cut the cucumber (already cooked) into pieces about the length of your little finger, dry them very carefully in a cloth, and fry them in butter. They can also be dipped in a good batter, and then fried in the same way as salsify. Particular care must be taken to have the vegetable very dry, as the slightest moisture will prevent them frying crisp.

410. **HARICOT BEANS** (1).—Ingredients—Half a pint of small white beans, enough cold water to cover them, ½ oz. of butter, teaspoonful of chopped parsley, a few slices of raw bacon.

Soak half a pint of small white beans over-night in just enough water to cover them; the next day, boil two hours, strain, and put into a pie dish with half an ounce of butter, a teaspoonful of finely chopped parsley previously fried, cover with slices of raw bacon, and bake a quarter of an hour.

411. **Do.** (2).—Ingredients—Beans, melted butter, 2 hard boiled eggs, fried parsley, a gill of milk, pepper, salt, 3 drops of lemon juice.

Soak and boil as before; then stir into them some well-made melted butter, and garnish with hard-boiled eggs cut in halves and set on end on the top of the beans, with a little pyramid of fried parsley in the centre of the dish. The melted butter must be carefully made, with half an ounce of butter and the same of flour stirred together over the fire until they are well blended; then add a gill of milk, pepper, and salt, and three drops of lemon juice; when this boils it is considered sufficiently cooked. An ordinary sized egg to be hard, should be boiled twelve minutes; if less it will be soft in the centre, if more it will be overdone, and have a black line round it near the shell.

412. **LIMA BEANS.**—Ingredients—One qt. Lima beans, salt, pepper, butter, 1 qt. of milk.

Take one quart of Lima beans, wash and soak them over-night in cold water; simmer over a slow fire four hours; then add salt, pepper, butter (the size of an egg), and one quart of sweet milk; boil for half an hour.

413. **LIMA AND BUTTER BEANS.**—Ingredients—Beans, boiling water, a little salt and butter.

Shell and place in cold water, allowing them to remain in the water half an hour; then put into boiling water with a little salt and cook until tender; drain, and butter and pepper them.

414. **FRENCH BEANS.**—Ingredients—Beans, boiling water, butter the size of an egg, salt.

Top, tail, and string the beans *carefully*; cut in pieces about an inch long; lay in cold salt and water for a quarter of an hour; drain and plunge into saucepan of boiling water and boil until tender; drain in a cullender; dish with the above proportion of butter stirred in.

415. FRENCH BEANS (to Preserve).

Get the beans, some salt, and any kind of salting tub or earthenware pan; put in a layer of beans, a layer of salt, and so on till full. When wishing to use, soak forty-eight hours; cut and boil till cooked. The water must be changed several times in which they soak. They will be of an excellent color and flavor.

416. TURNIPS (Boiled).—Ingredients—Turnips, boiling water, pepper, salt, a teaspoonful of sugar, a tablespoonful of butter.

Pare and cut in pieces; put them into boiling water well salted, and boil until tender; drain thoroughly and then mash and add a piece of butter, pepper and salt to taste, and a small teaspoonful of sugar; stir until they are thoroughly mixed, and serve hot.

417. Do. (German recipe for cooking).—Ingredients—Half a dozen large turnips, 3 oz. of butter, ½ pint weak stock, 1 tablespoonful of flour, pepper and salt.

Heat the butter in a stewpan, pare and cut the turnips into pieces the size of dice and season with pepper and salt; then place in the hot butter, toss over the fire for five minutes, add the stock and simmer gently until the turnips are tender. Brown the flour with a little butter; add this to the turnips and simmer five minutes. Boiled mutton may be served with this dish.

418. Do. (a la Creme).—Ingredients—One oz. of butter, a dessertspoonful of flour, pepper and salt, grated nutmeg, a little milk or cream.

Take small new turnips, peel and boil them in salted water; drain them thoroughly. Melt one ounce of butter in a saucepan, add to it a dessertspoonful of flour, pepper, salt, grated nutmeg, and a small quantity of milk or cream; put in the turnips; simmer gently a few minutes, and serve.

419. Do. (a la de Maitre).—Ingredients—Small new turnips, a little butter, chopped parsley, pepper and salt, and a squeeze of lemon.

Boil some small new turnips as in the preceding recipe; drain them thoroughly, and melt some butter in the saucepan; put the turnips in, give them a toss or two, add a little chopped parsley, pepper and salt, a squeeze of lemon juice, and serve.

420. **CARROTS (to Boil).**—Ingredients—6 young carrots, a tablespoonful of salt.

Place upon the stove two qts. of warm water with the above proportion of salt, bring to a boil ; wash and scrape the carrots, remove any black specks, cut in halves, plunge into the boiling water, and boil until tender ; drain, and serve upon a hot dish.

421. **Do. (Stewed).**—Ingredients—Carrots, a little weak broth, salt, butter, a dessertspoonful of flour, pepper.

Wash and scrape the carrot ; split the largest. Then whiten them in hot water, and drain them on a sieve ; then boil them in weak broth, with salt ; then put some butter in a saucepan, with a dessertspoonful of flour ; stir it and brown it. Add the carrots to it, broth and pepper. Stir, and let all simmer together.

422. **CAROTTES (Glacees).**—Ingredients—Carrots, butter, white powdered sugar, a little stock.

Trim up to resemble little pears in shape some new red carrots, and soak for a few minutes in water. Then fry in butter with the addition of some white powdered sugar and a little good stock. When the pieces are sufficiently cooked increase the heat of the fire, so that evaporation goes on rapidly ; let the carrots glaze, and then serve.

423. **SALSIFY (Boiled).**—Salsify, vinegar, water, butter, lemon juice, parsley, salt.

Scrape the roots, cut them in short lengths, and throw them into vinegar and water as they are being done. Boil them till tender in salted water, drain them, toss them into a saucepan with a piece of butter, a little lemon juice, and some minced parsley ; add salt and serve.

424. **EGG PLANT (Baked).**—Ingredients—Egg plant, salt, a cup of crumbs, 2 oz. of salt pork, an onion, pepper, nutmeg, butter.

Parboil fifteen minutes. Then make a triangular cut in the top ; remove the piece and take out the seeds. Let it lie for an hour in water to which a tablespoonful of salt has been added. Make a stuffing of one cup of crumbs, two ounces of salt pork, and an onion chopped fine, one teaspoonful of salt, half a one of pepper and of nutmeg mixed ; wet with half a cup of boiling water or stock, and fill the egg plant, tying a string around it to keep the piece in place. Bake an hour, basting often with a spoonful of butter in a cup of water.

425. **VEGETABLE MARROW (Stewed).**—Ingredients—1 marrow, 1 onion, a piece of butter, pepper, salt, nutmeg, parsley, a little stock.

Chop up half an onion very small, and put it in a saucepan

with a piece of butter; when it begins to color put in the vegetable marrow (cut in slices), add pepper, salt, and grated nutmeg; moisten with stock, and stew till done, adding some finely minced parsley just before serving

426. **VEGETABLE MARROW (Fried).**—Ingredients—1 marrow, a little salt, flour, dripping or lard.

Having peeled and removed the seeds of a good-sized vegetable marrow, cut it in strips one and a half inches long by three-quarter inches square; put these on an inverted plate placed in a basin, and strew plenty of finely powdered salt over them. In a couple of hours take up the pieces of marrow and dry them in a cloth by wringing it at both ends, not so hard, however, as to break them; then put them in another cloth with some flour and shake them well, so that they are individually well covered with flour; lastly, put them in a frying basket and plunge this in very hot fat; as soon as the marrow strips begin to color, lay them, sprinkled with salt, in front of the fire to drain, and serve hot.

427. **Do. (Boiled).**—Ingredients—Allow 1 tablespoonful of salt to ½ gallon of water, marrow.

Having prepared the water as above bring to the point of boiling; peel the marrow and plunge into the boiling water, and boil until tender; remove from the water with a slice, halve, and should it be very large quarter it. Dish on toast, and send to table accompanied with a tureen of melted butter.

428. **GREEN CORN (Stewed).**

Having cut the corn from the cob, put into boiling water and allow to stew a quarter of an hour; remove nearly all the water and cover with milk, and allow to stew until tender; before dishing, roll some pieces of butter in flour and mix with the corn, adding a little pepper and salt; give one boil and serve.

429. **Do. (Boiled).**

Strip off all the outer husks, allowing the innermost to remain; remove the silk and re-cover the ear with the remaining husk, secure with a piece of thread, plunge into boiling salted water, and boil half an hour. Cut off stalks and dish upon a napkin.

430. **Do. (Roasted).**—Ingredients—Corn, butter, salt, pepper.

Open the husks, remove the silk, close the husks closely, and roast in the ashes of a wood fire until tender; serve with butter, pepper, and salt. This is frequently eaten in camp.

431. **SUMMER SQUASHES.**—Ingredients—Squash, butter, pepper, salt.

Pare the outer rind, remove the seeds, quarter, and lay in

ice water ten minutes; put into boiling water, a little salt, and cook until tender; press all the water from them. Mash smooth, season with the above ingredients, and serve *hot.*

432. WINTER SQUASH.

Proceed as above, allowing more time to cook; before putting into the boiling water, allow it to soak in cold water three hours.

433. CAULIFLOWER (Boiled).—Ingredients—Cauliflower, salt water.

Wash in two or three waters. Cut off the end of stalk and outer leaves, allow to lie in salt and water five minutes, plunge into boiling salted water, and boil fifteen or twenty minutes; drain and serve hot.

434. Do. (Fried).—Ingredients—Cauliflower, salt, vinegar, whole pepper, a few cloves, butter, lard.

Pick out all the green leaves from a cauliflower, and cut off the stalk close; put it head downwards in a saucepan full of boiling salted water; do not overboil it; drain it on a sieve, pick it out into small sprigs, and place them in a deep dish with plenty of vinegar, whole pepper, salt, and a few cloves. When they have lain about an hour in this drain them, dip them in batter, and fry in hot lard to a golden color.

435. Do. (Scalloped).—Ingredients—Cauliflower, 1 oz. butter, ½ gill of milk, 1 oz. bread-crumbs, cayenne, salt, 1 egg.

Choose a cauliflower of medium size, boil it twenty minutes; put into a saucepan one ounce of butter, half a gill of milk, and one ounce of bread crumbs; add cayenne and salt to taste, and stir till the bread has absorbed the milk and butter. Beat an egg and add this to the sauce, but be sure that it does not simmer after the egg has been added. Butter a flat tin dish, take off the fine leaves of the cauliflower and place them all round on it, break up the flower carefully and lay in the centre, making it as high as possible; pour the sauce over this, sprinkle a few bread-crumbs on the top, and bake ten minutes.

436. GREEN PEAS (to Keep).

Shell, and put them into a kettle of water when it boils; give them two or three warms only, and pour them in a cullender; when the water drains off, turn them out on a table covered with cloth, and pour them on another cloth to dry perfectly; then bottle them in wide-mouthed bottles; leaving only room to pour clarified mutton-suet upon them an inch thick, and for the cork. Rosin it down, and keep it in the cellar or in the earth. When they are to be used, boil them till tender, with a piece of butter, a spoonful of sugar, and a little mint.

437. GREEN PEAS (to Keep, as practised in the Emperor of Russia's kitchen).

When they are to be used, let them lie an hour in water; then set them on with cold water and a piece of butter, and boil them till ready. Put a sprig of dried mint to boil with them. Boiled peas should not be overdone, nor in much water; chop some scalded mint to garnish them, and stir a piece of butter in with them.

438. Do. (Stewed).—Ingredients—A quart of peas, 1 lettuce, 1 onion, butter, pepper, salt, 1 egg, a little flour.

Put a quart of peas, a lettuce and an onion both sliced, a piece of butter, pepper, salt, and no more water than hangs round the lettuce from washing; stew them two hours very gently. When to be served, beat up an egg, and stir it into them, or a little flour and butter. Some think a teaspoonful of white powdered sugar is an improvement.

439. Do. (a la Francaise).—Ingredients—For every pint of peas 1 gill of water, 1½ oz. of butter, a bunch of parsley, salt, pepper, 8 or 9 small white onions, 1 lettuce.

Put the required quantity of peas necessary for your dish into a perfectly clean and bright stewpan, with some water and butter in the following proportions: For every pint of peas one gill of water and one ounce of butter. When this is thoroughly amalgamated, add a little bouquet, tied together, of parsley, also salt, pepper, and another half ounce of butter, then eight or nine small white onions, and a whole lettuce. Simmer the whole well for an hour, or more if the peas and other vegetables are not completely tender. The time, in fact, must be regulated according to the judgment of the cook. When done, take out the bunch of parsley, the lettuce, and the onions, which are very serviceable for hashes, stews, or soups, even when used as above. The peas, when once cooking, must not be touched by a spoon or a fork, as it would bruise them and spoil the appearance of the entrée, but well tossed constantly to prevent them sticking to the stewpan, always kept briskly simmering, but never boiling, otherwise they will harden.

440. Do. (au Sucre).—Ingredients—Peas, white sugar.

Green peas prepared as above without the lettuce, onions, parsley, or pepper, but some finely powdered white sugar sprinkled in by degrees, and according to taste.

441. Do. (en Purée).—Ingredients—Two pints of peas, white sugar, bread-crumbs, flour, double cream, salt, a bunch of parsley, white pepper, butter and stock in adequate proportions, fried croûtons (heart-shaped).

The great secret of a well-concocted purée is the softness of the whole. It should pass over the palate like velvet, and leave no trace of its substance or material behind. To ensure this creamy softness there are three distinct methods. Firstly, by adding *before* passing through the hair sieve some very fine white sifted bread-crumbs; secondly, prepared flour mixed carefully to a smooth paste first, with some stock or bouillon; and thirdly by the aid of good double cream. A tiny pinch of fine white powdered sugar must always be added. It is a very necessary ingredient. For an artistic purée, then, take two pints, say, of young green peas, and throw them into a saucepan of boiling water with some salt, and a bunch of parsley. When they are tender, take them out and drain them thoroughly from all the moisture, and then pass carefully through a fine hair sieve. Season the purée thus made with a little white pepper and salt to taste, and reheat in a saucepan with a little butter and stock in adequate proportions, having of course previously, as directed above, employed one of the three methods for thickening and softening the purée. Serve with fried croûtons, cut out in heart shape. The husks of the very young green-pea shell will also make a purée, or prove serviceable in mixing with the other, if thoroughly well cooked until quite soft in boiling water, drained, bruised, and then passed through a sieve, seasoned in the same manner. For green-pea soup the husk is very useful, as the flavor obtained equals in every way the vegetable itself.

442. **ASPARAGUS**.—Ingredients—Asparagus, salt, toast, butter.

After scraping the stalks to cleanse them, place them in a vessel of cold water. Tie them up neatly into bundles of about twenty-five heads each, then place them in a saucepan of boiling water, sprinkling a handful of salt over it. When it is boiling remove any scum there may be; the stalks will be tender when they are done; they will take about twenty minutes or half an hour; be careful to take them up the minute they are done; have ready some toast, dip in it the liquor in which the asparagus was boiled; dish upon toast, and serve with a boat of melted butter.

443. **Do. (in Ambush)**.—Ingredients—2 bunches of asparagus, 8 stale biscuits (or rolls may be used), 4 eggs, about ½ pint of milk, butter the size of an egg, flour, pepper and salt to taste.

Take the green tops of the two bunches of asparagus, boil them tender and mince finely. While they are boiling, take the biscuits or rolls, divide them, keeping the top half for a cover; place them all in the oven to crisp; make the milk hot, and then pour in the eggs beaten; stir over the fire until it thickens, then add the butter rolled in flour, and lastly add the asparagus; spread the rolls with this mixture, put on the tops and serve hot.

444. ASPARAGUS (and Eggs).—Ingredients—26 or 30 heads of asparagus, good rich butter, salt and pepper, 5 or 6 eggs.

Boil the asparagus (after cutting them into pieces of about half an inch) for fifteen minutes; take a cup of rich butter and put it into a saucepan; drain the asparagus, and put it with the butter; heat them to a boil, seasoning with pepper and salt, and then pour into a buttered baking tin or dish; break five or six eggs neatly over the surface of this, sprinkle with pepper and salt, and put it in the oven until the eggs are set nicely. Serve hot.

445. Do. (Pudding).—Ingredients—Green tops of 2 bunches of asparagus, 3 tablespoonfuls of prepared flour, 4 or 5 well-beaten eggs, 2 dessertspoonfuls of melted butter, 1 teacup of milk, 1 pinch of soda, pepper and salt to taste.

Boil the asparagus and when cool chop finely; take the eggs, butter, pepper and salt, and beat them up together, then put in the flour; stir the soda into the milk, and add gradually; lastly put in the asparagus. Put this into a buttered mould with a lid, or if it has no lid tie it down tightly with a floured cloth; boil for two hours. When done, turn out on a dish, and pour melted butter round it.

446. ARTICHOKES (with White Sauce).—Ingredients—Salted water, ½ oz. butter, 1 tablespoonful of flour, white pepper and salt, the yolks of 2 eggs and the juice of a lemon.

Wash them well, peel and shape them to a uniform size; throw them into boiling salted water, and let them boil fifteen to twenty minutes; drain them at once thoroughly; put them on a dish and serve with the following sauce poured over them. Mix over the fire one and a half ounces of butter with a tablespoonful of flour; add half a pint of boiling water, white pepper, and salt to taste; stir till the sauce thickens, then take the saucepan off the fire, and stir in the yolks of two eggs, beaten up with the juice of a lemon, and strained.

447. Do. (with Cream).—Ingredients—The same ingredients as above, adding a little cream and grated nutmeg.

Prepare and parboil them as in the preceding recipe; then put them into a saucepan with a due allowance of white sauce, and let them finish cooking in this, adding at the last a small quantity of cream and grated nutmeg.

448. Do. (with Gravy).—Ingredients—As No. 1, adding gravy.

Prepare them as above, cutting them to the size of pigeon's eggs. Parboil them for ten minutes, drain them and toss them in a saucepan, with a piece of butter; then add a small quantity of good clear gravy and a dust of pepper. Let them simmer very gently till wanted.

449. **ARTICHOKES (Mashed)**.—Ingredients—Salted water, a piece of butter, a little cream, white pepper, nutmeg and salt.

Wash, peel, and boil them in salted water; drain, and pass them through a hair sieve. Squeeze all the water out of the pulp; put it into a saucepan, and work it on the fire, with a piece of butter and a little cream, adding white pepper, nutmeg and salt if necessary. When quite hot and sufficiently dry, serve.

450. **Do. (Fried)**.—Ingredients—A little flour, lard, butter.

Wash, peel, and parboil them whole for ten minutes, then cut them in strips the size of a little finger. Flour them carefully, and fry in hot lard; or they may be dipped in batter and fried. Serve piled up on a napkin.

451. **Do. (Stewed)**.—Ingredients—Two shallots, butter, a little stock, pepper, salt, lemon juice, parsley.

Mince a couple of shallots and fry them in plenty of butter; put in the artichokes parboiled and cut into pieces, moisten with a little stock, season with pepper, salt, and a little lemon juice; lastly add some finely-chopped parsley, and let the whole stew gently till quite done. A small quantity of Parmesan cheese may be added.

452. **Do. (au Gratin)**.—Ingredients—A shallot, baked bread-crumbs, pepper, salt, powdered thyme, lemon juice, butter.

Wash, peel, and boil them whole; cut them in slices the thickness of a cent. Butter a dish previously rubbed with a shallot; arrange the slices on it, strew over them some baked bread-crumbs, seasoned with pepper, salt, and a little powdered thyme, add a squeeze of lemon, put a few pieces of butter on the top, and bake for ten or fifteen minutes.

453. **PUMPKIN (Stewed)**.—Ingredients—Pumpkin, butter, pepper and salt.

Halve, remove the seed, pare and slice neatly. Soak for an hour in cold water; then place in a saucepan of boiling water on the fire. Allow it to stew gently until it falls to pieces. Stir often. Then take it out, drain, squeeze, and rub through a cullender, then put it back in the saucepan adding two dessertspoonfuls of butter, pepper and salt to taste. Stir quickly, and when nearly boiling dish, adding more pepper if required.

454. **Do. (Baked)**.—Ingredients—A nice rich pumpkin, butter.

Cut the pumpkin into quarters, remove seeds, cut into slices lengthwise about half an inch thick. Place in a baking dish suitable for the purpose and arrange in layers about three slices deep. Put a very little water in the bottom of the dish and bake very slowly until done (the water must have evaporated). It takes a long time to bake. Butter the slices on both sides and dish. It is eaten with bread and butter, and tea.

SALADS.

OBSERVATIONS ON SALADS.

The following vegetables are commonly used in compounding salads: Beetroot, lettuce, cucumber, mint, parsley, radish, mustard and cress, onions, and celery. Any remnants of boiled fresh fish make very good salads; they should be sliced and seasoned with anchovies, parsley, vinegar, &c.

455. **SALAD.**—Ingredients—Four or five heads of cabbage lettuce, 4 spoonfuls of olive oil, 1½ or 2 tablespoonfuls of tarragon vinegar, pepper and salt to taste, a small pinch of mint minced finely.

Take four or five heads of cabbage lettuce, remove all outside leaves, and cut off the stalks close; then cut each head apart into four or five "quarters," that is, cut through the stalk and then tear the rest. Put four tablespoonfuls of olive oil into the salad bowl, with two and one half tablespoonfuls of tarragon vinegar, pepper and salt according to taste, and beat the mixture with a fork for some minutes; then put in the lettuce, and keep it turning over swiftly for five minutes, adding a small pinch of mint, chopped as finely as possible.

456. **LETTUCE SALAD.**—Ingredients—Two heads of lettuce, yolks of 2 hard boiled eggs, a teaspoonful of French mustard, pepper and salt to taste, 4 tablespoonfuls of oil, 1 of tarragon, and 1 of plain vinegar, chervil, garden cress and tarragon.

Wash two heads of lettuce, dry them thoroughly, and break the leaves or cut them into convenient pieces. Put the yolks of two hard-boiled eggs into a basin with a teaspoonful of French mustard, pepper and salt to taste, and a tablespoonful of oil; work the mixture into a smooth paste, and add consecutively three tablespoonfuls of oil, one of tarragon, and one of plain vinegar; then a little chervil, garden cress, and tarragon finely chopped. Stir the mixture well, and lastly add the lettuce; turn it or work it well. Garnish the top with hard-boiled eggs.

457. POTATO SALAD (1).—Ingredients—Shallot, some cold boiled potatoes, 3 parts of oil to one part of tarragon vinegar, pepper and salt to taste, and a small quantity of any of the following: powdered sweet herbs, mint, parsley, chervil, tarragon or capers.

Rub a dish with shallot; dispose on it some cold boiled potatoes cut in slices; beat together three parts of oil and one part, more or less according to the strength of it, of tarragon vinegar, with pepper and salt to taste. Pour this over the potatoes, and strew over all a small quantity of any of the following: powdered sweet herbs, mint, parsley, chervil, tarragon or capers, or a combination of them all, finely minced.

458. Do. (2).—Ingredients—Cold boiled potatoes, anchovies, capers, tarragon or powdered sweet herbs, plain salad dressing as above, shallot, hard boiled eggs.

Cut cold boiled potatoes in small cubes. Bone and fillet a few anchovies and chop them up, take the same quantity of capers, mix all together with some finely-minced tarragon or powdered sweet herbs, and a plain salad dressing as above. Put on a dish rubbed with shallot, and make a border round it of pieces of hard-boiled eggs.

459. Do. (3).—Ingredients—Five cold boiled potatoes, $\frac{1}{2}$ a small beetroot, $\frac{1}{2}$ a Spanish onion, 3 inches of pickled cucumber, salad dressing as above, a little English mustard, sweet powdered herbs, hard boiled eggs.

Take four or five cold boiled potatoes, half a small beetroot, half a small Spanish onion plainly boiled, and about three inches of pickled cucumber. Cut them all in slices and arrange them on a dish. Pour over them a salad dressing as above, adding a little English mustard to it, and strew powdered sweet herbs over. Serve with a border of hard boiled eggs cut in slices.

460. Do. (4).—Ingredients—Half a dozen well-washed anchovies, 2 hard-boiled eggs, a dessertspoonful of French Mustard, a sprig or two of tarragon, salad oil, pepper and lemon juice to taste, salt, minced truffles, a dish of cold boiled potatoes.

Pound half a dozen well-washed anchovies in a mortar, with two hard-boiled yolks of eggs, a dessertspoonful of French mustard, and a sprig or two of tarragon, then gradually work in salad oil, add pepper and lemon juice to taste, and salt if necessary. Strain the sauce over a dish of sliced cold boiled potatoes, and strew over all plenty of minced truffles.

461. SALAD (Lobster).—Ingredients—Lettuces, endives, beetroots, dressing, 4 tablespoonfuls of oil, 2 of vinegar, 1 teaspoonful of made mustard, yolks of 2 hard-boiled eggs, ¼ of a teaspoonful of anchovy sauce, cayenne, salt, 1 hen lobster, 2 hard-boiled eggs.

Clean thoroughly some lettuces, endives and beetroots, cut them up and mix them with the following dressing : four tablespoonfuls of oil, two ditto of vinegar, one teaspoonful of made mustard, the yolks of two eggs, half a teaspoonful of anchovy sauce, and cayenne and salt. Pick out from the shells the flesh of one hen lobster, cut into well-shaped pieces, put half in the salad and garnish with the rest, also with the whites of two hard-boiled eggs chopped fine, and the yolks mixed with the coral and rubbed through a sieve.

462. **SALAD (Sardine).**—Ingredients—3 sardines for each person, 2 eggs, 1 teaspoonful each of French mustard, and essence of anchovies, strained oil from a box of sardines, adding enough Lucca oil to make three tablespoonfuls in all, Chili, shalot, and good malt vinegar to taste, lettuce, mustard and cress, some red capsicum.

Allow three sardines for each person ; bone and fillet these, carefully removing all the skin, and set them aside until required. Boil two eggs for three minutes ; shell them and break them up in your salad bowl with a spoon ; mix with them a teaspoonful each of French mustard and essence of anchovies, the strained oil from the tin of sardines with as much Lucca oil as will make three tablespoonfuls in all ; add Chili, shalot, and good malt vinegar to taste (vinegar varies so much in acidity that it is difficult to specify the exact proportion). Cut up some nice crisp lettuce, and mix it well with the dressing, but only just before it is to be served. Put a little heap of mustard and cress in the centre of the salad, with a whole red capsicum upon it. Arrange the sardines round, and outside these a border of mustard and cress, dotted here and there with thin slices of red capsicums.

463. **Do. (Anchovy).**

The anchovies sold in bottles, ready filleted and preserved in oil, will be found most convenient for this. Make the salad as for sardines, only omitting the essence of anchovies. The eggs may be boiled hard, the yolks used for the dressing, and the whites cut in rings and filled with mustard and cress.

464. **Do. (Game).**—Ingredients—Cold grouse, partridge or pheasant, pepper, salt, juice of a lemon, about 2 tablespoonfuls of fresh salad oil, lettuce, salad sauce, hard-boiled eggs, fillets of anchovies, sprigs of parsley.

Cold grouse, partridge or pheasant may be used in this way.

Cut them into joints, and put them into a pie dish; season with salt and pepper, and pour ver them the juice of a lemon and about two tablespoonfuls of very fresh salad oil; let them remain in this for three or four hours. Having cut up and well dried a fresh lettuce, place it on a flat dish and arrange the pieces of game which have been in the oil and lemon juice neatly in the centre; over the game pour a salad sauce, which should be of the consistency of thick cream. Ornament the top with slices of hard-boiled egg, fillets of well-washed and scraped anchovies, and garnish with tiny sprigs of parsley. Cold chicken, or the white meat from a cold turkey cut into small pieces, may be treated in this way. Cold salmon or turbot are also excellent.

465. **SALAD (Tomato).**—Ingredients—Some good-sized tomatoes, two parts of oil to one of vinegar, pepper and salt to taste, a few leaves of basil, some onions.

Peel some good-sized tomatoes, not over ripe, cut them in slices and remove the pips, lay them in a dish with oil and vinegar in the proportion of two to one, sprinkle pepper and salt over them according to taste, a few leaves of basil finely minced, and some onions very finely sliced. They should lie in the sauce for a couple of hours before serving.

466. **Do. (Egg).**—Ingredients—Hard-boiled eggs, chopped parsley, pepper, salt, vinegar, and oil.

Slice hard-boiled eggs, and dress them with chopped parsley, salt, pepper, vinegar, and oil. They must, of course, be very cold before they are sliced.

467. **Do. (Russian).**—Ingredients—Carrots, turnips, butter, beetroot, truffles, asparagus points, haricot beans, 2 tablespoonfuls of capers, 2 do. of French pickled gherkins and anchovies, 2 doz. stoned olives, 1 tablespoonful of tarragon and chervil, half that quantity of chives, sauce as follows—The raw yolks of some eggs, oil, vinegar, pepper and salt, some savory jelly, hard boiled eggs, caviare, lobster spawn, olives, pickles, truffles, etc.

Boil some carrots and some turnips in salted water with a small piece of butter, but do not let them be overdone; when cold cut out of them, with a vegetable scoop, a number of pieces the size of an olive; cut some beetroot in the same way, and likewise some truffles. Take equal parts—say a cupful—of each of the above, and a similar quantity of preserved fresh (not dried) haricot beans ready cooked, and of asparagus points preserved in the same way. Two tablespoonfuls respectively of capers, of French pickled gherkins, cut into the shape of capers, and of anchovies, perfectly cleaned, and cut into small pieces; a couple of dozen or more olives stoned, one tablespoonful of tarragon and chervil minced fine, and half that quantity of chives, also minced. Mix the whole lightly together into a sauce made with raw yolks of eggs, oil, vinegar, pepper, and salt, well worked together (proportions of oil to vinegar three to one). Dress within a border of savory jelly, and ornament with hard-boiled eggs, caviare, lobster spawn, olives, pickles, truffles, etc.

468. **SALAD (Beetroot).**—Ingredients—Beets, vinegar, salt, pepper, sugar, mustard, 1 tablespoonful of oil to 4 of vinegar.

Put the beets into a saucepan, and allow to boil until tender; then scrape clean. Drop them into a pan of cold water for 3 or 4 minutes to cool them; slice thinly and dress with the remaining ingredients. This salad will keep not more than two days.

N.B. This salad must be allowed to stand covered for two hours before serving.

469. **Do. (Celery).**—Ingredients—2 heads of celery, 1 tablespoonful of salad oil, half a teacup vinegar, a teaspoonful of granulated sugar, pepper and salt to taste.

Well wash the celery, removing any unsightly parts, lay in iced water until wanted; then cut into pieces about an inch in length. Season with remaining ingredients, mix well and serve in salad bowl.

470. **Do. (Red Cabbage).**—Ingredients—One small red cabbage, 1 small dessertspoonful of salt, ½ pint of vinegar, 1½ dessertspoonsful oil, a little cayenne pepper.

Secure a nice fresh cabbage, remove the outer leaves and cu the cabbage into nice thin slices, then mix in the above ingredients and allow to stand for two days when it will be fit for use. This salad will keep good for several days.

471. Rev. Sydney Smith's Receipt for Salad Dressing.

"Two boiled potatoes, strained through a kitchen sieve,
Softness and smoothness to the salad give;
Of mordant mustard take a single spoon—
Distrust the condiment that bites too soon,
Yet deem it not, thou man of taste, a fault
To add a double quantity of salt;
Four times the spoon with oil of Lucca crown,
And twice with vinegar procured from town;
True taste requires it, and your poet begs
The pounded yellow of two well boiled eggs.

Let onions' atoms lurk within the bowl,
And, scarce suspected, animate the whole:
And, lastly, in the flavored compound toss
A magic spoonful of anchovy sauce.
Oh! great and glorious, and herbaceous treat,
'Twould tempt the dying anchorite to eat;
Back to the world he'd turn his weary soul,
And plunge his fingers in the salad bowl."

472. **SALAD (Oyster)** —Ingredients—1 tin of oysters containing about a quart, 1 head of celery, 1 tablespoonful of oil, 1 small teaspoonful of salt, made mustard and pepper, 3 dessertspoonfuls of cider vinegar, a pinch of white sugar.

Strain off the liquor from the oysters and cut them up (do not chop them), mince the celery and blend with the oysters. Mix the remaining ingredients, putting in the vinegar last, then pour over the celery and oysters. Stir well, and serve directly, as this salad will not keep long.

PICKLES.

OBSERVATIONS ON PICKLES.

Enamelled kettles should always be used in preference to those of brass or copper, as the verdigris produced by the vinegar on these metals is extremely poisonous. For some pickles use cold vinegar, as in boiling most of the strength is lost by evaporation. For French beans, brocoli, cauliflowers, gherkins, etc., it is better to heat the vinegar, for which the following process is recommended:—Put the vinegar and spice in a jar, cover it tightly, let it simmer on the back of the stove or on a trivet. Shake occasionally. Pickles should never be put into glazed jars, as salt and vinegar penetrate the glaze, which is poisonous.

Glass or stone jars are preferable to any other; a small piece of alum in each jar will make the pickles firm and crisp. One tablespoonful of sugar to each quart of vinegar will be found a very great improvement to all pickles. Always use the very best cider or wine vinegar.

474. **ONIONS** (1).—Ingredients—Onions, best white wine vinegar, allspice and whole black pepper.

In the month of September, choose the small white round onions, take off the brown skin, have ready a very nice tin stewpan of boiling water, throw in as many onions as will cover the top; as soon as they look clear on the outside, take them up as quick as possible with a slice, and lay them on a clean cloth, cover them close with another, and scald some more, and so on. Let them lie to be cold, then put them in a jar, or glass, or wide-mouthed bottles, and pour over them the best white wine vinegar, just hot but not boiling. To each gallon of vinegar add one ounce of allspice and one of black pepper. When cold, cover them. Should the outer skin shrivel, peel it off. They must look quite clear.

475. **Do.** (2).—Ingredients—Onions, vinegar, allspice, whole black pepper.

To each quart of vinegar allow a dessertspoonful of allspice and one of whole black pepper; take off the outer skin with the fingers, the next skin should be taken off with a plated or silver knife; it may be found necessary to remove a third skin if the onions do not look perfectly clear. As the onions are prepared drop them into jars; then cover with cold vinegar, adding allspice and whole pepper as directed; cover very tightly and in three weeks they will be ready for use. This is a most excellent receipt for onions. They should be eaten within six or seven months, as they will not be crisp after that time.

476. **WALNUTS.**—Ingredients—Fifty walnuts (seasonable for pickling early in July). To each pint of vinegar allow 1 oz. of black pepper, half an ounce of allspice, and half an ounce of bruised ginger.

Prick the walnuts with a fork, and put them in a brine (composed of one pound of salt, to each quart of water). Let them remain in this nine days, changing the brine three times. Put them in the sun until they turn black; put them into jars, allowing sufficient room to cover them with vinegar; boil (or scald) vinegar and spices in the above proportions. Cover closely and keep dry. They can be used in six weeks.

477. **JUMBO PICKLE.**—Ingredients—Cabbage, salt, onion, pepper and celery seed, strong vinegar.

Take a head of cabbage; chop fine, sprinkle with salt; let it remain thus for twelve hours; then mix an onion finely minced with the cabbage; drain through a cullender; add a good quantity of pepper and celery seed. Put it in a jar and cover with vinegar. Ready for use in three days.

478. **RED CABBAGE.**—Ingredients—Cabbage, beetroot, vinegar, spice.

Slice it into a cullender, and sprinkle each layer with salt; let it drain two days, then put it into a jar, and pour hot vinegar enough to cover, and put a few slices of red beet-root. Observe to choose the purple red cabbage. Those who like the flavor of spice will boil it with the vinegar. Cauliflower cut in branches, and thrown in after being salted, will look of a beautiful red.

479. **MUSHROOMS.**—Ingredients—Button mushrooms, pepper, mace, salt and vinegar.

Buttons must be rubbed with a bit of flannel and salt; and from the larger take out the *red* inside, for when they are black they will not do, being too old. Throw a little salt over, and put them into a stewpan with some mace and pepper; as the liquor comes out, shake them well, and keep them over a gentle fire till all of it be dried into them again;

then put as much vinegar into the pan as will cover them, give it one warm, and turn all into a glass or stone jar. They will keep two years, and are delicious.

480. **LEMONS.**—Ingredients—Lemons, salt, vinegar, rape vinegar, Jamaica pepper and ginger, mustard seed, garlic.

They should be small, and with a thick rind; rub them with a piece of flannel; then slit them half down in four quarters, but not through to the pulp; fill the slits with salt hard pressed in, set them upright in a pan for four or five days, until the salt melts; turn them thrice a day in their own liquid, until tender; make enough pickle to cover them, of rape vinegar, the brine of the lemons, Jamaica pepper and ginger; boil and skim it; when cold, put it to the lemons, with two ounces of mustard seed, and two cloves of garlic to six lemons. When the lemons are used, the pickle will be useful in fish or other sauces.

481. **CAPERS.**—Ingredients—Vinegar, capers.

Add fresh vinegar that has been scalded, and become cold, and tie them close to keep out the air, which makes them soft.

482. **CUCUMBERS.**—Ingredients—Cucumbers, pepper, ginger, vinegar.

Cut the cucumbers into slices about half an inch thick; sprinkle with salt, and let them remain twenty-four hours, then drain for seven hours. Pour the hot vinegar over them. Keep them in a warm place for a short time. Tie them down with bladder and you may use them in a few days.

483. **PICALILLI.**—Ingredients—Small cucumbers, button onions, small bunches of cauliflower, carrots, ginger, grapes, strips of horse-radish, radishes, bean pods, cayenne pods, 4 quarts of white wine vinegar, 4 tablespoonfuls of salt, mustard and flour, 2 tablespoonfuls of ground ginger, pepper, allspice and turmeric.

The brine for this pickle is made by putting a pint of rock salt into a pail of boiling water. Put the vegetables for pickling into the brine and cover tightly to prevent the steam escaping. Allow them to stand a night and a day. Change the brine a second time and allow them to remain the same length of time. The second brine may be used a second time if skimmed and scalded. Choose pickles from the brine of an equal size and of various colors. Great taste may be displayed in the arrangement of the pickles when putting them in bottles. To four quarts of white wine vinegar add the spices. Simmer these together (the mustard and turmeric must be blended together with a little vinegar before they are added to the liquor); when the liquor is on the point of boiling, pour into a vessel; cover tightly. When sufficiently cold pour into the bottles containing the pickle, and make air-tight. It will be ready for use in five or six months.

484. **EGGS.**—Ingredients—Thirty-two eggs, 2 quarts of vinegar, 1 oz. of black pepper, 1 oz. of Jamaica pepper, 1 oz. of ginger.

Boil the eggs hard (ten or twelve minutes would be sufficient time). Dip them in a pan of cold water for a minute to prevent them turning black, and remove the shells. Allow the remaining ingredients to simmer gently in a saucepan for ten minutes or a quarter of an hour. Put the eggs into your pickling jar and pour over the boiling vinegar, pepper and ginger. Let them stand till cold and make air tight. Ready for use from a month to six weeks.

485. **BEETS.**—Ingredients—Vinegar, beets, 2 oz. of whole pepper, 2 oz. of allspice to every gallon of vinegar.

Carefully remove all dirt from the beets. Let them simmer in boiling water for one hour and a half, then take them out and leave to cool. Boil the remaining ingredients for ten or fifteen minutes and leave to cool. When cold pour it over the beets (which you have previously pared and cut into thin slices). Make air-tight and they will be ready for eating in a week or ten days.

EGGS.

OBSERVATIONS ON EGGS.

As a rule the quality of eggs largely depends upon the food given to the hen. The eggs of the common hen or barn door fowl are esteemed most delicate when new laid, and for invalids they are exceedingly nutritious beaten up raw. The white of the egg, from its tendency to coagulate into a hard and indigestible substance, is likely to disagree with some invalids when the yolk may prove perfectly harmless. About one-third of the entire weight of an egg may be regarded as nitrogenous and nutritious matter; a greater proportion than that of meat, which is rated at only from 25 % to 28 %. The lightest way of cooking them is by poaching. It is a good plan in testing new laid eggs to apply the tongue to the large end of the egg, and if perfectly fresh will feel warm, or they can be held to the light and if perfectly clear will be good; or try them in water—the freshest will sink first. Always keep them in a cool place.

It is said that covering eggs with a solution of beeswax in warm olive oil (one-third of beeswax, two-thirds of olive oil) will keep them fresh for two years.

The following recipe has been used by an old housekeeper for about fourteen years, and has never been known to fail: To five quarts of water put one pound of salt, and one ounce of saltpetre; boil them ten minutes, and when nearly cold add four spoonfuls of unslacked lime. Let this stand two days, stirring it very frequently, then put your eggs into a pipkin (*i.e.*, a large earthern jar with straight sides, about a foot or more deep), the narrow end of the egg downwards, and pour the mixture over when it is clear.

---

486. **POACHED EGGS (on Toast)**.—Ingredients—Two or more eggs, salt, vinegar, peppercorns, leaves of parsley, hot buttered toast.

If the eggs are not new laid, they will not poach well. Fill a shallow sauté-pan with water and salt *quantum suff.*, add a little vinegar, a few peppercorns, and some leaves of parsley. When the water is on the point of boiling (it should never be allowed to boil) break two or more eggs into it (according to the size of the pan), and put on the cover ; when done, take them out carefully, brush them clean on both sides with a paste brush, and cut each egg with a round fluted paste cutter, so as to get them of a uniform shape, lay them on slices of hot buttered toast, and serve.

487. **POACHED EGGS (on Ham toast)**.—Ingredients—Buttered toast, grated ham, poached eggs.

Make some buttered toast, and cut it in pieces of uniform shape, spread over them a small quantity of grated ham, then put a poached egg on each piece of toast, and serve hot.

488. **Do. (and Spinach)**.—Ingredients—Poached eggs, 2 or 3 lbs. of spinach, butter, a pinch of flour, pepper and salt to taste, milk, fried sippets.

Poach the eggs as above, and serve on a purée made as follows : Pick and wash perfectly clean two or three pounds of spinach, put it into a saucepan with a little water, and let it boil till quite done, turn it out on a hair sieve to drain, squeeze the water out, and pass the spinach through the sieve. Put a good lump of butter into a saucepan, fry it a light brown, add a pinch of flour, mix well, put in the spinach, pepper and salt to taste, and a little milk, stir well, dispose the spinach on a dish, laying the poached eggs on the top of it, and a border of fried sippets round it.

489. **Do. (and Minced Chicken)**.—Ingredients—Remnants of fowl, equal quantity of ham or tongue, truffles or mushrooms, butter, a pinch of flour, white pepper, salt, and powdered spices, white stock, yolk of an egg, juice of half a lemon, bread sippets, poached eggs.

Take some remnants of fowl, free from skin, etc., mince them with an equal quantity of ham or tongue, as well as a small quantity of truffles or mushrooms, all finely minced ; toss the whole in a saucepan with a good sized piece of butter mixed with a pinch of flour, add white pepper, salt, and powdered spices to taste, and moisten with a little white stock ; lastly, stir in, off the fire, the yolk of an egg beaten up with the juice of half a lemon and strained ; serve within a border of bread sippets fried in butter, and dispose the poached eggs on the top.

490. **Do. (on a Puree of Game)**.—Ingredients—Carcases of roast game, ½ an onion, a carrot, a bay-leaf, a small piece of celery, a couple of cloves, a little mace, some whole pepper, a large

pinch of salt, common stock, ½ lb. lean beaf, butter, poached eggs, fried sippets.

Take any carcases of roast game—say three snipe or two partridges—cut them up into convenient pieces, and pack them into a saucepan with half an onion, a carrot, a bay leaf, a small piece of celery, a couple of cloves, a little piece of mace, some whole pepper, and a large pinch of salt; pour in just enough common stock to cover the contents; let the whole boil for a couple of hours, strain the liquor and put it by; take half a pound of lean beef, chop it up and pound it in a mortar with all the flesh that can be picked out of the pieces of game, then pass the whole through a sieve, moistening now and then with some of the liquor; lastly, heat the purée, correct the flavoring if necessary, stir in a piece of fresh butter the size of a walnut, and serve with fried sippets round and poached eggs on the top.

491. **EGGS (au Gratin).**—Ingredients—Hard-boiled eggs, butter, grated Parmesan cheese, black pepper, powdered nutmeg, baked bread-crumbs.

Cut some hard-boiled eggs in slices, and lay them on a well-buttered dish, with grated Parmesan cheese, black pepper, and the least bit of powdered nutmeg; sprinkle some baked bread-crumbs over all, put the dish in the oven, and serve as the contents begin to color.

492. **Do. (Stuffed).**—Ingredients—Hard-boiled eggs, olives, capers, anchovies, truffle trimmings, tarragon, butter, pepper, sippets of bread.

Cut some hard-boiled eggs in half, mince the yolks with a few olives and capers, some anchovies thoroughly washed, a few truffle trimmings, and a little tarragon, add some pepper, and fill each half-egg with this mixture. Pour some liquefied butter over, and warm them in the oven. Then place each half-egg on a round sippet of bread fried in butter to a light yellow color, and serve.

493. **Do. (Stewed).**—Ingredients—Spanish onions, butter, flour, cream or milk, pepper and salt to taste, grated nutmeg, hard-boiled eggs, bread sippets.

Cut some Spanish onions in slices, and fry them in plenty of butter till they are quite done without taking color, add a small quantity of flour, and when this is amalgamated with the butter moisten with a due quantity of cream, or simply milk, then add some pepper and salt to taste, a little grated nutmeg, and a quantity—equal in bulk to the onions—of hard-boiled eggs cut in slices. Let the whole simmer gently till quite hot, and serve with bread sippets fried in butter.

494. EGGS (a la Soubise).—Ingredients—Onions, milk, pepper, salt, nutmeg, butter, flour, cream or milk, hard-boiled eggs.

Boil some onions in milk with pepper, salt, and nutmeg; when quite done pass them through a sieve. Put some butter into a saucepan with a little flour, when the butter is melted and well mixed with the flour put in the onion pulp, and add either milk or cream until the sauce is of the proper consistence, then add hard-boiled eggs cut in half, and as soon as they are quite hot serve.

495. Do. (a la Maitre D'Hotel).—Ingredients—Hard-boiled eggs, butter, pepper, salt, minced parsley, lemon juice,

Cut some hard-boiled eggs in half, toss them in butter till quite hot, add pepper, salt, minced parsley, and a little lemon juice, and serve.

496. Do. (with Sorrel).—Ingredients—Eggs, sippets of bread, butter, sorrel, salt, a tablespoonful of flour, pepper and salt to taste, cold stock.

Boil a number of eggs in their shells for three or four minutes, then dip them into cold water, carefully remove the shells, and place them again in hot water to make them quite hot; drain, and serve them on the following purée with sippets of bread fried in butter round the dish: Pick and wash a quantity of sorrel, put it into a saucepan with a little water and some salt, when thoroughly done drain off all the moisture and pass the sorrel through a hair sieve. Amalgamate a piece of butter and a tablespoonful of flour in a saucepan on the fire, put in the sorrel and stir well for some minutes, then add pepper and salt to taste, and the yolk of one egg beaten up with a little cold stock and strained.

497. Do. (in Cases).—Ingredients—Paper cases, butter, parsley, pepper, salt, cayenne, eggs, a teaspoonful of grated Parmesan, a sprinkling of baked bread-crumbs.

Oil some small paper cases as for ramakins, put into each a piece of butter the size of a hazel nut, with a small pinch of minced parsley, some pepper, salt, and the least pinch of cayenne. Break an egg into each case, add a teaspoonful of grated Parmesan and a sprinkling of baked bread-crumbs. Put the cases in the oven for about five minutes and serve. They may also be so prepared, a number at a time, in a silver dish, and served in it.

498. BUTTERED EGGS.—Ingredients—Four eggs, 2 oz. of butter, 2 tablespoonfuls of cream, a little grated tongue, pepper and salt to taste, pieces of buttered toast.

Break four eggs into a basin, and beat them well; put two

ounces of butter and two tablespoonfuls of cream into a saucepan; add a little grated tongue, pepper and salt to taste, when quite hot add the eggs, stir till nearly set, then spread the mixture on pieces of buttered toast and serve.

499 **FRIED EGGS** (1).—Ingredients—Butter, eggs, pepper, salt.

Melt a piece of butter in a small frying pan, break two eggs in it carefully so as not to break the yolks; when nearly set, trim the edges of the whites and slip them out on a hot dish, pour the butter over them, sprinkle with salt and pepper, and serve.

500. **Do**. (2).—Oil, dripping or lard, eggs.

Put a good allowance of either oil, dripping, or lard in a frying pan; when quite hot break an egg into it, and as soon as the white begins to set turn it over dexterously with the slice, so as completely to cover the yolk. The eggs must be fried one by one, and as one is done it must be carefully taken up and laid in front of the fire to drain and keep hot.

501. **Do. (with Black Butter)**.—Ingredients—Butter, eggs, tarragon vinegar, minced parsley, salt and pepper.

Fry them in butter as above, leave the butter in the frying pan over the fire till it is nearly black, add a few drops of tarragon vinegar, some minced parsley, a little salt and pepper. Pour over the eggs and serve.

502. **Do. (with Tomatoes)**.—Ingredients—Butter, French tomato sauce, pepper and salt to taste, fried eggs.

Melt a small piece of butter in a saucepan, put to it a small quantity of French tomato sauce, add pepper and salt to taste, and when quite hot turn it out on a dish, disposing on it the eggs fried in butter.

503. **Do. (with Bacon)**.—Ingredients—Thin slices of streaky bacon, fried eggs.

Cut some thin slices of streaky bacon, cut off the rind and trim them; put them into a frying pan on the fire, and turn them often until quite hot, then roll up each slice, make a border of them round the fried eggs in the dish.

504. **Do. (with Ham)**.—Ingredients—A slice of ham, fried eggs.

Trim a slice of ham, and either grill it on a clear fire or toast it in front of it. Serve with the fried eggs on it.

505. **SCRAMBLED EGGS**.—Ingredients—Four eggs, salt and pepper to taste, 1 oz. of butter, finely minced parsley.

Beat up four eggs, with salt and pepper to taste; put an ounce of butter into a saucepan, directly it is melted put in the eggs, and keep constantly stirring with a spoon until they are nearly set, adding at the last a little finely-minced parsley.

506. **SCRAMBLED EGGS (with Asparagus).**—Ingredients—Asparagus points, salted water, butter, scrambled eggs.

Parboil some asparagus points, cut the size of peas, in salted water, drain them and toss them in a little butter till quite hot. Scramble some eggs as in the preceding recipe, and when nearly set add the asparagus points instead of the parsley.

507. **Do. (with Tomatoes).**—Ingredients—Four eggs, 1 tablespoonful of French tomato sauce, or 1 large tomato, scrambled eggs.

Beat up four eggs with a tablespoonful of French tomato sauce, or one large tomato, peeled, freed from pips, and chopped small, and proceed as above.

508. **Do. (with Onions).**—Ingredients—2 slices of Spanish onion, butter, 4 eggs, pepper and salt to taste.

Take two slices of Spanish onion, and chop them coarsely; put them into a saucepan with plenty of butter, and when they are thoroughly cooked, without having taken any color, throw in four eggs beaten together with pepper and salt to taste; keep on stirring till the eggs are nearly set, and then serve N.B.—Equal parts of tomatoes and onions may be cooked together, and then the eggs added.

509. **Do. (with Fish).**—Ingredients—Remnants of fish, 4 eggs, pepper and salt to taste, finely minced parsley.

Pick out the meat of any remnants of fish, such as salmon, turbot, cod, haddock, or whiting, and with a silver fork break it up small; take two tablespoonfuls of this and four eggs; beat the whole together with a little pepper and salt to taste, and a little parsley finely minced, then proceed as in No. 505.

510. **Do. (with Ham).**—Ingredients—A tablespoonful of grated ham, 4 eggs, pepper to taste, butter.

Beat up a tablespoonful of grated ham with four eggs, and pepper to taste; put them into a saucepan with a piece of butter, and stir till nearly set.

511. **Do. (with Cheese).**—Ingredients—Four eggs, 3 tablespoonfuls of Parmesan cheese, a sprinkling of pepper.

Put four eggs and three tablespoonfuls of Parmesan cheese into a basin with a sprinkling of pepper; beat all together, and proceed as in the first recipe, omitting the parsley.

512. **SCRAMBLED EGGS (on Toast).**

Any of the above may be served on slices of buttered toast, but if so served they must be even less set, at the time of serving, than when served plain; or neat bread sippets, fried in butter, may be served round them.

513. **SIPPETS (Fried).**—Ingredients—A loaf of bread, butter.

Cut out of a loaf slices from a quarter to three-eighths of an inch thick, shape them into triangles or arrowheads all of a size; put some butter in a frying pan, and when quite hot lay the sippets in it; turn them frequently, adding more butter, as it is wanted, and taking care that they are all fried to the same golden color. A readier way, but producing not so nice a sippet, is to lay the pieces of bread in the frying basket, and dip it in a saucepan full of boiling fat. They must afterwards be laid in front of the fire to drain.

514. **OMELET (Plain).**—Ingredients—3 or 4 eggs, 1 dessertspoonful of finely minced parsley, pepper and salt to taste, butter size of an egg.

Beat up three or four eggs with one dessertspoonful of parsley very finely minced, and pepper and salt to taste; put a piece of butter, the size of an egg, into a frying pan, as soon as it is melted pour in the omelet mixture, and, holding the handle of the pan with one hand, stir the omelet with the other by means of a spoon. The moment it begins to set cease stirring, but keep on shaking the pan for a minute or so; then with the spoon double up the omelet and keep shaking the pan until the under side of the omelet has become of a golden color. Turn it out on a hot dish and serve.

515. **Do. (Savory).**—Ingredients—3 or 4 eggs, ½ a shallot, parsley, a small pinch of powdered sweet herbs, pepper and salt to taste.

Beat up three or four eggs with half a shallot very finely minced, some parsley similarly treated, and a very small pinch of powdered sweet herbs, add pepper and salt to taste; then proceed as above.

516. **Do. (Ham or Bacon).**—Ingredients—Three or 4 eggs, 1 heaped tablespoonful of ham or bacon, pepper to taste.

Beat up three or four eggs with a heaped tablespoonful of ham or bacon, half lean and half fat, cut up to the size of very small dice; add pepper to taste, and salt if necessary, and proceed as above.

517. OMELET (Cheese).—Ingredients—Three eggs, 1 or 2 tablespoonfuls of Parmesan cheese.

Beat up three eggs with one or two tablespoonfuls of grated Parmesan cheese. Cook as above, and serve with some more grated cheese strewn over the omelet.

518. Do. (Tomato, 1).—Ingredients—Plain omelet mixture, tomato sauce.

Add to a plain omelet mixture a small quantity of tomato sauce, mix well, then finish in the usual way.

519. Do. (Tomato, 2).—Ingredients—Equal parts of sliced onions and tomatoes; butter, pepper and salt, plain omelet.

Take equal parts of sliced onions and tomatoes peeled and freed from pips, chop them both coarsely. Fry the onions in butter. When cooked, without being colored, add the tomatoes, with pepper and salt, and keep stirring the mixture on the fire till it forms a sort of puree. Make a plain omelet, and insert this in the fold on dishing it.

520. Do. (Tomato, 3).—Ingredients—Tomato sauce, potato flour, butter, pepper and salt to taste, savory or plain omelet.

Take a little tomato sauce, add to it a little potato flour dissolved in water, then put it into a saucepan with a piece of butter, and pepper and salt to taste. When quite hot and thickened turn it out on a dish, and on it place a savory or a plain omelet. There must not be too much sauce on the dish.

521. Do. (Mushroom.)—Ingredients—Button mushrooms, white or brown sauce. (See Sauces.)

Parboil a small quantity of button mushrooms, slice them small, and stew them just long enough to cook them in a small quantity of either white or brown sauce; then use as in preceding recipe.

522. Do. (Fish.)—Ingredients—3 eggs, remnants of cold fish, minced parsley, pepper and salt to taste.

Beat up three eggs with a quantity equal in bulk to one egg of the remnants of any cold fish (salmon or turbot) finely shredded with a fork, a pinch of minced parsley, pepper and salt to taste.

523. Do. (Oyster.)—Ingredients—Oysters, butter, pinch of flour, cream, salt, pepper, nutmeg, least bit of cayenne, finely minced parsley, yolk of an egg, juice of $\frac{1}{2}$ a lemon, plain omelet.

Parboil some oysters in their own liquor, remove the beards, cut each oyster in four or six pieces; melt a piece of butter in a saucepan, add to it a pinch of flour, the liquor of the oysters, a little cream, salt, pepper, nutmeg, the least bit of cayenne, and some finely-minced parsley; put in the oysters, and toss them in this sauce just long enough to make them quite hot; stir into this off the fire the yolk of an egg beaten up with juice of half a lemon, and strained. Insert this in the fold of a plain omelet, or serve it round the omelet.

524. **Do. (Kidney.)**—Ingredients—Sheep's kidneys, butter, pepper and salt to taste, finely minced parsley, flour, white wine and stock, a squeeze of lemon.

Parboil some sheep's kidneys, cut them in slices, and toss them in butter, with pepper and salt to taste, and some finely-minced parsley; mix, in a saucepan, a small quantity of butter and flour, add equal quantities of white wine and stock, put in the kidneys, toss them until done, then add a squeeze of lemon and serve in or round the omelet.

525. **EGGS (to Keep Fresh for Several Weeks).**

Fill a saucepan with three or four quarts of boiling water. Put two dozen eggs into a cabbage or onion net and hold them in the *boiling* water for twenty seconds. Continue this operation until you have as many eggs as you wish to preserve. Have some sawdust in boxes and pack them in it. At the end of two or three months the eggs will be found quite good enough for culinary purposes. Eggs can be kept for a long time if the shells are smeared with butter or sweet oil, then packed in plenty of sawdust, not allowing the eggs to touch each other. Another way is to plunge them in lime water directly they have been laid, and allow the vessel to stand in a cool cellar. Eggs for preserving should not be more than twenty-four hours old, and should be collected in fine weather. Take care the eggs are covered with the lime water, and it is a good plan to lay a piece of board on the top of the eggs with a little lime and salt upon it.

KETCHUPS.

526. **MUSHROOM KETCHUP.**—Ingredients—To 2 gallons of mushrooms, ½ lb. salt; to every quart of mushroom liquor, allow a small saltspoonful of cayenne, a teaspoonful of allspice, a teaspoonful of ginger, 2 blades of pounded mace,

Select some freshly gathered (gather in dry weather or else the ketchup will not keep), full-sized mushrooms. Lay in an earthenware pan in layers, first a layer of mushrooms and then one of salt, and so on until all are used. Allow them to stand a while (say five or six hours). Then break to pieces with the hand, place in the refrigerator for three days, stirring or mashing them occasionally. Extract as much juice as possible, measure the liquor without straining, adding to each quart the above mentioned spices. Pour into a stone jar, exclude the air; place the jar in a saucepan of boiling water and allow to boil three hours. When this is done pour the contents of the jar into a stewpan and allow it to simmer *gently* for half an hour. Pour into a vessel, place in refrigerator till the next day. Pour off into another vessel and strain. Have ready some clean dry bottles and to each pint of ketchup it is a great improvement to add a few drops of brandy; pour into the bottles, taking care not to squeeze the mushrooms, and allow the sediment to remain at the bottom of the vessel, (if wanted very clear and bright, the liquor must be strained after the above operation through a flannel bag). Cork and seal. Examine occasionally and if there is any sign of spoiling boil again with a few peppercorns. The sediment may be bottled for immediate use.

527. **LEMON KETCHUP.**—Ingredients—One dozen lemons, ½ a breakfast cupful of white mustard seed, 1 eggcupful of turmeric and white pepper, ½ an eggcupful of cloves and mace, ½ a *small* teacupful of white sugar, 1 saltspoonful of cayenne, ½ a small teacupful of horse radish, ½ a small teacupful of salt, 4 shallots.

Finely grate the rind of lemons, pound the spices in a mortar, grate the horse-radish. Thoroughly blend these ingredients, then sprinkle the salt over all, extract the juice from the lemons and add to the mixture. Allow to stand in a cool place for three or four hours. Boil in an enamelled kettle thirty minutes, pour into a stone jar, cover tightly. Stir every day for fourteen days, then strain, bottle and seal.

528. **TOMATO KETCHUP** (1).—Ingredients—To 1 peck of tomatoes allow 1 tablespoonful of salt, mace, black pepper, cloves powdered, and one of celery seed; a teaspoonful of cayenne, ¼ lb. tin of mustard.

Make a small incision in each tomato, put into an enamelled saucepan, and boil until perfectly soft, and the pulp dissolved; work through a cullender, then through a hair sieve. Place upon the stove adding the remaining ingredients (the celery seed must be confined in a muslin bag), and boil six hours. Stir occasionally for the first five hours and all the last hour. Pour into a stone jar; allow to stand from twelve to fourteen hours in a cool place. When perfectly cool add a pint of strong vinegar. Remove the celery seed; bottle, cork, and seal. Exclude from the light.

529. **Do.** (2).—Ingredients—Ripe tomatoes, to every lb. of juice add a pint of vinegar, a dessertspoonful of sliced garlic, a small teaspoonful of salt and white pepper.

Take a number of ripe tomatoes; place in a jar; cover and bake till tender. Strain and work through a sieve, and add the above ingredients. Pour into a stewpan and boil until the ingredients are perfectly soft. Work through the sieve a second time and to every pound squeeze the juice of three lemons. Boil again until of the thickness of cream. Set aside to get cold. Bottle, cork and seal, and keep in a dry, dark place.

530. **WALNUT KETCHUP.**—Ingredients—Walnuts, salt, to every 2 quarts of walnut liquor allow 1 oz. each of allspice, ginger, black pepper, cloves, mace.

Wash the shells of walnuts, bruize them slightly, put them with salt in a stone jar for two or three weeks until they ferment, then boil them up, strain off the liquor, add to every two quarts one ounce each of allspice, ginger, black pepper, cloves, and mace; boil the whole one hour; let it cool, bottle it, and tie a bladder over the corks.

531. **MUSTARD (to make).**

Mix the best Durham flour of mustard by degrees with boiling water to a proper thickness, rubbing it perfectly smooth; add a little salt, and keep it in a small jar closely covered, and put only as much into the glass as will be used soon, which should be wiped daily round the edges.

532. **Another way, for immediate use.**

Mix the mustard with new milk by degrees, to be quite smooth, and add a little raw cream. It is much softer this way, is not bitter, and will keep well.

533. FRENCH MUSTARD.—Ingredients—One quart of brown mustard seed, 1 handful each of parsley, chervil, tarragon and burnet, 1 teaspoonful of celery seed, cloves, mace, garlic. Salt to taste, enough wine vinegar to cover the mixture.

Put the whole into a basin with enough wine vinegar to cover the mixture. Let it steep twenty-four hours, then pound it in a marble mortar. When thoroughly pounded pass it through a fine sieve; add enough vinegar to make the mustard of the desired consistency, and put into jars for use.

534. MINT VINEGAR.

Take a wide-mouthed bottle or bottles. Fill them (loosely) with nice fresh mint leaves, then add good vinegar to fill the bottle or bottles; cork well. Allow to stand for two or three weeks, and at the expiration of this time, strain into fresh bottles and cork securely. Useful when mint is not in season.

535. HORSE-RADISH VINEGAR.—Ingredients—Three oz. of scraped horse-radish, 1 oz. of minced shallot, 1 drachm of cayenne, 1 quart of vinegar.

Pour the vinegar upon the above ingredients; allow to stand ten days. This will be found exceedingly useful for cold joints, salads, &c., and a very economical relish.

536. An excellent substitute for Caper Sauce.

Boil slowly some parsley to let it become a bad color, cut, but don't chop it fine; put it to melted butter, with a teaspoonful of salt, and a dessertspoonful of vinegar. Boil up and serve.

537. NASTURTIUM (for Capers).

Keep m a few days after they are gathered, then pour boiling vinegar over them, and when cold cover. They will not be fit to eat for some months, but are then finely flavored, and by many preferred to capers.

538. CHILI VINEGAR.—Fifty fresh red Chilies, one pint of vinegar.

Cut the Chilies in half, steep in the vinegar for a fortnight, it will then be ready for use, and will be found a very nice relish to fish.

539. CHEROKEE.—Ingredients—One eggspoonful of cayenne, 5 cloves of garlic, an eggcupful of soy, ½ an eggcupful of walnut ketchup, 1 pint of vinegar.

Boil all the ingredients for half an hour. Strain, and bottle for use. Will keep good a long time.

540. GREEN GOOSEBERRY CHUTNEE.—Ingredients—Two pints of unripe gooseberries or green apples, 3 oz. mustard seed, 3 oz. powdered ginger, 5 oz. coarse sugar, 10 oz. raisins, 3 oz. salt, 2 pints vinegar, 3 oz. garlic.

Chop the gooseberries and the raisins (after being stoned) quite fine, also the onions and garlic almost to a paste; add one ounce cayenne, and a proper quantity of turmeric to make it a nice color. When well mixed, boil ten minutes or quarter of an hour, and rub through a sieve.

541. HERBS (to Dry).

Gather the herbs for drying before they begin to flower. Free from dirt and dust and tie in bunches having previously removed the roots. Dry in the oven or before the fire, in either case, dry *quickly* as the flavor is better preserved by quick drying. Upon no consideration allow them to burn. Tie up in paper bags and hang in a dry place. N. B.—Take care to gather the herbs on a dry day.

542. MY MOTHER'S CHUTNEE.—Ingredients—Half a lb. brown sugar. ½ lb. salt, ¼ lb. garlic, ¼ lb. onions, ¼ lb. ginger, ¼ lb. mustard seed, or cayenne pepper, ½ lb. raisins, stoned and chopped fine, 15 large apples (sour), 3 pints best vinegar.

Boil the apples, onions, and garlic in the vinegar, rub this through a sieve, steep the mustard seed in vinegar, then shred it fine; add all together and mix well. Bottle when cold. It is much more of a relish than pickles.

543. HIMALAYA CHUTNEE.—Ingredients—Eight lbs. green apples, 1 lb. sultana raisins, 1 lb. brown sugar, 1 oz. birds-eye chilies, 2 oz. whole mustard, 4 oz. garlic, 4 oz. coarse salt, 1½ bottles brown vinegar.

Chop all the ingredients very fine, then add the salt, vinegar, and sugar; put in a jelly pan on a slow fire and let it stew till soft like a pulp. This is very good when bottled and well corked.

544. HERB POWDER (for winter use).—Ingredients—Take 2 oz. each of winter savory, sweet marjoram, lemon, thyme, lemon peel and 4 oz. of parsley.

Thoroughly dry the herbs and take off the leaves. Grind to a powder and pass through a sieve. Dry the lemon peel and pound as finely as possible, then mix all together thoroughly. Keep in glass bottles tightly corked.

545. PARSLEY (to keep for winter use).

Take fresh bunches of parsley and plunge into boiling water slightly salted, boiling for three or four minutes. Remove from the water, and drain dry very quickly before the fire, and put in bottles for use. Soak in tepid water five minutes when required for cooking.

546. GARLIC VINEGAR.

Steep an ounce of garlic in two quarts of the best white wine vinegar; add a nutmeg scraped. This vinegar is much esteemed by the French.

547. A USEFUL KETCHUP.—Ingredients—Half pint of mushroom ketchup, ½ pint of walnut pickle, 2 tablespoonfuls of Chili vinegar, 2 shallots.

Take one and a half pts. of freshly made mushroom ketchup, peel the shallots and add them to the ketchup and allow it to simmer for ten minutes, then add the pickle and vinegar and boil again for ten minutes. Stand in a cool place, and when perfectly cold, bottle, and having placed a small piece of shallot in each bottle, cork and set by for use.

548. OYSTER KETCHUP (without the liquor).—Ingredients—One pint of oysters, 1 pint of sherry, 3 tablespoonfuls of salt, 1 drachm of cayenne, 2 drachms of ground mace.

Be sure the oysters are perfectly fresh, reserve the liquor and put it, the oysters and sherry into a stewpan to scald. Strain and pound the oysters in a mortar with the seasoning. When pounded to a pulp add the oyster liquor and boil five minutes. Skim, work through a sieve, allow it to stand until perfectly cool, and it is ready to bottle. Cork well, and seal the corks.

FORCEMEATS.

OBSERVATIONS ON FORCEMEATS.

Whether in the form of stuffing-balls or for patties, forcemeat makes a considerable part of good cooking, by the flavor it imparts to the dish it accompanies, and considerable care should be taken in cooking it. It is often the case, at many excellent tables where everything else is well done, to find very bad forcemeat or stuffing.

549. **FORCEMEAT (to force Fowls or Meat).**—Ingredients—A little ham or gammon, veal, or fowl, beef-suet, onion, parsley, lemon-peel, salt, nutmeg, pounded mace, white pepper or cayenne, bread-crumbs, 1 or 2 eggs.

Shred a little ham or gammon, some cold veal, or fowl, some beef-suet; a small quantity of onion, some parsley, very little lemon-peel, salt, nutmeg or pounded mace, and either white pepper or cayenne, and bread-crumbs. Pound in a mortar, and bind it with one or two eggs beaten and strained; for forcemeat patties the same mixture as above.

550. **Do. (for cold Savory Pie).**—Ingredients—As above.

The same; only substituting fat, or bacon, for suet. The livers (if the pie be of rabbit or fowls), mixed with fat and lean of pork, instead of bacon, and seasoned as above, is excellent.

551. **Do. (Common, for Veal or Hare).**—Ingredients—½ lb. of bread crumbs, 4 oz. of beef suet, the rind of half a lemon, 1 tablespoonful of *minced* savory herbs, pepper and salt to taste, a little nutmeg, 2 eggs.

Mince the lemon rind as fine as possible and blend with the other ingredients; mix well and bind with the beaten eggs.

552. **Do. (for Fish Soups).**—Ingredients—1 lobster, 1 small head of celery, butter the size of an egg, a cupful of bread-crumbs, 3 eggs, pepper, salt, and a little nutmeg.

Pick the meat from the lobster and pound in a mortar, boil the celery until soft, drain, and mix with the lobster, bread-crumbs, seasoning, and the yolk of one hard-boiled egg.

Pound well for a quarter of an hour, warm the butter, and mix with two beaten eggs ; add this to the lobster and other ingredients. Dip your hands in flour, form the mixture into little balls, fry in butter, and serve in fish soup.

553. **FORCEMEAT (for Fowls).**—Ingredients—Quarter lb. of suet, 2 oz. of ham, the grated rind of half a lemon, a dessert spoonful of minced parsley, 1 teaspoonful of minced sweet herbs, cayenne, salt, grounded mace to taste, 7 oz. of bread-crumbs, 2 eggs.

Cut the ham into small, thin strips, chop the suet finely, also the lemon peel ; add the seasoning, then the crumbs ; thoroughly blend, and after the eggs have been well beaten add to the other ingredients, and it is ready for use. If wished for balls, fry a golden brown in hot lard.

554. **FORCEMEAT BALLS (for Mock Turtle).**—Ingredients— Pounded veal, udder, or butter, bread-crumbs, milk, chopped parsley, shallot, yolks of 3 hard-boiled eggs, pepper, salt, curry powder or cayenne, yolks of 2 uncooked eggs.

Take the pounded veal and rub through a sieve, with an equal quantity of udder, for if there is no udder at hand one-third of the quantity of butter will do instead. Then place the bread-crumbs into a stewpan and mix with it a very small quantity of milk, enough to moisten it. Add to this the chopped parsley and shallot, and mix well until they have become a paste ; pour through a sieve and leave to cool. When cold pound it and mix well together. Have ready the yolks of three hard-boiled eggs, add these and some pepper and salt, curry powder or cayenne for seasoning ; then add the yolks of the two uncooked eggs, rub all well together, and shape into balls. Place in the soup ten or fifteen minutes before serving.

555. **Do. (very fine Balls for Fish Soups or Stewed Fish).** —Ingredients—Lobster, a little essence of anchovy to taste, boiled celery, yolk of a hard-boiled egg, cayenne, mace, salt, white pepper, 2 tablespoonfuls of bread-crumbs, one of oyster liquor, 2 oz. of butter, 2 eggs.

Beat the flesh and soft parts of a middling lobster, essence of anchovy to taste, a large piece of boiled celery, the yolk of a hard egg, a little cayenne, mace, salt, and white pepper, with two tablespoonfuls of bread-crumbs, one ditto of oyster liquor, two ounces of butter warmed, and two eggs well beaten ; make into balls, and fry of a fine brown in butter.

556. **Do. (Balls for Soup).**—Ingredients—8 oz of bread-crumbs, sweet herbs, salt and pepper to taste, 5 eggs.

Have the bread-crumbs finely grated, and the herbs pounded

to a powder; sprinkle with pepper and salt; boil two eggs hard and mince finely. Mix all together and bind the whole with the remaining eggs. Form into little balls, and drop into the soup about five or six minutes before serving.

557. **FORCEMEAT (Oyster, for Roast or Boiled Turkey).**—Ingredients—2 teacupfuls of bread-crumbs, ½ oz. of minced suet, 1 table-spoonful of savory herbs, a sprinkle of nutmeg, salt and pepper to taste, 2 eggs, 1½ doz. oysters.

Have the bread-crumbs and suet finely minced, add the herbs chopped as finely as possible ; mix well. Having opened the oysters, beard and chop them (not very small) and add to the other ingredients; beat up the eggs, and with the hand work all together thoroughly ; it is then ready for use.

558. **SAGE AND ONION STUFFING (for Pork, Ducks, Geese).**—Ingredients—2 teacups of bread-crumbs, 4 large onions, 12 sage leaves, butter the size of an egg, pepper and salt to taste, 1 egg.

Peel and boil the onions for five or six minutes, dip the sage leaves in the same water (while boiling) for a minute or two, then chop finely ; add seasoning, the bread-crumbs and butter ; beat up the egg, and work all together. It is then ready for use.

BREAD AND CAKES.

OBSERVATIONS ON BREAD.

Of all articles of food, *bread* is perhaps the most important, therefore it is necessary to be well acquainted with the quality of the ingredients and the art of making it. Flour ought to be a few weeks old before being used, and care must be taken to keep it perfectly dry. Genuine flour will hold together in a mass when pressed with the hand. American flour requires almost twice as much water to make it into bread, as is used for English flour, and therefore it is more profitable, for a stone of the American which weighs 14 lbs. will make 21½ lbs. of bread, but the best sort of English flour produces only 18½ lbs. In wet weather, or when wheat is badly stored, causing it to be damp, the soluble albuminoids which it possesses act upon the insoluble gluten causing it to decompose, and at once generating dextrin by their action on the starch of the grain, consequently the flour prepared from such grain is poor in gluten and rich in dextrin, the consequence being that when used it produces heavy bread, therefore it is of the utmost importance to purchase only the best quality of flour, for it is the truest economy. Do not place the sponge or dough too near the fire, as some cooks are liable to do in cold weather, or the quality of bread will be endangered. The proper heat should be gentle and equal for fermentation. Care must also be taken to mix and knead (brisk and long kneading will fully repay for the trouble) when it has reached the point for either. Some authorities say the heat of the oven should rise to 280° and after a quarter of an hour slacken to 220°, others from 300° to 400°. The cook must be guided by experience as to exact degree of heat. Doubtless the bread will require a brisk oven, and should take about an hour to an hour and a half to bake.

OBSERVATIONS ON CAKES.

For good cakes (as in bread) it is of great importance to use no ingredients, but those of the finest quality. The flour must be dry and sifted. It will be found a good plan after purchasing currants, to wash in three waters, pick and dry in a cloth. Then look them carefully over, discarding any stone, stalk, or grit. Lay before the fire or in the sun to dry. Put by in jar, and they will always be ready for use. Eggs should be well whisked, the whites and yolks beaten separately and strained. Butter must not be allowed to oil. Lemon peel should be cut thinly as possible. Sugar should be finely powdered. When soda is used it is a good plan to dissolve it in warm water. When all the ingredients are mixed, vigorous and patient beating will greatly add to the lightness of the cake. The heat of the oven is of great importance for cakes, especially those that are large. If not pretty quick, the batter will not rise. Should you fear its catching by being too quick, put some paper over the cake to prevent its being burnt. If not long enough lighted to have a body of heat, or it is become slack, the cake will be heavy. To know when it is soaked, take a broom straw, and pierce into the very centre, draw it instantly out, and if the least stickiness adheres, put the cake immediately in, and shut up the oven.

558. **YEAST** (1).—Ingredients—A double handful of hops, ½ doz. potatoes, ½ gal. of water, 1 or ½ cupful of ginger, small cup of flour, a cup of brown sugar, ½ cup of salt, a cupful of good yeast.

Allow the hops and potatoes to boil together in one-half gallon of water till done; strain and mash the ginger, then add remaining ingredients, excepting the yeast. Let stand until cool, then add the yeast. Next day cork up tight in a jug.

559. **YEAST** (2).—Ingredients—Two oz. of hops, 1 gal. of water, a handful of salt, 1 lb. of best flour, 3 lbs. of potatoes.

Boil the hops in a gallon of water for half an hour; strain it, and let it cool down to the heat of new milk; then put the salt and moist sugar; beat the flour with some of the liquor, and then mix all together. Two days after, add the potatoes, boiled and then mashed, to stand for four-and-twenty-hours; then put it into bottles, and it will be ready for use. Stir it frequently while making, and keep it warm. Before using, shake the bottle up well. It will keep in a cool place for two months.

560. **YEAST (Compressed).**

This yeast will make good and wholesome bread, but bread made from it will not keep as long as with brewers or home-made yeast. Potatoes mixed with the dough will keep it moist longer.

561. **POTATO YEAST.**—Ingredients—To every lb. of potatoes 2 oz. of treacle, 2 large spoonfuls of yeast.

This is made of mealy potatoes boiled thoroughly soft; they are skinned and mashed as smooth as possible; as much hot water should then be put on them as will make a mash of the consistency of good beer yeast. Add to the potatoes the treacle; and when just warm, stir in the yeast. Keep it warm till it has done fermenting, and in twenty-four hours it will be fit for use. One pound of potatoes will make nearly a quart of yeast; and it is said to be equally as good as brewers' yeast.

562. **HOME-MADE BREAD** (1).—Ingredients—Four lbs. of flour, 1 tablespoonful of solid brewers' yeast, 1½ pints of luke-warm milk and water, salt.

Put the flour into a deep pan, sprinkle a little salt into it, hollow out the middle with a wooden spoon (take care to leave the bottom of the pan well covered with flour). Next take the yeast, which has been made solid by liberally mixing with cold water and allowing it to settle twenty-four hours. Then proceed to pour the yeast into the hole in the flour, and mix with it as much flour as is round about it until it is of the consistency of thick batter; be careful there are no lumps. Sift plenty of flour over the top, cover with a clean cloth, and set it where the air is warm and equal. Allow to stand an hour or a little longer, and if the yeast has broken through it is then ready to be made into dough. Pour into the sponge the remaining milk and water. Mix into it as much of the flour as you can with the spoon. Now take plenty of the flour, sprinkle on the top of the leaven, and proceed to knead briskly, and when perfectly free from lumps and does not adhere to the hands, it may be covered with a cloth and left to rise a second time. When it begins to crack, which will be in about three-quarters of an hour, it can be formed into loaves and baked. In forming the loaves divide in two and make up the shape and size required, and with a sharp knife make incisions in the top of each loaf. If baked in tins, take care to grease them before using. When baked stand on end to allow the steam to evaporate. The dough can be made without making a sponge (if desired) by mixing the yeast with the best part of the milk and water, and after a little salt has been added proceed to work up the whole of the flour at once, and then act as above. The dough will soften in the rising, so it should be made firm at first.

563. HOME-MADE BREAD (2).

Put the flour into a large pan; mix in a dessertspoonful of salt; make a hole in the middle, and pour in the yeast (half a teacup of yeast to two quarts of flour), with about a pint of water or milk (which use warm in winter, and cold in summer), not mixing in all the flour; then put a blanket, or towel, over the pan, and let it stand to rise, near the fire in winter. This is "putting bread in sponge." When it has risen, mix all the flour with the sponge; knead it well, and let it stand two hours till quite light. Then mould the dough on a board till elastic, and put the loaves into greased or floured baking-tins; prick them two or three times through with a fork; let them rise again for a quarter of an hour, and bake them in a quick oven.

564. WHITE BREAD.—Ingredients—Sponge, a pan of buttermilk, or sour milk, flour, teacupful of yeast.

For the sponge take a pan of buttermilk or sour milk which has just turned thick. Put it on the stove and scald. When the curd is well separated from the whey strain or skim it out. Let the whey cool until it will not scald, then stir in the flour, beating thoroughly. It should be about as thick as batter for griddle cakes. Sweet milk, or even water may be used as wetting for the sponge, if good sour milk or buttermilk cannot be had. But fresh buttermilk is, perhaps, the best of all. When the sponge is about milkwarm, beat in a teacupful of yeast. One teacupful of the yeast is enough for three ordinary white loaves, one loaf of brown bread and a tin of rolls. The sponge should be made at night. Let it stand until morning. Unless the weather is very cold, it is not necessary to put it near the fire. In the morning, when the sponge is light, take out enough for your loaf of brown bread. Mix the remainder with flour, taking care not to put in too much, as that will make the bread dry and hard. Knead half an hour. The whiteness and delicacy of the bread will be much increased by thorough kneading. Put the dough away to rise again. When it is light, if you wish to make rolls, save enough of the dough for that purpose. Make the remainder into loaves. Set them away to rise. When light, bake.

565. **YEAST BREAD**.—Ingredients—Yeast, 12 potatoes, 3 large tablespoonfuls of flour, 2 each of sugar and salt, 2 yeast cakes, to every loaf of bread allow 1 pint of yeast.

To make the yeast pare twelve medium-sized potatoes and put them in a kettle to boil. While they are boiling put in a pan three heaped tablespoonfuls of flour, two each of sugar and salt. Pour slowly over these a pint of boiling water, stirring constantly to free from lumps. When soft mash the potatoes and add to the contents of the pan. Now pour in a quart of cold water and one of boiling water. Set aside till cool enough to bear your finger in. Stir in two yeast cakes dissolved in a little water. Keep warm till a foam rises over the top, when it is ready for use. For each loaf of the bread take one pint of the yeast, no other wetting being required. Make a hole in the centre of a pan of flour, pour in the yeast and stir it thick as possible, cover and set in a warm place to rise, which will be in about two hours—sometimes less—now mix into loaves, let it rise again, and bake from a half to three quarters of an hour. A great advantage of this bread is, it is so quickly made. If the yeast should become a little sour, a pinch of soda may be put in when first stirred for bread.

566. **PLAIN BREAD**.—Ingredients—Half lb. of white flour, 1 teaspoonful of baking powder, a pinch of salt, ¼ pint of milk and water.

The simplest way of making bread in small quantities is as follows:—Take ½ lb. of white flour, and, whilst in a dry state, mix in thoroughly a small teaspoonful baking powder and a pinch of salt. Then add about a quarter of a pint of milk and water, or water alone; knead it as quickly as possible, and put immediately into a very hot oven; the whole secret of making light bread after this fashion lies in attention to these last rules. If the oven is well heated, it will rise almost directly, and it should be baked until the outside is quite crisp and hard. I generally knead mine into the desired shape, but they can be baked in tins if preferred. For brown bread, I use three parts of brown and one of white flour, and a little extra baking powder; also adding a little more water, if necessary, to mix it.

567. **RICE and WHEAT BREAD.**—Ingredients—One lb. of rice, 2 quarts of water, 4 lbs. of flour, 4 large spoonfuls of yeast, salt.

Simmer a pound of rice in two quarts of water till it becomes perfectly soft; when it is of a proper warmth, mix it extremely well with four pounds of flour, and yeast and salt as for other bread; of yeast about four large spoonfuls; knead it extremely well; then set it to rise before the fire. Some of the flour should be reserved to make up the loaves. If the rice should require more water, it must be added, as some rice swells more than others.

568. **FRENCH BREAD.**—Ingredients—¼ pk. of fine flour, yolks of 3 and whites of 2 eggs, salt, ½ pt. of good yeast, ½ pt. of milk.

With a quarter of a peck of fine flour mix the yolks of three and whites of two eggs, beaten and strained, a little salt, half a pint of good yeast, that is not bitter, and as much milk, made a little warm, as will work into a thin light dough; stir it about, but don't knead it; have ready three quart wooden dishes, divide the dough among them, set to rise, then turn them out into the oven, which must be quick. Rasp when done.

569. **BROWN BREAD.**—Ingredients—Sponge as for white bread, 2 parts of Graham flour, one-third white flour, to every qt. of this add a large breakfast cup of Indian meal, 2 saltspoonfuls of salt, for a good sized loaf allow ½ a cup of molasses.

Take the Graham and white flour, Indian meal, and salt, in the above proportions, and mix this up with the sponge, then pour in the molasses. If it cannot be brought to the proper congruity (which should be very soft) with the sponge, add a little warm water; be careful to knead it well and for a long time; then allow it to rise; it will take longer than white bread; then make into loaves, and bake carefully. When baked allow to cool before cutting.

570. **Do.** (2).—Ingredients—1 pt. of brown flour, ½ cup of yeast, white flour, sweeten to taste.

Scald one pint of brown flour, make it as thick as stiff mush; then put in half a cup of yeast, and let this sponge stand over night; in the morning mix it up with white flour, and sweeten to taste. This quantity makes two small loaves. It requires longer to bake than white bread.

571. **Do.** (3).—Ingredients—Three teacups of corn meal, 2 cups of boiling sweet milk, 1 teacup of molasses, 1 cup of wheat flour, 1 cup of sour milk, 1 teaspoonful of soda, ½ teaspoonful of salt.

Take the corn meal, stir into it the boiling sweet milk;

when cold, add the molasses, wheat flour, and sour milk; into the sour milk stir well the soda; add also the salt; steam three hours.

572. BROWN BREAD. (4).—Ingredients—One pint of corn meal, 1 pint of rye flour, 1 tablespoonful of brown sugar, 1 teaspoonful of salt, 2 of baking powder, 1 tablespoonful of lard, ¼ pint of milk.

Sift together the above ingredients, excepting the lard and milk; rub into the mixture the lard and add the milk. Mix into a batter-like cake and bake one hour. Protect it with brown paper if it should brown too fast at first.

573. Do. (5).—Ingredients—One cup of corn meal, one cup of Graham flour, one cup of sour milk, one cup of warm water, one half cup of molasses, one teaspoonful of soda, a little salt.

Steam two hours. Serve at table hot.

574. Do. (Steamed).—Ingredients—One cup of sour milk, ½ cup of warm water, 1 cup of molasses, ½ teaspoonful of soda, 1½ cups of Indian meal, ½ cup of flour.

Steam three hours and bake one-half hour. It may seem thin but it will be just right when done.

575. Do. BOSTON (Delicious and Genuine).—Ingredients—One and a half cups of yellow meal, one cup of rye flour, one cup of Graham flour, one cup of New Orleans molasses, two full teaspoonfuls of baking powder and a little salt.

Mix all to a consistency of a thick batter with either milk or water, pour into a buttered mold or tin pail, and steam in boiling water four hours.

576. RYE BREAD.—Ingredients—Two cups of Indian meal, scalding water, a small cup of white bread sponge, sugar, salt, a teaspoonful of soda, rye.

Make the Indian meal into a thick batter with scalding water; when cool add the white bread sponge, a little sugar and salt, and the soda, dissolved. In this stir as much rye as is possible with a spoon; let it rise until it is very light; then work in with your hand as much rye as you can, but do not knead it, as that will make it hard; put it in buttered bread tins, and let it rise for about fifteen minutes; then bake it for an hour and a half, cooling the oven gradually for the last twenty minutes.

577. CORN BREAD STEAMED (Canadian recipe).—Ingredients—Three cups of corn meal, boiling water, 1 cup of flour, 2 cups of sour milk, 1 cup of molasses, 1 teaspoonful of soda, a little salt.

Scald two cups of corn meal with boiling water, add another

cup of meal and remaining ingredients. Mix thoroughly, and steam three hours.

578. CORN BREAD (Baked).—Ingredients—Half a pint of buttermilk, ½ pint of sweet milk, ½ a teaspoonful of soda, 2 eggs, 9 tablespoonfuls of sifted corn meal, lard, a teaspoonful of salt.

Half a pint of buttermilk, half a pint of sweet milk; add to the buttermilk half a teaspoon of soda; beat the eggs, whites and yolks together, pour the milk on to the eggs, and thicken with the sifted corn meal. Put the pan in which it is to be baked on the stove with a piece of lard the size of an egg; when melted pour in the batter, add the salt, stir well, and bake.

579. RICE BREAD.—Ingredients—A plate of boiled rice, 2 eggs, 1½ cups of flour, lump of butter size of a walnut, milk.

Take the boiled rice warm enough to melt the butter, beat the eggs separately, mix with them the flour, and milk enough to make a thick batter. Grease the pans and bake like bread or muffins.

580. BREAD OMELET.—Ingredients—A teacupful of breadcrumbs, 1 of sweet milk, 6 eggs, pepper, salt, a small lump of butter.

Let the milk come to a boiling point, pour it over the crumbs and let it stand a few minutes; take the eggs, beat them well and pour into the bread mixture; season with salt and pepper and a small lump of butter; when thoroughly mixed butter a hot skillet and pour the mixture in, letting it fry slowly; when one side is browned nicely cut it in squares and turn. Serve at once.

581. SODA BREAD.—Ingredients—Allow a teaspoonful of tartaric acid to every 2 lbs. of flour, 2 saltspoonfuls of salt, ¾ pint of milk with a teaspoonful of carbonate of soda dissolved in it.

Pound the tartaric acid and the salt to a powder. Then put them into a basin with the flour and mix well together. Take the milk with the soda well dissolved in it and pour in with the flour. Great expedition is required in working it into a dough. Form into two loaves and bake in a brisk oven for an hour.

582. AMERICAN CORN BREAD.—Ingredients—One large tablespoonful of lard, half a teacup of brown sugar, one teacup of flour, 3 teacups of Indian meal, two small teaspoonfuls cream of tartar, one small teaspoonful of carbonate of soda, one egg, one saltspoon of salt, enough sour milk to make a batter about as thick as for cake, or thinner.

Beat eggs, lard and sugar together, then add flour, meal and milk gradually with the salt and cream of tartar; when just ready for the oven, mix in the carbonate of soda, put in tins, and bake in a good oven, but not too hot. Bake about three-quarters of an hour or until done. If the tins have paper at the bottom they bake better, and do not stick. If you have not sour milk, sweet will do, but buttermilk is the best of all. These cakes can be kept in the tins and heated up the next day.

583. **RUSKS.**—Ingredients—One pint of new milk, 2 tablespoonfuls of yeast, flour, 2 tablespoonfuls of butter, 1 cupful of sugar, 2 eggs, 2 saltspoonfuls of salt.

Rusks require a longer time for rising than ordinary rolls or biscuits. Prepare a sponge of the yeast, milk and flour (sufficient to make a thin batter) and allow it to rise all night. Next morning add eggs, butter and sugar (which must have been mixed well together), salt and flour enough to produce a soft dough. Shape into neat balls of equal size, place in a pan and allow to rise until very light. Flavor according to taste. Bake in a quick, steady oven till of a pretty brown color; glaze with the yolk of an egg and sprinkle with powdered white sugar.

584. **BUTTER ROLLS.**—Ingredients—One quart of flour, half a teaspoonful of salt, two teaspoonfuls of baking powder, one egg, one pint of milk, one tablespoonful of lard.

Sift the flour, salt and baking powder together, rub in the lard cold, then add the egg and milk, mix as soft as possible. Roll it out one half inch in thickness and cut with a plain round biscuit cutter. Dip them in melted butter, fold one-third of each piece over the remainder and bake in a quick oven for fifteen minutes.

585. **VIENNA ROLLS.**—Ingredients—One quart of milk, one-half teaspoonful of salt, three teaspoonfuls of baking powder, one tablespoonful of lard, one pint of milk.

Mix into a dough easily to be handled without sticking to the hands; turn on the board and roll out to the thickness of half an inch, cut it out with a large cake cutter, spread very lightly with butter, fold one half over the other and lay them in a greased pan without touching. Wash them over with a little milk, and bake in a hot oven.

586. **FRENCH ROLLS.**—Ingredients—Two eggs, $\frac{1}{2}$ pint of milk, 1 tablespoonful of yeast, 1 oz. of butter.

Beat two eggs, and mix with them half a pint of milk and a tablespoonful of yeast; knead well and let it stand till morning; then work in one ounce of butter; mould into small rolls, and bake at once.

586. **SWISS ROLL.**—Ingredients—Two eggs, their weight in flour and sifted sugar and butter, lemon juice, jam.

Take two eggs as your weights and take their weight in flour, sifted sugar, and butter. First cream the butter and sugar, stir in the two yolks slightly beaten, then the two whites beaten to a stiff froth, and last of all the flour, strewn lightly in; mix thoroughly, and add a little lemon juice. Grease a Yorkshire pudding-dish, and pour in the mixture about half an inch in depth; bake in a hot oven for not more than seven minutes, as otherwise it would become too crisp to roll; strew a sheet of paper with sugar, and turn it out on this, and immediately spread with jam, and quickly roll it; if not done whilst very hot, it will break in the rolling. The top can be ornamented with bars of pink sugar icing, silver comfits, and preserved fruit.

587. **BREAKFAST ROLLS.**—Ingredients—Two quarts flour, one tablespoonful sugar, one tablespoonful butter, one-half cup of yeast, one pint scalded milk, or water if milk is scarce, and a little salt.

Set to rise until light; then knead until hard and set to rise, and when wanted make in rolls; place a piece of butter between the folds, and bake in a slow oven.

588. **GRAHAM BISCUITS.**—Ingredients—One quart water or milk, butter the size of an egg, three tablespoonfuls sugar, two of baker's yeast, and a pinch of salt; enough white flour to use up the water, making it the consistency of batter cakes, and as much Graham flour as can be stirred in with a spoon.

Set it away till morning; in the morning grease pan, flour hands; take a lump of dough the size of a large egg; roll lightly between the palms; let them rise twenty minutes and bake in a tolerably hot oven.

589. **SODA BISCUITS.**—Ingredients—Eighteen oz. of flour, ¼ of a breakfast cup of lard, 2 small cups of new milk, 2 teaspoonfuls of cream-tartar, 1 of soda, a pinch of salt.

Take care that the cream-tartar and the soda are of the finest powder and mix well with the flour; add the salt and lard, and with the hands rub well into the flour; pour in the milk and work up the dough as *quickly* as possible, taking care to have it as soft as is possible to handle. Roll, cut into cakes, and bake in a brisk oven.

590. **MILK BISCUITS.**—Ingredients—Quarter lb. of butter, 1 qt. of milk, 1 gill of yeast, salt to taste, as much flour as will form the dough.

Stir flour into the milk so as to form a very thick batter, and add the yeast; this should be done in the evening; in the morning cut up the butter and set it near the fire where it will melt, but not get hot, pour the melted butter into the sponge, then stir in enough flour to make a dough; knead well and leave to rise; as soon as it is perfectly light, butter your tins, cut the dough into cakes and let them rise; when they have risen bake in a *very* quick oven. When done, rub over the tops with water and serve hot.

591. **BAKING POWDER BISCUIT.**

Take one quart of flour, three teaspoonfuls of baking powder, mix thoroughly, then rub in butter or lard the size of an egg, and wet with milk, stirring with a spoon till thick enough to lay on the moulding-board. Cut thin and bake in a quick oven.

592. **SALLY LUNN.**—Ingredients—Two pounds of flour, half a pound of butter, three eggs, one pint of milk, half a gill of yeast, salt according to taste.

Cut up the butter in the flour, and with your hands rub it well together; beat the eggs; add them gradually to the flour alternately with the milk; stir in the yeast and salt. Bake it in an earthen mould, or iron pan, one hour.

593. **BREAKFAST MUFFINS.**—Ingredients—Three eggs, 1 breakfastcupful of milk, 1 tablespoonful of butter melted, 1 of sugar, a pinch of salt, 2 heaped teaspoonfuls of baking powder.

Whisk the eggs and mix with the milk; put the melted butter into a basin with the above ingredients, mixing in flour enough to make a batter. Bake in round tins, and when almost done wash the top of each with a feather dipped in milk.

594. **GRAHAM MUFFINS.**—Ingredients—One quart of Graham flour, two teaspoonfuls of baking powder, a piece of butter the size of a walnut, one egg, one tablespoonful of sugar, one-half teaspoonful of salt, milk enough to make a batter as thick as for griddle cakes.

Bake in muffin-rings, about twenty minutes, in a quick oven.

595. **RICE MUFFINS.**—Ingredients—Two cups of cold boiled rice, 1 pint of flour, 1 teaspoon of salt, 1 tablespoon of sugar, two teaspoons of baking powder, $\frac{1}{2}$ pint of milk, 3 eggs.

Mix into a smooth and rather firm batter, and bake as above.

596. **OATMEAL MUFFINS.**—Ingredients—One cup oatmeal, 1$\frac{1}{2}$ pints flour, 1 teaspoonful of salt, 2 teaspoonfuls of baking powder, 1 pint of milk, 1 tablespoonful of lard, 2 eggs.

Mix smoothly into a batter rather thinner than for cup cakes. Fill the muffin rings two-thirds full and bake in a hot oven.

597. **CRUMPETS** (1).—Ingredients—Two eggs, 1 teaspoonful each of salt and sugar, 4 teaspoonfuls of baking powder, 1 quart of milk, 3 pts. flour.

Mix into a stiff batter and bake in greased muffin rings on a hot greased griddle.

598. **CRUMPETS** (2).—Ingredients—Two pts. flour, 1½ teaspoonfuls of sugar, 1 teaspoonful of salt, 2½ teaspoonfuls of baking powder, 2 eggs, 1 pt. milk, 1 teaspoonful of cinnamon.

Mix thoroughly, adding the eggs and milk last. Stir to a stiff batter, and bake on a hot, well greased griddle.

599. **WAFFLES**.—Ingredients—Two eggs, 1 pint of milk, ½ oz. of butter, ½ gill yeast, salt to taste, and flour enough to form a thick batter.

Warm the milk and butter together; beat the eggs, and add them by turns with the flour; stir in the yeast and salt. When they are light, heat your waffle-irons and butter them, pour in some of the batter, and brown them on both sides; butter them, and serve them with or without sugar and cinnamon.

600. **RICE WAFFLES**.—Ingredients—One gill of rice, 3 gills of flour, salt to taste, 1 oz of butter, 3 eggs, as much milk as will make it a thick batter.

Boil the rice in very little water until it is soft; drain it and mash it fine. Then add the butter to the rice whilst it is warm; whisk the eggs very light, the yolks and whites separately. Add the yolks to the rice, and as much milk as will form a batter. Beat the whole very hard, then stir the whites of the eggs gently into the mixture. Grease your waffle-irons, and bake them. If the batter should be too thin, add a little more flour.

601. **WAFFLES** (without yeast).—Ingredients—Three eggs, 1 pint of milk, 1 teaspoonful of butter, as much flour as will make a batter.

Beat the yolks and whites separately; melt the butter, and while lukewarm stir it into the milk; whisk the yolks very light; add to them the milk and flour alternately; beat it well; lastly stir in the whites, which should be whisked very dry. The batter should not be beaten after the whites are in. Grease your waffle-irons after having heated them; fill them nearly full of the batter, close them, and place them over the fire; turn the irons so as to bake the waffle on both sides. When done, take it out and butter it. These must be baked the moment they are mixed.

602. **SPANISH BUNS**.—Ingredients—One lb. of flour, ¾ of a lb. of sugar, ½ lb. of butter, 4 eggs, 1 gill of yeast, 1 teaspoonful of cinnamon, ½ teaspoonful of nutmeg, ½ pint of milk, 2 tablespoonfuls of rose water.

Cut up the butter, and rub it well with the flour, add the sugar, beat the eggs very light, and stir in lastly the spices and rose-water, with milk enough to form a very thick batter, then add the **yeast**. The next morning stir it again, and let it rise the second time. Butter your pans, and fill them three parts full. When they are done and cold, sift sugar over, and with a sharp knife cut them in squares.

603. **BUNS**.—Ingredients—One pound of flour, 3 oz. butter, ¼ lb. sugar, 2 eggs, 3 half gills of milk, 1 gill of home-made yeast, 1 tablespoonful of rose-water, 2 teaspoonfuls of powdered cinnamon.

Warm the butter in the milk; beat the eggs; mix the eggs with the milk and butter, and pour altogether into the pan of flour; then add the rose-water, cinnamon, and yeast. Mix all thoroughly, knead the dough well, let it rise; when light, make it out into cakes; put them in buttered pans, let them stand till they rise again, and bake them.

604. **EASTER BUNS**.—Ingredients—Half quartern of white bread dough, 6 oz. fresh butter, 6 oz. white sugar, 4 eggs.

Beat the sugar and eggs together and mix them well with the dough (if it is stiff the best plan is to beat it with your hand, but if not a spoon will answer the purpose). When this is done add the butter. Put the mixture into tins or cups, and bake for about twenty minutes in a quick oven.

605. **POP-OVERS**.—Ingredients—Take of equal proportions (say 2 cups) milk and flour, 2 eggs, a little salt butter the size of an egg.

Mix the salt in the flour, beat the eggs, add to it the milk and pour upon the flour; mix well, melt the butter and add to other ingredients; the last thing, grease and half fill the tins; bake quickly.

606. **DOUGHNUTS**.—Ingredients—One quart of water, 1 cake of yeast, 1 coffee-cupful of lard, 2 of white sugar, 3 large mashed potatoes, a small nutmeg.

Set sponge for them about two or three o'clock; fry them the next forenoon. Make a sponge, using the above proportions of water and yeast. Let it rise until very light (five hours is usually sufficient); then add the other ingredients; let it rise again until very light; roll, and cut or pull off bits of dough and shape as you like; lay enough to fry at one time on a floured plate, and set in the oven to warm ; drop in boiling lard, and fry longer than cakes made with baking powder. If the dough is light enough, and you heat it before dropping in the lard, your doughnuts will be delicious.

607. **BUTTERMILK CAKES**.

Take one pint of buttermilk, and stir into it as much flour as will form a dough, with one tablespoonful of dissolved carbonate of ammonia ; roll the dough out in sheets, cut the cakes, and bake them in a moderate oven. The carbonate of ammonia may be obtained at any of the druggists ; it is the common smelling-salts, without any of the aromatic drugs. It never imparts any taste to the food, as the heat disengages the carbonic acid gas and the ammonia.

608. **MUSH CAKES**.—Ingredients—One qt. of milk, ¼ pound of butter, flour enough to make a dough, salt according to taste, Indian meal sufficient to thicken the milk, half a pint of yeast.

Boil the milk, and stir into it as much Indian meal, mixed with cold milk, as will make a mush as thick as batter ; add the butter and salt while the mush is hot; as soon as it becomes lukewarm stir in the yeast and as much flour as will form a dough ; cover it and stand it to rise. When light, make it out into biscuits, put them in buttered pans, and, as soon as they rise again, bake them in a hot oven. These cakes are very nice.

609. **BUCKWHEAT CAKES**.—Ingredients—One pint of buckwheat meal, 1 qt. of water, salt according to taste, 1 gill of home-made yeast.

Mix the water (which should be lukewarm if the weather is cold) with the meal ; add the salt and yeast ; beat it well ; when light, bake them on a griddle. Grease the griddle; pour on a little of the batter ; spread it so as to form a cake about the size of a breakfast-plate ; the cakes should be very smooth at the edges. When they are done on one side, turn them; when brown on both sides, put some butter on the plate, put the cake on it, butter the top, bake another and put on it, butter hot, and send them to the table. Buckwheat cakes are much better if they are sent to the table with only one or two on the plate.

610. **RYE BATTER CAKES**.—Ingredients—One pint of rye meal enough lukewarm milk to make a thin batter, salt according to taste, one gill of home-made yeast.

Add enough lukewarm milk to the rye to make a thin batter, with salt ; beat it well, then add the yeast ; when they are light, bake them on a griddle, as buckwheat cakes.

611. **MILK AND BUTTER CAKES.**—Ingredients—Three-quarters of a pound of flour, ½ lb. of butter, ½ lb. of sugar, 1 teaspoonful of grated nutmeg, as much milk as will form a dough.

Cut up the butter in the flour, add the sugar and spices by degrees; stir in as much milk as will make a dough; knead it well, roll it out in sheets, cut in cakes, butter your tins, lay them on so as not to touch, and bake in a moderate oven.

612. **SPONGE JELLY CAKE.**—Ingredients—3 eggs, 4 oz. of sugar, 1 cup of flour, 1 dessertspoonful of baking powder, 3 tablespoonfuls of boiling water.

Mix the baking powder with the flour, and beat each of the eggs separately. Then mix all the ingredients together, and bake in jelly tins in a brisk oven. When cool, chocolate frosting put between the cakes makes them very delicious, or jelly if preferred.

613. **JELLY ROLLS.**—Ingredients—3 eggs, ½ a cupful of butter, 1½ teaspoonsful of baking powder, ⅔ of a cup of pulverized sugar, 1 cupful of flour, a little salt.

Bake in shallow pans—a dripping-pan well buttered is good for this purpose; put in the dough till it is about half an inch thick; take it carefully from the tins when baked and lay on a cloth; spread jelly over it evenly with a knife; roll while hot; if this is not done the cake will crumble.

614. **SPONGE JELLY CAKE (Rolled.)**—Ingredients—5 eggs, 1 cup of sugar, 1 cup of flour, and 1 teaspoonful of baking powder.

Beat the yolks and sugar to a cream, add the whites, beaten to a stiff froth; then the flour, in which the baking powder has been mixed. Bake in a dripping-pan. When done, turn out on a cloth, spread jelly on the bottom of the cake, and roll from the side.

615. **ROLL JELLY CAKE.**—Ingredients—1½ cups of brown sugar, 3 eggs, 1 cup of milk, 2 cups of flour, 1 teaspoonful of cream of tartar, 1 teaspoonful of soda, 1 teaspoonful of lemon or vanilla essence.

Thoroughly beat the eggs and sugar together; mix the cream of tartar and soda with the milk, stirring in the flavoring also; next mix in the flour; spread them upon a long pan, and as soon as done spread jelly on the top and roll.

616. **JOHNNY CAKE.**—Ingredients—1 pt. of Indian meal, 1 teacupful of sugar, 1 pt. of milk, 2 eggs, 1 teaspoonful of butter, salt to taste, 1 teaspoonful of dissolved saleratus.

Mix the butter and sugar with the meal; boil half the milk.

Add the dissolved saleratus and the eggs, after they have been well beaten, to the remaining half of cold milk. Pour the boiling milk over the meal and let it cool. Then add the cold milk and saleratus. Bake in a shallow pan.

617. **INDIAN MEAL BREAKFAST CAKES.**—Ingredients—
1 qt. of Indian meal, 2 eggs, 1 teaspoonful of *dissolved* saleratus, ½ oz. of butter, salt to taste, milk sufficient to make a thick batter.

Beat the eggs very thick and light. Cut up the butter into the meal; then pour over enough boiling water to wet it. When it is cool add the eggs and salt; pour the dissolved saleratus into the milk, and add as much milk as will make it into a thick batter. Butter square tin pans, fill them about two-thirds full, and bake in a quick oven. When done, cut into squares and serve hot.

618. **ICING FOR CAKES** (1).—Ingredients—Four eggs, 1 lb. of finely powdered white sugar, vanilla, strawberry, lemon, or any other flavoring.

Take the whites of the eggs, and beat well adding the sugar to stiffen in small quantities; continue until you have beaten the eggs to a stiff froth; it will take about half an hour if well beaten all the time; if not stiff enough then add more sugar; spread carefully on the cake with a broad bladed knife; to color icing yellow, put the grated peel of a lemon (or orange) into a piece of muslin, strain a little juice through it and press hard into the other ingredients. Strawberry juice or cranberry syrup colors a pretty pink color.

619. **ICING FOR CAKES** (2).—Ingredients—The whites of two eggs, ½ lb. of castor sugar, and the juice of a lemon or a few drops of orange flower water.

Beat the mixture until it hangs upon the fork in flakes, then spread over the cake, dipping the knife in cold water occasionally; stand it before the fire, and keep turning the cake constantly, or the sugar will catch and turn brown; as soon as it begins to harden it may be removed; the icing must not be put on until the cake itself is cold, otherwise it will not set. A few drops of cochineal will color it if desired.

620. **EXCELLENT FROSTING.**

Take one cup of granulated sugar and four tablespoons of hot water, boil them together until it threads from the spoon, stirring often. Beat the white of one egg until firm; when the sugar is ready set it from the stove long enough to stop boiling, then pour on to the egg slowly, but continually, beating rapidly; continue to beat until of the right consistency to spread on the cake and flavor while beating; it hardens very quickly after it is ready to put on the cake, so it is best to have the white of another egg ready to add a little if it gets too hard to spread smoothly. Boil the sugar the same as for candy; when right for candy it is right for frosting; if at last it hardens very rapidly it has been boiled too hard; but a little white of egg will rectify it. Or if not boiled enough (that is, if it remains too thin after beaten until cold) put in pulverized sugar, adding a little and beating hard, then if not just right, a little more and beat again until thick enough.

The one thing is to have the sugar boiled just right; if you hit that point you will not have a bit of trouble, if not, it will require "doctoring," as I have told you. A good deal depends upon stirring the sugar into the white of the egg at first; if too fast or too slow it will cook the egg in lumps; if you should not get it just right at first do not be discouraged; when once you get it perfect you will never make it any other way. This quantity is for one cake.

621. **ALMOND ICING FOR CAKES.**—Ingredients—Four eggs, a small quantity of rose water, and to every lb. of sweet almonds add 1 lb. of powdered loaf sugar.

Blanch and pound the almonds until of the consistency of thick cream, wetting now and then with a little rose-water, next beat the whites of the eggs to a firm froth; add to the almonds mixing in the sugar, and stir all well together (be sure it is nice and smooth). After spreading on the cakes cover with plain icing, after this, if desired, pop it in the oven to dry, and harden.

622. **CHOCLATE ICING FOR CAKE (Simple).**—Ingredients—¼ cake chocolate, ½ cup sweet milk, 2 dessertspoonfuls of corn starch, a teaspoonful of vanilla.

Mix together the chocolate, milk, and starch; boil for two minutes, flavor with the vanilla, and sweeten with powdered white sugar to taste.

623. **PLAIN FRUIT CAKES.**—Ingredients—One lb. of flour, ¼ lb. of dripping, 2 teaspoonfuls of baking powder, a little allspice and salt, ¼ lb. of currants, ¼ lb. of white sugar, and ½ pint of milk.

Mix into the flour the baking powder and salt, then with the hands rub the dripping in the flour until it resembles bread-crumbs. Add the currants, allspice and sugar. Take care that the ingredients are well mixed; pour in the milk and mix with a wooden spoon. Grease a quartern tin and pour the mixture into it; bake for one hour. To ensure the cake being done stick a piece of broom straw into it. This answers the same purpose as a knife and is better, as the knife is apt to make the cake heavy. Turn the cake on end to allow the steam to evaporate.

624. **PLAIN FRUIT CAKE** (2).—Ingredients—One lb. of flour, ½ lb. of raisins, 4 oz. of dripping, 4 oz. of white sugar, a teacup of milk, 1 egg, 2 teaspoonfuls of baking powder, a little salt, 1 oz. of lemon peel.

Add to the flour the baking powder and salt; rub the dripping into the flour with your hands. Take care it is well incorporated. Stone the raisins, grate the lemon rind, and with the sugar add to the other ingredients. Well whisk the egg, and mix in the milk, adding to the mixture; thoroughly mix. Grease a cake tin and bake for an hour. Proceed to test if done, as above.

625. **SODA CAKE**.—Ingredients—One pound of flour, 3 oz. of butter, eight oz. of sugar, a quarter of a pint of milk, three eggs, ½ lb. of currants; one teaspoonful of carbonate of soda, grate in a quarter of a nutmeg.

Beat the whole well and lightly together. Remember that the soda should only be stirred into the ingredients just before putting it (in a well buttered pan) into the oven. Bake it for about an hour and a quarter.

626. **ECONOMICAL FRUIT CAKE**.—Ingredients—Five oz. of butter, 2 lbs. of flour, ½ lb. of sugar, one lb. of currants, one gill of yeast, enough milk to make a thick batter, one tablespoonful of powdered cinnamon.

Mix the flour, leaving out a quarter of a pound, with the butter cut in small pieces, the sugar, cinnamon and fruit; add milk enough to form a thick batter, and lastly stir in the yeast. Mix it over night, and set it away to rise; in the morning stir in the remainder of the flour, and let it rise; when light, mould it out very lightly; butter your pan, and bake it in an oven about as hot as for bread.

627. **NEW YORK PLUM CAKE**.—Ingredients—One lb. of butter, 1 lb. of flour, 2 lbs. of raisins, seeded, 2 lbs. of currants, ¼ oz. of ground cloves, one wineglassful of brandy, 1 lb. of sugar, 1 lb. of citron, cut in small, thin pieces, 8 eggs, ¼ oz. of ground cinnamon; ¼ oz. ground mace, ¼ oz. of grated nutmeg.

Slice the citron, pick, wash and dry the currants, seed the raisins, and mix the fruit together, and dredge over it as much flour as will adhere to it. Prepare the spice. Stir the butter and sugar till it is smooth and light. Beat the eggs very light, and stir them into the butter and sugar. Add the flour and fruit gradually; beat the batter till the fruit is thoroughly mixed with it, then add slowly the spice and liquor. Beat the mixture very hard for ten or fifteen minutes. Line your pans with two thicknesses of stout white paper, which should be well buttered: pour in the batter, and bake from four to five hours. Rose-water and lemon may be used to flavor it instead of the liquor; a wineglass of rose-water, and as much lemon as to give it a taste.

628. **PLUM CAKE**.—Ingredients—One pound each of butter, sugar and flour, 10 eggs, 1 lb. of raisins, ½ lb. each of currants and sliced citron, a teaspoonful of ground cloves, one of mace, one nutmeg, the juice and grated peel of a lemon, half a coffee cup of molasses.

Beat the butter till it is soft and creamy, then add the sugar. Beat the whites and the yolks of the eggs separately; stir the yolks in with the butter and sugar; stir the flour in gradually (having first mixed one heaping teaspoonful of cream of tartar with it). When the flour is about half worked in, put in half a teaspoonful of soda dissolved in as little water as is possible to use; then add the whites of the eggs, and lastly the fruit, which is well covered with the rest of the flour. Bake in a large tin, with a buttered paper on the sides as well as on the bottom; it will need to bake slowly for five hours. Then, do not attempt to lift it from the tin until it is perfectly cold. This should be made several days before it is used.

629. **A RICH PLUM CAKE**.—Ingredients—One lb. of fresh butter, 1 lb. of powdered loaf sugar, 1 lb. of flour, 1½ lbs. of currants, 2 lbs. candied peel, 1 lb. sweet almonds, 2 oz. allspice, ¼ oz. of cinnamon (both these in powder), 10 eggs, a glass of brandy.

Beat the butter to a cream, and add the sugar; stir till light, and put in the spices; in fifteen minutes work in the eggs two or three at a time, then add the orange, lemon, and citron peel and currants, and mix them well with the almonds, blanched and cut small; last of all add the flour and brandy; bake in a hot oven for three hours, in a tin hoop with plenty of paper underneath.

630. **SEED CAKE**.—Ingredients—Ten oz. of flour, 2 oz. of sugar, 2 teaspoonfuls of baking powder, and one of carraway seeds, 1 egg, 3 oz. of butter, a little salt, and half a glass of milk.

Mix the baking powder and salt in the flour, rub in the butter also (with the hands). Add the sugar and carraway seeds, taking care to thoroughly blend them. Well whisk the egg and add the milk to it, add to the other ingredients and beat well for about ten minutes. Grease a baking tin and pour the mixture in. It will take about one hour to bake.

631. **ANOTHER SEED CAKE** (Good).—Ingredients—1 lb. of butter, 12 oz. of sifted white sugar, 6 eggs, nutmeg grated and powdered mace to taste, 1 lb. of flour, 2 oz. of carraway seeds, ½ a gill of brandy.

Beat the butter until of the consistency of a thin paste; sift in the flour. Add the remaining ingredients excepting the eggs, mixing all well together. Beat the eggs separately and stir in the brandy, add to the other ingredients and beat the mixture for ten or twelve minutes. Line a tin with buttered paper and put the cake in and allow to bake for about one and a half or two hours.

632. **SEED BISCUITS.**—Ingredients—18 oz. of flour, 6 oz. of sugar, 6 oz. of butter, ½ oz. of carraway seeds, 3 eggs.

Beat the butter until it is of the consistency of cream. Work in gradually the flour, sugar, and carraway seeds. When thoroughly mixed add the eggs, well whisked. Roll out the paste, cut into fancy shapes, and bake for a quarter of an hour. It is an improvement to brush over the tops with a little milk, strewing a little white sugar over them.

633. **RICE CAKE.**—Ingredients—Two handfuls of rice, a little less than a quart of milk, sugar to taste, rind of a lemon cut in one piece, a small stick of cinnamon, 4 eggs, a small quantity of candied citron.

Pick and wash in two or three waters the rice and put it to cook in the milk, sweeten to taste, add the lemon rind and cinnamon. Let the rice simmer gently until tender and has absorbed all the milk. Turn it into a basin to cool, and remove the lemon rind and cinnamon. Then stir into it the yolks of four and the white of one egg. Add a little candied citron cut in small pieces. Butter and bread-crumb a plain cake mould; put the mixture into it and bake in a quick oven half an hour.

634. **RICH RICE CAKE.**—Ingredients—One lb. of ground rice, 1 lb. of flour, 1 lb. of sugar, 17 eggs, 36 drops of of essence of lemon, or, if preferred, the rind of 2 lemons, ½ lb. of butter.

Whisk the eggs separately; beat the butter to a cream, and add the yolks of the eggs, mixing well. Then add the flour, rice and lemon (if lemon rind take care it is finely minced). Beat the mixture for about ten minutes, and lastly add the whites of the eggs. Beat again for a quarter of an hour; put into a buttered mould. It will take about an hour and a half to bake.

635. **RICE CAKES.**—Ingredients—Eight oz. of rice flour, 4 oz. of white sugar, 4 oz. of butter, 3 eggs.

Work the butter to a creamy substance, add the sugar and flour, and mix in the well-whisked eggs. Roll upon pastry board and shape into cakes with a cake cutter. Bake in a slow oven.

636. **JUMBLES** — Ingredients—Two pounds of flour, 1¼ lb. of sugar, half a pint of milk, 3 eggs, ½ lb. of butter, one teaspoonful of *dissolved* saleratus, essence of lemon according to taste.

Beat the butter and sugar to a cream; add the eggs, which must have been whisked till very thick, and some essence of lemon; then pour in the milk and saleratus. The saleratus should be dissolved in water, and a teaspoonful of this solution be mixed with the milk. Bake in the form of jumbles.

637. **INDIAN LOAF CAKE.**—Ingredients—One lb. of Indian meal, ¼ lb. of butter, 2 eggs, ½ lb. of sugar, ¼ lb. of raisins, ¼ lb. of currants.

Cut up the butter in the Indian meal; pour over it as much boiling milk as will make a thick batter; beat the eggs very light; when the batter is cool pour them into it. Seed the raisins; wash, pick, and dry the currants; mix them with the raisins, and dredge as much wheat flour on them as will adhere to them. Stir the fruit into the batter, and add the sugar. Bake it in a moderate oven two hours.

638. **ALMOND CAKE.**—Ingredients—Ten eggs 1 lb. of sugar, ¼ lb. of flour, 1 wineglass of rose water, 1 oz. of bitter almonds.

Beat the eggs—the yolks and whites separate. When the yolks are very light, add the sugar and the almonds, which must have been blanched and pounded with the rose water. Beat the whole well. Whisk the whites to a dry froth, and stir in one half of the white with one half of the flour till it is thoroughly mixed; then add the other half of the white and flour. Do not beat it after the white is in, as that will make it tough and heavy.

639. **CREAM CAKE AND CHOCOLATE.**—Ingredients—Two-thirds of a cupful of butter, 2 cups of white sugar, 4 eggs, ½ a glass of milk, 3 cups of prepared flour.

Beat the butter and sugar to a cream; add the yolks of the

eggs, well beaten, the milk and then the whites of the eggs also well beaten to a froth, alternately with the flour; when cold spread with the following filling:—A cup of milk, a dessertspoonful of corn starch, an egg, a teaspoonful of vanilla, ¼ a cup of sugar. Scald the milk; mix in the corn-starch, previously moistened with a little cold milk; pour over the well-beaten eggs and sugar; allow to remain on the fire until thick, stirring well. Flavor when cold. Serve with chocolate.

640. **QUEEN CAKES.**—Ingredients—One lb. of dried flour, same of sifted sugar and of washed-clean currants, 1 lb. of butter, 8 eggs.

Mix the flour, sugar and currants; wash the butter in rose-water, beat it well, then mix with it the eggs, yolks and whites beaten separately, and put in the dry ingredients by degrees; beat the whole for one hour; butter little tins and put the mixture in, only filling half full, and bake; sift a little fine sugar over just as you put into the oven.

641. **QUEEN'S CAKE** (2).—Ingredients—One lb. of fine flour, ½ lb. of powdered white sugar, the same of butter, and of currants, ½ pt. of cream, 3 eggs, a teaspoonful of carbonate of soda, flavoring, either lemon or almond.

When the butter is beaten to a cream, sift in the flour, then put in the currants and sugar, being careful to mix the ingredients well together; beat the eggs, pour in the cream and flavoring and pour into the flour, etc. Finally, mix in the carbonate of soda, and mix well for quarter of an hour. Pour the paste into little buttered tins and bake about twenty minutes.

642. **SPICE CAKE.**—Ingredients—Two cups of flour, 2 cups of sugar, 3 eggs, 4 teaspoonfuls of baking powder, 1 cup of butter, 1 gill of boiling water.

This is a very handy cake; any filling convenient may be used.

643. **GINGER CUP CAKE.**—Ingredients—Two cups of butter, 2 cups of sugar, 1 cup of molasses, 1 cup of cream, 3 eggs, 1 tablespoonful of *dissolved* saleratus, 4 heaping cups of flour, half a cup of ginger.

Beat the butter and sugar to a cream; whisk the eggs light, and add to it; then stir in the other ingredients. Butter a pan or earthen mould, and pour in the mixture. Bake in a moderate oven, or it may be baked in queen cake pans.

644. **GINGER NUTS.**—Ingredients—Half lb. of butter, ½ lb. of sugar, 1 pint of molasses, 2 oz. ginger, 2 tablespoonfuls

of cinnamon, as much flour as will form a dough, ½ an oz. of ground cloves and allspice mixed.

Stir the butter and sugar together; add the spice, ginger, molasses, and flour enough to form a dough. Knead it well, make it out in small cakes, bake them on tins in a very moderate oven. Wash them over with molasses and water before they are put in to bake.

645. **GINGER NUTS** (2).—Ingredients—Half lb. of butter, 2 lbs. of flour, 1 pt. of molasses, 2 eggs, 6 oz. ground ginger, 3 oz. ground allspice, 1 oz. powdered cinnamon.

Mix in the same manner as for gingerbread. Roll out the dough into ropes about half inch thick; cut these transversely into pieces, which roll into small balls; place these at a little distance apart, upon greased baking sheets, and flatten them down with the palm of your hand; when the sheet is full, wash them over the tops with a brush dipped in thin molasses, and bake in a moderate oven.

646. **GINGER BREAD**.—Ingredients—Half lb. of moist sugar, 2 oz. of ground ginger 1 lb. of flour, ½ lb. of butter, ½ lb. of treacle.

Put the butter and treacle into a jar near the fire; when the butter is melted mix it with the flour while warm, and spread the mixture thinly on buttered tins, mark it in squares before baking, and as soon as baked enough separate it at the marks before it has time to harden. Time to bake, fifteen minutes.

647. **HONEYCOMB GINGERBREAD**.—Ingredients—½ lb. of flour, ½ lb. of the coarsest brown sugar, ¼ lb. of butter, one dessertspoonful of allspice, two ditto of ground ginger, the peel of half a lemon grated, and the whole of the juice; mix all these ingredients together, adding about ½ lb. of treacle so as to make a paste sufficiently thin to spread upon sheet tins.

Beat well, butter the tins, and spread the paste very thinly over them, bake it in a rather slow oven, and watch it till it is done; withdraw the tins, cut it in squares with a knife to the usual size of wafer biscuits (about four inches square), and roll each piece round the fingers as it is raised from the tin.

648. **DROP GINGER CAKES**.—Ingredients—Put in a bowl one cup of brown sugar, one of molasses, one of butter, then pour over them one cup boiling water, stir well; add one egg, well beaten, two teaspoonfuls of soda, two tablespoonfuls each of ginger and cinnamon, a half teaspoonful of ground cloves, five cups of flour.

Stir altogether and drop with a spoon on buttered tins; bake in a quick oven, taking care not to burn them.

649. **GINGER BISCUITS.**—Ingredients—Rub 4 oz. of fresh butter into ½ lb. of flour, add 3 tablespoonfuls of sugar, ½ oz. of ground ginger, and one egg beaten up with a little milk to a smooth paste.

Bake on buttered paper for ten minutes. Keep the biscuits in a tin in a dry place.

650. **GINGER SNAPS.**—Ingredients—Two cups of butter, 2 cups of molasses, 2 teaspoonfuls of ginger, 2 teaspoonfuls of saleratus dissolved in one cup of boiling water.

Knead soft, roll thin, and bake in quick oven.

651. **TIPSY CAKE.**—Ingredients—A moulded sponge cake, strawberry preserve, a little wine, brandy and water, about ¼ lb. of sweet almonds, custard.

Scoop out carefully the centre of the moulded sponge cake, so as to leave the shape intact; fill the cavity with strawberry preserve, then cover with a layer of cake, and place it in a glass dish to soak with a little light wine and brandy and water. This should be poured gently over it with a spoon until all the wine is absorbed; then stick it all over with the sweet almonds blanched and cut finely, and lastly fill the dish with custard, or, if preferred, hand the latter round in custard cups.

652. **TIPSY CAKE.**(2)—Ingredients—A large stale sponge cake, ½ pt. of sherry, a wineglassful of brandy, ¼ lb. of sweet almonds, a little orange flower water, 1 pt. of milk, yolks of six eggs, sugar to taste, crystallized fruit.

Take the sponge cake, cut the bottom of it so as to make it stand even on a glass dish. Make numerous incisions in it with a knife, and pour over it the sherry and brandy; let the cake soak these all up. Blanch, peel, and slice the sweet almonds, and stick the cake all over with them. Blanch, chop and pound in a mortar a quarter pound of sweet almonds, moistening with a little orange-flower water to prevent their oiling, add one pint of milk and the yolks of six eggs, sweeten to taste with pounded loaf sugar. Stir over the fire till the custard thickens, but do not let it boil. Keep stirring now and then till it is quite cold, then pour it round the cake. Garnish the dish with crystallized fruit, and it is ready.

653. **SMALL NOUGATS.**—Ingredients—1 lb. of sweet almonds, ½ lb. white sugar, oil of sweet almonds.

Blanch the almonds, and cut each lengthwise into thin narrow pieces, lay them on a dish in front of the fire, or in the oven (with the door open), to get perfectly dry; melt in a sugar-boiler the sugar; when the sugar is a rich brown put in the almonds, mix them well but carefully together, and you will have a soft paste, which will harden when cold. Make some small moulds very hot; slightly but thoroughly oil them with oil of sweet almonds, put some of the mixture in one of them, and with the handle of a teaspoon previously oiled, spread it out so as completely to line the mould; trim the edges, and when cold turn out the nougat. Having made a number in the same way, serve them with sweetmeats inside each. The nougats should be very thin. Any kind of mould, large or small, may be used, but the work must be done quickly, for the sugar soon becomes too stiff to be spread into position.

654. **APPLE CAKE.**—Ingredients—1½ lb. of apples cut and cored, 1 lb. lump sugar, the juice of three lemons, and about half the rinds grated.

Simmer in a stew-pan for four hours until it becomes quite stiff. Then put into a mould, in which let it remain all night. Before turning out plunge the mould in warm water to prevent it sticking.

655. **WASHINGTON CAKE.**—Ingredients—1 lb. of sugar, ¾ lb. of butter, 4 eggs, 1 lb. flour, 1 teacupful of milk, 2 teaspoonfuls of dissolved saleratus, 3 tablespoonfuls of brandy, ½ a teaspoonful of cinnamon, half a nutmeg, 1 lb. dried currants, washed, picked, and wiped dry.

Beat the butter and sugar until it is smooth and light. Whisk the eggs till they are thick, and add them to the butter and sugar. Stir in the flour, brandy, and spice. Flour the fruit, and stir it in. Beat the whole very hard for fifteen minutes. Then stir in the saleratus. Line the sides and bottom of your pan with thick paper; butter it well, pour in the mixture, and bake it in a moderate oven.

656. **METROPOLITAN CAKE.**—Ingredients—Light part: 2 cups sugar, ¾ cup butter, 1 cup sweet milk, 2½ cups of flour, whites of 5 eggs, 3 teaspoonfuls baking powder. Dark part: ½ cup molasses, ½ cup flour, 1 cup raisins, 1 teaspoonful cinnamon, ½ teaspoonful cloves, 2 large spoonfuls of the light part.

Bake the light part in two cakes. Bake the dark part in one cake and place between the two light cakes with jelly or frosting.

657. **GATEAU DE SAVOYE (French Sponge Cake.)**—Ingredients—(Take the weight of 8 eggs in their shells) of finely powdered white sugar and half their quantity of potato flour, 2 eggs, juice of half a lemon, some (glacé) sugar (icing), preserved cherries, and sugar plums.

Put the sugar and the yolks of the eggs in a basin, and beat them well together with an egg whisk or with a fork until the mixture assumes a white creamy appearance. Add essence of lemon to taste. Sprinkle in (beating the mixture all the time) half the potato flour, and add the whites of four eggs whisked to a stiff froth. Then put in, in the same manner, the rest of the flour; and lastly add the remaining four whites beaten to a froth. As soon as the composition is smoothly mixed together—and this must be done quickly—pour it into a buttered plain mould, and bake it in a slow oven. When quite done, turn the cake out of the mould and leave it to get cold. In the meantime put the whites of two eggs into a basin, with the juice of half a lemon and some *glace* sugar; stir the mixture briskly with a wooden spoon, adding more *glace* sugar as it gets thin, until it becomes a smooth white paste of the consistency of butter. Lay the mixture all over the cake with a knife, and lay it on as smoothly as possible. Put the cake in the oven just long enough for the icing to glaze. Take it out, and before the icing has time to cool ornament the cake with preserved cherries, small coloured sugarplums, &c., in any pattern you please.

658. **SPONGE CAKE.**—Ingredients—Five eggs, ½ lb. loaf sugar, the grated rind and juice of one lemon, ¼ lb. flour.

Separate the yolks from the whites. Beat the yolks and sugar together until they are very light; then add the whites, after they have been whisked to a dry froth; alternately with the flour stir in the lemon, put the mixture in small pans, sift sugar over them, and bake them.

659. **ITALIAN SPONGE CAKE.**—Ingredients—One lb. of white sugar, 18 eggs, 1 lb. potato flour.

Put into a large basin the sugar and half the number of eggs; beat for ten minutes with an egg-whisk. Then place the basin in a large vessel containing hot water. Add the rest of the eggs, and continue beating the mixture for ten minutes longer. sprinkle in the potato flour and continue beating, taking care that it is mixed very slowly with the eggs and sugar. Pour into a buttered mould and bake in a slow oven.

660. **HICKORY NUT CAKE.**—Ingredients—One and one half cupfuls of sugar, half a cupful of butter, a scant half-cupful of sweet milk, two cupfuls of flour, three eggs, two teaspoonfuls of cream-tartar, one of soda or three teaspoonfuls of baking powder.

Bake in layers. Filling for same:—One cupful of sweet cream or milk; let it come to a boil; then stir in one tablespoonful of corn starch which has previously been wet with cold milk; sweeten to taste; let it just boil up; remove from the fire, and stir in one pint of pulverized hickory nut meats. Flavor to taste, and when partially cool spread between each two layers.

661. **LADY FINGERS.**—Ingredients—4 oz. of sugar, 4 yolks of eggs, mix well; 3 oz. flour, a pinch of salt.

Beat the four whites and stir in gradually; butter a shallow pan and squirt the mixture through a piece of stiff paper rolled up; dust with sugar and bake in a not too hot oven.

662. **SQUASH CAKES.**—Ingredients—Sieve two and one-half cups of cooked squash; add a pint of milk, two eggs, a pint of flour, one teaspoonful of sugar, two teaspoonfuls of baking powder and a little salt.

Beat together until smooth and fry brown in butter.

663. **STRAWBERRY SHORT-CAKE.** — Ingredients— Butter, flour, strawberries, sugar, whipped cream.

Make a rich, short crust with butter and flour, allowing one ounce more of flour than butter; bake in flat tins of equal size (the pastry when baked should be about an inch thick); open the shortcake, butter it well, and cover one-half with a layer of strawberries previously mixed with sugar; have alternate layers of berries and pastry, finishing with the former, over which place a layer of whipped cream.

664. **SHORT-CAKE (Spanish).**—Ingredients—Three eggs, half a cup of butter, one cup of sugar, two-thirds of a cup of sweet milk, a little cinnamon, two cups of flour and one teaspoonful of baking powder.

Stir the flour in, do not knead it; the eggs, butter and sugar should be beaten together till very light; bake in a shallow tin; when it is done spread a thin frosting over the top; make this of the white of one egg, a little pulverized sugar and a teaspoonful of cinnamon; set it in the oven to brown.

665. **SHORT-CAKE (Blackberry).**—Ingredients—Two qts. of flour, 3 tablespoonfuls of butter, 2 of lard, 2½ cups of buttermilk, or thick sour milk, yolks of 2 eggs, a teaspoonful of soda and salt.

Mix the salt in the flour, then work in the shortening; beat the yolks of the eggs; dissolve the soda in a little hot water and add to the above proportion of milk; add these to the first mixture; quickly make into a paste, roll out half an inch thick, having upper and under crust. Lay the paste in a well greased baking tin, cover thickly with berries, sprinkle with sugar, cover with the top crust. Bake about half an hour; cut into squares and eat (splitting these open) with sugar and butter.

666. SHORT-CAKE (Scotch).—Ingredients—Four oz. of white sugar, ½ lb. of slightly salted butter, 1 lb. of flour.

Mix the flour and butter with the hands; then add the sugar, and work all into a smooth ball; then roll out until it is an inch thick; prick over with a fork and pinch round the edges, and bake for one-half hour in an oven with a moderate fire, in a round or square pan, according to taste.

667. SHORT-CAKE (Raspberry or Huckleberry).—Ingredients—One qt. of flour, 2 tablespoonfuls each of butter and lard, 2 half cups of buttermilk, yolks of 2 eggs, a teaspoonful of soda and salt, 1 qt. of raspberries or huckleberries.

Sort the flour; chop up the lard and butter in the flour, whisk well the yolks of the eggs; dissolve the soda in a little warm water. Make all these ingredients into a soft paste. Roll lightly in two sheets; lay the bottom crust in a greased square pan; strew thickly with berries, sprinkle with sugar and cover with the upper crust. Bake about half an hour; cut into squares and send to table piled upon a dish. Split and eat with butter and sugar.

668. CHOCOLATE CAKE.—Ingredients—Half a lb. of butter, yolks of 12 eggs, ½lb. of white sugar, same of ground almonds, ¼ lb. of chocolate, 2 tablespoonfuls of cinnamon, ½ teaspoonful of pounded cloves.

Melt the butter and stir it until it froths, beat the yolks of the eggs and stir into the butter; add the sugar and pounded almonds, grated chocolate, cinnamon and pounded cloves, beat well for fifteen minutes; then beat the whites of the eggs to a froth, and add these to the above mixture; butter the mould, and bake the above in a moderate oven for an hour and a quarter.

669. CHOCOLATE CAKE (2).

Beat for ten minutes the yolks of three eggs, stir them into the butter, add two ounces of sugar, two ounces of Jordan almonds, blanched and pounded, two ounces of powdered chocolate, half a teaspoonful of cinnamon, and the same of cloves, pounded. Stir well for a quarter of an hour, then add the whites of the eggs, beaten to a froth; butter a mould and bake in a moderate oven for an hour.

670. RATAFIAS.—Ingredients—8 oz. of sweet almonds, 4 of bitter, 10 oz. of white sugar, 4 eggs.

Blanch and skin the almonds, and pound them in a marble mortar with the white of an egg; add gradually the sugar, and the whites of three eggs, having previously well whisked them.

Take a large sheet of cartridge paper and drop the mixture through a biscuit syringe upon it and bake for about twelve minutes. The oven should be rather quick, and the cakes should not be larger than a 25c. piece.

671. LEMON CAKE.—Ingredients—10 oz. each of white sugar and flour, 9 eggs, 3 large spoonfuls of orange flower water, 1 lemon.

Beat separately the whites and yolks of the eggs. When the former is a stiff froth add the flower water, the sugar, and grated lemon rind. Mix these ingredients for about ten minutes; now mix in the yolks of the eggs and lemon juice; lastly dredge in the flour, beating the mixture all the time. Fill a buttered mould with the mixture, and bake for an hour.

672. MACAROONS.—Ingredients—4 oz. of almonds, 4 spoonfuls of orange flower water, 1 lb. of white sugar, wafer paper, 4 eggs.

Blanch the almonds, and pound with the orange-flower water; whisk the whites of four eggs to a froth, then mix it, and a pound of sugar sifted with the almonds, to a paste; and laying a sheet of wafer-paper on a tin, put it on in different little cakes, the shape of macaroons. Bake from fifteen to twenty minutes.

673. CAKE WITHOUT EGGS.—Ingredients—2 lbs. flour, 1 lb. currants, 1 lb. sugar (half white and half brown), ½ lb. clarified dripping or butter, rather more than 1 pint of milk or buttermilk, 1 large teaspoonful of salt, 4 drachms of bicarbonate of soda, 4 drachms of muriatic acid.

Beat the dripping to a cream, dissolve the soda in some of the milk, and pour the muriatic acid into the rest; mix all the ingredients well together; it should be a very thick batter. Candied peel may be added or used instead of the currants; the flour should be dried. Mix the milk with the carbonate of soda well into the other ingredients before adding the muriatic acid. The strength of the muriatic acid should be 1—165. The best tin for baking cakes is round, nine inches in diameter, with a chimney up the middle, where a round hole is cut out of the bottom of the tin. Anyone adopting these cakes should be provided with a small box containing scales and weights, and a minim or drop measure.

674. MALAGA CAKE.—Ingredients—1 cup of butter, 2 cups of sugar, ½ cup of sweet milk, 2 teaspoonfuls of baking powder, 3 cups of flour, whites of 6 eggs. Filling:—Whites of 3 eggs beaten with sugar, 1 cup of seeded and chopped raisins, 2 teaspoonfuls of extract of lemon.

Beat to a cream the butter and sugar, add the milk; mix the baking powder with the flour; beat the whites of the eggs to a froth, stir all together and flavor with lemon. Bake in sheets, and when done spread with the above filling.

675. CHARLOTTE A LA POLONAISE.— Ingredients — A sponge cake, cream, sugar, sweetmeats.

Make a sponge cake, cut it transversely, dip each piece in cream, and then place them back where they were, so as to give the cake its original form as near as possible. When thus reformed, cover it with cream, dust with sugar, and decorate it with any kind of sweetmeats. Besides the sweetmeats that are placed here and there all around, some currant jelly may be used to decorate. Place on ice for some time and serve.

676. SILVER CAKE.—Ingredients—¾ lb. of sugar, ½ lb of flour, ¼ lb. of butter, whites of 8 eggs, 1 heaped teaspoonful of essence of bitter almonds.

Cream the butter and sugar; whisk the eggs to a stiff froth and add; lastly the flour and flavoring. Flavor icing of this cake with rose water.

677. COCOANUT CAKE.—Ingredients—6 oz. of butter, 1 lb. of sugar, 1 lb. of flour, 1 large cupful of milk, 1 teaspoonful of soda, 2 of cream-of-tartar.

Rub the butter into the flour; add the sugar and cream-of-tartar; well whisk the eggs; dissolve the soda in a little warm water, adding these to other ingredients. Bake in layers as for jelly cake. Icing to place between the layers :—8 oz. of white sugar, whites of two eggs. Well whisk the eggs and sugar, add the grated cocoanut and place between the layers.

678. SCOTCH SNOW CAKE.—Ingredients—7 oz. white sugar, 1 lb. arrowroot, ½ lb. butter, whites of 7 eggs, any flavoring that is preferred.

Beat the butter until like cream, and while beating add gradually the arrowroot and sugar. When the whites of the eggs are beaten to a stiff froth, mix with the other ingredients and beat for a quarter of an hour. Flavor to taste, pour into buttered mould and bake for an hour and a quarter.

679. SCOTCH OAT CAKE.—Ingredients—8 oz. Scotch oatmeal, a small spoonful of butter, as much carbonate of soda as will lay on a 5c. piece.

Place the butter in a teacup with the above proportion of soda, and pour upon this half a teacup of hot water. Mix until both are melted. Having put the meal into a basin (holding about a pint) pour quickly the contents of the teacup upon it, and mix well with the point of a knife. Place upon the paste-board and with the knuckles spread it out gradually. Care must be taken that the edges do not crack. Sprinkle plenty of dry meal over it and roll with a crimped roller to the thickness of a quarter of an inch. Take care to keep the paste round. Then put the knife in the centre and divide into three. Place them upon a hot griddle, and as they get done move in order from a cool spot to a warmer. When they are done enough they will not be doughy. Remove from the fire on to a toaster before the fire and allow them to dry gradually, and as done remove from the fire, stand them on edge to allow to get cold. Proceed in this manner till the mixture is used.

680. **RICH BRIDE CAKE.**—Ingredients—5 lbs. sifted flour, 3 lbs. fresh butter, 2 lbs. white sugar, 5 lbs. currants, 1¼ lbs. of sweet almonds, ¾ lb. of candied citron, 6 oz. each of candied orange and lemon peel, ¼ oz. of mace, half a ¼ of cloves, 17 eggs, 1 gill each of brandy and wine, 2 nutmegs, a little orange-flower water.

Blanch and pound the almonds, adding a little orange-flower water to prevent oiling. Then proceed to work the butter with the hands until of the consistency of cream. Add the sugar. Whisk the whites of the eggs to a stiff froth and add to the butter and sugar. Beat the yolks of the eggs for twelve minutes, and add them to the flour, grated nutmeg, and finely powdered mace and cloves, beating the whole for three-quarters of an hour. Then proceed to add lightly the almonds, with the thinly sliced peel, and lastly the brandy and wine. Then beat for one half an hour. Line your cake tin with buttered paper, and fill with the mixture. The oven should be tolerably quick, but great care must be taken that it is not too fierce, or the cake will brown before it begins to soak. It will take about 6 hours to bake. Test if done as in Recipe for plain Fruit cake No. 623. Turn on end to allow the steam to evaporate, and spread with icing when cold. See Recipe for "Almond Icing," No. 621.

681. **WHITE BRIDE CAKE.**

Take one pound of butter, put it into a basin and beat it with your hand till it comes to a fine cream, then add one and one-quarter pounds of pulverized sugar, and beat together until it is fine and white : then add one pound of sifted flour, give it a stir and then add the whites of fourteen eggs ; continue to beat it and add another pound of flour and fourteen more whites ; beat well; mix all together, paper your dish around the sides and bottom, put in your batter and bake in a moderate oven.

682. **PLAIN LUNCHEON CAKE**—Ingredients—¼ lb. of butter, 2 oz. of dripping, 3 eggs well beaten, ¼ lb. moist sugar, ¼ lb.

of currants, ¼ lb. sultanas, 2 oz. candied peel, ⅜ lb. of flour, 2 teaspoonfuls of baking powder.

Melt the butter and dripping in the oven, let it stand till cool, then add the eggs, moist sugar, currants, sultanas, and candied peel, cut up finely. Have ready in a separate basin the flour mixed with two teaspoonfuls of baking powder; and add this gradually to the other ingredients; bake an hour and a half in a moderate oven. These cakes are excellent.

683. **SHREWSBURY CAKE.**—Ingredients—One lb. of sugar, pounded cinnamon, a little grated nutmeg, 3 lbs. of flour, a little rose water, 3 eggs, melted butter.

Sift the sugar, cinnamon and nutmeg into the flour (which must be of the finest kind); add the rose water to the eggs and mix with the flour, etc., then pour in enough melted butter to make it a good thickness and roll out. Mould well, roll thinly, and cut into such shapes as you like.

684. **MARBLE SPICE CAKE.**—Ingredients—Three-quarters of a pound of flour, well dried; 1 lb. white sugar, ½ lb. of butter, whites of 14 eggs, 1 tablespoonful of cream tartar mixed with the flour.

When the cake is mixed, take out about a teacupful of batter and stir into it one teaspoonful of cinnamon, one of mace, one of cloves, two of spice and one of nutmeg. Fill your mould about an inch deep with the white batter, and drop into this, in several places, a spoonful of the dark mixture; then put in another layer of white, and add the dark as before; repeat this until your batter is used up. This makes one large cake.

685. **CORN STARCH CAKE.**—Ingredients—Four eggs, whites only; 1 cup of butter, ¾ cup of corn starch, ½ cup of sweet milk, 1 cup flour, 2 teaspoonfuls baking powder, lemon or rose water flavoring.

Cream the butter and sugar thoroughly either with the hand or a silver spoon; mix the corn starch with the milk, and add; then add the eggs, beaten stiff, next the sifted flour, into which the baking powder has been stirred. Put into well greased mould and bake.

686. **POTATO CAKE.**—Ingredients—A few mashed potatoes melted butter, flour.

Take the potatoes and stir in melted butter according to the quantity of potatoes used; thicken to a paste with flour, bake in a quick oven and serve hot.

687. **CRACKNELS.**—Ingredients—One qt. of flour, ½ a nutmeg, 4 eggs, 4 spoonfuls of rose water, 1 lb. of butter.

Mix with the flour, the nutmeg grated, the yolks of the eggs, beaten, and the rose water, into a stiff paste with cold water; then roll in the butter and make into cracknel shape; put them into a kettle of boiling water, and boil them till they swim, then take out, and put them into cold water; when hardened, lay them out to dry and bake on tin plates.

688. **ORANGE BISCUITS.**—Ingredients—Four whole Seville oranges, loaf sugar pounded.

Boil the oranges in two or three waters until most of the bitterness has gone; then cut them and remove the pulp and juice; beat the outside very finely in a mortar, and add to it an equal weight of fine white sugar, well pounded and sifted. When well mixed to a paste, spread it thinly on china dishes, and set to dry before the fire; when half dry, cut into shapes, turn the other side up, dry that well, and then pack in boxes with layers of papers between

689. **OATMEAL BISCUITS.**—Ingredients—Six oz. of flour, 3 oz. of oatmeal and white sugar, 3 oz. of butter, enough carbonate of soda to lie on a 5c. piece, 1 large egg.

Melt the butter and add to the flour, oatmeal, sugar, and soda; mix thoroughly; put a tablespoonful of cold water into a basin and break the egg into it and whisk slightly; add this to the other ingredients and mix smoothly; turn on to a well-floured board, roll as thinly as possible and cut into shapes with a cake-cutter. Grease a baking tin, and bake for about twenty minutes.

690. **ROCK BISCUITS.**—Ingredients—Half a dozen eggs, 1 lb. of white sugar, 9 oz. of flour, ¼ lb. of currants.

Beat the eggs until very light, add the sugar and mix thoroughly; add the flour and currants, gradually mixing all the time. Place upon greased tins in the form of small pieces of rock. This is best done with a fork. Bake half an hour, and keep in a tin canister.

691. **LEMON BISCUITS.**—Ingredients—One lb. of flour, ½ lb of white sugar, ¼ lb. of fresh butter, 1 oz. of lemon peel, 1 tablespoonful of lemon juice, 3 eggs.

Add the butter to the flour and rub finely with the hands; mince the lemon peel and stir it and the sugar into the former mixture; well whisk the eggs and lemon juice, and thoroughly mix the whole. Drop from a spoon to a greased baking tin about two inches apart. Bake for twenty minutes.

692. COCOANUT BISCUITS.—Ingredients—Six oz. of cocoanut grated, 9 oz. of white sugar, 3 eggs.

Whisk the eggs for about twelve minutes, then sprinkle in the sugar gradually, lastly the cocoanut; form with your hands into little pyramids; place upon white paper, and the paper on tins. Bake in a cool oven until slightly brown.

693. BISCUIT POWDER (for babies).

Dry plain biscuits in a slow oven. Roll them with a rolling pin. Then grind in a marble mortar till reduced to powder. Keep in a tin canister.

694. RICE BISCUITS.—Ingredients—Half lb. of ground rice, 5 oz. of white sugar, 4 of butter, 2 eggs.

Well beat the butter; stir in gradually the ground rice and sugar; well whisk the eggs and add to the other ingredients. Roll out on the paste board and cut into shapes with paste cutter. Place upon greased tin and bake a quarter of an hour in a *slow* oven.

695. SODA BISCUITS.—Ingredients—Three pints of flour, 1 tablespoonful of butter and 1 tablespoonful of lard, a teaspoonful of salt and a teaspoon even full of cream of tartar, 1 teaspoonful of soda.

Sift the cream of tartar with the flour dry, rub the butter and lard very thoroughly through it; dissolve the soda in a pint of milk and mix all together. Roll out, adding as little flour as possible; cut with a biscuit cutter, and bake twenty minutes in a quick oven.

696. PLAIN AND VERY CRISP BISCUITS.—Ingredients— One lb. of flour, yolk of 1 egg, some milk.

Make into a very stiff paste; beat it well, and knead till quite smooth; roll very thin, and cut into biscuits. Bake them in a slow oven till quite dry and crisp.

697. HARD BISCUITS.—Ingredients—2 oz. of butter, skimmed milk, 1 lb. of flour.

Warm the butter in as much skimmed milk as will make a pound of flour into a very stiff paste, beat it with a rolling-pin, and work it very smooth. Roll it thin and cut it into round biscuits; prick them full of holes with a fork. About six minutes will bake them.

698. BISCUITS OF FRUIT.—Ingredients—To the pulp of any scalded fruit put an equal weight of sugar sifted.

Beat it two hours, then put it into little white paper forms, dry in a cool oven, turn the next day, and in two or three days box them. 13

PASTRY & PUDDINGS.

OBSERVATIONS.

A good hand at pastry will use less butter and produce lighter crust than others. Salt butter is very good, and if well washed makes a good flaky crust. If the weather is warm the butter should be placed in ice water to keep it as firm as possible; when lard is used take care it is perfectly sweet.

In making pastry (*See Recipes Nos. 820 to 846*), as in other arts, "practice will make perfect;" it should be touched as lightly as possible, made in a cool place, and with hands perfectly cool; if possible, use a marble slab instead of a pastry board; if the latter is used, it is better to procure it made of hardwood.

It is important to use great expedition in the preparation of pastry, and care must be taken not to allow it to stand long before baking, or it will become flat and heavy. A brisk oven will be required for puff pastry; a good plan to test the proper heat is to put a small piece of the paste in before baking the whole. Be sure that the oven is as near perfection as possible; for, "an oven in which the heat is not evenly distributed can never produce a well-baked pie or tart; where there is an unequal degree of heat the pastry rises on the hottest side in the shape of a large bubble and sinks into a heavy indigestible lump on the coolest." This is a truism which many people must have discovered for themselves, as they would be well accustomed to the sight of miniature mountains and tableland on their tarts and pies. Raised pie crust should have a good soaking heat, and glazed pastry rather a slack heat. When suet is used it must be perfectly free from skin and minced as finely as possible; beef suet is considered the best.

All moulds, pie-dishes, patty-pans, and vessels of all descriptions used for baking or boiling must be well buttered.

The outside of a boiled pudding often tastes disagreeably, which arises from the cloth not being nicely washed, and kept in a dry place. It should be dipped in boiling water, squeezed dry, and floured when to be used.

If bread, it should be tied loosely, if batter, tightly over.

The water should boil quickly when the pudding is put in; and it should be moved about for a minute, lest the ingredients should not mix.

Batter pudding should be strained through a coarse sieve when all is mixed. In others the eggs separately.

A pan of cold water should be ready, and the pudding dipped in as soon as it comes out of the pot, and then it will not adhere to the cloth.

Very good puddings may be made *without* eggs; but they must have as little milk as will mix, and must boil three or four hours. A few spoonfuls of fresh small beer, or one of yeast, will answer instead of eggs.

Snow is an excellent substitute for eggs either in puddings or pancakes. Two large spoonfuls will supply the place of one egg, and the article it is used in will be equally good. This is a useful piece of information, especially as snow often falls at the season when eggs are the dearest. Fresh small beer, or bottled malt liquors, likewise serve instead of eggs. The snow may be taken up from any clean spot before it is wanted, and will not lose its virtue, though the sooner it is used the better.

Note.—The yolks and whites beaten long and separately, make the article they are put into much lighter.

699. **ALMOND PUDDING**.—Ingredients—Three quarters lb. sweet almonds, a large spoonful of rose water, 6 eggs, 3 spoonfuls of pounded white sugar, 1 quart of milk, 3 spoonfuls of powdered crackers, 4 oz. of clarified butter, same of citron cut into pieces.

Blanch, and pound the almonds in the rose water; beat the eggs to a stiff froth with the sugar, mix the milk with the crackers, butter and citron; add almonds, etc.: stir all together, and bake in a small pudding dish with a lining and rim of pastry. This pudding is nicer eaten cold. Bake an hour and a half in a quick oven.

700. **AMBER PUDDING**.—Ingredients—One lb. of fresh butter, ½ lb. loaf sugar, 8 eggs, jam.

Line a pudding dish with good puff paste, take the yolks of

the eggs, mix with the sugar and butter on the fire till it becomes thick, but not boiling, whip the whites of the eggs to a froth, and mix with the other when cold. Put any sort of jam on the bottom of the dish, according to taste, and pour the mixture of eggs, etc., over it, and bake half an hour.

701. APPLE PUDDING (Boiled).—Ingredients—Suet or butter crust, apples, sugar to taste, a little minced lemon peel, 2 tablespoonfuls lemon juice.

Butter a pudding mould, line with the paste, pare, core and cut the apples into small pieces. Fill the basin and add the sugar, finely minced lemon peel and juice. Cover with the crust, press the edges firmly, cover with a floured cloth. Tie securely and plunge into boiling water. Allow to boil two hours. Remove from basin and send to table quickly.

702. APPLE DUMPLING (Boiled). — Ingredients — Apples, quince or orange marmalade, or sugar, some cold paste.

Peel the apples, remove the core with an apple scraper, and fill the hole with the marmalade or sugar: then take a small piece of the cold paste and place the apple in it, then take another piece of the same shape and place on the top, join the paste as neatly as possible. Tie in a cloth and boil three quarters of an hour. Pour melted butter over them and serve.

703. CURRANT DUMPLING.—Ingredients—One lb. of flour, 5 oz. of beef suet, 7 oz. of currants, 1 glass of water.

Mince the suet finely, mix with the flour and currants, which of course have been washed, picked and dried: mix with the above proportion of water or milk, divide into dumplings about the size of an orange: tie in cloths, plunge into boiling water, and boil from an hour to an hour and a quarter. Serve with butter and white sugar.

704. NORFOLK DUMPLINGS.—Ingredients—One lb. of dough, wine sauce.

Divide one pound of dough into six equal parts; mould these into dumplings, drop them into a pan of fast-boiling water, and boil quickly for about a quarter of an hour. Send to table with wine sauce, or melted butter well sweetened.

[Note—These dumplings should never be cut, but torn apart with two forks.]

705. LEMON DUMPLINGS.—Ten oz. of fine bread-crumbs, 1 large tablespoonful of flour, ½ lb. finely chopped beef suet, the grated rinds of 2 small lemons, 4 oz. of powdered sugar, 3 large eggs beaten and strained, and last of all the juice of the 2 lemons, also strained.

Mix the ingredients well, divide into four dumplings, tie them in well-floured cloths, and let them boil an hour.

706. **APPLE PUDDING** (baked.)—Ingredients.—10 apples, 4 oz. of brown sugar, 3 oz. of butter, 4 eggs, 2½ breakfast cups of bread-crumbs.

Pare and cut into quarters the apples, removing the cores. Boil them to a pulp. Well whisk the eggs and put them and the butter into the apple pulp. Stir the mixture for five minutes. Grease a pie dish and place a sprinkling of bread-crumbs, then of apple, and proceed in this manner until all are used. Bake for three quarters of an hour. N. B.—Care must be taken that the top layer is of bread-crumbs.

707. **BAKEWELL PUDDING.**—Ingredients—Puff-paste, jam, few strips of candied lemon-peel, yolks of four eggs, whites of two, ½ lb. of clarified butter, ¼ lb. of pounded sugar, 2 oz. of almonds.

Line a shallow dish with the puff paste, spread over it any kind of jam and the candied lemon-peel. Fill the dish with the rest of the ingredients, beating the yolks of the eggs, and blanching and pounding the almonds. Mix well and pour over the jam. Bake in a moderate oven.

708. **BATTER PUDDING.**—Ingredients—1½ cupful of flour, 1 teaspoonful baking powder, ½ teaspoon salt, 1 tablespoon butter, 2 eggs, 1 pint of milk.

Steam one hour, and serve with sauce. By adding a cupful of raisins, or any other desirable fruit, either fresh or dried, to the above pudding, makes a most delicious dish.

709. **BREAD PUDDING.**—Ingredients — Bread, boiling milk, allowing ½ a pint to 1 lb. of soaked bread, 2 beaten eggs, a little nutmeg, sugar.

Soak the bread in cold water, then squeeze it very dry, take out any lumps, and add the milk, beat up the eggs, sweeten to taste, add nutmeg, and bake the pudding slowly until firm. If desired, a few sultanas may be added to the pudding ; or, if the bread is light, such as the crusts of French rolls, it may be soaked in as much cold milk as it will absorb, and when it is perfectly soft have sugar, eggs, and flavoring added to it.

710. **BROWN BREAD PUDDING**.— Ingredients — ¼ lb. stale brown bread finely and lightly grated, the same of suet chopped fine, the same of sultanas ; ¼ of a saltspoon of salt, 1½oz. of sugar, ¼ of a nutmeg (grated), the grated rind of 1 lemon, 2 well-beaten eggs, ½ a glass of brandy or 1 glass of sherry.

Mix all the ingredients thoroughly, and boil in the mould for three hours. A warm jam sauce should be poured over the pudding, or round it, when sent to table.

711. CARAMEL PUDDING.—Ingredients—A handful of white sugar, ¾ pint of water, yolks of 8 eggs, 1 pint of milk.

Boil the sugar and water until of a deep brown color, warm a small basin, pour the syrup in and keep turning the basin in your hand until the inside is completely coated with the syrup, which, by that time, will have set. Take the yolks of the eggs and mix gradually and effectually with the milk. Pour this mixture into the prepared mould. Lay a piece of paper on the top. Set it in a saucepan full of cold water, taking care that the water does not come over the top of the mould, put on the cover, and let it boil gently by the side of the fire for one hour. Remove the saucepan to a cool place, and when the water is quite cold take out the mould, and turn out the pudding very carefully.

712. CARROT PUDDING.—Ingredients—½lb. of grated potatoes, ½lb. grated carrots, ½lb. flour, sugar, suet, plums and currants, spices and candied lemon peel.

Mix well together and boil for eight or nine hours. Serve with brandy or wine sauce.

713. CARROT PUDDING (2).—Ingredients — 10 oz. of bread-crumbs, 5 oz. of suet, 5 oz. of raisins, 12 oz. of carrots, 4 oz. of currants, 4 oz. of sugar, 4 eggs, a little nutmeg, milk.

Boil the carrots until tender. Mash them. Stone the raisins and well whisk the eggs. Mix all the ingredients together with enough milk to make a thick batter. This pudding can either be boiled or baked. If for baking, put in a pie dish and bake for an hour. If for boiling, put into a buttered mould, secure with a cloth and boil for three hours. Serve with white sugar sifted over.

714. MARTHA'S PUDDING.—Ingredients — ½ pint of milk, laurel leaf, a piece of cinnamon, 1 cupful of bread-crumbs, 3 eggs, nutmeg and lemon-peel, teaspoonful orange flower water.

Put the laurel leaf and cinnamon into the milk and boil, then pour over the bread-crumbs, add the eggs well beaten, the nutmeg, lemon-peel and flower water. Sweeten to taste, butter a basin, stick currants or split raisins in rows upon it. Stir all the ingredients well together and pour into the basin. Cover with a cloth and boil one hour and a half.

715. PEAS PUDDING.—Ingredients—1 quart of split peas, a piece of butter, the yolk of an egg.

Dry the peas before the fire, then tie up loosely in a cloth; plunge into warm water, boil them two hours or more, until tender, take them up, beat in a dish with a pinch of salt, yolk of an egg and butter, make it quite smooth, tie it up again in a cloth, and boil one hour longer.

716. CHOCOLATE PUDDING.—Ingredients—1 quart of milk, 14 even tablespoonfuls of grated bread-crumbs, 12 tablespoonfuls of grated chocolate, 6 eggs, 1 tablespoonful vanilla; sugar to make very sweet.

Separate the yolks and whites of four eggs; beat up the four yolks and two whole eggs together very light with the sugar. Put the milk on the range, and when it comes to a perfect boil pour it over the bread and chocolate; add the beaten eggs and sugar and vanilla; be sure it is sweet enough; pour into a buttered dish; bake one hour in a moderate oven. When cold, and just before it is served, have the four whites beaten with a little powdered sugar, and flavor with vanilla and use as a meringue.

717. CURRANT PUDDING (boiled).—Ingredients — 14 oz. of flour, 7 oz. of suet, 7 oz. of currants, a little milk.

Have the currants washed and dried, mixed with the finely minced suet and flour. Moisten the whole with sufficient milk to form a stiff batter. Place in a floured cloth and plunge into boiling water. Boil four hours and serve with butter and sugar.

718. CURRANT BUN PUDDING.—Ingredients—4 buns, jam, white of 1 egg, 2 oz. of sugar.

Line a pie dish with the buns previously soaked in milk, put between them a layer of jam and bake half an hour. Whip the white of the egg up with the sugar, and place on the top when done. These last two receipts are nursery puddings.

719. GINGERBREAD PUDDING.— Ingredients—2 oz. lard or butter, 2 tablespoonfuls brown sugar, 2 ditto golden syrup, 1 egg, 1 teacupful milk, 1 teaspoonful ground ginger, 8 oz. flour, one teaspoonful baking powder.

Work the butter and sugar together, then add the egg beaten well, the ginger, treacle and milk, and then the flour and baking powder. Steam four hours.

720. GINGER PUDDING.—Ingredients—9 oz. of flour, 5 oz. of suet, 5 oz. of sugar, 1 large tablespoonful of grated ginger.

Chop the suet finely. Add to the flour sugar and ginger; mix well. Butter a mould and put the ingredients in perfectly dry. Cover securely with a cloth and boil three hours. To be eaten with sweet sauce

721. **ORANGE PUDDING** (1).—Ingredients—Puff paste, ½ lb. of butter, 9 eggs, 1 Seville orange, ¼ lb. of white sugar, a teaspoonful of orange flower water, 2 teaspoonfuls of rose water, ¼ pint of cream, ½ glass of sherry, 1 hard biscuit.

Make some puff paste and lay it thin in a dish and round the rim ready to receive the pudding. Melt the butter, break the eggs and add them (the yolks of all, the whites of five) well beaten, to the melted butter. Shake well together, then grate the yellow part of the rind of the orange, add the sugar finely sifted ; mix all well together, add the orange-flower water and rose water, cream, and sherry ; grate into the mixture a hard biscuit ; mix all the ingredients thoroughly, pour into the dish lined with paste, and bake very carefully as long as you would a custard pudding.

722. **ORANGE PUDDING** (2).—Ingredients— The rind of 1 Seville orange, 6 oz. of fresh butter, 6 oz. of white sugar, 6 eggs, 1 apple, puff paste.

Grate the rind and mix with the butter and sugar, adding by degrees the eggs well beaten ; scrape a raw apple and mix with the rest ; line the bottom and sides of a dish with paste, pour in the orange mixture, and lay it over crossbars of paste. It will take half an hour to bake.

723. **ORANGE PUDDING** (3). — Ingredients — Two Seville oranges, 1 sweet orange, 6 eggs, ½ lb. of white sugar, ½ lb. of butter, puff paste.

Boil the oranges, changing the water four times to remove all bitterness. When they are quite tender take them out, cut them in halves, and remove the seeds and inward skins and stringy portions. Beat the rinds and juice in a stone mortar, squeeze in the juice of a sweet orange through a sieve, beat up the yolks of six eggs and whites of three, and half a pound of white sifted sugar. Mix all well together, and stir in the melted butter. Bake in a dish lined and ornamented with puff paste in not too quick an oven.

724. **SHROPSHIRE PUDDING**.—Ingredients—Half lb. of suet, ¼ lb. of bread-crumbs, 1 lemon, juice and rind, 1 nutmeg, ½ lb. of sugar, 5 eggs.

Boil three hours, and serve with brandy sauce.

725. **LEMON PUDDING** (1).—Ingredients—Two eggs, two cupfuls of sugar, 4 tablespoonfuls of corn starch, 2 lemons, butter.

Beat the yolks of the eggs light, add the sugar ; dissolve the corn starch in a little cold water, stir into it two teacupfuls of boiling water ; put in the juice of the lemons, with some of the grated peel. Mix all together with a teaspoonful of butter. Bake about fifteen minutes. When done spread over the top the beaten whites of the eggs and brown.

726 **LEMON PUDDING** (2).—Ingredients—Three quarters of lb. of bread-crumbs, 1 quart of milk, 3 oz. of butter, 1 lemon, 4 oz. of white sugar, 4 eggs, 1 tablespoonful of brandy, paste.

Place the milk in a stewpan and bring to a boil; add the butter and when melted pour over the bread-crumbs. Mince the lemon peel and with the sugar add to the other ingredients. Well whisk the eggs, adding the brandy; beat the whole for a few minutes. Line a pie dish with paste and pour the mixture in. Bake for nearly an hour.

727. **FAVORITE PUDDING.**—Ingredients—Three eggs, flavoring, grated rind and juice of a lemon, $\frac{1}{2}$ teaspoonful of grated nutmeg, 1 cup of grated bread-crumbs, 1 cup of finely chopped apples, 1 cup of English currants and $1\frac{1}{2}$ cups of sugar.

Beat the eggs very lightly, flavor; to this add the bread-crumbs and remaining ingredients. Stir thoroughly; then put in a buttered pudding dish and boil at least two and a half hours. Serve with any good sauce.

728. **MARMALADE PUDDING** (1).—Ingredients—Two oz. of lard or butter, 2 tablespoonfuls of brown sugar, 4 oz. of marmalade, 1 egg, 1 teacup of milk, 8 oz. of flour, 1 teaspoonful of baking powder.

Well mix the butter and sugar, then add the eggs well beaten, the marmalade and milk, then the flour and baking powder. Steam four hours.

729. **MARMALADE PUDDING** (2).—Ingredients—Quarter lb. of suet, $\frac{1}{4}$ lb. of grated bread-crumbs, $\frac{1}{4}$ lb. of sugar, 2 eggs, a full tablepoonful of marmalade.

Well mix the suet and bread-crumbs, then add the sugar, the eggs well beaten, and the marmalade. Shred some lemon peel, and squeeze the juice over four or five large lumps of sugar; add a glass of white wine, and a quarter of a pint of water. Let this mixture simmer for twenty minutes. Put in a buttered china mould and boil for four hours.

730. **SAUCE (for Marmalade Pudding).**—Ingredients—Some lemon peel and juice, 4 or 5 large lumps of sugar, a glass of white wine, $\frac{1}{4}$ pint of water.

731. TEACAKE PUDDING.—Ingredients—A teacake, butter, custard, milk, 2 eggs, sugar to taste.

Cut the teacake into thin slices, butter and line a pie-dish with them; make the custard, pour in and bake forty minutes.

732. COMPANY PUDDING.—Ingredients—Dried cherries or sultanas, some small sponge cakes, sherry or marsala and a tea spoonful of brandy, cold custard, vanilla flavoring.

Butter a mould thickly; stick it all over with the dried cherries or sultanas; fill the mould with the sponge cakes three parts full; soak them through with the sherry or marsala and the brandy; fill up the mould with cold custard flavored with vanilla; butter a paper to cover over the top. Tie up tightly with a floured cloth and boil one hour; turn out carefully and serve with cold custard poured over.

733. HOLIDAY PUDDING.—Ingredients—A plain sponge cake, strawberry jam, icing, a rich custard, some preserved ginger.

Make the sponge cake in a round mould, take out the inside of the cake with a cutter not too near the edge, put in a good layer of strawberry jam, not too thickly spread. Cut the inside of the cake you have taken out in slices, spread some jam between each slice (different sorts of jam may be used but strawberry does very nicely), and replace the cake. Ice it nicely over; put it into a very slow oven to try the icing. Then make the custard and pour into it small pieces of preserved ginger. Pour into the cake and serve hot.

734. SPONGE CAKE PUDDING.—Ingredients—Six or eight sponge cakes, 2 oz. of ratafias, a few sultanas, a wineglassful of sherry or cognac, or curacoa, some sweet almonds.

Take the sponge cakes and ratafias, break them into small pieces, split and stick the sultanas on the inside of a mould, and put the cake into it; pour over them a wineglassful of sherry or cognac, or curacoa. Blanch and pound the almonds; sprinkle them over the cakes. Fill up the mould with *cold* custard, steam the pudding for one hour; turn it out of the mould. Serve with some of the custard over it.

735. CABINET PUDDING.—Ingredients—1½ pts. of new milk, white sugar, 1 lemon, cinnamon, mace, cloves, 5 eggs and the yolks of 4, butter, 4 or 5 sponge cakes.

Boil the milk with enough white sugar to sweeten it, the peel of a fresh lemon cut thinly, the cinnamon, mace and cloves. Boil these ingredients as for a custard. Beat up the eggs. Pour the boiling milk, etc., on to these, stirring continually, then strain the whole through a hair sieve and leave to cool. Take a good sized pudding mould, butter it well and line with sponge cakes, cut into thin slices. Pour the custard into the mould and tie it close. It will take an hour and a half to boil. It is an improvement after buttering the mould and before placing the sponge cakes, to arrange some stoned raisins, slices of candied peel and nutmeg. Serve hot with sauce.

736. **COLLEGE PUDDING.** — Ingredients—Eight oz. breadcrumbs, 8 oz. suet, 8 oz. currants, 1 oz. citron peel, 1 oz. orange peel, a little sugar and nutmeg, 3 eggs, beaten yolks and whites separately, and a glass of brandy.

Mix well and shape them into balls, rub them over with egg, and roll them in flour. Fry a nice brown in boiling butter or lard, and drain them on blotting paper. Or they may be put into small moulds and baked in the oven. In either case serve with wine or brandy sauce.

737. **STEAMED PUDDING.**—Ingredients—1 cup of suet, chopped fine, 1 cup of molasses, 1 cup of currants—washed and dried—1 cup of sour milk, 1 teaspoonful of soda, a little salt, flour.

Mix well, using flour enough to make a stiff dough; pour into a mould and steam four hours.

738. **OXFORD DUMPLINGS.**—Ingredients—2 oz. grated bread, 4 oz. currants, 4 oz. suet chopped fine, 1 large spoonful of flour, 1 oz. pounded sugar, 3 eggs, grated lemon peel and a little spice.

Mix with the yolks of the eggs well beaten and a little milk. Divide into five dumplings half an inch thick, and fry a nice brown in plenty of lard. Serve with wine sauce and sifted sugar on them.

739, **MARROW PUDDING.**—Ingredients—1½ pints of boiling milk, ½ pt. of bread-crumbs, 4 eggs, 6 oz. of shreded marrow, 2 oz. of raisins and dried currants, grated nutmeg, and sugar to taste.

Pour the milk on the bread-crumbs, cover up and allow to soak thoroughly, then beat the eggs with the marrow and add to the bread-crumbs with the raisins and currants, grated nutmeg and sugar. Put into a buttered mould, boil two and a half hours, turn it out and serve with pounded sugar.

740. **MARROW PUDDING.**—Ingredients—2 teacupfuls of flour, 1 of suet chopped very fine, 1 egg beaten in a cup and the cup filled up with treacle, 1 teaspoonful of carbonate of soda, ½ teaspoonful of tartaric acid and a little flavoring.

Mix well together; put into a basin, but do not fill the basin, or tie it down, as the pudding will rise. Steam for two or three hours. Serve with wine sauce.

741. **FRUIT PUDDING.**—Ingredients—Crust—4 oz. of suet to 6 of flour; pinch of salt, and water enough to make a thick paste, fruit, sugar.

Make the crust of the suet, flour, salt and water; roll it out thin before putting into a buttered basin, then add the fruit mixed with the sugar except in the case of apples, which are sometimes hardened by boiling with sugar; put on a lid of paste, and boil the pudding an hour and a half. Care should be taken to roll the crust thin, in order to get as much fruit as possible into the pudding. It is a good plan to stew a little fruit, and serve it with the pudding, as it should be given to children in large proportion to the crust.

742. **LAYER PUDDING.**—Crust as for fruit pudding, jam or treacle.

Make a crust as for fruit pudding. Roll it out and line a buttered basin with it, lay at the bottom a layer of jam or treacle, then a thin layer of crust, and so on until the basin is full. Boil an hour and a half.

743. **MINCEMEAT (without meat).**—Ingredients for four different receipts—3 lb. raisins, 3 lb. currants, 3 lb. almonds, well chopped, 3 lb. apples, 2 oz. mixed spices, 1 oz. candied peel, juice of one lemon, peel of three lemons, half a wine glass of brandy, sugar to taste.

1½ lb. suet, 1½ lb. raisins, 1½ lb. currants, 1½ lb. sugar, 2 lb. apples, chopped fine, of mace, cinnamon, and salt ¼ oz. pounded together, four cloves, the grated rind of two lemons and the juice of one, 1 oz. of sweet almonds, pounded, ½ lb. of candied peel, and a wineglassful each of port, white wine, and brandy.

Two lb. raisins, stoned, 2lb. currants, 2lb. beef suet, 3lb. raw sugar, ¼ lb. candied citron, ¼ lb. candied lemon, ¼ lb. candied orange, the juice and rind of four lemons, 2 lb. apples, and a teacupful of brandy.

Currants and raisins 2lb. each, brown sugar 1¼lb., suet 1¼lb., salt ½ oz., cloves, mace, cinnamon, less than ¼ oz. each, apples 4, lemon 1, orange and lemon peel ¼ lb. each, all chopped up together, when add rather more than half a bottle of the best brandy. When well soaked, put in a jar for use.

744. **MINCEMEAT (with meat).**—Ingredients—1½ lb. lean beef, 3 lb. beef suet, 2 lb. raisins, 2 lb. currants, 2 lb. sugar, 2 lb., mixed peel, 1 nutmeg, the rind of two lemons, the juice of 1, 2 lb. of apples.

Stone the raisins and cut in halves, add the sugar, have the currants washed, dried and ready for use. Slice the peel, grate the nutmeg, mince the apples, beef suet, and lemon peel. strain the juice, and lastly add the brandy. Mix *well* and cover air tight. Will be ready for use in three weeks.

745. PLUM PUDDING.—Ingredients—2 lb. beef suet, 1½ lb. bread-crumbs, 1½ lb. of flour, 2 lb. raisins, 2 lb. currants, ½ lb. mixed peel, 1½ lb. foots sugar, 14 eggs, a little nutmeg, ginger, allspice (powdered), a large pinch of salt, ½ pint of milk.

Chop the suet as finely as possible, and any stale piece of bread can be used for grating, allowing the above quantity; mix with the suet and flour. Stone the raisins, and have the currants perfectly washed and dried, the peel cut into thin slices and added to the suet, bread and flour, mixing well for some minutes, then add the sugar and continue working with the hands for five minutes. Put the eggs into a bowl (breaking each into a cup first to ascertain that it is fresh and to remove the speck), add to them grated nutmeg, powdered ginger, and powdered allspice, according to taste, and a large pinch of salt; then stir in half a pint of milk; beat all up together, and pour it gradually into the other bowl, working the whole mixture with the hand for some time. If the mixture be too stiff add more milk, and continue to work it with a wooden spoon for at least half an hour. Scald two pudding cloths, spread each in a bowl and dredge them well with flour. Divide the composition in two equal parts, put each in its cloth and tie it up tightly. To boil the puddings place two inverted plates in saucepans filled with water, and when the water boils fast put each pudding into its saucepan. Let them boil six hours, keeping the saucepans full by adding more water as it is required, and taking care that it never ceases boiling. Then take the puddings out, and hang them up till the next day, when the cloth of each pudding should be tightened and tied afresh, and three hours' boiling as in the first instance will make them ready for table. Serve with a sprig of holly stuck on the top, and plenty of brandy poured round the pudding, and set alight outside the dining room door.

746. An EXCELLENT PLUM PUDDING.—Ingredients—One lb of bread-crumbs, 1 lb. of suet, 1¼ lb. raisins, ¾ lb. of currants, 10 oz. of mixed candied peel, 9 eggs, ½ a gill of brandy.

Wash the currants carefully, pick and dry them; then stone the raisins and halve them carefully with a knife; chop the suet until very fine; slice the candied peel thinly, and when grating the bread-crumbs be sure they are nice and fine. Mix all well together, wetting with the well beaten eggs and the brandy mixed in. Give the mixture a good stirring and empty into a mould previously well buttered. Press it down firmly. Cover with a floured pudding cloth and tie tightly. Boil for from five and a half to six hours. When done hang the pudding up until it is required. If the pudding is to be eaten hot boil two hours on Christmas day, or on the day it is wanted, and serve with brandy sauce.

747. **A TEETOTALLER'S CHRISTMAS PUDDING.**—Ingredients—Pick and stone two pounds of good Valentias; pick, wash and dry 1 lb. of currants; chop 2 lb of beef suet; have ready ½ a lb. of brown sugar, 6 oz of candied peel, cut thin, 2½ lb. of flour, 6 eggs, a quart or more of milk, an ounce of mixed spice, and a tablespoonful of salt.

Put the flour into a large pan, add the plums, currants, suet, sugar, peel, spice, and salt, and mix them well together *while dry*. Beat the eggs well up in a large basin, and add a portion of the milk, stirring it at the same time. Make a well in the middle of the flour, and pour in the milk and eggs. Keep stirring till all the ingredients are thoroughly mixed. Add more milk, if necessary, and stir up again; the batter should be rather stiff. Have a good stout cloth ready; wet and flour it well, lay it over a pan, pour in the batter, and tie it firmly up. When the water in the copper or large kettle *boils*, put the pudding in and let it boil gently for five or six hours. Turn it carefully out of the cloth. Serve with or without sauce.

748. **SWISS PUDDING.**—Ingredients—7 eggs, ½ oz. of isinglass, 1 pint of milk, sugar to taste, for the sauce ¼ of a pt. of white wine, ¼ lb of sugar, the juice and rind of a lemon (the rind pared very thin).

Take the yolks, eggs, and isinglass, beat them well, add a pint of good milk, and sugar to taste. Put this in a mould, and boil the pudding three-quarters of an hour exactly. Let it stand in the mould till cold. The sauce for this pudding is made with the above ingredients. Boil this till it becomes like a syrup. When cold, pour it round the pudding, but not till it is ready to be sent to table, then put a few strips of orange marmalade or apricot jam on the top and round the pudding.

749. **ICE PUDDING.**—Ingredients—Half lb. white sugar, a stick of vanilla, 10 eggs, 1 gill of cream, 12 lbs. of ice, 6 lbs. of fine salt, dried fruits.

Put the milk into a stewpan with white sugar and a stick of vanilla; leave it to boil ten minutes. Mix the yolks of ten eggs with the cream, pour in the milk, then put it back into the stewpan, and stir until it thickens, but do not let it boil; strain it into a basin, and leave it to cool. Take the ice, pound it small, add the salt; **mix** together quickly, cover the bottom of an ice pail (a common pail will do), place the ice pot in it, and build it around with the ice and salt. This done, pour the cream into the pot, put on the cover, and never cease turning until the cream becomes thick; move it from the sides occasionally with the ice scoop, to prevent it getting into hard lumps. The mould to be used to set the pudding should be put on ice to get quite cold. It is then filled with the cream to the level, and three or four pieces of white paper wetted with cold water are placed on it before you put on the cover, which should fit very tight. The mould is then buried in the same mixture of ice and salt used for freezing the cream in the first instance, and is left until wanted, when it is dipped in cold water, turned out on a napkin, and served. Dried fruits, cut small, may be put in the cream when the mould is being filled.

750. **ROLY POLY JAM PUDDING.**—Ingredients—Suet crust, 10 oz. of any kind of jam.

Having made a nice suet crust, roll to the thickness of about half an inch. Place the jam in the centre and spread equally over the paste, allowing a margin of about half an inch for the pudding to join. Roll up lightly, join the ends securely, place upon a floured cloth, and secure with tape, allowing a little room for the pudding to swell. Plunge into boiling water and boil two hours.

751. **RED CURRANT PUDDING.**—Ingredients—Some red currants and raspberries, sugar, slices of bread.

Stew the red currants and raspberries with sugar till thoroughly done, pour off all the juice, and put the fruit while hot into a pudding basin lined with bread made to fit exactly; fill the basin up with fruit, and cover it with a slice of bread made to fit exactly; let it stand till quite cold with a plate on it. Boil up the juice which was poured off with a little more sugar, and let that get cold. When served the pudding must be turned out on a dish and the juice poured all over it so as to color the bread thoroughly. It can be served with custard or cream.

752. **RASPBERRY PUDDING.**—One pint of bread-crumbs, 1 quart of milk, 2 cupfuls of sugar, 1 lemon, butter, a cupful of preserved raspberries, 4 eggs.

Mix the bread-crumbs, milk, 2 cupfuls of sugar, the peel of the lemon grated, the yolks of the eggs, and a small piece of butter, and bake. When done spread over the top a cupful of preserved raspberries; put over that a meringue made with the whites of the eggs, a cupful of sugar and the juice of the lemon. Return it to the oven to color; let it partly cool and serve it with rich cream.

753. SWEET POTATO PUDDING.—Ingredients—Two cups of mashed sweet potato (the potato must first be boiled), a cup of sugar, a small cup of butter, 3 eggs, ¼ teaspoonful of soda dissolved in a little hot water, a teaspoonful of lemon extract, and half teaspoonful of grated nutmeg.

Beat the eggs until they are very light, rub the butter and sugar to a cream, and mix all with the potato; cover a deep plate or shallow pudding dish with a thick crust; then put in the mixture, and bake slowly for three-quarters of an hour.

754. A GOOD BAKED PUDDING.—Ingredients—One pint of new milk, 3 spoonfuls of flour, ¼ lb. of butter, 5 eggs, salt to taste, rind of lemon, brandy and sugar.

Make the milk and flour into a hasty pudding, mix with the butter; when cold add the eggs well beaten, and the remaining ingredients. Bake three-quarters of an hour.

755. RICE AND RAISIN PUDDING.—Ingredients—Five eggs, 1 cup of rice, 1 cup of sugar, butter the size of an egg, 2 handfuls of raisins.

Simmer the rice in a quart of milk until tender; remove from the stove to cool. Well whisk the yolks of the eggs and add to the rice, also the rest of the milk, sugar, and butter. Then well beat the whites of the eggs, stone the raisins, and add to the other ingredients. Grate nutmeg on the top and bake one hour.

756. SIR WATKIN WYNN'S PUDDING. Ingredients—Four oz. ground rice, ½ lb. suet, ½ lb. bread-crumbs, 4 yolks and 2 whites of eggs, 4 tablespoonfuls of orange marmalade.

Mix well together the day before using. Put it in a well-buttered mould that will just hold a quart, taking care to beat it up well just before you mould it, and do not press it tightly. Let it boil four hours. Serve with or without wine sauce.

757. NEWCASTLE PUDDING.—Ingredients—Four oz. butter, 6 oz. rice flour, 6 oz. white sugar, 4 eggs, a pinch of carbonate of soda, 10 drops of essence of lemon.

Beat the rice flour, sugar, eggs and soda in a basin until very light and white; then beat the butter to a cream, and put it into the pudding with ten drops of essence of lemon. Beat all together for five minutes. Butter a mould, pour the pudding into it, and boil for two hours. Serve with or without wine sauce.

758. PLAIN RICE PUDDING.—Ingredients—One quarter lb. best rice, 1 pint of new milk.

Wash the rice, put it in a pie dish with a pint of new milk, and allow it to bake rather quickly for three quarters of an hour. If the pudding is required to be moist, half a pint more milk must be allowed. A good nourishing rice pudding may be made with a quarter of a pound of rice, a pint of milk, half a pint of water, and one ounce of finely-shred beef suet. Sugar and flavoring may, if desired, be stirred into the pudding before sending to the table. Children generally like rice thus cooked with sugar and lemon juice, which should be added when served to them.

759. RICE CUSTARD PUDDING.—Ingredients—Quarter lb. best rice, 1½ pints of milk, an egg or two, sugar, flavoring.

Bake the rice as in the preceding recipe; when done, add to it half a pint of milk, into which an egg or two, sugar to taste, and flavoring have been whisked. Bake very gently for three quarters of an hour.

760. RICE AND APPLE PUDDING.—Ingredients—A cupful of rice, 6 apples, a little chopped lemon peel, 2 cloves, sugar.

Boil the rice for ten minutes, drain it through a hair sieve until quite dry. Put a cloth into a pudding basin and lay the rice round it like a crust. Cut the apples into quarters, and lay them in the middle of the rice with a little chopped lemon peel, cloves and some sugar. Cover the fruit with rice, tie up tight, and boil for an hour. Serve with melted butter, sweetened and poured over it.

761. GROUND RICE PUDDING.—Ingredients—Two oz. of ground rice, 1 pint of cold milk, 6 lumps of sugar, 1 egg.

Mix the rice in half a pint of cold milk, pour on it half a pint of boiling milk, in which the sugar has been dissolved, and stir over the fire for ten minutes. Put in the pudding, the egg well beaten, and bake in a buttered tart dish for three quarters of an hour.

762. CREAM TAPIOCA PUDDING.—Ingredients—Three tablespoonfuls of tapioca, 4 eggs, 3 tablespoonfuls of sugar, 3 tablespoonfuls of prepared cocoanut, 1 quart of milk.

Soak the tapioca in water over night, put it in the milk and boil three quarters of an hour. Beat the yolks of the eggs into a cup of sugar, add the cocoanut, stir in and boil ten minutes longer; pour into a pudding dish; beat the whites of the eggs to a stiff froth, stir in three tablespoonfuls of sugar; put this over the top and sprinkle with cocoanut and brown five minutes.

763. TAPIOCA PUDDING.—Ingredients—Ten tablespoonfuls of tapioca, 1 quart of rich milk, 2 tablespoonfuls of butter, 6 tablespoonfuls of white sugar, 1 lemon.

Take the tapioca, wash it in warm water, drain and put the tapioca in a pan with the milk. Set the pan over a kettle of boiling water and stir till it thickens; then add the butter, sugar and lemon, grated (or flavor to suit the taste with good lemon or vanilla extract.)

764. FRENCH TAPIOCA.—Ingredients—Two oz. of fine tapioca, ½ pint of milk, 1 well-beaten egg, sugar and flavoring.

Take the tapioca de la couronne, and boil it in half a pint of water until it begins to melt, then add the milk by degrees, and boil until the tapioca becomes very thick; add the egg, sugar, and flavoring to taste, and bake gently for three quarters of an hour. This preparation of tapioca is superior to any other, is nourishing, and suitable for delicate children.

765. VELVET PUDDING.—Ingredients—Five eggs, 1½ cupfuls of sugar, 4 tablespoonfuls of corn starch, 3 pints of milk.

Dissolve the corn starch in a little cold milk, and add one cupful of sugar and the yolks of the eggs beaten. Boil three pints of milk and add the other ingredients while boiling; remove from the fire when it becomes quite thick; flavor with vanilla and pour into a baking dish; beat the whites of the eggs to a stiff froth, add half a cup of sugar, turn over the pudding, and place it in the oven and let brown slightly.

766. SAUCE (for Velvet Pudding.)—Ingredients—Yolks of 2 eggs, 1 cupful of sugar, 1 tablespoonful of butter, 1 cup of milk.

Well beat the yolks, sugar and butter; add to the milk (boiling), and set on the stove till it comes to boiling heat; flavor with vanilla.

767. FLORENTINE PUDDING.—Ingredients—One quart of milk, 3 tablespoonfuls of corn starch dissolved in a little cold milk, 3 eggs, ½ a teacupful of sugar, flavoring, lemon or vanilla, or according to taste, white sugar.

Put the milk in a saucepan and allow it to boil. Add to the corn starch (mixed in the milk) the yolks of the three eggs beaten, the sugar and flavoring; stir in the scalding milk, continue stirring until the mixture is of the consistency of custard. Pour into baking tin; beat the whites of the eggs in a teacup of pulverized sugar and when the pudding is cooked spread on the top; place in the oven to brown. Can be eaten with cream, but is very nice without.

768. SEMOLINA PUDDING.—Ingredients—2 oz. of semolina, 1 pint of milk, sugar, flavoring, 1 egg.

Boil the semolina in the milk, sweeten and flavor, and beat in the egg; put the pudding in a buttered tart dish; bake an hour in a slow oven.

769. SWEET MACARONI.—Ingredients—¼lb. of best macaroni, 2 quarts of water, a pinch of salt, 1 teacupful of milk, ¼ lb. of white sugar, flavoring.

Break up the macaroni into small lengths, and boil in the water (adding the salt) until perfectly tender; drain away the water, add to the macaroni, in a stew pan, the milk and sugar, and keep shaking over the fire until the milk is absorbed. Add any flavoring and serve with or without stewed fruit.

770. MACARONI PUDDING.—Ingredients—¼ lb. of macaroni, custard, 2 eggs, 1 pt. of boiling milk, sugar and flavoring to taste.

Boil the macaroni as for the above dish, when done drain away the water, and put the macaroni into a tart dish; pour over it custard, the sugar and flavoring to taste; bake very slowly for an hour.

771. CUSTARD PUDDING (baked).—Ingredients—½ pt. of milk, a little white sugar, 2 eggs, flavoring.

Boil the milk, with sufficient sugar to taste, and whip into it the eggs (the whites and yolks previously well beaten together), add flavoring to taste; put the pudding into a pie dish, and place it in another vessel half full of boiling water, put into the oven, and bake gently for about half an hour; or, if more convenient, the pie dish may be placed in a stew pan half filled with water, by the side of the fire, and allowed to cook slowly.

772. OATMEAL PUDDING.—Ingredients—2 oz. of fine Scotch oatmeal,¼ pt. of cold milk, 1 pt. of boiling milk, sugar to taste, 2 oz. of bread-crumbs, 1 oz. of shred suet, 1 or 2 beaten eggs, lemon flavoring or grated nutmeg.

Mix with the oatmeal, first the cold milk, and then add the boiling milk; sweeten, and stir over the fire for ten minutes, then add the bread-crumbs; stir until the mixture is stiff, then add the suet and eggs; add flavoring. Put the pudding in a buttered dish and bake slowly for an hour.

773. INDIAN CORN FLOUR PUDDING.—Ingredients—2 oz. of Indian corn flour, ¼ pt. of milk, ¾ pt. of boiling milk, sweetening and flavoring to taste, 1 egg.

This must not be confounded with corn flour sold in packets, which in some cases is the starch of Indian corn or maize, deprived of much of its nutritive value by the process it undergoes to render it white and smooth. Indian corn flour is the finely-ground flour of maize, and is largely used in America. Dr. Pavy says: "properly prepared, it furnishes a wholesome, digestible, and nutritious food." Like oatmeal, it requires to be thoroughly well boiled. Vanilla is the most suitable flavoring for this pudding, but any other may be used. Mix the corn flour smooth in the cold milk and then stir in the boiling milk. Sweeten and flavor. Put into a clean stew pan and stir over the fire until it becomes thick; beat in the egg, put the pudding in a buttered tart dish and bake very slowly for three-quarters of an hour.

774. SUNDAY PUDDING.—Ingredients—¼ lb. of bread-crumbs, ½ pt. of milk, sugar and flavoring to taste, 2 eggs, strawberry jam.

Boil the bread-crumbs in the milk, sweeten and flavor, and when the bread is thick stir in the yolks of the eggs. Put the pudding into a buttered tart dish, bake slowly for three quarters of an hour. Then spread over the top a layer of strawberry jam, and on this the whites of the eggs beaten with a teaspoonful of sifted sugar to a strong froth. Dip a knife in boiling water, and with it smooth over the whites, put the pudding again into a moderate oven until the top is a light golden brown. Serve immediately.

775. YORKSHIRE PUDDING (1).—Ingredients—1 egg, a pinch of salt, milk, 4 tablespoonfuls of flour.

Take the egg and salt and beat with a fork for a few minutes. Add to this three tablespoonfuls of milk and the flour; beat (with a spoon) very well, whilst in a batter, for ten minutes. Then add milk till it attains almost the consistency of cream. Take care to have the dripping hot in the pudding tin. Pour the batter into the tin to the thickness of about a quarter of an inch, then bake under the roasting joint. The above will make a pudding of moderate size, perhaps one dozen squares. The great secret of a pudding being light is to mix it two hours before cooking it.

776. YORKSHIRE PUDDING (2).—Ingredients—6 tablespoonfuls (heaped) of flour, 1½ pints of milk, 3 eggs.

Put the flour in a basin with a little salt, stir in enough milk to make it a stiff batter. When quite smooth put in the eggs, well beaten, and the rest of the milk. Beat again, put in shallow tin rubbed with beef dripping. Bake for an hour, then put under the meat half an hour to catch a little dripping. Cut in small squares to serve. The secret of lightness is to have smooth batter highly beaten, hot oven, and serving very quickly—in fact, that intelligent care in small details which gives perfect cooking.

777. **STEAK PUDDING.**—Ingredients—½ lb. of suet, 18 oz. of flour, a large teaspoonful of baking powder, pepper and salt to taste, 1¾ lbs. of steak, 6 oz. of bullock's kidney.

Chop the suet finely. Add the baking powder and salt to the flour, and then mix in the suet. Add gradually a glass of cold water (about half a pint), mixing all the time; roll into a sheet. Cut the steak into pieces and the kidney into slices, sprinkling well with pepper and salt. Grease a pudding mould and line it with the paste. Place the meat in and pour in about two wine glasses of cold water. The meat must only come level with the top. Cover with the paste, tie down in a floured cloth, plunge into boiling water and boil for two and a quarter hours.

778. **GRAHAM PUDDING.**—Ingredients—2 cups of Graham flour, 2 eggs, 1 quart of milk, butter the size of an egg, salt to taste.

Put a pint of milk into a buttered stew pan, and allow to heat slowly. Mix the rest of the milk in the flour, and beat lightly with the butter, eggs and salt. Then pour the hot milk upon it, mix well, return to the fire surrounded by *boiling* water, and stir constantly for a quarter of an hour; grate nutmeg upon it. Serve in uncovered dish, and eat with butter and sugar.

779. **COTTAGE PIE.**—Ingredients—Two lbs. of potatoes, scraps of cold meat, 1 onion, 1½ oz. of butter, pepper and salt to taste, ½ a glass of milk.

Boil and mash potatoes (or if there are any cold ones at hand, they will do as well); put the milk and butter on the fire to boil, and when boiling pour upon the mashed potatoes and mix to a paste; place the meat in a pie dish with a little fat in layers, mince the onion and sprinkle each layer with it, also pepper and salt; half fill the dish with water or gravy and cover with the potatoes, smoothing neatly and marking with a fork into a pattern; bake half an hour.

780. PORK PIE.—Ingredients—For paste, ¼ lb. of lard, ½ oz. of butter, 1 lb. of flour.

Make a paste thus: Melt the lard and butter in hot milk (not boiling); when it rises to the top of the stewpan skim it off, and mix it warm with the flour; raise the crust, when sufficiently kneaded, on a round block of wood about four inches in circumference and six inches in height. Take lean pork, cut it up in small square pieces, season with pepper and salt, fill the pie, put on a lid of paste, and decorate with paste ornaments, cut out with tin cutters.

781. EEL PIE.—Ingredients—Eels, salt, pepper, and nutmeg, puff paste, 1 onion, a few cloves, a little stock, 1 egg, butter, flour, and lemon juice.

Skin and wash some eels, remove the heads and tails; cut up the fish into pieces about three inches long, season them with salt, pepper, and nutmeg. Border a pie dish with puff paste, put in the eels with a chopped onion, and a few cloves, add a little clear stock; cover with puff paste, brush over the crust with the yolk of an egg, and bake; make a sauce with the trimmings of the eels, some white stock seasoned with salt and pepper; thicken it with a *liaison* of butter and flour, add some lemon juice, strain and pour it quite hot through a funnel into the pie.

782. EEL PIE (2).—Ingredients—eels, pepper, salt, butter, paste.

Cut the eels in length of two or three inches, after skinning them; add seasoning and place in the dish with some pieces of butter and a little water, and cover with the paste. Middle-sized eels are the best for this purpose.

783. PIGEON PIE.—Ingredients—Pigeons, pepper and salt, a piece of butter, a bunch of parsley, a beef steak, 2 hard boiled eggs, 1 cup of water, a few pieces of ham, crust.

Rub the pigeons with pepper and salt, inside and out; in the former put a piece of butter, and if approved, some parsley chopped with the livers, and a little of the seasoning; lay the steak at the bottom of the dish, and the birds on it; between every two a hard egg. Put the water in the dish; and if you have any ham in the house, lay a piece on each pigeon, it is a great improvement to the flavor. Observe when the ham is cut for gravy or pies, to take the under part rather than the prime. Season the gizzards, and the two joints of the wings, and put them in the centre of the pie; and over them in a hole made in the crust, three feet nicely cleaned to show what pie it is.

784. **RAISED BEEF STEAK PIE**.— Ingredients — Rump steak, butter, pepper and salt, lemon juice, shalots chopped finely, oysters, crust, ketchup.

Remove any skin there may be adhering to the fat of the steaks, heat them over the fire with the butter, pepper, salt, lemon juice and finely chopped shalots; when half cooked, remove from the fire and place on a dish to cool; blanch the oysters, strain off the liquor, preserving for future use, make a crust and place a layer of steaks at the bottom of the dish, and then put in some oysters, and continue to do this until all are used; cover with crust, ornament the top with a pretty device and put in the oven to bake. When done put into a cullis with the oyster liquor mixed with some nice ketchup and serve.

785. **VENISON PASTRY**.—Ingredients—A neck and breast of venison, pepper, salt, best part of a neck of mutton, glass of red wine, coarse paste, 1 lb. of butter, puff paste.

Bone the venison and season plentifully with pepper and salt; put into a saucepan with the mutton sliced and laid on them; pour in the wine, cover with a coarse paste, bake two hours, then remove the venison to a dish, pour over the gravy and add the butter; lay the puff paste round the edge of the dish. Roll out the cover, which must be a little thicker than that round the edge and lay it on, ornament to fancy. If kept in the pot it was cooked in, it will keep eight or ten days, but the crust must be kept on to keep air tight.

786. **HARE PIE**.—Ingredients—A hare, pepper, salt, nutmeg, mace, ½ lb. of butter, forcemeat, ¼ lb. scraped bacon, 2 onions, glass of red wine, bread-crumbs, winter savory, the liver of the hare, nutmeg, and yolks of 3 eggs.

Cut the hare into neat pieces, season with the pepper, salt, nutmeg and mace; put it into a jug with the butter, close up, and set in a saucepan of boiling water with the forcemeat; season highly with pepper and salt; mix well with the yolks of the eggs, raise the pie, and lay the forcemeat at the bottom of the dish; then put in the hare with the gravy that came from it; lay on the crust and bake an hour and a half.

787. **RAISED FRENCH PIE**.—Ingredients—Pie crust, some veal, a few mushrooms, a few slices of ham, a chicken cut up, a sweetbread cut into slices, pepper, salt, sweet herbs, 6 yolks of hard boiled eggs.

Raise a crust about three inches high, lay in some slices of the veal, then a few of the mushrooms, then a few slices of ham, then the chicken, a few more mushrooms and the sweetbread; add seasoning, cover in and bake for two hours in a slack oven : when done pour off the fat and add the eggs.

788. **MACARONI PIE.**—Ingredients—Quarter lb. of macaroni, ½ lb. of sausages, a small bunch of parsley, water, a gill of stock, a pinch of salt, chopped parsley. Pastry,—8 oz. of flour, 6 oz. of lard (or well clarified dripping).

Stew the macaroni till tender in a pint of water to which add the stock and salt ; open the sausages lengthwise and scrape out the meat : then put a layer of macaroni in a small pie dish, another of sausage meat and a sprinkling of pepper, salt and chopped parsley, and so on in alternate layers until all are used. Moisten with two tablespoonfuls of water ; cover with the pastry and bake half an hour.

789. **CHICKEN PIE.**—Ingredients—2 young fowls, seasoning : —white pepper, salt, a little mace, and nutmeg all of the finest powder, and cayenne. Some fresh ham cut in slices, or gammon of bacon, some forcemeat balls, and hard eggs Gravy from knuckle of veal or a piece of scrag, shank bone of mutton, herbs, onion, mace, and white pepper.

Cut up the fowls ; add the seasoning. Put the chicken, slices of ham, or gammon of bacon, forcemeat balls and hard eggs by turn in layers. If it be baked in a dish put a little water, but none if in a raised crust. By the time it returns from the oven have ready a gravy made of the veal or scrag, shank bones of mutton and seasoning. If to be eaten hot you may add truffles, morels, mushrooms, etc., but not if to be eaten cold. If it is made in a dish, put as much gravy as will fill it ; but in raised crust the gravy must be nicely strained, and then put in cold as jelly. To make the jelly clear, you may give it a boil with the whites of two eggs, after taking away the meat, and then run it through a fine lawn sieve.

790. **GIBLET PIE.**—Ingredients—Some goose or duck giblets, water, onion, black pepper, a bunch of sweet herbs, a large teacupful of cream, sliced potatoes, plain crust, salt.

Line the edge of a pie dish with a plain crust. Stew the giblets in a small quantity of water with the seasoning till nearly done. Let them grow cold and if not enough to fill the dish, lay a beef, veal or two or three mutton steaks at the bottom. Add the giblets that the liquor was boiled in. Lay slices of cold potatoes on the top and cover with the crust ; bake for an hour and a half in a brisk oven.

791. **BEEFSTEAK AND OYSTER PIE.**—Ingredients—Steak, seasoning : pepper, salt, eschalot minced finely. Oysters,

lemon peel, mace and a sprig of parsley, 1 oz. of butter rolled in flour.

Prepare your steaks by beating them gently with a circular steak-beater, add the seasoning, put layers of them and of oysters. Stew the liquor and beards of the latter, with the lemon-peel, mace, and the sprig of parsley. These ingredients are to be boiled in about three spoonfuls of water and butter rolled with flour, then strained off, and put into the dish when the pie is baked.

792. **OYSTER PIE.**—Ingredients—Oysters, sweetbreads, salt, pepper, mace, ½ a teacupful of liquor, some gravy, a teacupful of cream, white gravy.

Open the oysters, and strain the liquor from them; parboil them after taking off their beards. Parboil sweetbreads, cut them in slices, lay them and the oysters in layers, add seasoning, then put the liquor, and the gravy. Bake in a slow oven, and before you serve, add the cream, a little more oyster liquor, and a cupful of white gravy, all warm, but not boiling.

793. **VEAL PIE.**—Ingredients—3 or 4 lb. of veal, a few slices of ham or bacon, powdered mace, cayenne, nutmeg, salt, forcemeat, 3 eggs.

Cut the veal into convenient pieces, place in saucepan and cover with cold water. Allow to come slowly to a boil then remove from the stove and place in a pie dish; pour the liquor over the meat, add the ham or bacon and seasoning, boil the eggs hard and cut into rings, place neatly over the meat, have ready veal forcemeat made into balls about the size of marbles. Line the edge of the pie dish with any paste preferred and cover the whole with the same, make a hole in the centre and bake about one to one and a half hours.

794. **VEAL, CHICKEN & PARSLEY PIE.**—Ingredients—Slices of neck or leg of veal, salt, parsley, milk, crust, ½ pint of cream.

Take the slices of veal (if from the leg, about the knuckle), season them with the salt; scald some parsley picked from the stems, and press it dry; cut it a little, and lay it at the bottom of the dish; then put the meat, and so on, in layers. Fill the dish with milk, but not so high as the crust; cover it with crust, and when baked pour out a little of the milk, and put in the scalded cream. Chickens may be cut up and cooked in the same way.

795. **MUTTON PIE.**—Ingredients—Loin of mutton, 2 kidneys pepper and salt to taste, ½ pint of gravy or water, a little minced parsley, a little onion if liked.

Cut the meat into chops, remove the bone and trim them

neatly, allowing a very small piece of fat to each chop. Cut the kidneys into small pieces also and mix with the mutton; arrange neatly in pie dish, sprinkle parsley and seasoning, pepper and salt over it, then pour in the gravy and cover with puff or any paste preferred. Bake one and a half hours.

796. **LEMON PIE.**—Ingredients—Crust, 1 lemon, 1¼ cups of white sugar, 1 cup of water, a piece of butter the size of an egg, 1 tablespoonful of flour, 1 egg.

First make your crust as usual; cover your pie-tins (I use my jelly-cake tins) and bake exactly as for tart crusts. If you make more than you need, never mind, they will keep. While they are baking, if they rise in the centre, take a fork and open the crust to let the air out. Now make the filling as follows: For one pie take a nice lemon and grate off the outside, taking care to get only the yellow; the white is bitter. Squeeze out all the juice; add white sugar, water, and butter. Put in a basin on the stove. When it boils stir in the flour, and the yolk of one egg, beaten smooth with a little water. When it boils thick take off the stove and let it cool. Fill your pie crust with this. Beat the white of an egg stiff; add a heaping tablespoonful of sugar; pour over the top of the pie. Brown carefully in the oven.

797. **LEMON PIE** (2).—Ingredients—1 cup of sugar, 1 tablespoonful butter, 1 egg, 1 lemon, juice and rind, 1 teacupful of boiling water and 1 tablespoonful corn starch.

Dissolve the corn starch in a little cold water, then stir it into the boiling water; cream the butter and sugar, then pour over them the hot mixture; cool, add the lemon juice, rind and beaten egg; bake with or without upper crust.

798. **LEMON PIE** (3).—Ingredients—3 eggs, 1 large spoonful of butter, 1 small cup of sugar, juice and rind of a lemon.

Beat the butter and sugar until like cream. Beat the yolks and whites of the eggs separately, grate the lemon peel and strain the juice, add the yolks and lemon to the butter and sugar, and mix well. Then bake in two open tins of paste. Beat the whites to a stiff meringue, with three tablespoonfuls of sugar and a few drops of rose water. When the pies are done spread the meringue over and return to the oven for five minutes.

799. **PEACH PIE.**—Ingredients—Puff or short crust, peaches, sugar.

Line a dish with a nice crust, skin the peaches, remove the stones, and put the fruit into the dish, with a little sugar and water. Cover with crust and bake a golden brown.

800. RHUBARB PIE.—Ingredients—Rhubarb, a little lemon peel, sugar, water, short crust.

Take a deep pie dish, wipe with a clean damp cloth the stalks, cut into pieces about an inch in length, mince the lemon peel, line the edge of the dish with the crust, then fill the dish with rhubarb, sugar and lemon, adding a cup of water. Cover with crust, making a hole in the middle. Bake about three quarters of an hour.

801. GOOSEBERRY PIE.— Ingredients — Gooseberries, sugar, crust.

Top and tail the berries, line the edge of a deep dish with short crust. Put the berries into it with at least six ounces of moist sugar and a little water. Cover with upper crust and bake from half to three-quarters of an hour.

802. DAMSON PIE.—Ingredients—Damsons, $\frac{1}{4}$ lb. moist sugar, crust.

Line the edge of a deep dish with crust, place a small cup in the middle, fill the dish with the fruit, sprinkling the sugar over; cover with crust and bake about three-quarters of an hour. If puff paste is used, just before it is done remove from the oven and brush over with the white of an egg, beaten to a froth. Sift a little white sugar over and return to the oven till finished.

803. RED CURRANT AND RASPBERRY PIE.—Ingredients—1 quart of currants, $\frac{1}{2}$ pint of raspberries, 6 oz. of moist sugar, crust.

Pick the currants, and proceed as above.

804. BLACK CURRANT PIE.—The same manner as Damson Pie, adding a little more water.

805. COCOANUT PIE.—Ingredients—1 cup of grated cocoanut, $\frac{1}{2}$ pint of milk, 2 crackers, 3 eggs, butter, salt, rind of $\frac{1}{2}$ lemon, sugar if desired, puff crust.

Make a nice puff crust, line a dish and bake, when done, set aside to cool; soak the cocoanut in the milk, pound the crackers, well whisk the eggs, and grate the rind of the half lemon. Mix all together, adding a little salt, sugar and butter. When well mixed place in the pie-dish, and put in the oven to slightly brown.

806. PUDDING PIES.—Ingredients—1$\frac{1}{2}$ pints milk, $\frac{1}{4}$ lb. ground rice, $\frac{1}{4}$ lb. of butter, $\frac{1}{4}$ lb. of white sugar, 6 eggs, puff paste, a few currants, flavoring.

Put the lemon rind in the milk, and set on the stove to infuse; when well flavored strain, add the rice, and allow it to come to a boil slowly, and boil ten or fifteen minutes, stirring all the time. Remove from the fire and add butter and sugar; well whisk the eggs and add also. Line patty-pans with puff paste, put about a tablespoonful in each pie. Strew a few currants on each pie and bake about twenty minutes.

807. **PUMPKIN PIE.**—Ingredients—1 pint of well stewed and strained pumpkin, 1 qt. of scalding hot rich milk, 1½ cups of sugar, 4 eggs, 1 teaspoonful of salt, 1 tablespoonful of ginger and 1 of ground cinnamon.

Bake in pie plate lined with good paste; do not let mixture stand after it is put together, but bake at once.

808. **PUMPKIN PIE** (2).—Ingredients—1 qt. of stewed pumpkin pressed through a sieve, 9 eggs, whites and yolks beaten separately, 2 qts. milk, 1 teaspoonful of mace, 1 of cinnamon and 1 of nutmeg, 1½ cups of sugar.

Beat all together and bake with one crust.

809. **PUMPKIN PIE** (3).—Ingredients—A pumpkin, 1 good cupful of molasses, to a whole pumpkin allow 3 pints of rich milk, 4 eggs, some salt, a little cinnamon, brown sugar to taste, crust.

Prepare the pumpkin by cutting into small pieces. Stew rapidly until it is soft and the water is stewed out, then let it remain on the stove to simmer all day. When well cooked add the molasses, and cook all down until dry. Then sift through a cullender, it will nearly all go through if properly cooked. Then add the milk, spices and eggs. Too much spice destroys the flavor of the pumpkin. Sweeten to taste. Then bake in a crust the same as for custard. Let it cook until of a dark brown color. This is a very wholesome dish.

810. **MARLBOROUGH PIE.**—Ingredients—6 tart apples, 6 oz. of sugar, 6 oz. of butter or thick cream, 6 eggs, the grated peel of 1 lemon, and ½ the juice.

Grate the apples, after paring and coring them; stir together the butter and sugar, as for cake; then add the other ingredients, and bake in a rich under-paste only.

811. **FRENCH PANCAKES.**—Ingredients—5 eggs, nearly a pint of cream, 1 oz. of butter.

Beat the cream till it is stiff, and the yolks and whites separately, and add to the cream and beat the mixture for five minutes; butter the pan and fry quickly, sugar and roll, and place on a hot dish in the oven. Serve very hot.

812. FRENCH PANCAKES (2)—Ingredients—½ pint of milk, 2 oz. of butter, 2 oz. of loaf sugar, 2 oz. of flour, 2 eggs.

Put milk, butter and sugar into a saucepan to dissolve (not boil), beat eggs and flour together till quite smooth, then add the other ingredients and well mix. Divide this quantity and put it in four saucers to bake for twenty minutes; lay two pancakes on a dish, and spread preserve over, cover them with the other two pancakes; serve very hot.

813. RICE PANCAKES.—Ingredients—½ lb. of rice, 1 pint of cream, 8 eggs, a little salt and nutmeg, ½ lb. of butter, flour.

Boil the rice to a jelly in a small quantity of water; when cold, mix it with the cream, well whisk the eggs and add also, with a little salt and nutmeg. Then stir in the butter, just warmed, and add, slowly stirring all the time, as much flour as will make the batter thick enough. Fry in as little lard as possible.

814. IRISH PANCAKES.—Ingredients—8 eggs, 1 pint of cream, nutmeg and sugar to taste, 3 oz. of butter, ½ pint of flour.

Beat 8 yolks and four whites of eggs, strain them into the cream, put in grated nutmeg and sugar to taste; set three ounces of fresh butter on the fire, stir it, and as it warms pour it to the cream, which should be warm when the eggs are put to it; then mix smooth almost half a pint of flour. Fry the pancakes very thin; the first with a piece of butter, but not the others. Serve several on one another.

815. ENGLISH PANCAKES.—Ingredients—4 oz. flour, 2 eggs, a little more than ½ pt. of milk, a pinch of salt, 2 oz. of lard, a few drops of lemon juice, 2 oz. of sugar.

Add the salt to the flour, break the eggs into the flour with a spoonful of milk, and mix well; then add slowly the rest of the milk, mixing all the time; grease the pan with a small piece of lard, and proceed to fry them (they should be very thin); and as they are done put two or three drops of lemon juice and a sprinkling of sugar on each.

816. APPLE PIE.—Ingredients—Some nice cooking apples, sugar, some shred lemon peel, juice or a glass of cider.

Pare and core the fruit having wiped the outsides with a damp cloth. Then boil the apples in a little water with the cores until it tastes well, strain, and put a little sugar, and a piece of bruised cinnamon, and simmer again. In the meantime place the apples in a dish, a paste being put round the edge; when one layer is in, sprinkle half the sugar, and shred lemon-peel, and squeeze some juice, or a glass of cider if the apples have lost their spirit ; put in the rest of the apples, sugar, and the liquor that you have boiled. Cover with paste. You may add some butter when cut, if eaten hot ; or put quince-marmalade, orange-paste, or cloves, to flavor.

817. ANOTHER APPLE PIE.—Ingredients—Puff paste, apples, sugar (brown will do), a small quantity of finely minced lemon peel, and lemon juice.

Prepare the paste (See Recipe No. 833), spread a narrow strip round the edge of your baking dish, and put in the fruit which you have previously peeled, cored and cut into convenient slices. Sweeten according to taste and add the flavoring. Cover with a pie crust, making a small hole in the middle, and place in the oven to bake. When nearly done ice the crust with the white of an egg, beaten to a froth and spread lightly over it. Sprinkle with white sugar and replace in the oven until done.

818. ORANGE AND APPLE PIE.—Ingredients—Puff paste, oranges, apples, sugar.

Cover a tin pie-plate with puff pastry and place a layer of sliced oranges, with the pips removed, on it, and scatter sugar over them. Then put a layer of sliced apples, with sugar, and cover with slices of oranges and sugar. Put an upper crust of nice pastry over the pie, and bake it for half an hour, or until the apples are perfectly soft. Take the pie from the tin-plate while it is warm, put into a china plate and scatter sugar over the top.

819. APPLE TART.—Ingredients—Puff paste, apple marmalade, 1 egg.

Lay a disc of puff paste on a round tin, spread a layer (about three-eighths of an inch thick) of apple marmalade over it, leaving a rim an inch wide clear all round ; roll out, and cut some of the paste in strips the size of a straw ; form a trellis work with them over the marmalade, then put a border of paste all round over the rim. Glaze the top of the border and trellis with beaten-up egg, and bake in quick oven.

820. RICE PASTE FOR TARTLETS.—Ingredients—7 oz. of rice, 1 tablespoonful of butter, 2 eggs.

Simmer the rice until tender, drain, place in a marble mortar with the butter and well whisked eggs ; beat thoroughly, and with the hands make into paste.

821. TO ICE OR GLAZE PASTRY.—Ingredients—The whites 3 eggs, 4 oz. sugar.

Place the whites upon a plate (beaten with a knife to a stiff froth), just before the pastry is done remove from the oven ;

brush with the beaten egg and sprinkle the white sugar upon it Return to the oven to set.

822. GLAZE.—Ingredients—The yolks of 3 eggs, a small piece of warm butter, white sugar.

Beat the yolks and butter together, and with a pastry brush brush the pastry just before it is finished baking, sift white sugar upon it and return to the oven to dry.

823. LIGHT PASTE FOR TARTS.—Ingredients—1 egg, ¼ lb. of flour, ½ lb. butter.

Beat the white of an egg to a strong froth, then mix it with as much water as will make the flour into a very stiff paste ; roll it very thin, then lay the third part of half a pound of butter upon it in little pieces ; dredge with some flour left out at first and roll up tight. Roll it out again and put the same proportion of butter, and so proceed till all be worked up.

824. GENOISE PASTRY (1).—Ingredients—¼ lb. of the freshest butter, 4 oz. of white sugar, 4 eggs, ¼ lb. of fine flour.

Take the butter, put it in a bowl, and warm it until it can be beaten with a spoon ; add to it the sugar, and beat the two together until a smooth white cream is obtained, then add one egg, and keep on beating the mixture till it is smooth again, then add three more eggs in the same manner. The speck of the eggs should be removed. Lastly, incorporate quickly with the mixture the flour, and as soon as it is smooth pour it out to the thickness of half an inch on a buttered flat tin, and put it into the oven at once. When done (in about ten to fifteen minutes) turn out the slab of Genoise, and put it to cool, under side uppermost, on a sieve. There is a great knack in beating this paste to prevent its curdling. Should this happen, it can generally be remedied by beating as quickly as possible until the mixture is smooth again.

825. GENOISE PASTRY (2).—Ingredients—¼ lb. of fresh butter, ¼ lb. of fine flour, 4 oz. of white sugar, 6 eggs, ½ a wine glass of brandy.

Beat the butter (warmed) with the flour, add the sugar and brandy. Then beat in one by one the eggs, and bake as above.

826. CHOCOLATE GENOISE.—Ingredients—Icing, ½ lb. white sugar, 2 oz of grated chocolate, and about a gill of water. Genoise pastry as above, apricot jam.

Prepare the icing as follows :—Put the sugar in a sugar boiler and add the chocolate and water ; stir over the fire until the mixture assumes the consistency of a smooth thick cream.

Take a slab of Genoise, spread on the top of it the thinnest possible coating of apricot jam, then a coating of the icing. Put it into a very hot oven for rather less than a minute, take it out, and place it in a cold place to get cool; then cut it up with a sharp knife in lozenges or any other shape, and serve piled up on a napkin.

827. **ALMOND GENOISE**.—Ingredients—2 oz. of blanched almonds, a little orange flower water, 2 oz. of fresh butter (warmed), 4 oz. of white sugar, yolks of 4, and whites of 2 eggs, 4 oz. of fine flour, essence of vanilla, apricot jam Icing: whites of 2 eggs, lemon juice, a little *glace* sugar.

Beat in a mortar the almonds, moistening with the orange flower water to prevent oiling. Beat in a bowl the butter and sugar, add the almonds and the yolks and whites of the eggs, one at a time, then very gradually add the flour. Continue beating until the mixture is perfectly smooth, then flavor it with some essence of vanilla, and bake as above. Spread the Genoise with apricot jam as above, and, instead of chocolate, use icing made as follows:—Put the whites of the eggs into a basin with a little of the lemon juice and some of the sugar. Work the mixture well with a wooden spoon, and, as it gets thin, add more sugar, until a smooth paste of the consistency of butter is obtained. Lay this icing on the slab of Genoise with a palette knife, put it in the oven for a minute to set the icing, and take it out at once in a cool place, then cut up the slab as above.

828. **ALMOND PASTRY**.—Ingredients—¼ lb. of flour, ¼ pt. of milk, a piece of butter the size of an egg, juice of 1 lemon, white sugar to taste, a handful of sweet almonds, yolks of 4 eggs, whites of three eggs.

Make a batter with the flour, milk, lemon juice and sugar. Mix in (off the fire) the sweet almonds, chopped up, and the yolks. Let the whole get cold, then work into it the whites, whisked to a froth, and spread out the batter on a baking sheet. Sift plenty of powdered sugar over, bake ten minutes in a slow oven, and cut it out in strips; serve hot or cold.

829. **ALMOND PASTRY** (2).—Ingredients—3 oz. of almonds, ¼ lb. butter, 2 oz. of loaf sugar, a little rose water.

Pound the almonds, butter, and loaf sugar with a little rose water till it becomes a thick paste. Spread it on a buttered tin, bake in a slow oven. When cold divide it into eight pieces, put a spoonful of preserve on each piece, and cover with whipped cream.

830. **PYRAMID PASTE.**—Ingredients—A sheet of puff paste, raspberry or apricot jam, or currant jelly, dried greengages, cherries or barberries.

Roll out the puff paste to half an inch thick; cut or stamp it into oval shapes; the first, the size of the bottom of the dish in which you serve it, the next smaller, and so on till it forms a pyramid; then lay each piece separately on paper in a baking plate, egg the tops of the pieces, and bake them of a light color. When done, take them off the paper, lay them on a large dish till cold, set the largest piece in the dish, put on it either of the above preserves, lay the next size on that, and more sweetmeats, and proceed in the same way with the other pieces till they are all placed on each other. Put dried green gages, barberries, or cherries round, and serve. Instead of stamping the pieces, they may be cut with a sharp knife; small pieces may be cut out round the edges to appear like spires, which will cause the paste to appear still lighter.

831. **PASTE FOR MINCE PIES.**—Ingredients—2 lbs. of the finest pastry flour, 2 lbs. of fresh butter, the yolks of 4 fresh eggs, 2 pinches of salt, the juice of half a lemon, tepid water.

Work the butter in a napkin till it is well freed from water. Place the flour on the pastry slab in a heap, make a hole in the middle of it, put in it the yolks of the eggs, freed from the speck, salt, the juice of half a lemon, and the fourth part of the butter cut up in very small pieces; work the paste as quickly as possible with the fingers of one hand, adding as much moderately tepid water as will make the paste smooth, and of the same consistence as the remaining one and a half pounds of butter. Beat the latter out into a flat square piece an inch in thickness; roll out the paste to four times the size of the piece of butter, lay this in the centre of the paste, which you fold over on each side, and roll out again to three times its original size, then fold over two sides only of the piece of paste, and roll it out again as before. Repeat this operation twice, cover the paste with a woollen cloth, and let it rest for half an hour. The operation of rolling out and folding up the paste is called "giving a turn." After the paste has rested, two more turns are to be given to it, and it will be ready.

832. **PASTRY FOR SWEET SANDWICHES.**—Ingredients—7 tablespoonfuls of flour, 7 tablespoonfuls of butter, 6 tablespoonfuls of sugar, 7 eggs.

Place the butter in a stewpan on the stove to melt; sift the flour, add the sugar to the eggs (having removed them from the shell), place the basin containing the eggs and sugar in a sauce pan of boiling water and whip the contents a quarter of an hour; then remove from the fire; now add the butter and sift in the flour, lightly stirring all the time. Bake in tins lined with buttered paper, put into a quick oven and test with broom straw.

N. B.—When the butter is on the stove take care it does not burn, only allow it to melt.

833. **PUFF PASTE.**—Ingredients—One lb. of flour, 1 lb. of butter, 1 egg, cold water.

Mix the flour with a lump of butter the size of an egg, and the egg to a very stiff paste with cold water; divide the butter into six equal parts, roll the paste and spread on one part of the butter, dredging it with flour; repeat until all the butter is rolled in.

834. **SHORT CRUST.**—Ingredients—Half lb. of flour, 3 oz. of butter, 2 oz. of white sugar, a pinch of salt, yolks of 3 eggs.

Rub into the flour the butter and the powdered loaf sugar; beat up the yolks of the eggs, the salt, and enough milk or water to make the flour into a paste; work the paste lightly, and roll it out thin. If not wanted sweet, the sugar can be left out.

835. **AN EXCELLENT SHORT CRUST.**—Ingredients—Two of white sugar, 1 lb. of flour, 3 oz. of butter, cream, yolks of two eggs.

Dry the sugar, pounding and sifting it, then mix it with the flour well-dried; rub into it the butter so finely as not to be seen. Into some cream put the eggs well beaten and mix all to a smooth paste; roll thin and bake in a moderate oven.

836. **FLEAD CRUST.**—Ingredients—1¼ lbs. of flour, 10 oz. of flead, salt to taste, a glass of water.

Remove skin, and cut into thin flakes and rub into the flour; add a sprinkling of salt and work the whole into a paste with the water; fold the paste over three times, beat it well with a rolling pin, roll out, and it is ready for use. This will be found extremely light if well prepared.

837. **DRIPPING CRUST FOR KITCHEN USE.**—Ingredients—1 lb. of flour, 5 oz. of clarified beef dripping, a glass of water.

Work the flour into a paste, with the water; roll into a sheet and spread upon it two ounces of the dripping; repeat this twice, be sure to use good beef dripping. If wanted for a short crust, half a teacupful of moist sugar may be added.

838. **SUET CRUST FOR MEAT PUDDINGS**—Ingredients—
Eight oz. of flour, 5 oz. of beef suet, a little salt.

Remove all skin from the suet, chop finely, and mix with the flour, adding a little salt, mix well, and add by degrees a little cold water and make into a paste; flour the paste board and place the paste upon it, roll out to the thickness of a quarter of an inch. It is then ready for use.

839. **POTATO PASTE.**—Ingredients—Potatoes, butter, an egg.

Pound boiled potatoes very fine, and add, while warm, a sufficiency of butter to make the mash hold together, or you may mix it with an egg; then before it gets cold, flour the board pretty well to prevent it from sticking, and roll it to the thickness wanted. If it has become quite cold before it be put on the dish, it will be apt to crack.

840. **FLAKY CRUST FOR PIES OR TARTS.**—Ingredeints—
One lb. of flour, ½ lb of butter, 1½ teaspoonfuls baking powder, 2 eggs, ¼ pint of water.

Mix the baking powder with the flour, whip the whites of the eggs to a stiff froth, then add to the flour and mix into a stiff paste with quarter of a pint of water; flour the paste board, and roll out the paste to a thin sheet, divide the butter into three, take one part and spread over the paste, sprinkle a little flour over and fold into three, roll again and spread second portion of butter, fold as before and add the rest of the butter, fold again and roll the thickness required; bake in quick oven.

841. **BUTTER CRUST FOR BOILED PUDDINGS.**—Ingredients—Half lb. of flour, 3 oz. of butter, a gill of water.

Make the flour into a paste with the water, roll thin and place the butter upon it cut in small pieces, sprinkle a little flour over and fold the paste, roll again into a sheet the thickness required.

842. **BAKED SUET CRUST.**—Ingredients—Equal proportions of sifted flour and beef suet, sprinkling of salt.

Shred beef suet very thin; take equal proportions of sifted flour, roll a little suet with a little flour; put it aside as you do it, and continue the process until all the suet and flour are rolled together into flakes; gather them into a heap on the board, sprinkle them with water, using as little as possible, to make the mass into paste; when it is worked into a smooth smooth paste, beat it a little with the rolling pin, and roll out as thin as possible; fold it over to the required thickness, and put it on the pie; bake rather quickly. This crust should be eaten before quite cold, and, if properly made, will be a very good and light puff paste.

843. **ORANGE FRITTERS** (1).—Ingredients—A few oranges, 1 wineglassful of brandy, 1 spoonful of sugar for batter, 2 oz. of melted butter, ¾ lb. of flour, yolks of 2 eggs, ½ pint of tepid water, whites of 3 eggs.

Cut some oranges in halves, use a sharp knife to remove the peel, pith and pips. Stand the bits of orange in a basin with the brandy and sugar for one hour. When ready to fry them drain them first on a sieve, then dip them separately in a batter made thus: Add melted butter to the flour, and two yolks of eggs. Mix these ingredients together with a wooden spoon, working in at intervals half a pint of tepid water: it must be worked up with the spoon until it looks creamy, and just before you use it add lightly the whites of eggs, whisked previously to a fine froth.

844. **ORANGE FRITTERS** (2).—Ingredients—5 tablespoonfuls of water, 2 of fine flour, 1 of melted butter or salad oil, 1 egg, salt, sugar.

Mix the water, flour, melted butter, or salad oil, the yolk of the egg, and a very little salt. When ready to be used, mix the white of one egg whisked to a froth lightly with the batter. Divide two oranges as in the preceding recipe, sprinkle sugar over them; let them remain an hour, then dip each piece separately in the batter. Get some frying fat ready at the right heat, and put in your fritters; a few minutes will cook them enough. Remove them from the pan with a wire spoon, drain them on paper, and sift sugar over them; serve very hot.

845. **SPANISH FRITTERS.**—Ingredients—Crumbs of a French roll, cream, nutmeg, sugar, pounded cinnamon, 1 egg, butter, wine, and sugar sauce.

Cut the crumb of the French roll into lengths about three quarters of an inch thick, in any shape you please. Soak in the cream, nutmeg, sugar, pounded cinnamon and egg. Fry a nice brown and serve with the wine, butter, and sugar sauce.

846. **CREAM FRITTERS.**—Ingredients—3 tablespoonfuls of potato flour, 1 pint of new milk, 2 whole eggs, yolks of 4 eggs, a pat of very fresh butter, powdered white sugar to taste, a few drops of essence of almonds, bread crumbs.

Make a smooth paste with the flour, and a part of the milk; then gradually add the remainder of the milk, the eggs, and yolks, the butter, white sugar to taste, and essence of almonds. Put the mixture into a saucepan on the fire, stirring all the while till it is quite thick. Spread out on a slab until of thickness of half an inch. When quite cold cut into lozenges; egg and bread crumb them, or dip in the butter; fry a nice color in lard and serve sprinkled with white sugar.

847. **RICE FRITTERS.**—Ingredients—3 tablespoonfuls of rice, 4 well beaten eggs, ¼ lb. of currants, grated lemon peel, nutmeg and sugar to taste, flour.

Boil the rice until it has fully swelled, then drain quite dry, and mix with the eggs, the currants, grated lemon peel, and nutmeg and sugar to taste. Stir in as much flour as will thicken it, and fry in hot lard.

848. **APPLE FRITTERS.**—Ingredients—Some large apples, ½ pt. of ale, 2 eggs, flour, nutmeg and sugar to taste.

Pare, core, and slice the apples into round pieces. Beat into the ale and eggs sufficient flour to form a thick batter. Add nutmeg and sugar to taste. Dip the slices of apple into the batter, fry crisp, and serve with sugar grated over and wine sauce in a wine boat.

849. **PLAIN FRITTERS.**—Ingredients—Crumbs of bread, 1 pt. of milk, yolks of 5 eggs, 3 oz. of sifted white sugar, and grated nutmeg, melted butter, wine and sugar.

Grate the breadcrumbs and add the hot milk, mix smooth and when cold add the yolks, sugar and nutmeg. Fry them and when done serve, with melted butter, wine and sugar poured round.

850. **CUSTARD FRITTERS.**—Ingredients—Yolks of 8 eggs, 1 spoonful of flour, ½ a nutmeg, salt, a wine glass of brandy, 1 pt. of cream, sugar to taste. Batter:—½ pt. of cream, ¼ pt. of milk, 4 eggs, a little flour, and a little grated ginger.

Beat the yolks with the flour, nutmeg, salt, and brandy, put in the cream, sweeten to taste and bake on a small dish. When cold cut into slices and dip into a batter made in the above proportions. Fry them and when done sprinkle with white sugar.

851. **CHEESE FRITTERS.**—Ingredients—About a pint of water, a piece of butter the size of an egg, the least piece of cayenne, plenty of black pepper, ¼ lb. of ground Parmesan cheese, yolks of two or three eggs, and whites of two beaten to a froth, salt, flour.

Put the water into a saucepan with the butter, cayenne, and black pepper. When the water boils throw gradually into it sufficient flour to form a thick paste; then take it off the fire and work into it the Parmesan cheese, and then the yolks and whites of the eggs. Let the paste rest for a couple of hours, and proceed to fry by dropping pieces of it the size of a walnut into plenty of hot lard. Serve sprinkled with very fine salt.

852. **STRAWBERRY FRITTERS.**—Ingredients—1 spoonful of sweet oil, one of white wine, some rasped lemon peel, whites of 2 or 3 eggs, some large strawberries, white sugar.

Make a batter with the oil, white wine, rasped lemon peel, and the whites of the eggs. Make the batter thick enough to drop from the spoon. Mix the strawberries with it, and drop them with a spoon into the hot fritters. When of a good color, take them out and drain them on a sieve. As soon as done sprinkle with sugar.

853. **RASPBERRY FRITTERS.**—Ingredients — Crumbs of a French roll, 1 pt. of boiling cream, yolks of 4 eggs, well beaten, raspberry juice, some blanched sliced almonds.

Grate the crumb of the French roll, and mix with the cream. When cold add the yolks of the eggs. Mix altogether with the raspberry juice; drop them into a pan of boiling lard in very small quantities. When done stick over with the almonds.

854. **ALMOND PUFFS.**—Ingredients—2 oz. of sweet almond, a little orange flower water, whites of three eggs, some sifted sugar.

Blanch and beat the almonds, moistening with a little orange-flower water; whisk the whites of the eggs to a froth, strew in sifted sugar; mix the almonds with the sugar and eggs, and continue adding the sugar till the mixture is as thick as paste. Lay it in cakes and bake on paper in a cool oven.

855. **PUFFS FOR DESSERT.**—Ingredients—1 pt. of milk and cream, the white of 4 eggs beaten to a stiff froth, 1 heaping cup of sifted flour, 1 scant cup of powdered sugar; add a little grated lemon peel and a little salt.

Beat these all together till very light, bake in gem pans, sift pulverized sugar over them and eat with sauce flavored with lemon.

856. **PLAIN PUFFS.**—Ingredients—Yolks of 6 eggs, 1 pint of sweet milk, a large pinch of salt, whites of 6 eggs, flour.

Beat the yolks of the eggs till very light, stir in the milk, salt and the whites beaten to a stiff froth, and flour enough to make a batter about as thick as a boiled custard. Bake in small tins in a quick oven.

857. **SPANISH PUFFS.**—Ingredients—A teacupful of water, a tablespoonful of white sugar, a pinch of salt, 2 oz. of butter, flour, yolks of 4 eggs.

Put the water into a saucepan, the sugar, salt and butter; while it is boiling add sufficient flour for it to leave the saucepan; stir in one by one the yolks of the four eggs; drop a teaspoonful at a time into boiling lard; fry them a light brown.

858. **CREAM PUFFS**.—Ingredients—1 pt. of water, ½ lb. of butter, ¾ lb. of sifted flour, 10 eggs, 1 small teaspoon of soda, mock cream, 1 cup of sugar, 4 eggs, 1 cup of flour, 1 qt. of milk, flavoring.

Boil the water, rub the flour with the butter; stir into the water while boiling. When it thickens like starch remove from the fire. When cool stir into it the well-beaten eggs and the soda. Drop the mixture on to the buttered tins with a large spoon. Bake until a light brown, in a quick oven. When done, open one side and fill with mock cream made as follows in the above proportions: beat eggs to a froth; stir in the sugar, then flour; stir them into the milk while boiling; stir till it thickens; then remove from the fire and flavor with lemon or vanilla. It should not be put into the puffs until cold.

859. **ORANGE PUFFS.**—Ingredients—Rind and juice of 4 oranges, 2 lbs. of sifted sugar, butter.

Grate the rind of the oranges, add the sugar, pound together and make into a stiff paste with the butter and juice of the fruit; roll it, cut into shapes and bake in a cool oven. Serve piled up on a dish with sifted sugar over.

860. **GRAHAM PUFFS.**—Ingredients—To one quart of Graham flour add ½ pt. fine white flour, and enough milk or water, a little warm, to make a thick batter; no salt or baking powder.

Have your oven hotter than for biscuit, and your gem pans standing in the oven till you get ready. Beat batter thoroughly, grease your pans, and drop in while the irons are smoking hot. Bake quickly a nice brown.

861. **LEMON PUFFS.**—Ingredients—One lb. of double refined sugar, juice and rinds of 2 lemons, white of 1 egg, 3 whole eggs.

Bruise the sugar, and sift through a fine sieve, put it into a bowl with the juice of the lemons and mix well together. Beat the white of egg to a very stiff froth, put it into your bowl, add the remaining eggs, with the rinds of the lemons grated. Mix well up and throw sugar on your papers, drop on the puffs in small drops and in a moderately heated oven.

862. **CHOCOLATE PUFFS.**—Ingredients—½ a lb. of double refined sugar, 1 oz. of chocolate, white of an egg.

Beat and sift the sugar, scrape into it, very finely, the chocolate and mix well together. Beat the white of the egg to a stiff froth and strew in the chocolate and sugar, beat till as stiff as paste. Then sugar the paper, drop them in very small quantities and bake in a slow oven.

863. **LEMON CHEESECAKES.**—Ingredients—Boil the peel of 2 large lemons, pound well in a mortar, with a ¼ of a lb. of loaf sugar, the yolks of 6 eggs, ½ a lb. of fresh butter, and some curd beaten fine.

Mix all together, lay a puff paste on the pattypans, fill them half full, and bake them. Orange cheesecakes are done the same way; but the peel must be boiled in two or three waters, to take off its bitter taste before it is put in.

864. **CURD CHEESECAKES.**—Ingredients—2 qts. of milk, ½ lb. of butter, salt, sugar, 3 rolled biscuits, a little spice and cloves. 8 eggs (using only 4 whites), 2 spoonfuls of wine and orange flower water, ½ lb. of currants.

Turn the milk; then dry the curd by pouring it through a sieve; put it in a pan and rub in the butter, add the salt, sugar, biscuits, spice, cloves and eggs, well beaten up in the wine and orange flower water; wash all well together through a coarse sieve, adding the currants.

865. **MAIDS OF HONOR.**—Ingredients—Puff paste, 1 lb. of sugar (white), yolks of 12 eggs, 1 oz. of sweet blanched almonds, and 12 bitter almonds, 4 tablespoonfuls of orange flower water.

Line small tartlet tins with puff paste and fill with this mixture; beat the sugar with the yolks in a mortar, adding the almonds and orange flower water just before filling the tarts. Bake in a moderately heated oven.

866. **PETITS CHOUX A LA CREME.**—Ingredients—About 1 pt. of water, a little salt, a piece of butter the size of an egg, same of sugar, plenty of grated lemon peel, flour enough to make a thick paste, 3 or 4 eggs, white sugar, jam, jelly or French custard *creme a choux*.

Put the water into a saucepan with the salt, butter, sugar and lemon peel. When the water boils throw gradually into it the flour; then remove from the fire, let it remain ten minutes, and work in the eggs. Butter a baking sheet and lay the paste upon it in neat little heaps, about one teaspoonful to each. Bake a nice color in a moderate oven, take them out, sprinkle some sugar over them, and put them in again for a few minutes. Make an incision in the under side of each, and insert a small piece of jam or jelly, or some French custard *creme a choux*.

867. **ALMOND TARTS.**—Ingredients.—Sweet almonds, white wine, sugar (1 lb. of sugar to 1 lb. of almonds), grated bread, nutmeg, cream, and the juice of some spinach.

Blanch and beat fine the almonds with the other ingredients. Bake in a gentle oven, and when done thicken with candied orange or citron.

868. **GREENGAGE TART.**— Ingredients — Some greengages, sugar, ½ a glass of water, short paste, 2 whites and 3 yolks of eggs, 1 oz. of butter, 1 oz. of sugar, a pinch of salt, flour, rice.

Stone the fruit and stew them for an hour, with plenty of sugar and the water. Make a short paste with one of the whites and the three yolks of the eggs, the butter, sugar, salt, water and flour *quant. suff.* Roll it out to the thickness of a penny piece, line a *tourte* mould with it uniting the joints with white of egg, fill it with rice and bake it. When done remove the rice, put in the stewed fruit, and serve.

869. **RASPBERRY AND CURRANT TARTLETS.**—Ingredients—Short paste, white of 1 and yolks of 3 eggs, 1 oz. of sugar, 1 oz. of butter, a pinch of salt, and flour *quant. suff.*, uncooked rice, raspberries and currants, syrup, sugar, brandy or sherry.

Make the short paste in the above proportions; work it lightly, roll out to the thickness of a quarter of an inch. Line some patty pans with it, fill them with uncooked rice to keep their shape, and bake them in a moderate oven till done. Remove the stalks from the raspberries and currants, add some syrup made with the sugar, and a little brandy or sherry, empty the tartlets of the rice, fill each with the fruit, put them into the oven to get hot, and serve. They may also be served cold.

870. **CHERRY TART.**—Ingredients—Short paste as above; 1½ lbs. of stewing cherries, sugar, a little sherry, a few drops of cochineal, rice.

Work the paste lightly, roll it out to the thickness of a quarter of an inch; line a flat mould with the paste, uniting the joints carefully with the white of egg, fill the mould with rice and bake it. Stone the cherries and cook them with the sugar, sherry, and cochineal to give them a nice color. Remove the rice and put in the stewed cherries. Serve hot or cold.

871. **APPLE TARTLETS.**—Ingredients—A few large apples, the juice and rind of a lemon, 1 lb. of sugar, 1 qt. of water, 2 cloves. For paste 2 oz. of sugar, 2 oz. of butter, the yolks of 4 eggs, a little water, a pinch of salt, a little flour and rice.

Peel, core, and halve some large apples, trimming them so as to get them all of one size; drop them as they are done into cold water with the juice of a lemon squeezed into it, to prevent their turning brown. Have ready a syrup (made with 1 lb. of sugar and 1 qt. of water) boiling hot, put the apples into this, with the thin rind of a lemon and two or three cloves. As soon as they are cooked (great care must be taken that they do not break), take them out and leave them to get cold, then set the syrup on the fire to reduce. Make some short paste with the above ingredients, work it lightly and roll it out to the thickness of one-eighth of an inch. Line some patty pans with it, fill them with uncooked rice to keep their shape; bake them in a moderate oven till done. Remove the rice, and place on each tartlet half an apple, the concave side uppermost, pour a little of the reduced syrup on each tartlet, and lastly, put a piece of guava or currant jelly in the cavity of each apple.

872. **APPLE TART** (1).—Ingredients—Puff paste, apple-marmalade, apples, sugar.

Lay a disc of puff paste on a round tin, and place a strip of paste all round it as for an ordinary jam tart. Spread on the inside a layer of apple marmalade a quarter of an inch thick. Peel and core the apples, cut them in slices a quarter of an inch thick, trim all the slices to the same shape, dispose all these over the marmalade, overlapping each other, and in some kind of pattern; strew plenty of sugar over, and bake in a quick oven till the apples are a good color.

873. **APPLE TART** (2).—Ingredients—Short paste, 6 apples, thin rind and juice of a lemon, white sugar, 4 or 5 eggs.

Line a *flan* mould (a flat tin with an upright edge one inch to one and a half inches high) with a thin crust of short paste. Stew the peeled, cored, and quartered apples with a little water, the thin rind of the lemon, and white sugar *quant. suff*; when quite tender, beat them up with a fork; add the juice and grated rind of the lemon, and work in one by one the yolks of the eggs, pour this mixture in the mould, and bake in a quick oven about half an hour.

874. **APPLE TART** (3).—Ingredients—Some uncooked rice, apple marmalade, apricot jam, icing, glacé sugar, white of eggs.

Line a *flan* mould as above, fill it with the rice, and bake it;

when done remove the rice and garnish it with a layer of apple marmalade. Spread over it a thin layer of apricot jam, and over that a thick layer of icing, made with the glacé sugar and whites of egg beaten up. Put the tit. in a very slack oven, just long enough to set the icing without coloring it, and serve cold. It may be ornamented with blanched pistachio nuts, strips of angelica, and candied cherries laid on the icing, before putting the tart in the oven. N.B.—To make icing, as much sugar should be beaten up with the white of egg as it will absorb until the mixture is of the consistency of the thickest double cream; whereas to make meringue, not more than half an ounce of sugar should be used for each white of egg.

875. **APPLE PUFFETS.**—Two eggs, 1 pint of milk, sufficient flour to thicken, as waffle batter, 1½ teaspoonfuls of baking powder.

Fill a teacup alternately with a layer of butter and then of apples chopped fine; steam one hour. Serve hot, with flavored cream and sugar.

876. **APPLE TURNOVERS.**—Ingredients—One lb. of flour, 5 oz. of dripping or butter, small teaspoonful of baking powder, 4 apples (allowing 1 for each turnover), 4 teaspoonfuls of brown sugar.

Pare, core and slice the apples. Mix the baking powder into the flour, then add the dripping or butter mixing well together. Moisten with cold water and stir to a paste. Roll out, cut into circles about seven inches in diameter. Put the apple on one of the rounds and sprinkle with sugar. Moisten the edges of the paste and shape in the form of a turnover.

SWEET DISHES.

877. **LEMON SYLLABUB.**—Ingredients—To 1 pint of cream allow 1 lb. of double refined sugar, juice of 7 and the rind of 2 lemons, 1 pt. of white wine, ½ pt. of sack.

Add to the cream and sugar the juice of the lemons. Grate the rinds of the two lemons into the wine and sack. Then put all these ingredients into a saucepan and beat for thirty minutes; then pour into glasses the evening before you serve. It would be better for standing a day or two.

878. **WHIPPED SYLLABUB** (1).—Ingredients—½ pt. cream, 1 gill of sherry, ½ gill of brandy, 3 oz. of white sugar, ½ a small nutmeg, the juice of ½ a lemon, whipped cream.

Mix all the ingredients (excepting the cream); put the syllabub into glasses, and heap on the top of them a small quantity of the whipped cream.

879. **WHIPPED SYLLABUB** (2).—Ingredients—3 pints of thick cream, 1 pt white wine, the juice of 2 Seville oranges, the yellow rind of 3 lemons, 1 lb. double refined sugar, 1 spoonful orange flower water.

Grate the rind of the lemons, mix all the ingredients, whisk half an hour, and take off the froth; lay it on a sieve to drain then fill the glasses; they will keep more than a week, but should always be made the day before they are used. The best way to whip a syllabub is to keep a large chocolate mill on purpose, and a large deep bowl to mill it in, as it will do quicker, and froth stronger. With the thin part left at the bottom, mix strong calf's foot jelly, and sweeten it to taste; give it a boil, then pour it into basins, and when cold and turned out it will be a fine flummery.

880. **SOLID SYLLABUB**—Ingredients—1 quart of cream, 1 pint of white wine, the juice of 2 lemons, the rind of 1 grated, sugar to taste.

Mix the ingredients, having done so whip it up, and take off the froth as it rises. Put it upon a hair sieve, and let it stand in a cool place till the next day. Half fill your glasses with the skimmed part, and heap up the froth as high as you can. The bottom will look clear; it will keep several days.

881. **FLUMMERY** (1).—Ingredients—1 oz. bitter almonds, 1 oz. of sweet, a little rose water, 1 pt. jelly stock, sugar to taste, 1 pt. thick cream.

Blanch, and then throw into cold water, the almonds; take them out, and beat them in a marble mortar, with a little rose water, to keep them from oiling, and put them into the jelly stock. Sweeten with white sugar; when it boils strain it through a piece of muslin, and when a little cold, put it into the cream, stirring often till thick and cold. Wet moulds in cold water, pour in the flummery, and let them stand six hours before turned out; if made stiff, wet the moulds, and it will turn out without putting them into warm water, which destroys their brightness.

882. **FLUMMERY** (2).—Ingredients—3 large handfuls of small white oatmeal, 1 large spoonful of white sugar 2 large spoonfuls of orange flower water

Put three large handfuls of very small white oatmeal to steep a day and night in cold water; then pour it off clear, and add as much more water, and let it stand the same time. Strain it through a fine hair-sieve, and boil it till it be as thick as hasty-pudding; stirring it well all the time. When first strained, put to it the white sugar, and flower water. Pour it into shallow dishes; and serve to eat with wine, cider, milk, or cream and sugar. It is very good.

883. **RICE FLUMMERY**.—Ingredients—1 pint of milk a small piece of lemon peel and cinnamon, rice, flour, sugar to taste, a dessert spoonful of peach water or a bitter almond beaten.

Put the lemon peel and cinnamon into the milk and bring to a boil, mix with a little cold milk as much rice-flour as will make the whole of a good consistence, sweeten, and add the flavoring, then boil it observing it does not burn; pour in a shape or pint basin, removing the spice. When cold turn the flummery into a dish and serve with cream, milk, or custard round.

884. **DUTCH FLUMMERY**.—Ingredients—2 oz. of isinglass, 1½ pints of water, 1 pt. of white wine, the juice of 3 lemons, the thin rend of 1 lemon, a few lumps of sugar, the yolks of 7 eggs.

Boil two ounces of isinglass in the water very gently half an hour; add the wine, the juice of three, and the thin rind of one lemon, and rub a few lumps of sugar on another lemon to obtain the essence, and with them add as much more sugar as will make it sweet enough ; and having beaten the yolks of the eggs, give them and the above, when mixed, one scald, stir all the time, and pour it into a basin ; stir it till half cold ; then let it settle, and put it into a melon shape.

885. **ISINGLASS BLANC-MANGE**.—Ingredients — 1 oz. of isinglass, 1 qt. of water, whites of 4 eggs, 2 spoonfuls of rice-water, sugar to taste, 2 oz. of sweet and 1 oz. of bitter almonds.

Boil the isinglass in the water till it is reduced to a pint ; then add the whites of the eggs with the rice-water to prevent the eggs poaching, and sugar to taste ; run through the jelly-bag; then add the almonds ; give them a scald in the jelly, and pour them through a hair sieve ; put it in a china bowl ; the next day turn it out, and stick it all over with almonds, blanched and cut lengthways. Garnish with green leaves or flowers.

886. **CLEAR BLANC-MANGE**.—Ingredients—1 qt. of strong calf's foot jelly, whites of 4 eggs, 1 oz. of bitter and one of sweet almonds, a spoonful of rose water, 3 spoonfuls of cream.

Skim off the fat and strain the calf's foot jelly ; beat the whites of the eggs, and put them to the jelly ; set it over the fire, and keep stirring it till it boils ; then pour it into a jelly-bag, and run it through several times till it is clear ; beat the sweet and bitter almonds to a paste, with the rose-water squeezed through a cloth ; then mix it with the jelly and the cream ; set it over the fire again, and keep stirring it till it is almost boiling ; then pour it into a bowl, and stir it very often till it is almost cold ; then wet the moulds and fill them.

887. **RICE BLANC-MANGE**.—Ingredients—6 oz. of the best rice, 1 pt. of water, ½ pt. of milk or cream, 3 oz. of white sugar, vanilla flavoring, any kind of preserve.

Put the rice into a pipkin with the water and let it simmer slowly in the oven for 2 or 3 hours. Then add the cream or milk, sugar, and flavoring. Boil up over the fire, and pour into a mould. When quite cold serve with any kind of preserve.

888. **CORNFLOUR BLANC-MANGE**.—Ingredients — 4 or 5 tablespoonfuls of corn-flour, a little over a quart of milk.

Mix the corn to a stiff paste with a little of the milk. Put rest of the milk in a stewpan and set on the fire. Put the rind of a lemon in to infuse. Add sugar to taste, and when on the point of boiling, strain, and add to the corn flour ; return to the stewpan and boil ten minutes. Wet a mould and pour the blanc-mange into it. Serve with jelly, or milk and sugar.

889. **RIBBON BLANC-MANGE**.—Ingredients—two thirds of a package of gelatine, 1 pt of hot milk, 6 tablespoonfuls of sugar, 2 eggs, lemon and vanilla flavoring, 2 large tablespoonfuls of grated chocolate.

Soften the gelatine in the milk. Sweeten, and divide the milk into three parts. Into the first put the whites of the eggs previously beaten to a froth and flavor with lemon. Beat the yolks and vanilla flavoring into another part. Then wet the chocolate in a little warm water, flavor with vanilla and add to the remaining third of milk. As each part stiffens, whip with an egg beaten, turn into a wet mould, first yellow, then chocolate, then white.

890. **CHOCOLATE BLANC-MANGE**.—Ingredients—½ a package of gelatine dissolved in water, 1 pt. milk, 1 cup of grated chocolate, 1 cup of sugar.

Dissolve the gelatine. Let the milk come to a boiling point then stir in the sugar and chocolate. Stir until both are dissolved, then set the saucepan on the back part of the stove and stir the gelatine in slowly, a little at a time, so that it will be thoroughly distributed through the milk. Then pour into cups or moulds. This is to be eaten cold with sugar and cream. Flavor the cream with vanilla.

891. **JAUNEMANGE**.—Ingredients—1 pint of boiling water 2 oz. of isinglass, ¼ pt. of white wine, juice of 2 oranges, 1 lemon, sugar to taste, yolks of 8 eggs.

Dissolve the isinglass in the water, and then add the wine, the juice of the oranges and of the lemon, the peel of the lemon shred finely, sweeten to taste and add the yolks of the eggs; let it simmer gently, strain and pour into moulds. Turn out the next day.

892. **ALMOND BLANC-MANGE**.—Ingredients—2 pts of milk, 1 oz. gelatine, 3 ozs. of sweet almonds, a little orange flower water, ¾ of a cup of sugar.

Soak the gelatine in a cup of cold milk for three quarters of an hour. Put the milk on the fire until it is at boiling point. Pour in the gelatine, add the almonds (which must previously have been blanched and pounded and moistened with the orange flower water), and stir all together for about ten minutes; then add the sugar. As soon as the gelatine is dissolved remove from the boiling water in which it has been cooked, and strain through muslin. Pour into a wetted mould and stand in a cool place to get firm.

893. COMPOTE OF ORANGES.—Ingredients—3 oranges, 4 oz. of sugar, a gill of water, a small glass of brandy.

Pare the rind off the oranges as thinly as possible, and set it on one side ; divide the fruit into halves, remove the pithy cord which is in the centre, and cut off the rind and pith into strips down to the quick, leaving the halves of the oranges transparently bare ; dish these up in a high compote glass. Throw the rind into the sugar, boiled with the water for five minutes. Strain this syrup into a basin, add the brandy, pour over the compote, and serve.

894. ORANGE FOOL.—Ingredients—juice of 3 Seville oranges, well beaten eggs, ½ pt. of cream, a little nutmeg and cinnamon, white sugar to taste.

Mix the orange juice with the eggs, cream and spices. Sweeten to taste. The orange juice must be carefully strained. Set the whole over a slow fire, and stir it until it becomes about the thickness of melted butter ; it must on no account be allowed to boil ; then pour into a dish for eating cold.

895. GOOSEBERRY FOOL.—Ingredients—1 quart of gooseberries, water, sugar, 1 quart of cream, macaroons or ratafias.

Pick one quart of quite young gooseberries, and put them into a jar with a very little water and plenty of sugar ; put the jar in a saucepan of boiling water till the fruit be quite tender, then beat it through a cullender, and add gradually one quart of cream with sufficient sugar to sweeten ; garnish the dish with macaroons or ratafias.

896. CHARLOTTE RUSSE (1).—Ingredients—For a small mould : Savoy biscuits, ½ pt. of double cream, 3 teaspoonfuls white sugar, rather more than ¼ oz. gelatine, a few drops of vanilla flavoring, 1 slice sponge cake.

These are best made in a plain round tin. Take some Savoy biscuits, using half at a time, and keeping the rounded side next the mould ; form a star at the bottom by cutting them to the shape you require to fit into each other ; touch the edges of the biscuits lightly with white of egg to hold them together, but be very careful not to let the egg touch the mould, or it will stick and prevent it from turning out. Having made a star for the centre, proceed in the same way to line the sides by placing the biscuits standing upright all round it, their edges slightly overlapping each other : these must also be fastened to each other, and to the centre star by a slight application of white of egg, after which the tin must be placed in the oven for a few minutes to dry the egg. The cream must be whisked to a stiff froth with the previously melted gelatine, the sugar, and a few drops of vanilla flavoring; pour this mixture into the mould, covering it with a slice of sponge cake the size of the mould, to form a foundation when it is turned out; the biscuits forming the sides must have been cut evenly with the top, and must be touched lightly with the white of an egg to make them adhere to this foundation slice. Place the mould on ice until required, then turn it out on a dish and serve at once. This requires great care in the turning out.

897. **CHARLOTTE RUSSE** (2).—Ingredients—Half an ounce of isinglass, 1 pint of milk, sugar and vanilla to taste, 1 pint of cream, Savoy biscuits, a few ratafias.

Dissolve the isinglass in the milk; whip the cream to a strong froth, and when the isinglass and milk have cooled and become a little thick, add it to them, pouring the cream with force into the bowl, whipping it all the time. Grease a mould (which must be scrupulously clean) and place Savoy biscuits in each flute; sprinkle a few ratafias at the top, and when nearly cold pour in the mixture. Serve with preserved apricots.

898. **CHARLOTTE RUSSE** (3).—Ingredients—One oz. of gelatine, 1 pint of milk, 1 egg, flavor 1 qt. of cream with vanilla and sugar to taste, lady-fingers.

Soak the gelatine in the milk for half an hour, then dissolve the same by placing the vessel containing the gelatine and milk in a pot of hot water, that it may not burn while heating. Next, beat the yolk of one egg and pour it into the milk and gelatine while hot; strain it into a bowl and while cooling beat it thoroughly; next flavor the cream with one large teaspoonful of extract of vanilla and sugar to suit the taste, beat the white of the egg to a stiff froth; stir the cream and egg together and beat to a light froth with an egg-beater; next pour the two mixtures together and whip them thoroughly; pour into moulds lined with lady-fingers. Do not pour into moulds until the mixture is stiff enough to prevent the cakes from rising to the surface.

899. **A VERY NICE TRIFLE**.—Ingredients—Macaroons and ratafias, raisin wine, a *very* rich custard, raspberry jam, whipped cream, some rich cream, whites of 2 eggs (well beaten), sugar, lemon peel.

Lay the macaroons and ratafias over the bottom of a dish, and pour in as much of the raisin wine as they will soak up, then pour on them the custard cold; it must stand two or three inches thick; then put a layer of the jam and cover the whole with a whip (which must have been made the day before) in the above proportions.

900. **GOOSEBERRY OR APPLE TRIFLE.**—Ingredients—Apples or gooseberries, ½ pint of milk, ½ pint of cream, yolk of 1 egg, sugar to taste.

Scald enough of either apples or gooseberries so that when pulped through a sieve, will form a thick layer at the bottom of your dish. If apples, mix the peel of half a lemon grated finely, and to either of the fruits add sugar to taste; mix the milk, cream, and the yolk of egg; give them a scald over the fire, stirring all the time; do not let it boil; then add a little sugar, and allow to get cold. Lay this mixture over the apples with a spoon, and then put on it a whip made the day before.

901. **STEWED APPLES AND RICE.**— Ingredients — Some good baking apples, syrup, 1 lb. of sugar to 1 pt. of water. Some shred lemon peel, jam, some well boiled rice.

Peel the apples, take out the cores with a scoop so as not to injure the shape of the apples, put them in a deep baking dish, and pour over them a syrup made by boiling sugar in the above proportion, put a little piece of shred lemon inside each apple, and let them bake very slowly until soft, but not in the least broken. If the syrup is thin, boil it until it is thick enough; take out the lemon peel, and put a little jam inside each apple, and between each a little heap of well-boiled rice; pour the syrup gently over the apples, and let it cover the rice. This dish may be served either hot or cold.

902. **SPICED APPLES.**—Ingredients—4 lbs. of apples (weigh them after they are peeled), 2 lbs. of sugar, ½ an oz. of cinnamon in the stick, ¼ of an oz. of cloves, and 1 pt. of vinegar.

Let the vinegar, spices and sugar come to a boil; then put in the whole apples, and cook them until they are so tender that a broom-splint will pierce them easily. These will keep for a long time in a jar. Put a clean cloth over the top of the jar before putting the cover on.

903. **APPLE CHARLOTTE.**—Ingredients—Some good cooking apples, sugar (1 lb. of apple pulp to ½ lb. of sugar), lemon flavoring, fried bread.

Bake good cooking apples slowly until done; scrape out all the pulp with a teaspoon, put it in a stewpan in the above proportion; stir it until the sugar is dissolved and the pulp stiff. Take care it does not burn. Add a little lemon flavoring, and place the apple in the centre of a dish, arranging thickly and tastefully round it neatly-cut pieces of the carefully-fried bread. If it is desired to make this dish very nice, each piece of fried bread may be dipped in apricot jam. Rhubarb Charlotte may be made in the same manner. The rhubarb must be boiled and stirred until a good deal of the watery portion has evaporated, and then sugar, half a pound to one pound of fruit, being added, it should be allowed to boil until it is thick.

904. ORANGE CHIPS.— Ingredients — Some Seville oranges, sugar.

Cut the oranges in halves, squeeze the juice through a sieve; soak the peel in water; next dry; boil in the same till tender, drain and slice the peels, pour the juice over them; take an equal weight of sugar, put sugar, peels, and juice into a broad earthenware dish, and set it over the fire, not close enough to crack the dish, stir frequently until the chips candy; then set them in a cool place to dry, which process will take three weeks.

905. ORANGE SOUFFLE.—Ingredients—6 oranges, sliced and peeled, sugar, custard, yolks of 3 eggs, a pint of milk, sugar to taste, grating of orange peel for flavor, white of the eggs.

Put into a glass dish a layer of oranges, then one of sugar, and so on until all the oranges are used, and let it stand two hours; make a soft boiled custard in the above proportions, and pour over the oranges, when cool enough not to break the dish. Beat the whites of the eggs to a stiff froth, sweeten to taste and pour over the top. Serve cold.

906. FLOATING ISLAND.—Ingredients—1½ pt. of thin cream, ¼ of a pt. of raisin wine, a little lemon juice, orange flower water, and sugar to taste.

Mix together, pour into a dish for the middle of the table, and put on the cream a froth made as below.

907. FOR FROTH.—Ingredients—½ lb. of damson pulp, sugar to taste, the whites of 4 eggs.

Sweeten the pulp, well whisk the whites, then mix with the pulp and beat until it will stand as high as you choose; put on the cream with a spoon, it will take any form, it should be rough, to imitate a rock.

Note—Any other sort of scalded fruit will do if desired.

908. DEVONSHIRE JUNKET.—Ingredients—2 qts. of new milk, 1¼ wine glasses of brandy, 4 dessert spoonfuls of sugar, 6 dessert spoonfuls of prepared rennet, clotted cream, a little nutmeg.

Just allow the milk to become blood warm, mix in the brandy and set in a deep dish, now add the sugar and rennet, stir well and put aside to set. When required for use, cover with the cream and a sprinkle of nutmeg.

DESSERT.

OBSERVATIONS ON FRUITS, &c.

Every intelligent person must admit that the free use of ripe fruit is one of the greatest promoters of health. But it is also obvious that fruits as an exclusive article of diet do not meet all the wants of the system. The chemistry of the apple, the pear, the tomato, the grape, and other fruits, is well understood, and it can be stated how much nutriment or assimilable food each is capable of affording; but this does not answer all the questions connected with the subject of the healthfulness of fruit. Besides furnishing nutriment, fruit exerts other influences upon the animal economy of the highest importance. The acids of fruits are not properly nutritive substances, but they produce physiological effects of a cooling or corrective nature which are highly salutary. Fruits are largely composed of water, and this fluid has come to them through extraordinary channels. The tiny root fibres have collected it in the dark earth, and by vital action it has been forced through the most minute tubes, until it is finally deposited in the fruit cells. So far as we know, the water undergoes no modifications; it is water in the soil, and it is the same in its wonderful associations in fruits. It, however, holds saccharine elements and other principles which modify its physical appearance and taste. The great amount of water contained in fruit is in itself an advantage, as it aids in cleansing the alimentary canal and other excretory ducts, and thus promotes healthy action.

Fruits are capable of sustaining life for long periods, but the lack of the nitrogenous elements detracts from their strength-giving power, and any one living exclusively upon them would not be able to labor effectively. We have all heard of the man who rowed his boat along the entire coast of New England, sustained alone by whortleberries; but if the voyage had lasted six months, or even three, his nerves and his muscles would have entirely failed him; so that to argue from all such brief experiments is delusive and unfair. If the fruit is largely consumed in connection with a proper proportion of animal or nitrogenous foods, a much higher standard of health will be attained among all classes.

Much can be done with a tastily arranged dessert of bright bonbons, crackers, dried fruit, apples, pears, oranges and nuts.

Delicate or quaint specimens of old Worcester, Chelsea, or Dresden will be found to exercise a most telling effect by introducing the proper harmony of colors in connection with the shining damask of the table linen, and the sparkling crystal of the glass service, nor can we altogether depreciate the use of colored grasses and artificial flowers. Some specimens of the latter which we have seen are so really artistic in conception and perfect in execution that, although abhorring all shams and make-believes, we cannot but consider them permissible by way of relieving with their gayer tints the somewhat sombre laurel. None of these suffer, as do the more delicate fruits of summer and autumn, from the baneful fumes of gas, and the heated atmosphere of the rooms. But, with regard to decorations suitable to the large festive gatherings and orthodox family dinner parties; in all the varied displays we have seen, glass ornaments seem usually to carry off the palm, owing to the superior delicacy and refinement of their shapes; china vases and figures, however, have an exceedingly good effect. One set of pure white china was very striking, contrasted as it was by a dessert set of exquisitely fine brilliantly colored china. The centre and side vases for the flowers were edged with open basket work, and supported with graceful figures of boys and maidens; the table was lighted with white china candelabras to match, and here and there were dotted about pure white baskets in imitation wicker work (also of china), decked out with graceful ferns and dainty sprays of flowers. As for the glass epergnes, the tall ones for the centre seem still to hold their own, and are likely to do so, being so far more elegant than the short stumpy ones.

Dessert would not be complete without chocolate, in different forms, all kinds of delicately flavored cakes, and the most costly and *recherche* wines. A good selection can be made from pines, grapes, oranges, apples, figs, melons, plums, nectarines, cherries, nuts, etc. See "Sweet Dishes" for several other suitable recipes for dessert.

909. ORANGES.

Oranges may be prepared for table in the following manner:—Cut gently through the peel only, from the point of the orange at the top to dent made at the stalk at the bottom, dividing the outside of the orange into cloves or sections, seven or eight in number. Loosen the peel carefully, and take each section off, leaving it only attached at the bottom. Scrape the white off the orange itself, and turn in each section double to the bottom of the orange, so that the whole looks like a dahlia or some other flower.

910. ALMONDS AND RAISINS.

Serve on a glass dish, the raisins piled **high in the** centre. Blanch the almonds and strew over them.

911. FROSTED CURRANTS.

Froth the white of an egg or eggs, dipping the bunches into the mixture. Drain until nearly dry, then roll in white sugar. Lay upon white paper to dry.

912. IMPROMPTU DESSERT.

Cover the bottom of a large glass dish with sliced orange; strew over it powdered sugar, then a thick layer of cocoanut. Alternate orange and cocoanut till the dish is full, heaping the cocoanut on the top.

913. DESSERT OF APPLES.—Ingredients—One lb. of sugar, 1 lb. of finely flavored ripe sour apples, 1 pint of rich cream, 2 eggs, ½ cup of sugar.

Make a rich syrup of the sugar; add the apples nicely pared and cored. Stew till soft, then mix smoothly with the syrup and pour all into a mould. Stir into the cream (or if there is none at hand, new milk must answer) the eggs well beaten, also the sugar, and let it just boil up in a farina kettle; then set aside to cool. When cold take the apples from the mould and pour this cream custard around it and serve. If spice or flavoring is agreeable, nutmeg, vanilla, or rose water can be used.

914. DISH OF FIGS.—Ingredients—One cup of sugar, one third of a cup of water, ¼ of a teaspoonful of cream of tartar.

Let the sugar and water boil until it is a pale brown color; shake the basin in which it is boiling gently, to prevent it burning, but do not stir it at all until just before you take it from the fire, then stir in the cream of tartar. Wash and cut open some figs; spread them on a platter, then pour the sugar over them. Take care to have each fig covered; set them in a cool place till the sugar has time to harden.

915. A DISH OF NUTS.

Arrange them piled high in the centre of a dish; a few leaves around the edge of the dish will greatly improve the appearance. In dishing filberts serve them with the outer skin on. If walnuts, wipe with a damp cloth before serving.

916. A DISH OF STRAWBERRIES.

If there are any inferior ones they should be placed in the bottom of the dish and the others put in rows to form a pyramid, taking care to place the stalks downwards. A few fern leaves placed at the bottom of the dish before building the pyramid will add to the good appearance of the dish. N. B. Secure the fruit with long stalks as they will support the pyramid.

917. DISH OF FRENCH PLUMS.

Arrange on a glass dish with highly colored sweet-meats, which make a good effect.

918. A DISH OF MOULDED PEARS.—Ingredients—5 large pears, 7 cloves, water, a little piece of cinnamon, 1 gill of raisin wine, a small piece of lemon peel and the juice of ½ a lemon, sugar to taste, ½ oz. of gelatine.

Put nearly one pint of water into a jar, pare and cut the pears into quarters, place them in the jar with spices and sugar to taste, cover the jar tightly and bake the pears in a gentle oven until tender, do not allow them to be overdone or they will break, wash out a mould (plain) and lay in the pears, now take half a pint of the juice the pears were stewed in, the wine, lemon peel, gelatine, and strained juice, boil five minutes, strain and pour over the pears; stand in a cool place, and when firm serve on a glass dish.

919. APPLE GINGER.—Ingredients—2 lbs. white sugar, 2 lbs. hard apples, nearly 1 qt. water, 1 oz. of tincture of ginger.

Make a rich syrup of the sugar and water, adding, as soon as it boils, the ginger. Pare, core, and cut the apples into quarters or pieces to suit the fancy plunging into cold water to preserve the color, then boil in the syrup until transparent. Great care must be taken that they do not break, as this would spoil the appearance. Place in jars and cover with the syrup, put into glass bottles and seal air-tight. It is then ready at any time for dessert.

920. A DISH OF MIXED FRUITS.

Select a handsome dish, put a table glass in the centre, cover with moss or leaves. Place a nice pine-apple upon the top of the glass, and round it apples or pears with leaves between, then plums mingled with grapes. Much taste can be displayed in the arrangement of the fruit.

921. COMPOTE OF FRUIT.—Ingredients—Equal quantities of red and white currants, raspberries, and very ripe cherries, white sugar, a wineglassful of pale brandy, sponge cake.

Remove the stalks and stones from the cherries, and pick the currants carefully, sprinkle plenty of white sugar over the fruit, add the brandy. Toss them lightly until the sugar is dissolved. Serve within a border of sponge cake.

922. STRAWBERRIES AND CREAM.

Pick the fruit carefully (which should be ripe, but not too much so), and put into a dessert dish, sprinkle two tablespoonfuls of white sugar over, then pour over the cream, allowing one pint to every three pints of fruit.

923. TO FROST LEAVES.

Free from all moisture the leaves, by wiping them with a clean cloth. Lay them upon a dish near the fire to get dry, (not too close or they will shrivel), oil a little butter, and dip them into it, sprinkle a little powdered sugar over them, and dry near the fire. This is pretty for garnishing dessert.

COLORINGS FOR CONFECTIONERY.

924. *Pink Color.*—You may make a pink color with either archil, lake, Dutch pink, or rose pink. Take as much of either of them as will be enough for your purpose, and moisten it with spirits of wine; grind it on a marble slab, till quite fine, and add spirits of wine, or gin, till it is of the thickness of cream.

925 *Red.*—Red color is made with cochineal. Grind half an ounce of cochineal fine enough to go through a wire sieve, put into a two-quart copper pan, half an ounce of salts of wormwood and half a pint of cold spring water; put the cochineal into it, and put it over a clear fire; let them boil together for about a minute; mix in three quarters of an ounce of cream of tartar, and let it boil again; as soon as it boils, take it off, and put in of powdered roche-alum rather less than half a teaspoonful; stir it well together, and strain into a bottle; put in a lump of sugar, to keep it; cork it up, and put it by for use.

926. *Cherry Red.*—Boil an ounce of cudbear in three half pints of water over a slow fire, till reduced to a pint, then add an ounce of cream of tartar, and let them simmer again. When cold, strain them, add an ounce and a half of spirits of wine to it, and bottle for use; this is rendered red when mixed with acid, and green with alkali; it is not a good color, and Dutch grappe madder may be substituted for it; take two ounces, tie it in a cloth and beat it in a mortar with a pint of water, pour this off and repeat the same operation until you have used four or five pints, when the whole of the color will be extracted; then boil it for ten minutes, and add one ounce of alum dissolved in a pint of water, and one ounce and a half of oil of tartar; let it settle, and wash the sediment with water; pour this off and dry it, and mix some of it with a little spirits of wine or gin.

A tincture made by pouring hot water over sliced beet-root, will give a good red for ices and jellies.

927. *Blue.*—Dissolve a little indigo in warm water, or put a little warm water into a plate, and rub an indigo stone on it till you have sufficient for your purpose. This will do for ices, &c.

But to use indigo for sugars, you must first grind as much as you will require as fine as you can on a stone, or in a mortar, and then dissolve it in gin or spirits of wine, till of the tint you wish.

You also make a good blue by grinding Prussian or Antwerp Blue fine on a marble slab, and mixing it with water.

928. *Yellow.*—You may get a yellow by dissolving turmeric, or saffron, in water or rectified spirits of wine. Tincture of saffron is used for coloring ices, &c. The roots of barberries prepared with alum and cream of tartar, as for making a green, will also make a transparent yellow for sugars, &c. Saffron or turmeric, may be used in like manner.

929. *Green.*—Boil an ounce of fustic, a quarter of an ounce of turmeric, two drams of good clear alum, and two drams of cream of tartar, in half a pint of water, over a slow fire, till one third of the water is wasted; add the tartar first, and lastly the alum; pound a dram of indigo in a mortar, till quite fine and then dissolve it in half an ounce of spirits of wine. When the ingredients you have boiled (and which make a bright yellow) are cold, strain the solution of indigo, and mix it with them. You will have a beautiful transparent green, strain it, and put it into a bottle, stop the bottle well, and put it by for use. You may make it darker or lighter by using more or less indigo. This may be used for coloring boiled or other sugars, or any preparation in ornamental confectionery.

A good green for coloring ices, &c. may be made as follows: Carefully trim the leaves of some spinach, and boil them in a very little water for about a minute, then strain the water clear off, and it will be fit for use.

930. *Brown.*—Burnt umber, ground on a marble slab with water, will make a good brown color, and you need not use much to obtain the tint you require. Burnt sugar will also answer the same purpose.

ICES, CREAMS, &c.

931. **COFFEE ICE CREAM.**—Ingredients—5 oz. of coffee berries, a breakfast cup of milk, 2 of cream, a tablespoonful of arrowroot, ¼ lb. of sugar.

Add the cream and milk together and boil, then pour into a can. While this has been going on, let the coffee berries be put on a tin in the oven for five or six minutes; then put them with the cream. Leave to cool and then strain through a sieve and add the remaining ingredients. Boil again (stirring all the time) until it thickens. Freeze in the usual way.

932. **CHOCOLATE ICE CREAM.**—Ingredients—6 tablespoonfuls of grated chocolate, 2 breakfast cups of cream, 1 of fresh milk, and ½ lb. of sugar.

Stir the chocolate into the milk, **mixing well, add remaining** ingredients and freeze.

933. **ICE CREAM.**—Ingredients—1¼ lbs of any kind of preserved fruit, 1 qt. of cream, juice of two lemons, sugar to taste.

Take the whole of the ingredients, and work through a sieve. Then freeze in a freezing can, and work until it is frozen. Then turn out and serve.

934. **ITALIAN ICE CREAM.**—Ingredients—One qt. of cream juice and peel of two lemons, 1 small wineglass of brandy, ¾ lb. of sugar.

Add the sugar to the cream, and beat in the lemons by degrees. Add the brandy and freeze in a patent freezer.

935. **ANOTHER ICE CREAM**—Ingredients—1 quart of milk 2 eggs, ¾ lb. of sugar, 2 tablespoonfuls of corn starch or arrowroot, 1 qt. of cream.

Scald the milk, yolks of eggs, sugar, and corn starch or arrowroot, until it is of the consistency of custard. Then allow to cool. When cool add the cream whipped, and the whites of the eggs whisked to a stiff froth. Sweeten to taste, flavor, and freeze in the usual way.

RECIPES FOR MAKING ICE CREAM, FRUIT, AND WATER ICE.

NOTE.—When pure cream is used, half the number of quarts that the can will hold will be sufficient, as the beater will make it light and spongy so that it will nearly fill the can. In using milk the can may be three-fourths filled.

936. Dissolve in two quarts of pure fresh cream, 12 to 14 oz. of best white sugar; flavor as given below, strain into the freezing can and freeze according to above directions.

937. *Making Ice Cream from Milk.*—Bring two quarts rich milk to a boiling point; stir in two tablespoonfuls of arrowroot or Corn starch, previously rubbed smooth in a cupful of cold milk. Remove from the fire and add four eggs and three quarters of a pound of sugar well beaten together; stir all well together and then set aside to cool. Flavor and freeze as before directed.

FLAVORS.

938. *Vanilla.*—One tablespoonful of good extract of Vanilla.

939. *Lemon.*—About three teaspoonfuls each of extract of Lemon and Lemon juice.

940. *Bisque.*—Add about two handfuls of powdered sifted dry sponge cake and a dessert spoonful of extract of Nectarine.

941. *Chocolate Ice Cream.*—Melt in a porcelain dish two ounces of Baker's chocolate, and about three ounces of water and four ounces of fine white sugar, dissolve and strain into the cream in freezing can, and proceed as directed above.

942. *Fruit Ice Cream.*—To two quarts of cream add about one quart of juice of such fruits as cherry, currant, strawberry, peach, orange, etc., finely strained, and one and a half pounds of fine white sugar, and freeze as above.

943. *Fruit Ices.*—Dissolve three pounds of fine white sugar in two quarts of water and one quart of finely strained juice of any of the above named fruits, and freeze the same as ice cream. It requires more time than the latter, and will not increase so much in bulk. For orange and strawberry ices add the juice of one large lemon.

These recipes are kindly furnished us by the "American Machine Co.," Philadelphia.

944. SUBSTITUTE FOR CREAM.

We have just met with the following in an Indian recipe book " Beat the white of an egg to a froth, and mix well with it a very small lump of butter. Add it to a hot liquid gradually, so that it may not curdle."

945. BURNT CREAM (1).—Ingredients— One pint of cream, 1 stick of cinnamon, a little lemon peel, the yolks of 4 eggs, sugar to taste.

Boil the cream with a stick of cinnamon, and lemon peel; take it off the fire, and pour it very slowly into the yolks of the eggs, stirring till half cold ; sweeten, and take out the spice, &c. ; pour it into the dish ; when cold, strew white pounded sugar over, and brown it with a salamander.

946. BURNT CREAM (2).

Make a rich custard without sugar, boil lemon peel in it. When cold sift a good deal of sugar over the whole, and brown the top with a salamander.

947. PARISIENNE CREAM.—Ingredients— One ounce of fine isinglass, 1 pt. of thin cream, 3 oz. of sugar broken into small lumps, ½ pt. of rich cream, 8 oz. of the finest apricot jam.

Dissolve the isinglass in the thin cream, and strain it through folded muslin ; put it into a clean saucepan with the lump sugar, and when it boils add the rich cream ; add it by spoonfuls to the apricot jam, which has been passed through the sieve when made. Mix the whole smoothly, and put it into a mould and stir till nearly cold, to prevent the jam sinking to the bottom. Put it on ice, and when set turn it out and serve. The strained juice of a lemon may be added when making the cream, and is a great improvement.

948. PINEAPPLE CREAM.—Ingredients—A tin of preserved pineapple, 6 oz. of sugar, ½ pt. of water, 7 sheets of best French gelatine dissolved in a little milk, 1 pt. of cream.

Pound the pineapple in a mortar, add the sugar and water ; boil for fifteen minutes and press through a tammy. Dissolve the gelatine in a little milk ; whip the cream to a froth ; mix the gelatine with the pineapple pulp, then quickly work in the cream. Pour the mixture into a mould, and put on ice to set. When wanted, dip the mould in hot water and turn out the cream.

949. DUTCH CREAM.—Ingredients—Six tablespoonfuls of sifted sugar, 6 of water, 6 of wine, 6 whole eggs well beaten, juice and peel of 1 lemon.

Boil all together. Serve cold.

Q

950. **CARAMEL CREAM.**—Ingredients—One qt. of rich milk, 3 yolks and 1 whole egg, caramel, 4 oz. of sugar, spoonful of water.

Boil the milk and mix in some caramel made in the above proportions thus :—Take the sugar and hold it over the fire in a spoonful of water until a rich golden color ; beat up the yolks and the whole egg together and add to the milk. Pass the whole through a hair sieve and put it in a basin in a saucepan of boiling water; cook until it thickens. Serve in glasses.

951. **STRAWBERRY CREAM.**—Ingredients—One pot of good strawberry jam, 9 sheets of the best French gelatine, 1 quart of cream.

Take jam, and pass through a tammy, add the gelatine dissolved in a little milk, then add the cream whipped to a froth ; put into a mould and lay on ice to set. When wanted dip the mould in hot water and turn out the cream.

952. **LEMON CREAM (made without cream).**—Ingredients—Four lemons, 12 tablespoonfuls of water, 7 oz. of powdered white sugar, yolks of 9 eggs.

Peel the lemons very thinly into the above proportion of water, then squeeze the juice into the sugar. Beat the yolks thoroughly and add the peel and juice together, beating for some time. Then strain into your saucepan, set over a gentle fire and stir one way till thick and scalding hot. Do not let it boil or it will curdle. Serve in jelly glasses.

953. **RATAFIA CREAM.**—Ingredients—Three or 4 laurel, peach or nectarine leaves, 1 pint of cream, yolks of 3 eggs, sugar to taste, and a large spoonful of brandy, a little ratafia.

Boil the leaves in the cream with a little ratafia. Remove the leaves ; beat the yolks of the eggs and strain, then add to the mixture. Sweeten to taste, and add the brandy stirred in quickly. Scald till thick, stirring all the time. Then pour into china dishes and when cold serve.

954. **ORANGE CREAM.**—Ingredients—One Seville orange, 1 spoonful of the best brandy, 4 oz. of white sugar, yolks of 4 eggs, 1 pint of boiling cream.

Boil the rind of the orange very tender ; beat it fine in a mortar ; add the brandy, the juice of the orange, the sugar, and yolks of the eggs. Beat all together for ten minutes. Then very gradually pour in the cream ; beat till cold. Put into custard cups, set into a deep dish of boiling water, and leave to stand till cold again. Place on the tops small strips of orange paring.

955. **RASPBERRY CREAM**.—Ingredients—One oz. of isinglass shavings, 3 pints of cream and new milk mixed, ½ pint of raspberry juice or syrup, 1 glass of brandy.

Boil the isinglass in the cream and milk until the former is dissolved, it will take about fifteen minutes. Strain through a hair sieve into a basin, when cool add the raspberry juice or syrup to the milk and cream; stir well, sweeten and add the brandy. Whisk until nearly cold; then put in a mould to get quite cold.

956. **BRANDY CREAM**.—Ingredients—2 doz. sweet and a few bitter almonds, a little milk, yolks of 5 eggs, 2 glasses of best brandy, sugar to taste, 1 quart of thin cream.

Boil the almonds (previously blanching and pounding them in the milk). When cold add to it the yolks of the eggs well beaten in a little cream, sweeten, and add the brandy. Mix well and add the cream; set over the fire but do not allow to boil. Stir one way till it thickens and then pour into cream glasses. When cold, serve with or without a ratafia drop in each. This cream will keep by scalding the cream previously.

957. **FRENCH RICE CREAM**.—Ingredients—Two tablespoons of Fayeux's creme de riz, ½ pint of cold milk, ½ pint of hot milk, 2 oz. of sugar, 2 well-whisked eggs.

Mix smooth the creme de riz in the cold milk; stir it into the hot milk (which must be boiling) in which the sugar has been dissolved. Stir over the fire till it boils, then beat in the eggs stirring for ten minutes over the fire. Add any flavoring and serve either hot or cold. This makes a very nice dish for delicate children.

958. **CRYSTAL PALACE CREAM**.—Ingredients—A rich custard, ¼ oz. of gelatine dissolved in a little boiling water, 2 sponge cakes, 2 macaroons, 2 tablespoonfuls of milk.

. Make the custard, dissolve the gelatine and when it is nearly cold pour into the custard, which must also be cool; soak the cakes and macaroons in the milk (or if preferred any fruit syrup, which must be rich and sweet). Put the cakes into a mould and gently pour the cream over them; let it stand till cold. A few glacé cherries may be added.

959. **VELVET CREAM**—Ingredients—One oz. of isinglass, ½ pint of sherry, juice of a lemon and half the rind, ¼ oz. of gelatine, 2 or 3 oz. of sugar, 1½ pints of cream.

Put into a pan all the ingredients except the cream. Let them boil till the isinglass is melted. Then strain through muslin into the cream. Keep stirring until nearly cold, and then put into moulds.

960. CHOCOLATE CREAM.—Ingredients—Yolks of 6 eggs (strained), 2 oz. of powered white sugar, 2 oz. of grated chocolate, 1 pt. of milk, 4 sheets of best French gelatine dissolved in a little milk, 1 pt. of well-whipped cream.

Mix the yolks of eggs with the sugar and chocolate, add the milk; set the mixture on the fire in a double saucepan, the outer one filled with hot water, and kept stirring till the cream thickens; add the dissolved gelatine and strain it into a basin; put this over ice, stirring till the mixture begins to set, then add the well-whipped cream. Put a mould in the ice, pour in the cream, cover it with ice, and when quite set, turn it out and serve.

961. COFFEE CREAM.—Ingredients—1 breakfastcupful of made coffee, a little more than ½ pt. of boiled milk, 8 yolks of eggs, a pinch of salt, ½ lb. sugar, 2 oz. of dissolved gelatine.

Put the coffee into a stew pan with the milk; add the yolks, salt and sugar; stir the cream briskly on the fire until it begins to thicken; stir for a minute longer and then run it through a sieve into a basin, add the gelatine, mix and set the cream in a mould embedded in rough ice.

962. LEMON CREAM.—Ingredients—One pt. of thick cream, yolks of two eggs, 4 oz. of fine sugar, rind of one lemon cut thinly, juice of the lemon.

Well beat the yolks and add to the cream, sugar and rind of the lemon; boil, and then stir it till almost cold; put the juice of the lemon into a dish and pour the cream upon it, stirring until quite cold.

963. LEMON CREAM SOLID.—Ingredients—Half a pint of cream, the juice of 3 lemons, and the rind of 2, ¾ lb. of loaf sugar in small lumps.

Rub the sugar on the lemons, and lay them at the bottom of the dish, pour the lemon juice over, make the cream a little warm, then, standing on a chair, and with the dish on the ground, pour the cream on so as to froth it.

964. ALMOND CREAM.—Ingredients—4 oz. of sweet almonds, a few bitter almonds, a quart of cream, juice of 3 lemons (sweetened), a little orange flower water.

Blanch and pound the almonds in a mortar moistening with a little orange flower water. Add the cream and the sweetened juice of the lemons. Beat to a froth, which take off on the shallow part of a sieve; fill glasses with some of the cream and some of the froth.

965. TEA CREAM.—Ingredients—One quart. of cream, some coriander seeds, 2 sticks of cinnamon, a piece of lemon peel, sugar to taste, ½ pt. of some very strong green tea, whites of 6 eggs.

Boil the cream with the spices, lemon peel, and sugar to taste, for about ten minutes; then add the tea, and the whites of the the eggs well beaten up. Beat over the fire till it thickens then pour into china cups and when cold serve with or without whole ratafias on each.

966. WHIPPED CREAM.—Ingredients—Whites of 8 eggs, 1 qt. of thick cream, ½ pt. of wine, sugar to taste, flavor with musk.

Mix the whites of the eggs with the cream and wine sweetening to taste. Add flavoring. Whip it up with a whisk with some lemon peel tied up in it. Take the froth with a spoon and lay in glasses. It looks nice over tarts.

967. WHIPPED CREAM FOR A TRIFLE.—Ingredients—One pt. of cream, wine, rind and juice of an orange, sugar to taste.

Put the cream into a freezer and freeze. Whip the cream. Mix together the remaining ingredients and add the cream. Then pour into the dish your trifle is to be in, and put the froth of the cream over it.

968. GINGER CREAM.—Ingredients—1 qt. of cream, yolks of 8 eggs, 2 tablespoonfuls of syrup, 6 oz. of preserved ginger, white sugar to taste, 2 oz. of isinglass shavings, melted and strained.

Cut the ginger into thin slices and mix with the syrup, yolks of eggs (well beaten) and the cream. Place in a saucepan over the fire not more than ten minutes and stir all the while. Then whisk till almost cold, add sugar to taste and the isinglass, and serve in cream dish.

969. TAPIOCA CREAM.—Ingredients—Two tablespoonfuls of tapioca, 3 eggs, 2 pts. of milk, any flavoring.

Dissolve the tapioca to a soft pulp, add the yolks of the eggs, well beaten, and sugar to taste; heat the milk to boiling and when cold add to the tapioca, etc. whip the whites of the eggs lightly and beat all together. Then put it on to boil about ten minutes and pour into cream cups.

970. SNOW SOUFFLE.—Ingredients—Half a package of fine gelatine, a smooth custard, whites of 2 eggs frothed, ½ lb. of sugar, juice of 2 lemons.

Put the gelatine into a pint of boiling water until it is dissolved; add sugar and lemon juice, stir in the eggs and mix the whole together until it is quite stiff and white, having a very good resemblance to snow. Put into a wetted mould, leave to cool and set, and serve with the custard round the dish.

971. **EGG SOUFFLE.**—Ingredients—Five eggs, ¼ lb. of white sugar, any flavoring, 3 oz. of butter, and 1 tablespoonful of rice-flour.

Add to the yolks of the eggs the rice flour, sugar, and flavoring and mix well together ; add lightly to this mixture the whites of the eggs well whisked. Put a little butter into a frying pan, and as soon as it is quite hot pour in the batter; when the omelet is firm, shape and slip on to a well buttered dish ; bake in the oven for nearly a quarter of an hour. Sprinkle with powdered sugar and serve instantly.

972. **SOUFFLE OF BREAD AND WALNUTS.**—Ingredients —Thirty sound and quite fresh walnuts, 2 oz. of white bread crumbs, ¼ lb. of butter, the same quantity of sugar, 6 eggs, and half a cupful of sweet cream.

Either pound or grate the walnuts with the fine skin which is on them ; soak the bread in milk, and squeeze it, beat the butter to cream, and add one after another the yolks of the eggs, then the sugar, bread, cream, and nuts, beat all the ingredients well together, and stir in lightly the whites of the eggs whipt to a stiff froth. Put into a proper souffle form, and bake it an hour, serve the moment it has properly risen.

973. **HOMINY** (1).

Wash it in two or three waters, pour boiling water on it, and let it soak for at least ten hours ; then put it into a stewpan, allowing two quarts of water to one quart of hominy, and boil it slowly four or five hours, or until it is perfectly tender ; then drain it, put it into a deep dish, add salt and a piece of butter, and serve as a vegetable with meat.

974. **HOMINY** (2).

Put some water on the fire, and when it boils add a little salt ; drop in gradually the hominy, and boil fifteen to twenty minutes, stirring well all the time with a wooden spoon ; serve with milk or cream. If preferred, it may be boiled in milk in the same way. It also makes excellent puddings cooked in the same way as rice or tapioca, but it should be well soaked before cooking ; it may also be made into shapes, and served with jam or custard.

975. **RICE SOUFFLE.**—Ingredients—One pint of milk, 5 eggs, ½ a breakfast cup of ground rice, sugar to taste, a piece of

butter the size of a peach, any flavoring that may be preferred.

Beat the yolks of the eggs, whisk the whites to a stiff froth. Mix into the rice half a breakfast cup of milk, and when smooth put into a stewpan with the rest of the milk and butter, stirring over the fire until it thickens. Now stir into the beaten yolks the mixture, adding a little sugar. (The less sugar the lighter the souffle.) Now mix the whites of the eggs to the preparation. Put into souffle dish and bake *directly*; it will take about twenty minutes to half an hour. Remove from the oven, brown with a salamander, sift a little sugar over the top, pin a napkin round the dish and serve *instantly*.

976. **APPLE SOUFFLE.**—Ingredients—6 tablespoonfuls of rice, 2 pints of milk, yolks of 4 and the whites of 6 eggs, butter the size of an egg, half the rind of a lemon, ¼ lb. of apple marmalade.

Put the milk to boil, throwing in the lemon rind until the desired lemon flavor is obtained. After straining, add the rice and allow to simmer gently until swollen sufficiently. Sweeten to taste. Pound the rice with a wooden beetle until it becomes a nice soft pulp; then line the sides and bottom with it neatly and pop it into the oven to get firm. When you are sure the rice is perfectly set, turn it out. Beat the yolks and add to the marmalade and the butter, and place on the fire till it thickens, stirring all the time. Then remove from the fire, add the whites of the eggs, frothed. Mix all well with a wooden spoon and pour gently into the rice. Bake from twenty-five to thirty minutes by which time the souffle will have become very high. Serve immediately after it is cooked.

977. **CHOCOLATE SOUFFLE.**—Ingredients—Eight eggs, ½ a small teacup of white sugar, 1 dessert spoonful of flour, 7 oz. of chocolate.

Beat the yolks and whites of the eggs separately. Grate the chocolate, and with the sugar, and flour, add to the yolks and stir for seven minutes. When the whites are a stiff froth add lightly to the mixture and work nice and smooth. Butter a dish and pour the preparation into it; bake about half an hour. Send to table *immediately*.

978. **ANOTHER CHOCOLATE SOUFFLE**—Ingredients—Two tablespoonfuls of flour, 2 of powdered white sugar, 2 oz. of butter, ¼ pint of milk, yolks of 4 eggs, 2 bars of chocolate, whites of the eggs, allowing to each egg 1 tablespoonful of sifted sugar.

Put the flour, sugar, butter and milk into a saucepan, and

boil; let it become nearly cold and stir in the yolks and chocolate. When ready for the oven, add the whites of the eggs beaten to a stiff froth with the above proportion of sugar. Bake three quarters of an hour.

979. **SMALL CHEESE SOUFFLE.**—Ingredients—Half oz. of fresh butter, 1 tablespoonful of flour, milk, 3 oz. of Parmesan cheese, white pepper, salt, yolks of 3 eggs, whites of 5 eggs.

Melt the butter in a saucepan, stir in the flour. When the two are well mixed put in a little milk, and the Parmesan cheese. Stir the mixture on a slow fire till it assumes the appearance of thick cream, but be careful not to let it boil; then add some white pepper, mix thoroughly, and if required, add a little salt. Keep on stirring the mixture at a moderate heat for about ten minutes; take the saucepan off the fire and stir the contents occasionally until quite cold, then stir in the yolks of the eggs beaten up with a little milk and strained, and finally add the whites whisked to a froth. Half fill some small paper cases with the mixture; put them into the oven to bake till done—from ten to fifteen minutes.

980. **SOUFFLE A LA VICEROY (hot)**—Ingredients—One pint of milk, ½ pint of cream, 3 oz. of flour, 5 oz. of white sugar, 5 eggs, 1 glass of noyeau, 1 glass of brandy, 2 oz. of ratafias, a small piece of chocolate, 3 oz. of butter.

Put into a stewpan the milk, cream, butter and sugar; boil these and whilst boiling stir in the flour, and keep stirring until the panada is cooked and leaves the sides of the stewpan quite clean. Take it off the fire and let it get cold, then stir in the yolks of the eggs, noyeau, and the brandy, two ounces of ratafias, roughly crushed, and about one ounce of grated chocolate, then whisk up the five whites into a firm snow, and gently stir in the mixture; turn it into a buttered mould and steam it for two hours. Serve it very hot, with a little sauce made as follows: Quarter pt. of water, a piece of cinnamon, two ounces of sugar, and a little red currant jelly; boil these well together and strain, then pour the sauce round the pudding souffle.

981. **BOILED CUSTARD.**—Ingredients—one quart of sweet milk, a stick of cinnamon, rind of one lemon, a few laurel leaves or bitter almonds, sugar to taste, yolks of 8 eggs, whites of 4.

Boil the milk with the cinnamon, lemon rind, and laurel leaves or bitter almonds, and sugar. Beat the yolks of the eggs with the whites, add a little milk, and strain into another dish.

When the milk boils remove from the fire, and strain; then add the egg to it. Return the whole to the saucepan and set on the fire, stirring diligently. Let it come to the boiling point, then pour into a jug and stir till nearly cold. It should be as thick as rich cream. Pour into glass, grate a little nutmeg over them and serve.

982. **BOILED ALMOND CUSTARD.**—Ingredients—Four bay leaves, 1 pt. of cream, a stick of cinnamon, 1 pt. of milk, 1 doz. bitter and 2 doz. sweet almonds, 4 whole eggs, 8 yolks of eggs, white sugar to taste.

Put the bay leaves with the cinnamon, cream, and milk into a clean saucepan on a slow fire, till they boil. While this is doing grate the sweet and bitter almonds into a basin, break in the whole eggs and the yolks one by one into a teacup, and as you find them good, put them into a basin; mix in sufficient loaf sugar in powder to sweeten it to your palate, whisk all well together, and when the milk boils take it off the fire for a minute or two before you pour it in; mix it well with the whisk, and strain it through a hair sieve into the saucepan that the cream was boiled in. Put it again on the fire, which must be slow, and stir it well till it begins to thicken, (it must not boil, or you will spoil it); remove it from the fire, and keep stirring it well till it is cool, otherwise it may curdle. As soon as it is cold, you can put it into the glasses or cups; grate a little nutmeg on the top of each.

983. **ALMOND CUSTARD.**—Ingredients—1 pint of new milk, 1 cup of pulverized sugar ¼ lb. of almonds blanched and pounded, 2 teaspoonfuls rose water, the yolks of 4 eggs.

Stir this over a slow fire until it is of the consistency of cream, then remove it quickly and put into a dish. Beat the whites with a little sugar added to the froth, and lay on top.

984. **ORANGE CUSTARD**—Ingredients—One Seville orange, 1 spoonful of the best brandy, 4 oz. white sugar, yolks of 4 eggs, 1 pt. of boiling cream, preserved orange.

Boil the rind of half the orange very tender; beat it in a marble mortar very fine; put to it the brandy and the juice of the orange and the sugar with yolks of the eggs. Then pour in gradually the boiling cream. Continue beating until cold. Pour into custard cups and stand in a dish of hot water. Allow them to stand until they are set, then take them out and some preserved orange on the top and serve.

985. FROZEN CUSTARD WITH FRUIT.—Ingredients—Two pts. of milk, same of cream, 6 eggs, 3 teacups of sugar, 1 pt. of berries, or peaches cut up small.

Let the milk nearly boil; beat the yolks of the eggs with the sugar and add the milk by degrees. Whip the whites of the eggs to a froth and add to the mixture; put all in a saucepan, stirring till it is a nice thick and smooth custard. When perfectly cold whisk in the cream and freeze. If the custard is allowed to freeze itself, stir in the fruit after the second beating.

986. CUSTARD.—Ingredients—One and a half quarts rich milk, one cup sugar, ½ box gelatine, four eggs, vanilla to taste.

Dissolve the gelatine in the milk; add the yolks and sugar; let it come to a boil, then remove from the fire. When cool, add whites of eggs, etc. Pour into mould. To be eaten with cream, if preferred.

987. BAKED CUSTARD.—Ingredients—Some nice pastry, 4 eggs, 3 gills of new milk, sugar to taste.

Line a good sized dish with the pastry; beat the eggs well, add slowly the new milk, sweeten to taste; pour on to the paste; bake in a moderate oven. Can be eaten hot or cold.

988. CUSTARD (for Cake).—Ingredients—One egg, ½ pint of milk, one teaspoonful of corn starch, 1 tablespoonful of flour, 2 tablespoonfuls of sugar.

Scald the milk, beat the sugar, flour, eggs and corn starch together; add the milk, boil until thick. Flavor, and when cold, spread between cake.

989. APPLE CUSTARD.—Ingredients—One pint of apple sauce, 1 pint of sweet milk, 3 eggs.

Flavor and sweeten to taste. Bake with an under crust.

990. CHOCOLATE CUSTARD.—Ingredients — One quart of milk, yolks of 6 eggs, 6 tablespoonfuls of sugar, ½ a cup of grated vanilla chocolate.

Boil the ingredients until thick enough, stirring all the time. When nearly cold flavor with vanilla. Pour into cups, and put the whites of the eggs beaten with some powdered sugar on top.

991. FRENCH CUSTARD.—Ingredients—One tablespoonful of *Fecule de pommes de terre*, or potato flour, 3 tablespoonfuls of cold milk, 1 pint of boiling milk, 2 oz. of white sugar, 2 eggs, a little flavoring.

Take the *Fecule de pommes de terre*, or potato flour, mix it smooth with the cold milk, then stir in the boiling milk in which the sugar has been dissolved ; boil the custard gently, stirring all the time until the custard becomes thick, then add the eggs well beaten, and the flavoring, and stir over the fire for four or five minutes. Pour the custard into a basin, stirring occasionally as it gets cold, to prevent a skin forming at the top. Note.—Corn flour may be substituted for the *Fecule de pommes de terre*, but it is not so delicate or appropriate for this purpose.

992. **CARAMEL CUSTARDS**.—Ingredients—A handful of loaf sugar, 6 eggs (yolks), 1 pint of milk.

Put the loaf sugar in a saucepan with a little water, and set it on the fire until it becomes a dark brown caramel, then add some more water (boiling). To produce a dark liquor take strong coffee. Beat up the yolks of the eggs with a little milk ; strain, add the milk, (sugar to taste), and as much caramel liquor (cold) as will give the mixture the desired color. Pour it in a well buttered mould ; put this in a *bain marie* with cold water ; then place the apparatus on a gentle fire, taking care that the water does not boil. Half an hour's steaming will set the custard, which then turn out and serve. By using the whites of one or two eggs in addition to the six yolks, the chances of the custard not breaking are made more certain.

993. **SNOW CUSTARD**.—Ingredients—Half a package of gelatine, 3 eggs, 1 pt. of milk, 2 teacups of sugar, juice from 1 lemon.

Soak the gelatine thoroughly in about two-thirds of a glass of water ; pour into a pint of boiling water. Stir till the gelatine is perfectly dissolved. Add two-thirds of the sugar and lemon juice. Whip the whites of the eggs to a stiff froth and when the gelatine is cold beat it into the whites, a spoonful at a time, for at least an hour. Whip steadily, and when firm pour into a mould wetted with cold water and set on the refrigerator. In five hours turn into a custard dish.

PRESERVES.

OBSERVATIONS ON PRESERVING.

Fruit for preserving must be gathered in dry weather, and should be carefully selected, discarding all bruised fruit, and purchasing only that of the largest and finest quality. Use only the best white sugar, or the preserve cannot be perfect, and nothing is saved. If common sugar is used, it causes a greater amount of scum, and of course this must be taken off, consequently evaporation reduces the quantity. In making syrups the sugar must be pounded and dissolved in the syrup before setting on the fire; no syrups or jellies should be boiled too high. Fruits must not be put into a thick syrup at first. Fruits preserved whole or sliced may be boiled in a syrup made of two lbs. of sugar to every one lb. of water, the quantity of syrup differing in some cases, but the general rule is one and a half the substance of fruit. We have found the following very good: To clarify six pounds of sugar, put into a preserving pan, and pour to it five pints of cold spring water; in another pint beat lightly up the white of one small egg, but do not froth it very much; add it to the sugar, and give it a stir to mix it well with the whole. Set the pan over a gentle fire when the sugar is nearly dissolved, and let the scum rise without being disturbed; when the syrup has boiled five minutes take it from the fire, let it stand a couple of minutes, and then skim it very clean; let it boil again, then throw in half a cup of cold water, which will bring the remainder of the scum to the surface; skim it until it is perfectly clear, strain it through a thin cloth, and it will be ready for use, or for further boiling.

All unripe fruit must be rendered quite tender by gentle scalding, before it is put into syrup, or it will not imbibe the sugar; and the syrup must be *thin* when it is first added to it, and be thickened afterwards by frequent boiling, or with additional sugar ; or the fruit will shrivel instead of becoming plump and clear. A pound of sugar boiled for ten minutes in one pint of water will make a very light syrup ; but it will gradually thicken if rapidly boiled in an uncovered pan. Two pounds of sugar to the pint of water, will become thick with a little more than half an hour's boiling, or with three or four separate boilings of eight or ten minutes each ; if too much reduced it will candy instead of remaining liquid.

In making jams many cooks after allowing the proper proportion of sugar to the fruit, put into the preserving pan without removing stones or skins until after boiling, as the flavor is thought to be finer by adopting this method. Glass bottles are preferable to any other as they allow inspection to detect incipient fermentation, which may be stayed by re-boiling. Copper or brass preserving pans are the best kind to use, but they require a great deal of care to keep clean ; the enamelled are very nice and easily kept in order. Jams should be kept in a dry, cool place, and if properly made will only require a small round of writing paper, oiled, and laid on to fit ; now tie down securely with a second paper brushed over with the white of egg to exclude the air. If you should have the least fear of the store closet being damp, it would be better for the first paper to be dipped in brandy. Inspect them every two or three months.

994. PLUM JAM.—Ingredients—Allow ¾ lb. of white sugar to 1 lb. of fruit.

It is difficult to give the exact quantity of sugar to be used in plum jam, in fact it entirely depends upon the quality of the plums used, therefore your own judgment will be necessary. After weighing the plums, halve them and remove the stones ; then place on a large dish and sprinkle with the sugar, leave them thus for twenty-four hours ; then put into a preserving pan and let them simmer gently on the back of the stove for about twenty-five or thirty minutes, then boil very quickly, for a quarter of an hour, skimming carefully, and stirring with a wooden spoon to prevent the jam sticking. It greatly improves the jam to put some kernels from the plum stones into it.

995. RED CURRANT JAM.—Ingredients—Three quarters of a lb. of white sugar to every pound of fruit.

Let the fruit be very ripe, remove from the stalks with a silver fork; dissolve the sugar over the fire, then put in the currants and boil for half an hour, stirring and skimming all the time. Put into jars and cover air tight.

996. BLACK CURRANT JAM.—Ingredients—One gill of water, 1 lb. of fruit to 1 lb. of sugar.

Purchase the fruit ripe and dry; having stripped from the stalk which can be done nicely with a silver fork, place them and the water into your preserving pan; boil for ten minutes; then add the sugar, and allow to boil three-quarters of an hour from the time it begins to simmer; keep it constantly stirred; carefully remove the scum. When done pot in the usual manner.

997. RASPBERRY JAM.—Ingredients—Allow 1 lb. of white sugar to 1 lb. of fruit, and 2 wineglasses of red currant juice.

Directly this fruit is purchased preserve it, if allowed to stand the jam and the flavor will not be so good; place in preserving pan and allow to boil twenty minutes, stirring constantly; add the sugar and currant juice and boil for half an hour. Be particular to skim well as this will make the jam nice and clear. When done, place in pots and cover in the usual manner.

998. GOOSEBERRY JAM.—Ingredients—Some fine full-grown unripe gooseberries, their weight in sugar, to 1 pt. of liquor allow 1 lb. of sugar.

Cut, and pick out the seeds of the gooseberries; put them into a pan of water, green, and put them into a sieve to drain; beat them in a marble mortar, with their weight in sugar. Boil a quart of them to a mash in a quart of water; squeeze, and add to the liquor, sugar in the above proportions; then boil and skim it, put in your green gooseberries, and having boiled them till very thick, clear, and of a nice green, put them into bottles.

999. DAMSON JAM.—Ingredients—Equal quantities of fruit and jelly.

Choose the fruit without blemish; remove the stones from the fruit, and put it and the sugar into your preserving pan; stir slowly until the sugar is melted, and remove all scum. After the jam has begun to simmer, allow it to boil for an hour; it is necessary to stir diligently or the jam will burn. When done, pot in the usual way.

1000. MULBERRY JAM.—Ingredients—Some ripe mulberries, 1 lb. sugar and 1 pint of mulberry juice to every pound of picked fruit.

Boil and skim the sugar with the juice for five minutes after the sugar is thoroughly dissolved; then add the fruit, and boil quickly for half an hour, stirring well; take off the fire, and, if quite stiff when cold, it is done sufficiently, if not, boil for another quarter of an hour and proceed to bottle in the usual way.

1001. RHUBARB JAM.—Ingredients—Rhubarb, to a pound of pulp allow 1 lb. of sugar, 1 oz. of sweet almond sblanched and chopped, and half a lemon cut into slices.

Peel and cut up the rhubarb, boil till reduced to a pulp with a very little water, add the sugar, almonds, and lemon; boil for three-quarters of an hour, or an hour; remove the lemon peel, and put it into pots.

1002. GREEN GRAPE JAM.—Ingredients—To 1 lb. of grapes allow $\frac{3}{4}$ lb. of sugar

Pick them carefully, and reject any that are injured; wash them. Put the grapes into a preserving pan, then a layer of sugar, than a layer of grapes. Boil on a moderate fire, stirring it all the time to prevent its burning, and as the grape stones rise take them out with a spoon, so that by the time the fruit is sufficiently boiled—about one hour—the stones will all have been taken out. Put into jars and cover in the usual way.

1003. BLACKBERRY JAM.—Ingredients—To every lb. of picked fruit allow 1 lb. of loaf sugar, and $\frac{1}{4}$ lb. of apples peeled and cored, and cut quite small.

Boil the fruit for ten minutes, add the sugar, boil, stir, and remove all scum; it will take from half to three-quarters of an hour.

1004. APRICOT OR PLUM JAM.—Ingredients—Take equal quantities of fruit and sugar.

Pound the sugar, pare and cut up with a silver knife some ripe apricots, or magnums, remove the stones, lay the fruit in a dish, strew over them half the sugar, and leave them till the following day; then boil and skim the remainder of the sugar, add the fruit, boil it up quickly, well skimming and stirring for twenty minutes; add the blanched kernels halved, boil for ten minutes more, and the jam will be ready to pot.

1005. **STRAWBERRY JAM.**—Ingredients—To 1 lb. of fruit allow ¾ lb. or 1 lb. of sugar, to 4 lbs. of strawberry add 1 pt. of red currant juice.

Put the currant juice and strawberries on to boil for thirty minutes, and stir carefully all the time. Then put in the sugar and boil up very quickly for twenty or twenty-five minutes removing any scum that arises. Put into your jars, covering air tight. If a pound of sugar is used there will be more jelly.

1006. **STRAWBERRY OR BARBERRY JAM.**—Ingredients— Some ripe but not too ripe strawberries, to every lb. of fruit allow 1 lb. of white sugar and ¼ pt. of currant juice.

Pick the fruit; pour the currant juice on the sugar. Boil the strawberries for twenty minutes, stirring well with a wooden spoon. Add the sugar and currant juice, and boil together on a trivet or hot plate for half an hour, carefully removing all the scum as it rises.

1007. **CHERRY JAM.**—Ingredients—To 1 lb. of cherries allow 1 lb. of sugar.

For this use ripe fruit, but carefully reject any which is bruised or over ripe. The Kentish are the best for this purpose, having a pleasant acid taste; other kinds are too sweet for the quantity of sugar necessary in preserving frut. To the stoned fruit, add the sugar; it will require stirring occasionally from the first, and continuously after it once comes to the boil, after which it must continue boiling for three-quarters of an hour; then try a little on a cold plate to see if it sets or jellies; if it does, pour it off into jars, and set in a cool dry place till the following day, when it should be covered down for keeping, if not, continue boiling until it will so set. It will not require skimming during the process of boiling, the scum will all boil away. The easiest way of stoning cherries is to tie a little loop of iron wire about the shape of a hairpin, on to a stick the length of a pencil; bind the two ends firmly to the stick, leaving the loop standing up about an inch long, and slightly bent forward. With this the stones are easily extracted.

1008. **QUINCE JAM.**—Ingredients—To 1 lb. of quinces allow ¾ lb. of sugar.

Peel and quarter your quinces, leaving the seeds in, as they readily impart their mucilage to water and thus thicken the syrup. Put the fruit and sugar into a preserving pan, and half a teacupful of water to moisten the bottom of the pan; stir the fruit and sugar frequently, and when it boils keep it boiling rapidly until the fruit is soft, and a clear red color. It will take about an hour, reckoning from the first boiling up. Put into jam pots, and cover when cold.

1009. APPLE JAM.—Ingredients—Allow to every 1 lb. of pared and cored fruit ¾ lb. of white sugar, the rind of one lemon, and juice of half a lemon.

Having peeled and cored the apples weigh them, and slice them very thin. Place in a stone jar and surround with boiling water, allow them to boil until tender; when tender place in a preserving pan, add the sugar, grated lemon rind and juice. Boil slowly half an hour from the time it begins to simmer, remove the scum, put into jars and cover in the usual manner.

1010. GREEN FIG PRESERVE.—Ingredients — Equal quantities of fruit and sugar, peel of 1 large lemon, a little ginger.

Lay the figs in cold water for twenty four hours, them simmer them till tender; put them again into cold water, and let them remain for two days, changing the water each day. If not quite soft simmer again, and replace in cold water until next day. Take their weight in loaf sugar, and with two-thirds of it make a syrup, in which simmer the figs for ten minutes. In two days take the third of the sugar, pounded fine, and pour the syrup from the figs on it. Make a rich syrup with the peel of the lemon and a little raw ginger, and boil the figs in it, then mix altogether and put into large jam pots. The figs may be cut in half, if preferred, after they have simmered until soft.

1011. PRESERVED MELONS.—Ingredients—Melon, salt and water, best white ginger to taste. To make syrup, 1 qt. of water to 1 lb. of white sugar, the rind of 3 lemons, another 1 lb. of sugar to each quart of syrup.

Take away the rind and seeds, and cut the melon about the size of pieces of ginger. Put them in strong salt and water, and let them remain for ten days, when it must be poured off, and fresh water put instead; this must be changed twice daily for three or four days till all taste of salt is gone from the melon. Scrape the outside off the best white ginger (the quantity according to taste), put it into a thin syrup made of the above proportions of water and sugar, drain the fruit, and pour the syrup and ginger over it boiling hot. Repeat this for three days, then add another pound of sugar to each quart of syrup; when boiled and skimmed add the rind of three lemons, cut lengthwise to each quart, put in the melons, and simmer until clear. After the first day's simmering the ginger may be sliced to impart more flavor, but it must not be allowed to boil.

The syrup, when done, must be rich and thick. It is better when kept a year.

1012. TO PRESERVE CITRON.—Ingredients—Citrons, sugar, and water.

Purchase fine citrons, pare and slice one inch thick, cut again into strips, remove the seeds, weigh, and allow one lb. of sugar to one lb. of fruit. Make a syrup, say five lbs. of sugar, half pint of water; when boiling add the fruit and boil three-quarters of an hour, test if done by piercing with a broom straw, and a few minutes before removing from the fire slice and seed a lemon, and with one root of ginger put into preserving pan, pot and cover air tight.

1013. PRESERVED PUMPKINS.—Ingredients—Equal proportions of sugar and pumpkin, 1 gill of lemon juice.

Cut the pumpkin in two, peel and remove the seed, cut in pieces about the size of a fifty-cent piece, after weighing place in a deep vessel in layers, first sprinkling a layer of sugar then of pumpkin and so on, until it is finished; now add the lemon juice and set aside for three days; now for every three pounds of sugar add half pint of water and boil until tender. Pour into a pan, setting aside for six days, pour off the syrup and boil until thick, skim and add the pumpkin while boiling; bottle in the usual manner.

1014. QUINCES PRESERVED WHOLE.—Ingredients—Some ripe quinces, to every pint of water allow 3 lbs. of white sugar.

Pare the quinces and put them into the preserving pan, three-parts covered with cold water (if they should float while the water is being poured on them, press them down with a plate until you have gauged the exact height of the water); take out the quinces, measure the water and add the sugar. Let this boil rapidly in the preserving-pan for five minutes, and then put in the quinces. The syrup should not cover them at first, but when they are half-cooked it will then amply cover the fruit. Boil the quinces rapidly, until soft enough for a knitting-needle to pierce them easily, which should be in an hour and a half, reckoning from the first boiling up. Take the quinces out carefully, so as not to break them, and lay them on dishes to cool. Run the syrup through a jelly bag, or a piece of new flannel, put in a gravy strainer: this frees it of all odd little bits that may boil from the outside of the quinces, and makes it clearer. Put the the syrup back in the preserving-pan, and boil it rapidly until it will jelly when dropped on a plate; put the quinces into the boiling syrup, and let them simmer gently for ten minutes. Place each quince carefully in wide-necked jars, pour the hot syrup over them, and when cold cover in the usual way.

1015. **PRESERVED ORANGES**.—Ingredients—any number of oranges, with rather more then their weight in sugar, allow rather more than half a pint of water to each pound of sugar.

Slightly grate and score the oranges round and round with a knife, but not very deeply. Put them into cold water for three days, changing the water twice each day. Tie them up in a cloth and boil them until they are quite soft, that is, soft enough to be penetrated by the head of a pin. While they are boiling place the sugar on the fire with the water; let it boil for a few minutes, then strain it through muslin. Put the oranges into the syrup and boil till it jellies and is of a yellow color. Try the syrup by putting some to cool; it should not be too stiff. The syrup need not cover the oranges completely, but they must be turned so that each part gets thoroughly done. Place the oranges in pots, cover with syrup, and tie down with brandied papers. This is an excellent way of preserving oranges or shaddocks whole. Only they should be looked at now and then, and boiled up again in fresh syrup, if what they are in has become too hard, which, however, if they have been properly done, will not be the case. They form a nice dish for dessert or for serving, filled with whipped cream, or custard, either cold or gently warmed through in the syrup in a stewpan. Oranges can also be canned in the American fashion in wide-mouthed bottles.

1016. **QUINCE MARMALADE**.— Ingredients — Quinces, to every lb. of pulp allow 2 lbs. of sugar.

Rub off all the down from the quinces, and cut off the tops and stalks. Put the quinces in a preserving pan with plenty of water and boil till they are soft; then remove them from the fire, and pass the pulp through a hair sieve, and beat it till it is soft and white; put the sugar on the fire with water, and let it boil till it is thick, and will fall from the spoon in flakes, commonly called feather point. Take the pan off the fire, and mix in the pulp; it is best to put a little of the sugar to the pulp, and keep on adding by degrees till it is tolerably thin, when it will mix more readily with the larger quantity of sugar; when all is well mixed, return the pan to the fire, and let the mixture get thoroughly warm, but do not allow it to boil, and stir all the time, or it will get burnt. Put the jam into jars, and allow them to stand in the sun, for two or three days, when there ought to be a thick crust on the top. This marmalade is very good for colds, and a spoonful mixed in half a glass of wine is considered strengenthing.

1017. **ORANGE MARMALADE.**—Ingredients—Twelve fair sized Seville oranges, some spring water, juice of 3 or 4 oranges, to every pound of peel and juice allow 1½ lbs. of white sugar, allow to this amount of sugar, 1½ pts. of water.

Take the oranges with smooth, highly colored skins, score the peel off in quarters, taking with it as much of the white skin as you can without breaking the pulp; as you remove the peel, put it into a basin of spring water; put it all, when ready, into a stewpan, with enough spring water to cover the peel; change the water several times during the boiling process, and when the peel is quite soft and very tender, take it out of the pan and drain it on a hair sieve. Spread out the peel, when nearly dry, on a pasteboard, and cut it into fine shreds; squeeze the oranges, and add the juice of the lemons; then add the sugar; allow to this amount of sugar the above proportion of water obtained by washing and straining the pulp of the oranges. Boil and skim carefully fifteen or twenty minutes, then add the washed pulp and juice, and boil until it commences to thicken, then put in the pulp and boil for twenty or thirty minutes, or until it jellies properly.

1018. **APPLE MARMALADE.**—Ingredients—Some good cooking apples, ¾ lb. of of fruit, ½ teacupful of water to 6 lbs. of sugar, a few cloves, cinnamon or lemon peel for flavor.

Peel, core, and thinly slice the apples (apples that cook to a smooth pulp easily); put the sugar in a preserving pan (a tin or iron saucepan will turn them black), with the water; let it gradually melt, and boil it for ten minutes; then put in the sliced apple, and a few cloves, cinnamon, or lemon peel to flavor, if liked. Boil rapidly for an hour, skim well, and put in jam pots; it should be quite a smooth pulp, clear, and a bright amber color. Will keep good for twelve months.

1019. **VEGETABLE MARROW (with ginger).**—Ingredients— A nice firm marrow, to 1 lb. of marrow 1 lb. of sugar, ¼ lb. of bruised ginger, a little lemon peel if liked.

Peel a nice firm vegetable marrow, and cut it into small thick slices, then boil these till they get quite tender; put the slices on a strainer or sieve for twenty-four hours, till all the water has run out; weigh it and take an equal quantity of sugar. Boil the syrup and ginger in about a pint of cold water; when clear and skimmed, put the marrow in for two or three minutes, and then pour it out into a basin. Do this two or three times every two days, boiling only the syrup, keeping the marrow separate, and pouring the boiling syrup on the marrow. This is sometimes called " mock ginger," and is certainly an excellent substitute. It will keep well, but requires looking at occasionally.

1020. **SWEET TOMATO PICKLE**.—Ingredients—3½ lbs. of tomatoes, 1¾ lbs. of sugar, ½ oz. each of cinnamon mace, and cloves mixed, 1 pt. of vinegar.

Peel and slice the tomatoes, sticking into them the cloves; put altogether into a stewpan and stew an hour. When done pack in glass jars, and pour the syrup over boiling hot.

1021. **SWEET PEACH PICKLE**.—Ingredients—To 4 lbs. of peaches allow 2 lbs. of white sugar, ½ oz. each of mace, cinnamon and cloves mixed, and 1 pt. of the best white vinegar.

Pour scalding water over the peaches and remove the skins with a butter knife; drop into cold water; stick four cloves in each peach. Lay the peaches in preserving pan with the sugar sprinkled over them; bring gradually to the boil, add vinegar and spice, boil five or six minutes. Remove the peaches and place in bottles. Boil the syrup thick and pour over boiling hot.

1022. **PEACHES IN BRANDY**.—Ingredients—¼ lb. of sugar to 1 lb. of fruit, brandy.

Wipe, weigh, and pick the fruit, and have ready the fine sugar in fine powder. Put the fruit into an ice pot that shuts very close; throw the sugar over it, and then cover the fruit with brandy. Between the top and cover of the pot put a piece of double cap-paper. Set the pot into a saucepan of water till the brandy be as hot as you can possibly bear to put your finger in, but it must not boil. Put the fruit into a jar, and pour the brandy on it. When cold, put a bladder over, and tie it down tightly.

1023. **BRANDIED QUINCES**.—Ingredients—Half lb. of white sugar to 1 lb. of fruit, brandy.

Peel some small ripe quinces, and allow the above proportion of sugar and fruit; boil the quinces half an hour in barely sufficient water to cover them; drain them, and put aside to get cool; empty the water out of the preserving-pan and put in the sugar, moistening it with a little of the water in which the quinces were boiled, and let the sugar boil for ten minutes; put in the quinces and let them boil rapidly for half an hour. Place them in wide-mouthed jars, as free from syrup as possible, boil down the syrup until it jellies when dropped on a plate, set it aside in a large jug or bowl, and when quite cold mix an equal quantity of good brandy with the syrup, and pour over the quinces in the jars. Cover closely with paper dipped in white of egg.

1024. **GRAPES IN BRANDY.**

Take some close bunches of grapes, but not too ripe, either red or white, and put them into a jar, with a quarter pound of sugar candy; fill the jar with common brandy; tie it close with a bladder, and set in a dry place. Morello cherries are done the same way.

1025. **TO KEEP CHESNUTS (for Winter use).**

Dry them after removing them from their green husks; put in a box or barrel mixed with, and covered over by, fine and dry sand. Three gals. of sand to one gallon of chesnuts. If there be maggots in any of the nuts they will come out and work up through the sand to get the air, and thus you have the chesnuts sweet, sound and fresh.

1026. **TO KEEP WALNUTS FRESH.**

Put a dessert spoonful of salt into one quart of water. Put the nuts in and let them stand a day and a night, then with a clean cloth rub dry, and store.

CANNED FRUITS, &c.

CANNING FRUIT.

1027. PEACHES (to Can).

First prepare the syrup. For canned fruits, one quart of granulated sugar to two quarts of water is the proper proportion; to be increased or lessened according to the quantity of fruit to be canned, but always twice as much water as sugar. Use a porcelain kettle, and, if possible, take care that it is kept solely for canning and preserving—nothing else. Have another porcelain kettle by the side of the first, for boiling water (about three quarts). Put the peaches, a few at a time, into a wire basket, such as is used to cook asparagus, etc. See that it is perfectly clean and free from rust. Dip them, when in the basket, into a pail of boiling water for a moment and transfer immediately into a pail of cold water. The skin will then at once peel off easily, if not allowed to harden by waiting. This, besides being a neat and expeditious way of peeling peaches, also saves the best part of the fruit, which is so badly wasted in the usual mode of paring fruit. As soon as peeled, halve and drop the peaches into boiling water, and let them simmer —not boil hard—till a silver fork can be passed through them easily. Then lift each half out separately with a wire spoon and fill the can made ready for use; pour in all the boiling syrup which the jar will hold; leave it a moment for the fruit to shrink while filling the next jar; then add as much more boiling syrup as the jar will hold, and cover and screw down tightly immediately. Continue in this way, preparing and sealing only one jar at a time, until all is done. If any syrup is left over, add to it the water in which the peaches were simmered, and a little more sugar; boil it down till it "ropes" from the spoon and you have a nice jelly, or, by adding some peaches or other fruit, a good dish of marmalade. Peaches or other fruit, good, but not quite nice enough for canning, can be used up in this way very economically. Peaches to be peeled as directed above should not be too green or too ripe, else, in the first place, the skin cannot be peeled off; or, if too ripe, the fruit will fall to pieces.

1028 (Another way).

After peeling and halving as above directed, lay a clean towel or cloth in the bottom of a steamer over a kettle of boiling water and put the fruit on it, half filling the steamer. Cover tightly and let it steam while making the syrup. When that is ready, and the fruit steamed till a silver fork will pass through easily, dip each piece gently into the boiling syrup; then as gently place in the hot jar, and so continue till all have been thus scalded and put in the jar. Then fill *full* with syrup, cover and seal immediately. While filling, be sure and keep the jars hot.

1029. (Another way).

Peel, halve, remove the stones, and prepare the syrup as directed; and when it is boiling drop in enough fruit for one jar; watch closely, and the instant they are sufficiently tender, take out each half with care and put into a hot jar till full. Then dip in all the boiling syrup it will hold. Cover tightly, set aside, and prepare for the next jar. Be sure and skim the syrup each time before adding more fruit. After jars are filled and the covers screwed on, before setting them away, every little while give the screw another twist until it cannot be moved farther.

1030. PEARS.

The skin will not peel off so easily as the peach by dipping them in boiling water, but it will loosen or soften enough to be taken off with less waste of the fruit than if pared without scalding. Prepare the syrup and proceed as for peaches. They will require longer cooking; but as soon as a silver or well-plated fork will pass through easily, they are done. Longer cooking destroys the flavor.

1031. PINEAPPLES.

Pare very carefully with a silver or plated knife, as steel injures all fruit. With the sharp point of the knife dig out as neatly and with as little waste as possible, all the "eyes" and black specks, then cut out each of the sections in which the "eyes" were, in solid pieces clear down to the core. By doing this all the real fruit is saved, leaving the core a hard, round woody substance, but it contains considerable juice. Take this core and wring it with the hands as one wrings a cloth, till all the juice is extracted, then throw it away. Put the juice thus saved into the syrup; let it boil up five minutes, skim till clear, then add the fruit. Boil as short a time as possible, and have the flesh tender. The pineapple loses flavor by overcooking more readily than any other fruit. Fill into well-heated jars, add all the syrup the jar will hold; cover and screw down as soon as possible.

1032. PLUMS.

Plums should be wiped with a soft cloth or dusted, never washed. Have the syrup all ready, prick each plum with a silver fork to prevent the skin from bursting, and put them into the syrup. Boil from eight to ten minutes, judging by the size of the fruit. Dip carefully into the hot jars, fill full, and screw on the cover immediately. Cherries may be put up in the same way.—*Beecher.*

1033. PEARS (Canned).—Ingredients—Bartlett pears, 1 quart of fruit, 1 pint of water, ¼ lb. of white sugar.

Make the syrup and set on the stove to boil, peel the pears and plunge into cold water as soon as pared; when the syrup boils put the pears in, and boil until you can pierce them easily with a piece of broom straw; dip the cans in hot water, put in the fruit, pour boiling syrup over and seal.

1034. PLUMS (Canned).—Ingredients—Syrup, 2 wineglasses of water and ¼ lb. of sugar to each 3 quarts of fruit.

When the sugar is melted and the water luke-warm put the plums in. Let it come slowly to the boil. Let them boil *gently* for five minutes. Put the plums into bottles, *fill* them with the boiling syrup (take care that there is as much syrup in the bottles as they will hold). Screw up immediately and set in a dark dry place.

1035. STRAWBERRIES (Canned).—Ingredients—Allow to each 1 lb. of fruit ¾ lb. of sugar.

Put berries and sugar into a large flat dish and allow to stand about four hours, then draw off the juice and put into preserving pan and allow to come to a boil, removing the scum as it rises; then put in the berries, and let them come to a boil. Put into warm bottles and seal quickly.

1036. CHERRIES (Canned).—Ingredients—To every 1 lb. of fruit ½ lb. of sugar, 3 gills of water.

Put the sugar and water on the fire to heat, and as soon as it comes to a boil put in the cherries and only allow them to *scald* for a quarter of an hour; put into bottles boiling hot and seal. A few of the kernels put in to scald with the fruit imparts a fine flavor. Note—Be sure to skim well.

1037. PEACHES (Canned).—Ingredients—To every 1 lb. of fruit allow 5 oz. of sugar, 1 gill of water.

Pour hot water over the peaches and the skin will come off; drop into cold water to prevent them changing color. As soon as the syrup has come to a boil, put in the peaches and allow them them to boil till tender. Try them with a broom straw and if tender place in hot bottles, pour over the boiling syrup to nearly running over and seal immediately. NOTE—Care must be taken that they are not over boiled or they will break.

1038. TO BOTTLE FRUIT.—Ingredients—Any fresh fruit, large-mouthed bottles, new corks.

Secure the fruit not very ripe and picked on a fine day; have the bottles clean and dry, put in the fruit, cover with pieces of bladder tied securely, stand them in a boiler with cold water to the necks, put the boiler on the fire, and allow to boil; as soon as the bladders begin to swell, pierce them with a large pin. Now let the fire out and allow the bottles to stand until cold. The following day remove the bladders and fill up the bottles with sugar. Be careful to have the corks close at hand, and just before corking hold a couple of lighted matches in the mouth of the bottle, and, before the gas has had time to escape, cork and cover with resin.

1039. GREEN GOOSEBERRIES (To Bottle).

Top and tail the gooseberries, and then fill wide-mouthed bottles, shaking them down till no more can be put in; then tie down with damp (not wet) bladder, and place the bottles, surrounded by hay, in a boiler of cold water, over a slow fire; let them simmer till reduced about one-third, then take the boiler off the fire, and let the bottles remain in it till quite cold.

1040. STONE FRUITS (To Bottle).—

For this purpose wide-necked glass bottles must be used. Fill them with the fruit, as closely packed as possible, and into the mouth of each put quarter pound of finely powdered white sugar. Tie a piece of wet bladder, tightly stretched, over each mouth, to exclude the air; place them in a large fish kettle, packing them with hay, which should surround each bottle, and line the sides of the kettle, to prevent their either touching it or each other; this will prevent their breaking; fill the kettle with water, which must not come quite up to the bladder coverings; place it on the fire, or if a very hot one, to the side will be better, letting it simmer until you see that the fruit is cooked, by which time it will have considerably sunk in the bottles; the kettle must then be removed from the the fire, but the bottles must not be taken from it until the water is perfectly cold. During the time the kettle is on the fire, the bladders will require frequent moistening with a little water to prevent them from bursting; should this happen, at once tie on a fresh piece of wet bladder. The bottles must be wiped dry after removing from the water, and should be kept in a dry, cool place. The bladders must never be taken off till the fruit is required for use, as it will not keep after the bottle has been once opened.

1041 PEARS FOR DESSERT.

Take the finest pears just ripe, just cover with water, simmer till tender, but not in the least broken; lift them out into cold water. Now measure the water you have simmered them in; to each half pint put one pound of sugar. Boil up the syrup, then simmer the pears for five minutes; repeat this for three days, but allow ten minutes simmering the last day. Keep the pears in the syrup; the day before any are wanted remove from it and dry in a very cool oven. Or you may stew pears in a syrup of five oz. sugar, six cloves, six allspice, half pint water, and half pint port wine. This is the proportion for eight large pears. Pure claret may be used instead of wine and water. Simmer slowly till tender, probably three hours. A few drops of cochineal improve the color if water has been used. Pears and plumbs in equal quantities, with a few of the kernels of the latter chopped, preserve beautifully in the above syrup.

1042. SYRUP (1).

Take of sugar ten pounds; water three pints. Dissolve the sugar in the water with a gentle heat.

1043. SYRUP (2).

Take of pure sugar ten pounds; boiling water three pints. Dissolve the sugar in the water with the aid of a gentle heat.

1044. SYRUP (3).

In making syrups, for which neither the weight of the sugar nor the mode of dissolving it is specified, the following rule is to be observed:—Take of refined sugar, reduced to a fine powder, twenty-nine ounces; the liquor prescribed one pint. Add the sugar by degrees, and digest with a moderate heat, in a close vessel, until it is dissolved, frequently stirring it; set the solution aside for twenty-four hours, take off the scum, and pour off the syrup from the feces, if there be any.

1045. SYRUP (4).

Take of sugar two and a half pounds; water a pint. Dissolve the sugar in the water with the aid of heat, remove any scum which may form, and strain the solution while hot.

JELLIES.

OBSERVATIONS ON JELLIES.

Jelly is usually made from calves' feet or gelatine; made from the latter, the process is simple; made from the former, it is considered more nutritious and takes a longer time in the preparation, and it is also more expensive. The stock should be made the day before the jelly is required, while gelatine needs only to be dissolved. When veal is in season calves' feet will be cheap; they are usually sold scalded, but they will need blanching before using. The first operation will be to divide the foot into four pieces through the joints between the hoofs, and sawing the bone in two. Place in a stewpan with enough cold water to cover them; allow them to come to the boil (this is blanching). Remove from the stewpan, wash in cold water, and having thrown away the water they were boiled in, wash out the stewpan and replace the pieces. Cover with two quarts and one pint of cold water; allow it to come gradually to a boil. Remove the scum as it rises (be very particular about the skimming). Let it simmer about six hours; this done strain through a hair sieve and set aside to get cold. The following day remove any fat there may be on the top (be careful to remove every particle). It is ready now to be cleared and flavored. Place in a stewpan; take two lemons, pare off the rind (in paring the rind be careful not to take any of the white as it would impart a bitter taste). Add to the stock; strain into it also the juice from three lemons, and a quarter pound of sugar, four cloves and a stick of cinnamon. Now take the whites of two eggs, their crushed shells also, and add to the stock. Now stir well over the fire till the jelly boils; remove the pan to the back of the stove allowing the cover to be only half way on. Do not touch it for twenty minutes. Then it is ready to clear. Dip the jelly bag into hot water, wring dry, and if in winter place near the fire, if in summer far from it, and drain the jelly through the bag, having first placed a vessel to receive it. If not clear, drain through a second time. Now add a gill of sherry and half a gill of brandy. If a gelatine jelly is desired observe the following rules:—In warm weather a larger proportion of gelatine will be required for stiffening than is necessary in cold, and jelly will set much quicker in small moulds than large. It is not wise to make jellies too stiff. They should be stiff enough to retain their shape and yet tremble when touched. A good rule is to allow one ounce of gelatine to a pint and a half of liquid. Soak the gelatine in enough water to cover it for one and a half hours. Now take as much water as it is wise to use and add to the gelatine, add also sugar, lemon and flavoring ingredients. Place the stewpan over the fire, whisk till it rises; set it at the back of the stove, allow to stand twenty minutes, strain through a jelly bag, add the wine and set in moulds.

A good strainer for jelly may be made by using a wooden chair without rails on the inside, turn upside down on a table; take a perfectly clean teacloth, tie the four corners to the legs of the chair, setting a basin underneath to receive the jelly. The teacloth should be dipped in boiling water before using. Jellies may be strained a third time if necessary.

1046. FRUIT JELLIES.

The fruit should be placed in a jar, and the jar set in a stewpan of warm water, covered and allowed to boil until the fruit is broken; take a strong jelly bag and press a little of the fruit at a time, turning out each time the skins; allow two pounds of sugar to one quart of juice, set on the stove to boil again. Many good cooks heat the sugar by placing in the oven and stirring now and then to prevent burning. When the juice begins to boil (watch that it does not boil over twenty-five minutes), then add the heated sugar; stir well and just bring to a boil, remove directly from the stove, dip the vessels to contain it in hot water, and set them upon a dish cloth wrung out of warm water, pouring the boiling liquid into them; cover in the usual manner.

1047. **PINEAPPLE JELLY.**—Ingredients—A moderate sized pineapple, 1 qt. of jelly.

Peel the pineapple, halve lengthwise and cut into thin slices; infuse into the jelly the rind of the pineapple (well washed) and put first a layer of jelly, and when nearly set lay a border of pineapple over one upon another forming a ring, and cover with jelly, and so on till all are used.

1048. **MULLED JELLY.**—Ingredients—One tablespoonful of currant or grape jelly, white of 1 egg, a little loaf sugar. ½ pt. of boiling water, a slice of toast or 2 crackers.

Take the jelly, beat with it the white of the egg and the sugar; pour in the boiling water and break in the toast.

1049. **CRAB APPLE JELLY.**—Ingredients—Some nice crab apples (Siberian are the best for this purpose), 1 lb. of sugar to each pint of juice.

Cut the apples to pieces neither paring nor seeding them, as the seeds give a very pleasant flavor to the jelly; put into a stone vessel and place in a pot of hot water; allow to boil eight or nine hours; cover the vessel (with the fruit in) tightly and leave all night; next morning squeeze out the juice, add the sugar hot in the above proportions, stirring rapidly all the time, allow it just to come to the boil and remove directly from the stove. Dip your jars in hot water and fill with the scalding jelly.

1050. **QUINCE JELLY.**—Ingredients—Some ripe quinces, allowing 1 pt. of water to each pound of fruit, ¾ lb. of sugar to each pound of juice.

Prepare the quinces and put them in water in the above proportions; simmer gently till the juice becomes colored, but only very pale; strain the juice through a jelly bag, but do not press the fruit, allow it to drain itself. Put the strained juice in a preserving pan and boil twenty minutes, then stir in the sugar in the above proportions and stir over the fire for twenty minutes, taking off the scum, and pour into glasses to set. It should be rich in flavor, but pale and beautifully transparent. Long boiling injures the color.

1051. **RASPBERRY JELLY**—Ingredients—Some ripe, carefully picked raspberries, allow ¾ lb. of pounded sugar to every pound of fruit.

Boil the raspberries for ten minutes, strain and weigh the juice and add the sugar in the above proportions and boil for fifteen or twenty minutes. Skim and stir well.

1052. **CHERRY JELLY**.—Ingredients—Maydukes or Kentish cherries (allowing ¾ pt. of water to 1 lb. of fruit).

Boil the cherries in the water, strain the juice and proceed as for raspberry jelly.

1053. **RED CURRANT JELLY**.—Ingredients—Red currants, ¾ lb. of sugar to 1 lb. of juice.

Pick the the fruit and simmer it in water for about an hour, or until the juice flows freely; strain, boil up the juice, add the sugar, and boil again, skimming and stirring well for fifteen minutes. Put into small pots, and when cold and firm cover it.

1054. **BLACK CURRANT JELLY**.

Make in the same way, but use a larger proportion of sugar.

1055. **WHITE CURRANT JELLY**.—Ingredients.—Fruit, sugar.

Pick the fruit carefully, weigh it, and put into the preserving pan equal quantities of fruit and sugar. Boil quickly for ten minutes, and strain the juice into the pots; when cold and stiff cover them.

1056. **BLACKBERRY JELLY**.

Make it as directed for red currant, but use only ten ounces of sugar to each pound of juice. The addition of a little lemon juice is an improvement.

1057. **BARBERRY JELLY**.—Ingredients—Barberries, a little water, ¾ lb. of sugar to every pound of juice.

Take ripe barberries, carefully reject any spotted or decayed ones, wash, drain them and strip off the stalks. Boil with a very little water till quite tender, press out and strain the juice, boil up the juice, add the sugar, and boil for ten minutes, skimming and stirring as above.

1058. **MEDLAR JELLY**.—Ingredients—Some ripe medlars, sugar.

Put ripe medlars into a jar with a very little water, bruising them slightly as you put them in; tie down the jar, and put it into a slow oven for ten or twelve hours. Strain off the juice without pressure, weigh it, and allow equal weights of sugar and juice. Boil the juice, add the sugar, and boil again, skimming and stirring well till it jellies.

1059. **GREEN GOOSEBERRY JELLY**.—Ingredients—Some carefully picked gooseberries (allowing to each pound of fruit ¾ pint of water), to every lb. of juice allow 1 lb. of white sifted sugar.

Boil the fruit in the water, reduce them to a pulp—it will take half an hour—strain through a jelly-bag, weigh the sugar in the above proportions; boil up the juice quickly and add the sugar, boil till reduced to a jelly (about twenty minutes), skim and stir well; pour into pots.

1060. RED GOOSEBERRY JELLY.

Make it in the same way as the green, but three-quarters pound of sugar will be sufficient for each pound of juice. In straining the juice be careful not to press the fruit. The surplus fruit, with the addition of some currant juice, can be made into common jam for children, &c.

1061. MIXED FRUIT JELLY.—Ingredients—Fruit, strawberries, currants, cherries, etc., ¾ lb. of sugar to each pound of juice.

Take ripe fruit, strip off the stalks and remove the stones from the cherries, boil altogether for half an hour, strain the juice. Boil up the juice, add the sugar in the above proportions, stirring well till quite dissolved, boil again for fifteen or twenty minutes till it jellies, stirring frequently, and carefully removing all scum as it rises.

1062. QUINCE JELLY.—Ingredients—Some ripe quinces, to every lb. of quince allow 1 lb. of crushed sugar.

Peel, cut up, and core some fine ripe quinces. Put them in sufficient cold water to cover them, and stew gently till soft, but not red. Strain the juice without pressure, boil the juice for twenty minutes, add the sugar and boil again till it jellies— about a quarter of an hour—stir and skim well all the time. Strain it again through a napkin, or twice folded muslin, pour into pots or moulds, and when cold cover it. The remainder of the fruit can be made into marmalade with three-quarters pound of sugar, and quarter pound of juicy apples to every pound of quinces, or it can be made into compotes or tarts.

1063. QUINCE AND APPLE JELLY.—Ingredients—equal quantities of quinces and apples, to every pound of juice allow ¼ lb. of white sugar.

Stew the fruit separately till tender (the quinces will take longer), strain the juice, mix it and add the sugar. Proceed as in quince jelly.

1064. APPLE JELLY.—Ingredients—Some sound apples, allow ¾ lb. of sugar to each pound of juice.

Peel, core, and quarter some sound apples, and throw them into cold water as they are done; boil them till tender, then strain the juice from them through a fine sieve, and afterwards through a jelly bag—if necessary pass it through twice, as the juice should be quite clear, boil up the juice, add the sugar, stir till melted, and boil for another ten minutes, add the strained juice of a lemon to every one and half pound juice just before it is finished.

1065. **CHARTREUSE OF ORANGES.**—Ingredients—One-half pt. of water, 6 oranges, sugar to taste, 1 wineglass of sherry, 2 oz. isinglass, 1 pt. cream, some sweetened orange juice, make a very clear orange jelly with the water, 4 oranges, sherry, 1½ oz. of isinglass, sugar to taste.

Divide two or three oranges into quarters, and with a sharp knife carefully remove from each quarter every particle of skin of any sort. Have two plain moulds, one about an inch and a quarter more in diameter than the other. Pour a very little jelly at the bottom of the larger mould, and place in it a layer of orange quarters prepared as above (if too thick, they should be split in two lengthwise) ; cover them with more jelly, but only put enough to get a smooth surface. Lay this on ice to set. When it is nearly firm put the small mould aside the large one, taking care to place it exactly in the middle, so that the vacant space between the two moulds be of the same width. In this vacant space dispose prepared orange quarters, filling up the interstices with jelly as you go on, until the whole of the space is filled up. Place the mould upon ice and proceed to whip a pint of cream with half an ounce of isinglass and some sweetened orange juice, which must be added to it a very little at a time, else the cream will not rise into a froth. When the cream is ready and the jelly set, remove the inner mould by pouring warm water into it, and fill up the inner space of the chartreuse with the cream. Set it on ice for an hour, turn out and serve.

1066. **PEACH JELLY.**

Pare, stone and slice the peaches, crack some of the stones and remove the kernels, put the peaches and kernels into a jar and stand the jar in a pot of boiling water, stir frequently pressing the fruit against the sides of the jar; when it is well broken strain, and allow the juice of a lemon to every pint of juice, mix and allow one pound of sugar to one pint of juice, put the juice on to simmer half and hour then add the sugar hot; allow it just to come to a boil, and remove from the fire ; allow to get cold ; cover with paper soaked in brandy, then with paper brushed over with the white of egg.

1067. **ICELAND MOSS.**—Ingredients—One oz. of Iceland moss, 1 small teacupful of sugar, 1 quart of water.

Wash the moss in cold water and set in a vessel of cold water to soak all night, when soaked,, dry in a cloth and place in a stewpan with the above proportion of water, allow to boil one hour and a quarter stirring frequently, strain and add the sugar, serve with milk and wine.

1068. **MILK JELLY.**—Ingredients—One qt. and 1 gill of milk, 1 cow heel, sugar to taste, a small stick of cinnamon.

Cut the heel into pieces and place in a jar with the milk and cinnamon, cover the lid, tie a paper over the lid tightly, place in the oven and allow to stew for three and a half hours; strain and sweeten to taste.

1069. **LEMON JELLY.**—Ingredients—One qt. of calf's foot jelly, ½ pt. of lemon juice, 10 oz. of fine sugar, thin rinds of 3 lemons, whites of 5 and the broken shells of 2 eggs.

Melt the calf's foot jelly, mix with it the lemon juice, sugar and rind of lemon with yolks and shells of eggs. Let it boil and then simmer ten minutes; let it stand a little and then pour through a jelly bag till all is clear. A pinch of isinglass added during the simmering is of great assistance. Pour it into a mould when clear, let it stand till set, and then turn out in a glass dish.

1070. **ORANGE JELLY**—Ingredients—Rind of 2 Seville, and 2 sweet oranges, and 2 lemons, juice of three of each, ¼ lb. of lump sugar, ¼ pt. of water, 1 qt. of jelly, 2 oz. of isinglass.

Grate the rind of the fruit, squeeze the juice, and strain it. Take the sugar and water and boil it with the juice till it almost candies. Have ready the jelly, add the syrup to it and boil it up once, strain the jelly and let it stand some little time to settle before it is poured into the mould.

1071. **A NICE JELLY.**—Ingredients—Two tablespoonfuls of gum arabic, 2 of isinglass, 2 of white sugar candy, a grated nutmeg, a pint of Madeira, or port wine, or milk.

Put all into a jar, and set it by the fire, or in a pan of water until dissolved, then pour upon a plate; cut as desired.

1072. **HARTSHORN JELLY.**—Ingredients—Half lb. of hartshorn shavings, 3 quarts of water, ½ pint of Rhenish wine, ¼ lb. of white sugar, whites of 4 eggs, juice of 4 lemons.

Boil the hartshorn shavings in the water over a gentle fire till it becomes a jelly; when a little hangs on a spoon it is done enough. Strain it hot, put it into a well tinned saucepan and add to it the wine and a quarter pound of loaf sugar. Beat the whites of the eggs to a froth, and stir sufficiently for the whites to mix with the jelly. Boil it two or three minutes, then add the juice of the lemons and boil it again two minutes longer. When it is finely curdled and of a pure white, pass it through a linen bag into a basin until it becomes quite clear, and has the appearance of a fine amber color. This is a very nice dish for invalids.

1073. **IVORY JELLY.**—Ingredients—To each lb. of ivory powder put 3 quarts of water, juice and rind of 3 lemons, whites and shells of 2 eggs, ½ pint of good mild beer, and sugar to taste.

Stew the powder and water in an earthen vessel down to three pints, which will take about twelve or fourteen hours. When cold turn out and take the jelly carefully from the sediment. Put the jelly into a clean pan, adding the juice and rind of the lemons, eggs, beer and sugar. Stir all well together, letting it boil until the sediment rises to the top; remove the pan from the fire. Let it stand a few minutes before putting it into the jelly bag.]

1074. **PUNCH JELLY.**—Ingredients—Two calves' feet, 4 quarts water, sugar to taste, juice and rind of 1 lemon, whites of 3 eggs whisked to a froth, rum to flavor.

Take the calves' feet, chop into convenient pieces and put them into a saucepan with two quarts of the water. Set the saucepan on the fire; directly the water boils throw it away and wash the pieces of feet carefully, then put them on again with two more quarts of cold water, and let them boil slowly for three hours, removing the scum carefully during the process; then strain the liquor into a basin, and when quite cold and set take off all fat and wash the top of the jelly with hot water so as to get rid of every vestige of fat. Put the jelly into a saucepan on the fire; directly it is melted add sugar to taste, the juice and rind of the lemon, and the whites of the eggs whisked to a froth. Beat up the mixture till it boils. Place the thin rind of a lemon at the bottom of a jelly bag, and pour the mixture over it. The bag should have been previously rinsed in boiling water, and the first half pint of jelly that comes through must be returned to the bag. If the jelly does not come out quite clear, the operation of straining must be repeated; add sufficient rum to the clarified jelly to flavor it well, pour into a mould and place it on ice to set. At the time of serving dip the mould in hot water, and turn out the jelly.

1075. SWEET WINE JELLY.—Ingredients—One oz. of isinglass dissolved in a pint of water, ¼ lb. loaf sugar, a large glass of sweet wine (any that you prefer).

Add the dissolved isinglass to the sugar and simmer for ten minutes. Add the wine and mix well. Strain through muslin. Let it stand a little while to settle, but not long enough to get cold, then pour it off clear into a mould.

1076. APPLE JELLY.—Ingredients—One lb. of moist sugar, 1 lb. of apples, one lemon—the juice of the lemon to be used and the rind added—cut very fine.

Boil the whole until it becomes a perfect jelly; let it stand in a mould till quite firm and cold, turn it out and stick it with almonds; set custard round. If for dessert, use a small plain mould.

1077. SAGO JELLY.—Ingredients—Two lbs. of picked red currants, 1 pint of cold water, ½ lb. of white sugar, a cupful of sago.

Put the currants into the water and boil till soft, pass them through a sieve; put the juice to boil again with the sugar; when quite boiling add the sago previously soaked in cold water; boil twenty minutes until quite transparent, put into a mould and when cold turn out. Serve with or without custard around it.

1078. MACEDOINE de FRUITS a la GELLEE.—Ingredients—Some pears, apples, plums, cherries and apricots, or any variety of fruit that you choose, a gelatine jelly, a glass of champagne.

Stew the fruit carefully, and cut into pieces; prepare the gelatine jelly and flavor with the champagne; fill a mould with alternate layers of jelly and fruit, and serve after freez'ng. If the fruit is very ripe it is better not to cook it; indeed no soft fruit, strawberries, etc., ever requires cooking for a macédoine.

1079. ASPIC JELLY.—Ingredients—Two calves' feet, a little salt, 2 lbs. of knuckle of veal, 2 shalots, 35 peppercorns, 2 sprigs of parsley, 1 of thyme, 1 leek, 1 onion, 4 cloves, 2 carrots, 2 small turnips, 1 small head of celery, the rind of a lemon, the juice of 3 lemons, 1 gill of sherry, ⅔ of a wine glass of French vinegar, 1 sprig of chervil, 1 sprig of tarragon, 2 bay leaves, the whites of 2 eggs, 1 lb. of veal, 2 blades of mace, 1 clove of garlic.

Blanch the calves' feet, as explained in observations on jelly, cut the veal from the knuckle, now place the veal bone and feet into a stewpan, cover with about two quarts and one pint of water, set on the fire to boil, it must come slowly to the point (be careful to skim), and directly it boils add half a teaspoonful of salt, the peppercorns, mace, clove of garlic, shalots, thyme, and parsley. Stick the clove in the onions, wash the leek and celery in ice water, wash and scrape carrots, wash and peel the turnips, now add the ingredients to the stewpan, putting in also the tarragon, chervil, and bay leaves, allow to simmer six hours. At the end of this time strain through a hair sieve ; now set in a cool place and when perfectly cold remove all fat, dip a clean cloth in hot water and dab over the jelly to remove every particle of fat. Peel the lemon thinly and put the peel into a stewpan, strain the juice into it also, whip the whites of the eggs and put them and the shells with the veal chopped finely into the stewpan, now add the sherry and vinegar, salt and pepper to taste, and whip thoroughly, put in the jelly stock, whisking until it boils, skim if required ; now remove to the back of the stove for half an hour, strain, now put a clean basin under the strainer, pour a ladleful of the jelly over the meat left in the strainer and let it strain slowly into the basin. If the jelly is required for a border scald the mould in boiling water, then in cold, place the mould on ice (be sure it stands firmly), pour in sufficient jelly to cover the bottom of the mould, when slightly set garnish with vegetables or with what it is to be served; pour the rest of the jelly in and allow it to get quite cold. When needed for table, dip the mould in hot water and remove instantly, turn on dish and serve.

1080. **CLARET JELLY.**—Ingredients—One bottle of claret, juice and rind of a lemon, 1 pot of red currant jelly, ½ lb. loaf sugar, rather more than 1 oz. of isinglass, and a wineglass of brandy.

Boil all together for five minutes, strain into a mould and let it get cold. Serve with cream sauce (half pint cream, sweetened, flavored with vanilla, and slightly whisked) poured over it.

1081. **CRANBERRY AND RICE JELLY.**—Ingredients—Cranberries, enough boiled ground rice to thicken to a jelly, sugar.

Boil and press the fruit, mix in the rice, stirring it ; sweeten to taste. Put into a mould. When set serve with milk or cream.

1082. **A TASTY JELLY.**—Ingredients—Half a breakfast cup of calf's foot jelly, the same of rich cream, 1 wineglass of sherry, flavoring and sugar to taste.

Color the jelly brown with a little burnt sugar, see " Colorings," page 253, and add the flavoring ; have ready an open mould which has been soaked in cold water for thirty minutes. Put the jelly into it and leave it to set ; then turn on to a glass dish and fill up the middle with the cream well whipped, flavored with the sherry, and sweetened, and serve.

MILK, BUTTER & CHEESE.

OBSERVATIONS.

Great attention and cleanliness are required in the management of a dairy. The cows should be regularly milked at an early hour, and their udders perfectly emptied. In good pastures the cows produce, on an average, three gallons a day, from Lady Day to Michaelmas, and from thence to Christmas one gallon a day.

The quantity of milk depends on many causes; as the goodness, breed, and health of the cow, the pasture, the length of time from calving, the having plenty of clean water in the field she feeds in, etc. A change of pasture will tend to increase it.

When a calf is to be reared, it should be removed from the cow in ten days at the farthest. It should be removed in the morning and no food given to it till the following morning, when, being extremely hungry, it will drink readily; feed it regularly morning and evening, and let the milk which is given to it be just warm; skimmed milk will be quite good enough.

The milk when brought in should always be strained into the pans. In some of the best dairies the floors are covered with running water to the depth of about eighteen inches, in which the milk is set in buckets or cans eight or ten inches in diameter, and about twenty inches in height. The temperature should be about 56° F. Instead of having the water run over the floor, it is better to allow it to pass through vats or troughs. When the cans containing the recently drawn milk are placed in the water, which should rise a little above the level of the milk, the animal heat is soon reduced to between 56° and 58° F.; and the milk will keep sweet for thirty-six hours even in the hottest weather. This temperature allows the cream to rise with greater facility and with less admixture of other constituents than can be obtained in any other way. Some butter-makers allow the milk to stand for thirty-six hours; others say that twenty-four hours is sufficient for all the cream to rise. After the cream has risen it is to be removed by skimming, and after standing a suitable time is placed in the churn. The kind of churn generally preferred by the best butter-makers is the common dash churn, made of white oak. Much depends upon the manner in which the operation is performed, even with the same churn. The motion should be steady and regular, not too quick nor too slow. The time occupied in churning 12 or 15 gallons of cream should be from 40 to 60 minutes. When removed from the churn, it should be thoroughly washed in cold water, using a ladle and not the hands. It should then be salted with about one-twentieth of its weight of the purest and finest salt, which should be thoroughly incorporated with it, by means of a butter worker or ladle, the hands being never allowed to touch the butter. Twelve hours afterwards another working should be performed and the butter packed in strong and perfectly tight white oak firkins. When filled they should be headed up and a strong brine poured in at the top. It should then be placed in a cool, well-ventilated cellar.

Dr. Ure gives the following directions for curing butter, known as the Irish method: "Take one part of sugar, one of nitre, and two of the best Spanish great salt, and rub them together into a fine powder. This composition is to be mixed thoroughly with the butter as soon as it is completely freed from the milk, in the proportion of 1 ounce to 16; and the butter thus prepared is to be pressed tight into the vessel prepared to receive it, so as to leave no vacuities. This butter does not taste well till it has stood at least a fortnight; it then has a rich, marrowy flavor that no other butter ever acquires."

1083. **PRESERVING BUTTER.**

Two pounds of common salt, one pound of loaf sugar, and one pound of saltpetre. Beat the whole well together, then, to fourteen pounds of butter, put one pound of this mixture, work it well, and when cold and firm put it into glazed earthen vessels that will hold fourteen pounds each. Butter thus preserved becomes better by being kept, but it must be kept from the air, and securely covered down. If intended for winter use, add another ounce of the mixture to every pound of butter, and on the top of the pans, lay enough salt to cover them with brine.

1084. CLOUTED CREAM.

In order to obtain this, the milk is suffered to stand in a vessel for twenty-four-hours. It is then placed over a stove, or slow fire, and very gradually heated, to an almost simmering state, below the boiling point. When this is accomplished, (the first bubble having appeared), the milk is removed from the fire, and allowed to stand for twenty-four hours more. At the end of this time, the cream will have arisen to the surface in a thick or clouted state, and is removed. In this state it is eaten as a luxury; but it is often converted into butter, which is done by stirring it briskly with the hand or a stick. The butter thus made, although more in quantity, is not equal in quality to that procured from the cream which has risen slowly and spontaneously; and in the largest and best dairies in the Vale of Honiton, the cream is never clouted, except when intended for the table in that state.

1085. RENNET (to prepare).

Take out the stomach of a calf just killed, and scour it well with salt and water, both inside and out; let it drain, and then sew it up with two large handfuls of salt in it, or keep it in the salt wet, and soak a piece in fresh water as it is required.

1086. BUTTERMILK.

If made of sweet cream, is a delicious and most wholesome food. Those who can relish sour buttermilk, find it still more light and it is reckoned more beneficial in consumptive cases. Buttermilk, if not very sour, is also as good as cream to eat with fruit, if sweetened with white sugar, and mixed with a very little milk. It likewise does equally for cakes and rice-puddings, and of course it is economical to churn before the cream is too stale for anything but to feed pigs.

1087. CREAM (to Manage for Whey-Butter).

Set the whey one day and night, skim it, and so till you have enough; then boil it and pour it into a pan or two of cold water. As the cream rises, skim it till no more comes; then churn it. Where new-milk cheese is made daily, whey-butter for common and present use may be made to advantage.

1088. **MAITRE D'HOTEL BUTTER.**—Ingredients—2 oz. of fresh butter, juice of 1 lemon, white sugar and salt to taste, parsley blanched, freed from moisture and finely minced.

Put the butter in a basin with the other ingredients, incorporate the whole effectually and quickly, and put it by in a cool place till wanted.

1089. **WATER CRESS BUTTER.**—Ingredients—½ lb of nice fresh butter, a bunch of watercress.

Mince the watercress finely, and mix well in with the butter. Roll into little shapes with butter pats.

1090. **APPLE BUTTER.**—Ingredients—To 3 pecks of tart cooking apples allow 9 lbs. of brown sugar, and a little more than 2 gallons of water.

Put the sugar and water in your kettle, and let it boil; then add the apples. After they begin to cook stir constantly till the butter is done. Try it by putting a little in a saucer, and if no water appears around it the marmalade is ready for the cinnamon and nutmeg " to your taste."

1091. **BUTTER (to serve as a little dish).**

Roll butter in different forms; either like a pine, and make the marks with a teaspoon, or roll it in crimping rollers, work it through a cullender, or scoop with a teaspoon, and mix with grated beef, tongue, or anchovies. Make a wreath of curled parsley to garnish.

1092. **CURLED BUTTER.**

Procure a strong cloth, and secure it by two of its corners to a nail or hook in the wall; knot the remaining two corners, leaving a small space. Then place your butter into the cloth; twist firmly over your serving dish and the butter will force its way between the knots in little curls or strings. Garnish with parsley and send to table.

1093. **DAISY BUTTER.**—Ingredients—2 tablespoonfuls of white sugar, the yolks of 2 hard-boiled eggs, 2 teaspoonfuls of orange flower water, ¼ lb. of *fresh* butter.

Pound the yolks with the orange flower water (in a mortar) to a smooth paste, then mix in the sugar and butter. Now place in a clean cloth, and force the mixture through by wringing. The butter will fall upon the dish in pieces according to the size of the holes in the cloth.

1094. **MELTED BUTTER.**—Ingredients—5 oz. of butter, 1 tablespoonful of flour, 3 tablespoonfuls of water, salt to taste.

Put all the ingredients into a stewpan, and stir one way over the fire until all the ingredients are well mixed. Allow it just to boil, and it is ready to serve.

1095. A PRETTY DISH OF BUTTER.

With a pair of butter pats, form some butter into balls the size of marbles. Set in a pretty dish, with a piece of ice, and sprigs of parsley strewn over.

1096. CHEESE (to make).

Warm the milk till equal to new; but observe it must *not* be *too hot*; now add a sufficiency of rennet to turn it, and cover it over; let it remain till well turned, then strike the curd well down with the skimming-dish, and let it separate, observing to keep it still covered. Put the vat over the tub, and fill it with curd, which must be squeezed close with the hand, and more is to be added as it sinks, and at length left about three inches above the edge of the vat. Before the vat is in this manner filled, the cheese cloth must be laid at the bottom of it, and, when full, drawn *smoothly* over on all sides. The curd should be salted in the tub after the whey is out. When everything is prepared as above directed, put a board under and over the vat, then place it in the press; let it remain two hours, then turn it out, put on a fresh cheese cloth, and press it again ten hours; then salt it all over, and turn it again into the vat; then press it again twenty hours. The vat should have several small holes in the bottom to let the whey run off.

1097. CHEESE (to preserve Sound).

Wash in warm whey, when you have any, and wipe it once a month, and keep it on a rack. If you want to ripen it, a damp cellar will bring it forward. When a whole cheese is cut, the larger quantity should be spread with butter inside, and the outside wiped to preserve it. To keep those in daily use moist, let a clean cloth be wrung out from cold water, and wrapt round them when carried from table. Dry cheese may be used to advantage to grate for serving with macaroni, or eating without. These observations are made with a view to make the above articles less expensive, as in most families where much is used there is waste.

1098. CREAM CHEESE (1).

Put five quarts of strippings, that is, the last of the milk, into a pan with two spoonfuls of rennet. When the curd is come, strike it down two or three times with the skimming-dish just to break it. Let it stand two hours, then spread a cheese-cloth on a sieve, put the curd on it, and let the whey drain; break the curd a little with your hand, and put it into a **vat** with a two-pound weight upon it. Let it stand twelve hours, take it out, and bind a fillet round. Turn every day till dry, from one board to another; cover them with nettles, or clean dockleaves, and put between two pewter-plates to ripen. If the weather be warm, it will be ready in three weeks.

1099. CREAM CHEESE (2).

Have ready a kettle of boiling water, put five quarts of new milk into a pan, five pints of cold water, and five of hot; when of a proper heat, put in as much rennet as will bring it in twenty minutes, likewise a piece of sugar. When come, strike the skimmer three or four times down, and leave it on the curd. In an hour or two lade it into the vat without touching it; put a two-pound weight on it when the whey has run from it, and the vat is full.

1100. CREAM CHEESE (3).

Put as much salt to three pints of raw cream as will season it; stir it well and pour it into a sieve in which you have folded a cheese-cloth three or four times, and laid at the bottom. When it hardens, cover it with nettles on a pewter-plate.

1101. CREAM CHEESE (4).

To a quart of fresh cream put a pint of new milk warm enough to make the cream a proper warmth, a piece of sugar, and a little rennet. Set near the fire till the curd comes; fill a vat made in the form of a brick, of wheat-straw or rushes sewed together. Have ready a square of straw, or rushes sewed flat, to rest the vat on, and another to cover it; the vat being open at top and bottom. Next day take it out, and change it as above to ripen. A half-pound weight will be sufficient to put on it.

1102. CREAM CHEESE (5).—Ingredients—To one pint of fresh rich cream allow one teaspoonful of rennet and a little salt.

Let it stand for two days, stirring twice with a silver spoon. Tie up in a cloth (in the form of a dumpling), put this into another coarse cloth, and bury it for two days. Make into proper shape with butter utensils.

1103. CREAM CHEESE (6).—Ingredients—One pint of rich raw cream, a dessertspoonful of salt.

Put the salt into the cream; fold a napkin double on the shallow end of a hair sieve—a sieve of about six inches in diameter. Pour the cream into the hollow lined with the napkin. In eight or ten hours the cheese will be fit to turn. Take a fresh napkin, doubled, place it on the top of the cheese, and turn the sieve over, so that the cheese may drop out on the dry cloth. Replace it in the sieve, so that it may both drain and keep in shape. For the two following days the napkins should be changed at least three times each day. On the fourth day the cheese will be ready for use.

1104. **SAGE CHEESE.**

Bruise some young red sage and spinach leaves, express the juice, and mix it with the curd; then proceed as with other cheese.

1105. **APPLE CHEESE.**—Ingredients—Equal weight of white sugar and apples, juice of 2 lemons and the peel cut finely,—custard.

Peel, pare, and core the apples, and cut into small pieces. Add the sugar, lemon juice and peel. Put them on the fire and keep moving them about to prevent their burning. Boil until the apples are quite mashed up and look clear, and in stirring the bottom of the pan comes clean. Dip a mould in cold water, put in your cheese, and serve next day cold with a custard round it.

1106. **CHEESE STRAWS.**—Ingredients—6 oz. of flour, 4 oz. of butter, 3 oz. of grated Parmesan cheese, a little cream, salt, white pepper, and cayenne

Roll it out thin, cut it into narrow strips, bake in a moderate oven, and serve piled high and very hot and crisp.

1107. **POTTED CHEESE.**—Ingredients—4 oz. of Cheshire cheese, 1½ oz. of fine butter, a teaspoonful of white sugar, a little piece of mace, a glass of white wine.

Cut and pound the cheese and add to the other ingredients. Press it down in a deep pot.

1108. **ROAST CHEESE.**—Ingredients—3 oz. of Cheshire cheese, yolks of 2 eggs, 4 oz. of grated breadcrumbs, 3 oz. of butter, a dessert spoonful of mustard, salt and pepper.

Grate the cheese, add the yolks, breadcrumbs, and butter; beat the whole well in a mortar and add the mustard, salt and pepper. Make some toast cut into neat slices and spread the paste thickly on. Cover with a dish and place in the oven till hot through, then uncover and let the cheese color a light brown. Serve immediately.

1109. **MUSCLE-PLUM CHEESE.**—Ingredients—6 lbs. of fruit, 2½ lbs. of good Lisbon cheese.

Bake the fruit in a stone jar, remove the stones and add the kernels. Pour half the juice on the cheese; when melted and simmered a few minutes skim and add the fruit. Keep it doing very gently till all the juice is evaporated, stirring all the time. Pour into moulds.

1110. **CHEESE TOAST.**—Ingredients—Some nice butter, made mustard and salt, a little Gloucester cheese, toast.

Mix the butter, mustard and salt, spread on toast and sprinkle with the cheese, grated.

1111. **CHEESE DISH.**—Ingredients—Quarter lb. of good fresh cheese. We mean not very old, or much dried, 1 cup of sweet milk, ¼ of a teaspoonful of dry mustard. A little pepper and salt, tablespoonful of butter.

Cut the cheese into thin slices put it into a "spider" or saucepan, and pour over it the milk, mix in the other ingredients. Stir this mixture all the time while over the fire. Turn the contents into a hot dish and serve immediately.

1112. **CHEESE TOAST.**—Ingredients—Some rich cheese, pepper to taste, a beaten egg with sufficient milk to make it of the consistency of cream.

Grate the cheese and mix with the other ingredients; warm the mixture on the fire and when quite hot pour it over some slices of hot buttered toast; serve immediately.

1113. **PARMESAN FONDUE.**—Ingredients—Half oz. of fresh butter, a tablespoonful of flour, a small quantity of milk, 3 oz. of grated Parmesan cheese, 1 pod of garlic, a small quantity of flour of mustard, a dash of powdered nutmeg, some white pepper, yolks of 3 eggs beaten up in a little milk, whites of 5 eggs whisked to a stiff froth.

Melt the butter in a saucepan, stir into it the flour, when the two are well amalgamated put in a small quantity of milk and the Parmesan cheese; stir the mixture on a slow fire till it assumes the appearance of thick cream, but be careful not to let it boil; then add the garlic, flour of mustard, powdered nutmeg, and white pepper; mix thoroughly, and, if required, add a little salt; keep on stirring the mixture at a very moderate heat for about ten minutes, then remove the pod of garlic, take the saucepan off the fire, and stir the contents occasionally until quite cold, when you stir into them the yolks of the eggs beaten up with a little milk, and strained, and finally the whites of five eggs whisked into a stiff froth. Pour the mixture into a deep round tin, put it into the oven, which must not be too hot; in about twenty or thirty minutes the fondue will have risen and taken color. Pin a napkin round the tin, and serve quickly.

1114. STEWED CHEESE.—Ingredients—Half lb. of Gloucester cheese, a little ale or white wine, a spoonful of mustard, some thin toasted or fried sippets.

Cut the cheese into thin slices, put it into a stewpan with the ale or white wine and keep stirring over the fire till it is melted; put in a spoonful of the mustard, stir it a moment over the fire, then put into a small deep dish, and brown it with a very hot salamander; have ready the sippets, stick all round and in the middle. Serve hot and quickly.

1115. CURD FOR CHEESECAKES.—Ingredients—One quart of new milk, 1 tablespoonful rennet, alum the size of a nutmeg, 3 oz. of butter, 2 or 3 eggs, sugar to taste, a few currants.

Put a quart of new milk into a clean pan, and set it by the side of the fire so that it will keep blood warm; put the rennet into it, too much will make the curd hard and the whey very salt; in a short time, it will be separated into curd and whey, which cut into small pieces with a knife. Or, put in a small piece of alum, about the size of a nutmeg, into the milk, and let it boil. Strain the curd from the whey by means of a hair sieve, either let it drain, or press it dry; pass the curd through the sieve, by squeezing it into a basin. Melt the butter and mix with the curd, also two or three eggs, or else one egg and four yolks; add sugar to your palate; with a little grated nutmeg, and a few currants if approved of; mix the whole together, and fill the cases.

1116. A CHEAP AND NUTRITIOUS DISH.—Ingredients— 1 breakfast cup of rice, 1 quart of milk, ½ lb. of cheese.

Chop the cheese as finely as possible; simmer the rice in the milk, and when tender add the cheese; mix well and bake half an hour.

1117. HOMINY AND CHEESE.—Ingredients—½ lb. of hominy. ½ pint of milk, ½ lb. of cheese.

Soak the hominy in water all night; next day boil in the milk, then add the cheese finely chopped, and mix thoroughly; bake twenty minutes.

N.B.—These dishes can be eaten by the dyspeptic without discomfort.

1118. POTTED CHEESE.—Ingredients—3 lbs of Cheshire cheese, ½ lb. of butter, a large glass of sherry, a little mace, cayenne, pepper and salt.

Beat the cheese in a mortar with the above ingredients.

Mix all thoroughly together, put into pots, and pour a little clarified butter over the top.

1119. CHEESE (Pounded).—Ingredients—Allow ¼ lb. of butter to 1 lb. of cheese.

This dish is economical, as dry cheese may be used. Slice the cheese into small pieces, then add the butter. Proceed to put it in a stone jar, pressing down tightly; put a layer of clarified butter over the top. It may be flavored with cayenne or mixed mustard.

1120. CHEESE STRAWS.—Ingredients—Some trimmings of puff paste, grated Parmesan cheese, pepper, mustard and salt.

Roll out a piece of puff paste very thin, and sprinkle it all over very thickly with grated Parmesan cheese, a little mustard, pepper and salt, then roll it up and press it with the hand and roll out thinly with the rolling pin, cut it out in strips, five inches long and a quarter of an inch wide, bake a few minutes in a warm oven, pile them up on a napkin, and serve very hot.

1121. RICOTTA.

This is a delicious dairy produce, obtainable in southern Italy, and for anyone having a dairy, it is worthy of a trial. Here are two recipes for making ricotta. Take nine and a half pints of milk, dissolve four grammes (about one-eighth of an ounce) of rennet in a little of it, mix it with the rest, and pour the whole into a flat copper pan. Place this on a slow fire, and work it well with a *rotolo*—*i.e.*, a stick with a wooden disk attached to its extremity. As soon as the milk is warm remove the pan from the fire, and cover it with a cloth, and when cold work it again with the stick; gather all that is coagulated, put it in a grass basket, and leave it to season. With the liquid that remains in the pan the ricotta is made in this wise: Add half a pint of fresh milk to it, put it in the pan on a slow fire, and work it lightly with the rotolo. A white froth will rise to the surface, and this carefully skimmed off and put into deep narrow grass baskets, constitutes the ricotta. Another way is as follows: When the first cheese has been taken off, the liquid that remains is strained through a very fine cloth, a few drops of rennet are added, and the pan is put on a gentle fire; at a certain degree of heat (30° Reau.) the ricotta will rise in a white froth, then the pan must be removed from the fire and covered with a cloth; when the contents have cooled the ricotta is gathered up with a spoon, and placed in grass baskets, as above.

1122. **MACARONI.**—Ingredients—¼ lb. of butter, ½ lb. of tubular macaroni, 5 oz. of Parmesan cheese, 2 glasses of milk, 1 quart of water, pepper and salt to taste.

Mix the milk and water, salting it to taste, place in a stewpan on the fire, bring to a boil and drop in the macaroni. When tender, drain and dish. Grate three ounces of the cheese and mix with the macaroni. Now mix in half of the butter, sprinkling a little pepper over. Put the rest of the grated cheese on the top, covering with bread crumbs. Warm the rest of butter (do not let it oil), pour over the breadcrumbs. Brown before the fire or with a salamander.

1123. **MACARONI A LA RUNI.**—Ingredients—Eight oz. macaroni, 10 oz. of any rich well-flavored cheese, ¾ pt. of good cream, a little salt, seasoning of cayenne, ½ a salt spoonful of pounded mace, 2 oz. of sweet fresh butter.

Boil the macaroni in the usual way, and by the time it is sufficiently tender dissolve gently the cheese in the above quantity of cream, add a little salt and rather a full seasoning of cayenne. Now add the pounded mace and butter. The cheese should, in the first instance, be sliced very thin, and taken quite free of the hard part adjoining the rind; it should be stirred in the cream without intermission until it is entirely dissolved, and the whole is perfectly smooth: the macaroni, previously well drained, may then be tossed gently in it, or after it is dished, the cheese may be poured equally over the macaroni. The whole, in either case, may be thickly covered before it is sent to table, with fine crumbs of bread fried of a pale gold color, and dried perfectly, either before the fire or in an oven, when such an addition is considered an improvement. As a matter of precaution, it is better to boil the cream before the cheese is melted in it; rich white sauce, made not very thick, with an additional ounce or two of butter, may be used to vary and enrich this preparation. Do not use Parmesan cheese for this dish.

BEVERAGES.

TEA, ITS HISTORY AND COMMERCE.

All that can be affirmed regarding the early history of this beverage, is that it appears to have been used for ages in China, where it is believed by the natives to be indigenous. It first became known to Europeans at the end of the 16th century, though it is only mentioned by the Portuguese writer Maffei, in his historic Indicoea, who refers to it as a product of both China and Japan. The first reference to it by a native of Britain is in a letter dated 27th June, 1615, written by a Mr. Wickham, which is in the records of the East India Company, and it is curious to observe that both the Portuguese and English writers referred to use their own rendering of the native name, which is Tcha; Maffei calls it "Chia," and Mr. Wickham "Chaw." From this time it gradually became known to the wealthy inhabitants of London in the form of occasional presents of small quantities from India obtained from China, or by small lots in the market in Britain from time to time, but always at exorbitant prices, fetching sometimes as much as $50 per pound, and never less than $25. From that time to the present many changes have taken place, both as regards the duties levied and otherwise, until now, when the duty is only 6d. per pound. The import for the year 1880 being 206,698,971 pounds, valued at £11,631,398 sterling, shows how generally the beverage is used. In

THE PREPARATION OF TEA,

Black, Mixed or Green, care should always be taken that the tea-pot has been thoroughly scalded out and is perfectly dry inside before you proceed to make the tea. Put in, say, one spoonful for each person, the water all being put on at once in a thoroughly boiling state. Very great care should be given to this matter, as it requires the temperature of boiling water to extract the peculiar oil of tea. As a given quantity of tea is similar to a given quantity of malt, only imparting strength to a given quantity of water, therefore any additional quantity is a waste and gives a vapid flavor to tea; much better use two tea-pots instead of two drawings. It should be allowed to stand from eight to ten minutes, and if the teapot is placed under a cosy the drawing qualities of the tea are brought out much quicker.

With regard to Japan Teas, if the following instructions are strictly adhered to, we can assure our readers they will have a delicious beverage:

1. An earthenware tea-pot or pitcher should be used.
2. The boiling water should *all* be poured into the pot at one time, and tea put on top of the water.
3. The tea should be allowed to stand for twenty minutes on the stove, at near the boiling point—it should then be boiled for four or five minutes.

The above notes on tea and tea-making are contributed by the world-renowned Li-Quor Tea Co., one of the best authorities on any matter relating to tea known.

The employment of coffee, as a beverage, was introduced from Arabia in the 16th century into Egypt and Constantinople. Leonhard Rauwolf, a German physician, was probably the first to make coffee known in Europe by the account of his travels printed in 1573. Soon after the first introduction of coffee, coffee-houses arose almost everywhere. The trade now is of great importance. In 1880 the total quantity imported into the United Kingdom was 1,546,130 cwts., of which 850,000 cwts. were imported from Ceylon and other British possessions, the computed real value being £6,861,130, or about 10d. per pound.

1124. **COFFEE (how to prepare)** —Ingredients—Allow 2 large teaspoonfuls of coffee to each person, and to this quantity ½ pint of water.

It is a good plan to have an iron ring to fit the top of the coffee pot inside, and have a small muslin bag attached (be sure and not have muslin too thin), put into the pot the muslin bag and pour boiling water in it, and when the pot is well warmed put into the bag the quantity of ground coffee you are about to use, then pour over as much boiling water as is required and close the lid. When all the water has drained through remove the bag and the coffee is then ready for the table. Preparing coffee in this manner prevents the necessity of changing the coffee from one vessel to another, which cools and spoils it. Water should be poured on coffee very slowly, as this will cause the infusion to be much stronger. N. B. Be careful in making the bag that the seams are well sewn, or the grounds will escape and spoil the coffee. Send to table with a pitcher of scalded milk.

1125. **TEA OR COFFEE WITH EGG.**

Beat up a new laid egg well, in a breakfast cup till it is quite frothy, then fill up the cup with either tea or coffee, adding milk and sugar to taste. To a delicate person there is much more support given in a cup of tea or coffee made in this way than if taken plain.

1126. **COFFEE (another method of making).**

First, take an earthenware jug to hold the required quantity—it must not only be made in this, but served too, as it is sweeter than either silver or metal, and they can be bought both strong, and of suitable appearance for the table. We will suppose four cups are wanted. Put eight heaped teaspoonfuls of freshly ground coffee and one teaspoonful of pure chicory in, for whatever may be said against the latter article, it is, when good, and in proper proportion, a considerable improvement. Now, with the lid on it, put the jug where it is warm for five minutes, then pour on boiling water, let it stand in a very hot place three minutes, take a spoon and stir the coffee, place the jug on the cold stand, and in two minutes it will be perfectly clear. If for breakfast a dessert spoonful of really good thick cream for each cup is necessary. Should this meal be one over which there is no hurry, then a jug of boiled milk is preferable, but it should be fresh, not milk that has stood and had the cream taken from it. I will just add that many people would ike the mixture a little stronger when taken after dinner.

1127. **COCOA (to make).**—Ingredients—2 tablespoonfuls of cocoa, 1 breakfast cupful of boiling milk and water.

Put sufficient cold milk in to form the cocoa into a smooth paste. Now add equal proportions of boiling milk and boiling water, mixing well. N. B.—Great care must be taken that the milk does not burn, or it will impart a disagreeable flavor.

1128. **CHOCOLATE (to prepare).**— Ingredients — Allow 1 oz. chocolate, 1½ pts. water and same quantity of milk to every two persons.

Heat the milk and water, grate the chocolate into it and stir quickly until the chocolate is dissolved, bring it to the point of boiling, and serve with sugar to taste.

1129. **COFFEE MILK.**—Ingredients—1 dessertspoonful of ground coffee to a pint of milk, 2 or 3 shavings of isinglass.

Boil the coffee in the milk for nearly a quarter of an hour, then put in the isinglass to clear it; let it boil a few minutes and set on the back of the stove to clarify. This is very good for breakfast. It should be sweetened with sugar of good quality.

1130. **CRANBERRY DRINK.**—Ingredients—A teacup of cranberries, 1 large spoonful of oatmeal, a piece of lemon peel, sugar, ¼ pt. of white wine.

Put the cranberries into a cup of water and mash them. Boil in the meantime two quarts of water with the oatmeal and lemon peel; add the cranberries and sugar (taking care not to put too much, or else the fine sharpness of the fruit will be lost). Then add the wine; boil for half an hour and strain.

1131. **OATMEAL DRINK (Recipe by the late Dr. Parkes).**

"The proportions are a quarter pound of oatmeal to two or three quarts of water, according to the heat of the day and the work and thirst; it should be well boiled, and then an ounce or one and a half ounces of brown sugar added. If you find it thicker than you like, add three quarts of water. Before drinking it shake up the oatmeal well through the liquid. In summer drink this cold; in winter hot. You will find it not only quenches thirst, but will give you more strength and endurance than any other drink. If you cannot boil it you can take a little oatmeal mixed with cold water and sugar, but this is not so good; always boil it if you can. If at any time you have to make a very long day, as in harvest, and cannot stop for meals, increase the oatmeal to half pound or even three-quarters pound, and the water to three quarts if you are likely to be very thirsty. If you cannot get oatmeal, wheat-flour will do, but not quite so well." Those who tried this recipe last year found that they could get through more work than when using beer, and were stronger and healthier at the end of the harvest. Cold tea and skim milk are also found to be better than beer, but not equal to the oatmeal drink.

1132. **LEMONADE (1).**—Ingredients—Six large lemons and a lb. of loaf sugar.

Rub the sugar over the rinds to get out the flavor, then squeeze out all the juice on the sugar ; cut what remains of the lemons into slices and pour on them a quart of boiling water ; when this has cooled, strain it on to the juice and sugar, and add as much more water (cold) as will make it palatable. A teaspoooful of orange flower water added gives it a pleasant flavor, much liked by some people.

1133. **LEMONADE** (2).—Ingredients—One oz. tartaric acid, 1 lb. loaf sugar, 1 pint of boiling water, and 20 or 30 drops of essence of lemon.

To be kept in a bottle and mixed with cold water as desired.

1134. **MILK LEMONADE.**—Ingredients—2 lbs. of loaf sugar, dissolved in a quart of boiling water, ½ pint of lemon juice, 1 gill of sherry, 1 pint of new milk (cold).

Mix the dissolved sugar, the lemon juice, sherry and milk. Stir the whole well and strain ready for use.

1135. **ORANGEADE.**—Ingredients—Juice of 7 oranges (large), peel of three, syrup of sugar and water, glass of brandy.

Pour boiling water over the peel ; cover closely over until it is cold, boil water and sugar sufficient to make a thin syrup. Skim carefully while boiling. When all are cold mix the infusion, the syrup and the juice, together with as much more water as will make a rich drink ; strain through muslin, add the brandy, and ice it with lumps of clear ice.

1136. **ALE OR BEER (to recover flat).**—Ingredients—Five gals flat ale or beer, 5 lbs. of honey.

Boil the ale with the honey, skim well, and when cold put it back into the hogshead and bung up close.

1137. **MULLED ALE.**—Ingredients—1 quart of good ale, a little nutmeg, 6 eggs, a piece of butter, a glass of brandy.

Boil the ale with the nutmeg ; have the eggs beaten up in a little cold ale and then pour the hot ale to it and return several times to prevent it curdling ; warm and stir it till sufficiently thick ; add the butter and brandy, and serve with dry toast.

1138. **HOP BEER.**—Ingredients—One handful hops, 1 lb. treacle, 1 teacupful yeast.

Boil the hops one hour; strain and add the treacle and enough water to make the whole two gallons ; when milkwarm add the yeast and let it stand a night, then skim and pour it carefully off the yeast. Bottle for use.

1139. **NETTLE BEER.** — Ingredients — 1½ doz. fine nettles (stocks as well as leaves), 2 lbs. of raw sugar, 3 tablespoonfuls of ginger, 2 gals. water, 1 or 1½ cakes of compressed yeast.

Put all the ingredients in the water and allow them to become lukewarm. Add the yeast and keep boiling for twenty minutes. Strain and set aside to cool. It should be put in large stone bottles when cold, and will be ready for use in two days.

1140. **ANNISETTE.** — Ingredients — Two oz. of green anniseed, 1 oz. of coriander seed, 2 grammes of cinnamon, 1 gramme of mace, 5 pints of brandy, 2 lbs. of white sugar.

Crush all the ingredients excepting the sugar and brandy; put into a large wide-mouthed glass bottle with the brandy and sugar; leave the whole for a month, then filter and cork tightly.

1141. **QUINCE RATAFIA.** — Ingredients — Some ripe quinces, brandy, 1½ lbs. of white sugar, 1 gramme of cinnamon, and a clove.

Scrape some quinces to the core. Do not peel them on any account, taking out all the pips. Leave them to macerate for three whole days in some cool place, then press the fruit to get all the juice. Measure the pulp, and put exactly the same quantity of brandy, adding also the white sugar, cinnamon and clove. Let the whole infuse from six weeks to two months and then filter.

1142. **SUMMER DRINK.** — Ingredients — Half a tumblerful of cold spring water, 2 large teaspoonfuls of lemon syrup, ½ a teaspoonful of carbonate of soda, same of tartaric acid.

Put into the water the syrup and carbonate of soda; when quite dissolved, add the tartaric acid and, stirring smartly, drink during the effervescence.

1143. **LEMON KALI.** — Ingredients — 24 grains of highly dried citric or tartaric acid, 1 scruple of carbonate of soda, also highly dried, 2 drachms of white sugar, 1 or 2 drops of essence of lemon.

Mix these ingredients and put into a nice dry bottle and be careful that no damp gets to it. When wanted for use, a dessertspoonful in a glass of water makes a nice drink.

1144. **GINGER BEER POWDERS.** — Ingredients — Blue paper, ½ drachm of bi carbonate of soda, a grain or two of powdered ginger, ¼ oz. of sugar. White paper — twenty-five grains of tartaric acid.

1145. GINGER LIQUEUR.—Ingredients—2 lbs. of white sugar, ½ pint of boiling water, ½ gallon of strong malt whiskey, 3 oz. of bitter and 2 oz. of sweet almonds, 3 oz. of bruised ginger, and the rind of three lemons.

Dissolve the sugar in the water, add the whisky, almonds, ginger and lemon rind ; mix all in an earthenware pan and in five days strain and bottle.

1146. GINGER BEER (1).—Ingredients—4 lbs. of white sugar, 4 oz. of bruised sugar, 4 gals. water, 3 lemons, 1 oz. good measure of cream of tartar, ½ pt. of fresh beer yeast.

Boil the sugar, ginger and water for half an hour briskly, and then skim ; slice the lemons into a wooden tub (thoroughly scaled and cleaned previously), and add the cream of tartar. Pour the boiling liquid into the tub over the lemons, etc., and allow it to cool. Then add yeast ; let it work in the tub for three, or even four days is safer, and strain off the liquid, clear from the lees, letting it remain a fortnight. Then bottle it, and carefully wire down the corks. If the ginger beer is required for keeping it is necessary, when strained from the dregs, to add half a pint of brandy. It will then keep good any length of time.

1147. GINGER BEER (2).—Ingredients—16 oz. of ginger, 10 lbs. sugar or candy, 15 wineglassfuls of lemon juice, 30 quart bottles, boiling water, 10 wineglassfuls of toddy.

The toddy is to be added when nearly cold. When quite cold bottle and tie down the corks.

1148. GINGER CORDIAL.—Ingredients—To 1 lb. of well picked currants (red or black) add a quart of whisky and 1 oz of bruised ginger, ½ lb. of sugar.

Put all the ingredients excepting the sugar into a jar and let it stand two days. Strain through flannel and add sugar. When this is melted, bottle.

1149. SPANISH GINGERETTE.—Ingredients—To each gallon of water allow 1 lb. white sugar, ½ oz. best bruised ginger root, ¼ oz. cream of tartar, 2 sliced lemons, ½ pt. yeast.

In making five gallons boil the ginger and lemon ten minutes in two gallons of water. Dissolve the sugar and cream of tartar in cold water and mix all, adding the yeast. Let it ferment all night, strain and bottle next morning.

1150. GINGER POP.—Ingredients—5½ gals. water, ¼ lb. bruised ginger, ½ oz. of tartaric acid, 2½ lbs. white sugar, whites of 3 eggs well beaten, 1 teaspoonful of lemon oil, 1 gill of yeast.

Boil the ginger for half-an-hour in one gallon of water,

strain, add the oil while hot ; mix well. Make over night and in the morning skim and bottle.

1151. **CASSIS**.—Ingredients—3 lbs. very ripe black currants, 2 qts. of brandy, ½ lb. of ripe raspberries, 2 cloves, ¼ oz. of cinnamon, 2 lbs. of white sugar.

This requires infusion for six weeks. Crush the currants, put them in an old fashioned earthen jar, wide mouthed, with the brandy, raspberries, cloves and cinnamon. Infuse for six weeks, then draw off the liquid and press the remains, put back the liquid into the jar with the sugar. When the sugar is thoroughly melted, filter.

1152. **CHAMPAGNE CUP**.—Ingredients—One qt. champagne, 2 bottles soda water, 1 liqueur-glass of brandy, 2 tablespoons of powdered sugar, a few thin strips of cucumber rind, a large lump of ice.

Make just before it is required.

1153. **VINEGAR PLANT** (1).—Ingredients—¼ lb. coarse brown sugar, the same quantity of treacle, 2 quarts of water.

Mix together and boil for five minutes, and pour into a white earthenware vessel. When the mixture is cold put the vinegar plant on, cover it close with brown paper, and let it stand six weeks or two months, by which time the liquid will be turned into vinegar. Then remove the plant, boil the liquor, and strain it through flannel ; bottle for use.

1154. **VINEGAR PLANT** (2).—Ingredients—Quarter lb. moist sugar, ¼ lb. of treacle, 5½ pts. water.

Put into a large white-lip basin that will hold three quarts ; place the vinegar plant on this, and in six weeks or so it will have covered the surface of the mixture. Young plants will form underneath, which can be detached one at a time. Pour off the vinegar through muslin into bottles, cork, and keep it in a cool place. The plant must also be kept in a dry place.

1155. **SUGAR VINEGAR**.—Ingredients—1 qt. spring water, ¼ lb. of coarsest sugar, a piece of toast spread with yeast.

Mix the water and sugar, boiling and skimming as long as any scum rises. (To every quart of spring water put a quarter lb. of the coarsest sugar) ; Put it in a tub, let it stand till cool enough to work ; and put into it a toast spread with yeast, of a size proportioned to the quantity made. Let it ferment a day or two ; then beat the yeast into it, put it into a bag or barrel, with a piece of tile or slate over the bung hole, and place it where it may have the heat of the sun. Make it in March, or the beginning of April, and it will be fit for use in July or August. If not sour enough, which is seldom the case when not properly managed, let it stand a month longer before bottling off. While making, it must never be disturbed, after the first week or ten days; if in very fine weather the bung hole would be best left open all day, but must be closed at night. Before bottling it may be drawn off into a fresh cask ; and, if it fill a large barrel, a handful of shred isinglass may be thrown in or less, in proportion to the quantity ; this, after standing a few days, will make the vinegar fine, and it may be drawn off, or bottled for use. This vinegar, though very strong, may be used in pickling for sea-store or exportation without being lowered; but for home pickles it will bear mixing with at least an equal quantity of cold spring water. There are few pickles for which this vinegar need be boiled. Without boiling it will keep walnuts, even for the East or West Indies ; but then, as remarked in general of pickles for foreign use, it must not be mixed with water. If much vinegar be made, so as to require expensive casks, the outside should be painted, for the sake of preserving them.

1156. **PRIMROSE VINEGAR.**—Ingredients—To 15 qts. water, allow 6 lbs. white sugar, ½ pk. of primroses with the stalks on, a little barm on toast.

Boil the sugar and water, remove the scum, leave till cold, then add the primroses and barm ; let it remain four days, take off the barm, put liquor and flowers into a cask, set in a warm place with the bung out until it is sour. Then bung slightly. Allow to stand a few months before bottling ; cover the bung hole with muslin.

1157. **CURRANT VINEGAR.**—Ingredients—2 qts. black currants, 1 pt. of the best vinegar, 1½ lbs. white sugar.

Well bruise the currants and place into a basin with the vinegar. Let it stand three or four days and then strain into an earthen jar, add the sugar ; set the jar in a saucepan of cold water and boil for an hour. When cold bottle. It is the better for keeping.

1158. **RASPBERRY VINEGAR.**—Ingredients—To 4 qts. of red raspberries put enough vinegar to cover, 1 lb. of sugar to every pint of juice.

Let the raspberries and vinegar stand for twenty-four hours, scald and strain it; add sugar, boil twenty minutes, skim well, and when cold bottle.

1159. **RASPBERRY ACID.**—Ingredients—Two and a half oz. of tartaric acid dissolved in a quart of water, 6 lbs. red raspberries, to each pint of liquor add 1½ lbs. of white sugar.

Pour the dissolved acid upon the fruit, let it stand twenty-four hours; then strain without pressing the fruit except ever so slightly. Add the sugar and stir until it dissolves. Bottle, but do not seal for four or five days.

1160. **CLARET CUP.**—Ingredients—One quart of claret, one bottle of soda water, 1 lemon cut very thin 4 tablespoonfuls of powdered sugar, quarter of a teaspoonful of grated nutmeg, one liqueur glass of brandy, one wineglass of sherry.

Half an hour before it is wanted, add a good-sized lump of ice.

1161. **RASPBERRY DRINK.**—Ingredients—Three quarts of nice ripe raspberries, 1½ pints of cider vinegar, ¾ lb. of white sugar, 3 gills of best brandy.

Put the fruit into a jar, pour the cider vinegar over them and the sugar; mash the berries to a pulp; leave in the sun for three and a half or four hours, then strain out all the juice and add the brandy; bottle and seal. When wanted put two tablespoonfuls into a glass of ice water.

1162. **CREAM OF TARTAR WHEY.**—Ingredients—One qt. of milk, a tablespoonful of cream of tartar, sweetening and flavoring to taste.

Set the milk on the fire and when it begins to boil put in the cream of tartar; take it off and let it stand till the curd settles at the bottom. Pour off the whey carefully, sweeten and flavor, and drink milk-warm.

1163. **SHERBET POWDER.**—Ingredients—Half lb. of white sugar, ¼ lb. of carbonate of soda, and ¼ lb. of tartaric acid, 40 or 50 drops of essence of lemon.

Mix the sugar, tartaric acid, and carbonate of soda. They must be very dry; then stir all together and run through a hair sieve. Add the lemon drops, and put all into a wide-mouthed bottle and cork down close. When using be sure the spoon is dry that you take the powder out with.

1164. **PERSIAN SHERBET.**—Ingredients—6 or 8 green stalks of rhubarb, 3 pints of water, ¼ lb. of raisins or figs, sliced, a small quantity of rose water and orange or lemon syrup to taste.

Boil in the water the rhubarb, and raisins or figs. When the water has boiled about thirty minutes, strain and stir in the remaining ingredients.

1165. **NOYEAU** (1).—Ingredients—½ lb. of apricot kernels, the same of cherry kernels, 1 quart of brandy, 2 lbs. of white sugar.

Infuse the apricot and cherry kernels in the brandy. Stir from time to time for three weeks; then pour off the liquid from the kernels. Melt the sugar in the water. Mix all together and filter.

1166. **NOYEAU** (2).—Ingredients—1 gallon of whiskey, 3 lbs. of loaf sugar, the rind and juice of three large lemons, 1 lb. of bitter almonds blanched and bruised in a mortar.

Let all the ingredients stand in a covered jar for six weeks, stirring daily, then filter through blotting paper and bottle it.

1167. **SODA CREAM.**—Ingredients—2½ lbs. of loaf sugar, 2 oz. of tartaric acid, 1 qt. of hot water, beaten whites of 3 eggs, flavor to taste.

Dissolve the sugar and tartaric acid in the water; when cold add the beaten whites of the eggs, stirring well. Flavor with whatever is best liked—lemon, orange, raspberry, or currant. Bottle for use, and when wanted put two tablespoonfuls into a tumbler of water, adding as much carbonate of soda as will lie on a sixpence.

1168. **DISTILLED WATER.**

This, the purest state of water, may be readily obtained by fixing a curved tin tube, three or four feet long, to the spout of a tea-kettle, and conducting its free end into a jar placed in a basin of cold water, and enveloped with a wet towel. The softer the water is, the better solvent it is of all soluble animal and vegetable substances; hence *Distilled Water*, being free from any foreign ingredients, is necessarily the softest of all water, and consequently it is well adapted not only for diluting in febrile affections, but for pervading the minutest vessels, and improving their secreting powers. Distilled water is mawkish to the taste; this is easily corrected by pouring it from one jug to another, successively, for ten or fifteen minutes, so as to involve in it a quantity of atmospheric air.

1169. **GOOSEBERRY, CURRANT, RASPBERRY, AND STRAWBERRY WATERS.**

Mash either of the fruits when ripe, and press out the juice through a hair sieve; add a little water to it, and give it a boil; then filter it through a flannel bag; some syrup, a little lemon juice and water to make it palatable, but rich, although not too sweet, which is often a fault with these and compotes. Ice them the same as wine, and serve.

1170. **RHUBARB WATER.**—Ingredients—Some sticks of rhubarb, a quart of water, sugar and lemon juice.

Cut up the rhubarb (about six or eight sticks, but it depends on their length), without peeling them. Put them in a stewpan, add the water and boil for quarter of an hour. Then strain into a jug and add the sugar and lemon juice. When cool it is fit for use.

1171. **WHITE CURRANT CORDIAL.**—Ingredients—1 quart of whiskey or brandy, 1 pt. currant juice. 1 lb. white sugar, ¼ of an ounce of ginger (pounded), and the rind of 1 lemon.

Mix all well together, and let it stand ten days or a fortnight, then filter through blotting paper.

1172. **A STRONG CORDIAL.**—Ingredients—1 quart each of peppermint water and rectified spirits of wine, 1 lb. of lump sugar.

Melt the sugar in the peppermint water and add the spirits of wine.

1173. **SEIDLITZ POWDERS.**

Two drams of tartarized soda, and two scruples of bicarbonate of soda for the blue packet, and thirty grains of tartaric acid for the white paper.

1174. **EFFERVESCING SALINE DRAUGHTS.**

White sugar powdered, eight ounces; tartaric acid two ounces; sesquicarbonate of soda, two ounces; essence of lemon, a few drops. Mix well, and keep in a corked bottle.

1175. **CIDER.**

For making this agreeable beverage, take red-streaked pippins, pearmains, gennetings, golden pippins, &c., when they are so ripe that they may be shaken from the tree with tolerable ease; bruise or grind them very small, and when reduced to a mash, put them into a hair bag, and squeeze them out by degrees: next put the liquor, strained through a fine hair sieve, into a cask well matched: then mash the pulp with a little warm water, adding a fourth part, when pressed out, to the cider. To make it work kindly, heat a little honey, three whites of eggs, and a little flour, together: put them into a fine rag, and let them hang down by a string to the middle of the cider cask: then put in a pint of new ale yeast pretty warm, and let it clear itself from dross five or six days; after which draw it off from the lees into smaller casks or bottles, as you think proper. If you bottle it take care to leave the liquor an inch short of the corks, lest the bottles burst by the fermentation. Should any such danger exist, you may perceive it by the hissing of the air through the corks ; when it will be necessary to open them, to let out the fermenting air. Apples of a better taste produce the strongest cider ; but you must observe never to mix summer and winter fruit together.

1176. CURRANT AND RASPBERRY SYRUP.

Take eight pounds of very ripe currants, red and white ; pick off all the stalks, and put them into a wide earthen pan ; then take them up in handfuls and squeeze them till the juice is all crushed out of them, which will take some time. Leave them in the pan with the juice for twenty-four hours. Put two pounds of raspberries in a saucepan with two teacupfuls of water, and boil them for a few minutes till they are all crushed. Then pass all the currants and raspberries through a hair-sieve, pressing them with a wooden spoon to extract all the juice. If the juice should be very thick, pass it also through a jelly-bag. Weigh the juice, and for every pound of it put two pounds of loaf-sugar, broken into large pieces. Put the sugar into a preserving pan with one pint of water ; pour all the juice on it. Let it boil for half an hour, stirring frequently ; then put it into small bottles, and cork it for use. Two tablespoonfuls in a tumbler of water make a very refreshing drink in summer. Cherry-syrup may be made in the same way with Morella cherries.

1177. SARSAPARILLA (simple decoction).—Ingredients—
 5 oz. of sarsaparilla chips, 4 pints of water.

Digest the chips in the water, let it simmer gently for two hours ; take out the chips, bruise and replace them in the water; boil down to two pints and strain.

1178. SARSAPARILLA (compound decoction).

This is made by adding to the above quantity while boiling, sassafras (sliced), quaiacum wood (rasped), and liquorice-root (bruised), of each ten drachms. Meyereon roots, three drachms. Boil for fifteen minutes and strain.

WINES & BRANDIES.

The high price of foreign wine renders the making good wine an object of no mean importance in domestic economy, and many excellent wines may be made with very little trouble, and at a trifling expense. Every person who possesses an extensive garden will find it more advantageous to use their surplus fruit for making wine, than to dispose of it by sale.

The process of wine-making is by no means so troublesome or laborious as brewing; and wine, when well made, will keep almost any length of time: indeed age, instead of deteriorating, adds to its goodness; and very good domestic wines may be made at a trifling expense.

1179. **BOTTLING OF WINE.**

The secret of bottling wine with success consists in the simple exercise of care and cleanliness. The bottles should be all sound, clean, and dry, and perfectly free from the least mustiness or other odor. The corks should be of the best quality, and immediately before being placed in the bottles should be compressed by means of a "cork squeezer." For superior or very delicate wines, the corks are usually prepared by placing them in a tub or copper, covering them with weights to keep them down, and then pouring over them boiling water, holding a little pearlash in solution. In this state they are allowed to remain for twenty-four hours, when they are drained and re-immersed for a second twenty-four hours in hot water, after which they are well washed and soaked in several successive portions of clean rain-water, drained, dried out of contact with dust, put into paper bags, and hung up in a dry place for use. The wine should be clear and brilliant, and, if it be not so, it must undergo the process of "fining" before being bottled. In fact, it is a common practice with some persons to perform this operation whether the wine requires it or not; as, if it has been mixed and doctored, it "amalgamates and ameliorates the various flavors." The bottles, corks, and wine being ready, a fine clear day should be preferably chosen for bottling, and the utmost cleanliness and care should be exercised during the process. Great caution should also be observed to avoid shaking the cask so as to disturb the bottoms. The remaining portion that cannot be drawn off clear should be passed through the " wine-bag," and when bottled should be set apart as inferior to the rest. The coopers, to prevent breakage and loss, place each bottle, before corking it, in a small bucket, having a bottom made of soft cork. They thus seldom break a bottle, though they "flog" in the corks very hard. When the wine is all bottled it is stored in a cool cellar, and on no account on the bottles' bottoms, or in damp straw, but on their sides, in sweet dry sawdust or sand.

1180. TO REFINE LIQUORS.

Dissolve two ounces in one quart of cider, beer, or wine; it should not be boiled, though warmed sufficient to dissolve it; put in when dissolved into a barrel of the liquor, where it should be well stirred, and when clear racked off. It should be put into cider as soon as it is drawn from the press, and should be racked as soon as clear; if it be not racked off at a proper time, a fixed air will form and cause the sediment to mingle again with the whole mass.

1181. FALSIFIED WINE.

One of the chief means of disguising a falsified wine is the use of various coloring-matters, which are now offered everywherer in France by private trade circulars. Public attention has been directed to this in Paris; and it is stated that although chemistry is powerless to discover the presence of these dyes, there nevertheless exists a simple means of detecting them which cannot be too widely known. Some of the wine must be heated; and, when it boils, a piece of white flannel should be well dipped in it and allowed to dry. If the flannel, when washed, still retains a red or reddish tinge, it is stated to be proof positive that the color of the wine has been artificially obtained.

1182. TO MULL WINE.

Boil some spice in a little water till the flavor is gained, then add an equal quantity of port, sugar and nutmeg to taste; boil together and serve with crisp toast.

1183. Another Way.

Boil a small piece of cinnamon and some grated nutmeg a few minutes in a large cupful of water, then pour to it a pint of port wine, adding sugar to taste, heat it up and it will be ready to serve. British wine can be used in place of port if desired.

1184. LEMON WINE.—Ingredients—One gal. water, 3 lbs. of powdered loaf sugar, rinds of 4 lemons, juice of the lemons, ½ lb. sugar, 1 slice of toast, yeast.

Add the sugar to the water, boiling twenty minutes, skimming well, pare the rinds of the lemons very thin, squeeze out all the juice of the lemons and mix with the sugar ; boil until it becomes a thick syrup ; add it to the water and rinds, and when the whole is just lukewarm put in a slice of toast covered on both sides with yeast. Allow it to work in an open tub two days, then put it into a cask. Let it stand three minutes before bottling.

1185. GRAPE WINE.—Ingredients—20 lbs. of fresh fruit, 1½ gals. of water, 10 lbs. of granulated sugar.

Put the grapes into a crock, pour over the water, which must be boiling ; when conveniently cool, press well with the hands. Let it remain three days on the pomace covered over with a cloth. Then squeeze out all the juice and add the sugar. Leave for a week longer in the crock. Then remove the scum. Strain and bottle, leaving uncorked until the fermentation is over. Then strain and rebottle, corking tight. Place the bottles on their sides in a cool place.

1186. GRAPE WINE (2).—Ingredients—To a gallon of bruised grapes put a gallon of water ; to a gallon of wine put 3 lbs. of sugar.

Let the fruit and water stand a week, without stirring. Then draw it off and add sugar in the above proportion ; put it into a vessel, but do not stop it till it has done hissing.

1187. APRICOT WINE.—Ingredients—12 lbs. of apricots, 2 gals. of water, to every quart of liquor allow 6 oz. of white sugar.

Wipe, clean and cut the apricots, which must be ripe ; add the water and let them boil till the water has thoroughly imbibed the flavor of the fruit ; then strain the liquor through a hair sieve ; add the sugar, and boil it again ; skim carefully, and when the scum has ceased to rise pour into an earthen vessel. Next day bottle it off, putting a lump of sugar into every bottle.

1188. DAMSON WINE.—Ingredients—8 lbs. of fruit, 1 gallon of water ; to every gallon of liquor add 2½ lbs. of good sugar.

Gather the fruit dry, weigh, and bruise them with your hands. Boil the water ; then pour it upon your fruit scalding hot, and let it stand two days ; then draw it off, put it into a clean cask, and add sugar ; fill the cask ; the longer it stands the better. It will keep very well a year in the cask. Afterwards bottle it off. The small damson is the best. Put a very small lump of loaf sugar into every bottle.

1189. GOOSEBERRY WINE (1).—Ingredients—One peck of half ripe gooseberries, allow 3 lbs. white sugar to a gallon of fruit.

The fruit should be gathered in dry weather; pick and bruise them in a tub. Press as much as possible without breaking the seeds; add the sugar and stir until dissolved, then fill a cask or vessel with it. Let it stand for a fortnight or three weeks, and set in a cool place. Then strain off the sediment; leave again for two or three months and then bottle.

1190. GOOSEBERRY WINE (2).—Ingredients—Six lbs. of green gooseberries to every gallon of water, 3 lbs. of white sugar.

The gooseberries must be green (*not* ripe) and must be perfectly sound. Top and tail them, place in a tub and bruise them. Be particular that every berry is broken, but do not crush the seeds; warm the water and pour on the fruit. Now press and squeeze it to a pulp; cover for a day and a night. Meantime prepare a coarse bag, and at the end of the stated time strain through it, extracting *all* the juice. Put into a tub, add the sugar, stir until it is dissolved and set in a warm place; keep it closely covered, allowing it to ferment for two days. At the end of that time draw into clean casks, tilt them a little on one side, and when the scum has settled, remove it and fill with the remaining juice. As soon as the fermentation has stopped, plug the casks upright, filling a third time, if needful, put the bungs in loosely and when the fermentation is over drive the bungs in tightly, and a small hole made to give vent. After six months draw off from the dregs into casks rinsed with brandy. Allow to stand a month, then examine, and if clear, bottle, if not, clear with one ounce of isinglass to eight gallons of wine.

1191. GINGER WINE.—Ingredients—7 qts. of water, 6 lbs. of sugar, 2 oz. of the best ginger, bruised, and the rinds of 3 good-sized lemons, boiled together; $\frac{1}{4}$ lb. of raisins, 1 spoonful of yeast, $\frac{1}{2}$ oz. of isinglass, $\frac{1}{2}$ pint of brandy.

When lukewarm, put the whole into a cask, with the juice of the lemons, and the raisins; add the yeast, and stir the wine every day for ten days. When the fermentation has ceased, add the isinglass and brandy; bung close, and in two months it will be fit to bottle.

1192. CHERRY WINE.—Ingredients—To every gallon of liquor 2 lbs of coarse sugar.

Pull off the stalks of cherries, and wash the latter without breaking the stones; press it hard through a hair bag, and let it work as long as it makes a noise in the vessel; stop it up close for a month or more, and when it is fine, draw it into dry bottles. If it makes them fly, open them all for a moment, and stop them up again. It will be fit to drink in three mon:

1193. **STONE'S PATENT RHUBARB WINE.**—Ingredients
To every gallon of liquor, 3 lbs. of white sugar.

When the green stalks or stems of the rhubarb plant are arrived at their full size, which will generally be about the middle of the month of May, pluck them; then cut off the leaves and throw them away; bruise the stalks in a large mortar, or other convenient vessel, so as to reduce them to a pulp; put the pulp into an open vat or tub, and to every five pounds' weight of the pulp, add one gallon of cold spring water. Let it infuse for three days, stirring it three or four times a day. On the fourth day press the pulp in the usual manner, and strain off the liquor, which place in an open vat or tub, and to every gallon of the liquor add three pounds of white sugar, stirring it until the sugar is quite dissolved; then let it rest, and in from four to six days the fermentation will begin to subside, and a crust or head will be formed, which is to be skimmed off, or the liquor drawn from it, just when the crust or head begins to crack or separate; then put the wine into a cask, but do not then stop it down. If it should begin to ferment in the cask, rack it into another cask; in about a fortnight stop down the cask, and let it remain till the beginning of the month of March in the next year, then rack it, and again stop down the cask; but if, from continued slight fermentation in the cask, the wine then should have lost any of its original sweetness, put into the racked wine a sufficient quantity of loaf sugar to sweeten it, and stop down the cask, taking care in all cases that the cask should be full. In a month or six weeks it will be fit to bottle, and in the summer to drink; but the wine will be improved by remaining a year or more in the rack after it has been racked. The plant in the autumn will produce a second crop, when another quantity of wine can be made.

1194. **RHUBARB CHAMPAGNE.**—Ingredients—To every lb. of bruised rhubarb stalks add 1 qt. of cold spring water; to every gallon of the juice add 2½ lbs. of white sugar, and to 10 gals. allow a bottle of pale brandy, 1 oz. isinglass.

Put the rhubarb in the water, and let it stand three days, stirring twice a day. Then press and strain it through a sieve, and to every gallon of the juice add two and a half pounds of loaf sugar, barrel it, and to ten gallons allow a bottle of pale brandy. Put the isinglass in a muslin bag, and suspend it in the barrel by a string. When it has ceased fermenting fasten up the barrel closely. It will be ready to bottle in six months. Some black or red currant juice added improves the color.

1195. **BLACKBERRY WINE.**—Ingredients—Some ripe blackberries, boiling water sufficient to cover them, to 10 quarts of liquor allow 1 lb. of sugar, 4 oz. of isinglass, 1 pint of white wine.

Put the berries into a large vessel of wood or stone with a tap to it; pour on the boiling water as above directed, and, as soon as the heat will permit, bruise well with the hand; let it stand closely covered till all the berries begin to rise to the top, which will take place in three or four days, then draw off the clear part into another vessel, add the sugar and stir well; leave to stand for a week or ten days, then draw off through a jelly bag. Lay the isinglass in the wine to steep for twelve hours, the next morning boil it on a slow fire till dissolved, then take a gallon of the blackberry juice, put in the dissolved isinglass, boil them together, pour all into the vessel, and let it stand a few days to purge and settle; draw it off, and keep it in a cool place.

1196. **RAISIN WINE.**—Ingredients—To every gallon of spring water allow 8 lbs. of good raisins, brandy of the finest quality.

Stir the fruit and water in a large tub every day for a month; then press the raisins in a horsehair bag as dry as possible; put the liquor into a cask, and when it has done hissing pour in a bottle of the best brandy; stop it close for twelve months; then rack it off, but without the dregs; filter them through a bag of flannel of three or four folds, add the clear to the quantity, and pour one or two quarts of brandy according to the size of the vessel. Stop it up, and at the end of three years you may either bottle it or drink it from the cask. Raisin wine would be extremely good if made rich of the fruit, and kept long, which improves the flavor greatly.

1197. **FAMILY WINE (Excellent).**—Ingredients—Equal proportions of black, red, and white currants, ripe cherries (black hearts are the best), raspberries. To each gal. of the liquor 3 lbs. of sugar; lastly, to every 9 gals. 1 quart of good Cognac brandy.

To four lbs. of the mixed fruit, well bruised, put one gallon of clear soft water; steep three days and nights, in open vessels, frequently stirring up the *magma*; then strain through a hair sieve, press the residuary pulp to dryness, and add its juice to the former; in each gallon of the mixed liquors dissolve three pounds of good sugar; let the solution stand another three days and nights, frequently skimming and stirring it up; then turn it into casks, which should remain full, and purging at the bung-hole, about two weeks. Lastly, to every nine gallons put in the above proportion of brandy, and bung down.

** If it does not soon become fine, a steeping of isinglass may be stirred into the liquid, in the proportion of about half an ounce to nine gallons. The addition of one ounce of cream of tartar to each gallon of the fermentable liquor improves the quality of the wine, and makes it resemble more nearly the produce of the grape.

1198. **BLACK OR WHITE ELDER WINE**.—Ingredients—
To every pint of juice 1½ pints of water, to every gallon of this liquor 3 lbs. of good moist sugar, the whites of 4 or 5 eggs, ale yeast.

Gather the elder berries ripe and dry, pick them, and bruise them with your hands, and strain them; set the liquor by in glazed earthen vessels for twelve hours to settle; set in a kettle over the fire, and when it is ready to boil clarify it with the whites of four or five eggs, let it boil one hour, and when it is almost cold work it with strong ale yeast, and tun it, filling up the vessel from time to time with the same liquor, saved on purpose, as it sinks by working. In a month's time, if the vessel holds about eight gallons, it will be fine and fit to bottle, and, after bottling, will be fit to drink in twelve months: but if the vessel be larger it must stand longer in proportion, three or four months at least for a hogshead. All liquors must be fined before they are bottled, or else they will grow sharp, and ferment in the bottles.

** Add to every gallon of this liquid one pint of strong mountain wine, but not such as has the *borachio*, or nag's skin flavor. This wine will be very strong and pleasant.

1199. **RASPBERRY WINE** (1).—Ingredients—To 1 qt. of picked raspberries allow 1 qt. of water; to a gallon of fruit allow 3 lbs. of white sugar.

Pour the water on the fruit, bruise them and let them stand for two days; strain off the liquor and the sugar; when dissolved put the liquor into a barrel, and when fine, which will be in about two months, bottle it, and to each bottle put a spoonful of brandy, or a glass of wine.

1200. **RASPBERRY WINE** (2).—Ingredients—Fruit; to a quart of juice allow 1 lb. of sugar, and 2 qts. of white wine.

Bruise the raspberries with a spoon, and strain into a stone vessel; add the sugar, stirring well together, and cover closely; let it stand three days and then strain off clear. Add the white wine and bottle.

1201. **RASPBERRY AND CURRANT WINE.**—Ingredients— Allow a qt. of water to every 3 pts. of fruit; to a qt. of liquor add 1 lb. of sugar.

Bruise the fruit (after carefully removing any that are bad or mouldy), adding the water ; let it stand a day, then strain and add the sugar ; leave again for three or four days, removing the scum as it rises. Then bottle it.

1202. **BLACK CURRANT WINE**.—Ingredients—Allow equal quantities of juice and water, to every 3 qts. of liquor add 3 lbs. of pure moist sugar, 3 qts. of brandy to 40 of wine.

Put it into a cask, preserving a little for filling up ; put the cask into a warm, dry room and the liquor will ferment of itself ; skim off the refuse when the fermentation shall be over, and fill up with the reserved liquor; when it has ceased working, pour in brandy. Bung it close for nine months, then bottle it, and drain the thick part through a jelly-bag, until it be clear, and bottle that. Keep it ten or twelve months.

1203. **ORANGE WINE**.—Ingredients—To make 9 gals. take 11 gallons of soft water, in which boil the whites of 30 eggs, 200 oranges, 40 lemons, and 30 Seville oranges, should they be preferred to the lemons, 30 lbs. of white sugar. If required, ferment with ½ pt. of yeast, 1 gal. to 1½ of French brandy.

Pare the fruit as thin as possible, and upon the parings pour the water, boiling. Upon this juice, having stood ten or twelve hours, and being strained, run the expressed juice of the oranges and lemons, adding the sugar ; if required, ferment with half a pint of yeast four or five days, when the wine may be casked, and brandy added, when the fermentation subsides. Some substitute sherry, but it is inferior to brandy, and gives an alien flavor to orange wine ; bung down closely, but watch the process of fermentation ; in six months it will be perfectly fine, this wine being less liable to remain turbid than any of our other wines. By the directions already given a wine from any fruit may be made, observing that the more sugar is used, the longer time it will require to complete the vinous fermentation.

1204. **MALT WINE**.—Ingredients—To 28 lbs. of sugar allow 5 gals. of water, 6 qts. each of sweet-wort and tun, 2½ lbs. of raisins, 10 oz. of candy, 1 pt. of brandy.

Mix the sugar and water and simmer for a quarter of an hour, skim well and pour the liquor into a tub ; set aside to cool, then mix in the sweet-wort and tun ; allow to stand undisturbed for three days, then put into a barrel to allow it to ferment for another three days. Bung the cask and keep for two or three months ; at the end of this time add the raisins, brandy and candy, and in five or six months time bottle the wine.

1205. **ORANGE BRANDY**.—Ingredients—Chips of 18 Seville oranges, 3 qts. of brandy, 2 qts. of spring water, 1½ lbs. of white sugar, the white of an egg.

Put the orange chips in the brandy, let them steep a fortnight in a stone bottle stopped close ; boil the water with the sugar, gently for an hour, clarify the water and the sugar with the white of an egg, then strain it through a jelly-bag and boil it nearly half away ; when cold strain the brandy into the syrup.

1206. **LEMON BRANDY**.—Ingredients—Five qts. of water to 1 gal. of brandy, 2 doz. lemons, 2 lbs. of the best sugar, and 3 pints of milk.

Pare the lemons thin, steep the peel in the brandy twelve hours, and squeeze the lemons upon the sugar ; then put the water to it and mix all the ingredients together. Boil the milk and pour it in hot. Let it stand twenty-four hours and then strain it.

1207. **CHERRY BRANDY (Excellent)** (1).—Ingredients—To every lb. of Morella cherries allow ¼ lb. sugar, brandy

The cherries for this purpose must not be too ripe and should be fresh ; remove the stalks, and place into your bottles (which must be quite dry) and add sugar ; when you have filled your bottles with the cherries and sugar, cover with brandy ; cork and tie a bladder over. Be careful not to put too much sugar, or the cherries will become very hard. Whiskey is a very good substitute for brandy.

1208. **CHERRY BRANDY** (2).—Ingredients — Eight lbs. of cherries, a gallon of the best brandy.

Stone the cherries, and add to them the brandy ; bruise the stones in a mortar and add them to the cherries and brandy. Cover close and leave for six weeks ; then pour off clear from the sediment and bottle. This makes a rich cordial. Some prefer the fruit bruised instead of being whole.

1209. **CARAWAY BRANDY**.—Ingredients—One oz. of caraway seeds, 6 oz. of white sugar, 1 qt. of brandy.

Steep the caraway seeds and sugar in the brandy ; let it stand nine days, then draw it off and it will make an excellent cordial.

SICK ROOM COOKERY.

There is sickness everywhere, and as it falls to the lot of most women at some time in their lives to be nurse or cook for the sick, a few hints may be useful. Every woman with a tender, loving heart, no matter what her position, will try in such a case to tempt the appetite of the afflicted with her own delicate cooking and serving, the result being in many cases, returning health, and in any case having the satisfaction of knowing you have done what you could. An anonymous writer says:—

"Invalids soon realize their dependence on others. I will say this much to every family that has an invalid charge, be kind to them; don't be always reminding them of expenses; do not make them feel that they are a burden to you. God sends the affliction upon them. They would not be a burden to you if they could help it, and I believe when the final day of judgment comes, the great Ruler of the Universe will deal with you as you have dealt with the sick ones. And with many the sentence will be, "Ye knew your duty, but you did it not." It is said "No physician ever weighed out medicine to his patient with half so much exactness and care as God weighed out to us every trial; not one grain too much does He ever permit to be put in the scale." It is hard for us to feel that our afflictions are sent to us for some wise purpose. Our burdens seem more than we can bear, and it is still harder for us to say "Thy will, not mine, be done." Be kind to the sick ones; their lot in life is hard enough. Throw a ray of sunshine across their path. There are a thousand and one ways that you can brighten their lives, by a little attention. There are many ways we could make others happy if we only would try, and we would be so much happier ourselves. Just think of the poor invalid that is confined to the house, seeing the same things day after day (yes, and often year after year), until they know every seam in the carpet, every flower on the wall—yes, every spot on the furniture. Their eyes will ache from the very sameness, and they feel that it would be a blessing to close them in utter oblivion.

It ought to be not only a pleasure, but a stern duty for us to lighten their burdens and make life bearable to them."

In preparing dishes for the sick, it is needful to combine the strongest nourishment with the simplest seasoning, as they require food which will not need too much exertion of the digestive power. Sweet-breads, broiled to a nice brown; oysters roasted in the shell, or plainly stewed; clam broth, and even calves' brains, are highly recommended as articles of diet, which will give the most nutritious food in the smallest quantities. All kinds of gruel are unpalatable to some persons, but fortunately, tastes differ, and there are those who will take with a decided relish large bowlfuls of flour, oatmeal, and even Indian-meal porridge. Groats, however, are considered the most delicate of all such preparations, and if well made, and flavored with a tablespoonful of old Jamaica or whisky, with a little sugar added to it, it is not a disagreeable compound.

Never set before the sick a large quantity of food; tempt with a very small portion delicately cooked and tastefully served. If not eaten directly, remove from the sick room without delay, as no food should be allowed to stand there. Do not give the same food often, as variety is charming. Never keep the sick waiting, always have something in readiness—a little jelly, beef tea, stewed fruit, gruel, etc. It will be found more tempting to serve any of these in glasses. If much milk is used, keep it on ice. Let all invalid cookery be simple; be careful to remove every particle of fat from broth or beef-tea before serving.

The best diet for brain workers who take proper care of their health is brown bread, cream, fresh butter, oatmeal, fresh cheese (if it agrees), eggs, fish, and a moderate amount of meat. Oysters may be used freely in their season, and fruits should not be omitted. There should be variety and change as the season and health require. The diet should be varied in kind and form quite frequently, though not necessarily every day. Even in health, the best viands when continued from day to day become unpalatable, and even nauseous. An occasional change of diet, in short, is indispensable to a proper relish for food, and the maintenance of the appetite and good health.

1210. **VEAL BROTH**.—Ingredients—One and a half lbs of veal. 1 doz. sweet almonds, a qt. of spring water, a little salt, 1 pt. of boiling water.

Remove all the fat from the veal, and simmer gently in the spring water till it is reduced to a pint ; blanch and pound the almonds till they are a smooth paste, then pour over them the boiling water very slowly, stirring all the time till it is as smooth as milk ; strain both the almond and veal liquors through a fine sieve and mix well together, and add the salt and boil up again.

1211. **CHICKEN BROTH**.—Ingredients—An old fowl, 3 pints of water, a pinch of salt, a blade of mace, 6 or 8 peppercorns, a very small chopped onion, a few sprigs of sweet herbs.

Cut up the fowl and put it, bones as well, in a saucepan with the water, salt, mace, peppercorns, onion and sweet herbs ; let it simmer very gently till the meat is *very* tender, which will take about three hours, skimming well during the time. Strain carefully and set aside to cool.

1212. **EGG BROTH**.—Ingredients—An egg, ½ pint of good unflavored veal or mutton broth quite hot, salt, toast.

Beat the egg well in a broth basin ; when frothy add the broth, salt to taste, and serve with toast.

1213. **EEL BROTH**.—Ingredients—Half lb. of small eels, 3 pints of water, some parsley, 1 slice of onion, a few peppercorns, salt to taste.

Clean the eels and set them on the fire with the water, parsley, onion, and peppercorns ; let them simmer till the eels are broken and the broth good. Add salt to taste and strain. These ingredients should make about a pint and a half of broth.

1214. **BEEF BROTH** (1).—Ingredients—One lb. of good lean beef, 2 qts. of cold water ½ a teacup of tapioca, a small piece of parsley, an onion if liked, pepper and salt.

Soak the tapioca one hour, cut in small pieces the beef, put in a stewpan the above proportion of water, boil slowly (keeping well covered) one and a half hours, then add the tapioca, and boil half an hour longer. Some add with the tapioca a small piece of parsley, and a slice or two of onion ; strain before serving, seasoning slightly with pepper and salt. It is more strengthening to add, just before serving, a soft poached egg. Rice may be used instead of tapioca, straining the broth, and adding one or two tablespoons of rice (soaked for a short time), and then boiling half an hour.

1215. BEEF BROTH (2).—Ingredients—One and a half lbs. of finely-minced beef, 1 qt. of cold water, a little salt, and 2 oz. of rice or barley.

Simmer for four hours, then boil for ten minutes, strain, skim off the fat and serve.

1216. SCOTCH BROTH.—Ingredients—The liquor in which a leg of mutton, piece of beef or old fowl has been boiled, barley, vegetables chopped small, a cup of rough oatmeal mixed in cold water, salt and pepper to taste.

Add to the liquor some barley and vegetables, chopped small, in sufficient quantity to make the broth quite thick. The necessary vegetables are carrots, turnips, onions, and cabbage, but any others may be added ; old (not parched) peas and celery are good additions. When the vegetables are boiled tender add the oatmeal to the broth, salt and pepper to taste. This very plain preparation is genuine Scotch broth as served in Scotland ; with any coloring or herbs, etc., added, it is not real Scotch broth. It is extremely palatable and wholesome in its plain form.

1217. HASTY BROTH.—Ingredients—A bone or two of a neck or loin of mutton, ¾ pt. of water, a piece of thyme, some parsley, a slice of onion.

Remove the fat and skin from the meat, set it on the fire in a small tin saucepan that has a lid, with the water, the meat being first beaten and cut into pieces ; add the seasoning. Let it boil rapidly, skim it nicely ; take off the cover if likely to be too weak. Half an hour is sufficient to make it in.

1218. BROTH (a Splendid Broth for Weakness).—Ingredients—2 lbs. of loin of mutton, a large handful of chervil, 2 qts. of water.

Boil the meat with the chervil in the water till reduced to one quart. Take off part of the fat. Any other herbs or roots may be added. Take half a pint three or four times a day.

1219. BROTH (Beef, Mutton and Veal).—Ingredients—2 lbs. of lean beef, 1 lb. scrag of veal, 1 lb. of scrag of mutton, some sweet herbs, 10 peppercorns, 5 qts. of water, 1 onion.

Put the meat, sweet herbs, and peppercorns into a nice tin saucepan, with the water, and simmer till reduced to three quarts. Remove the fat when cold. Add the onion, if approved.

1220. CALVES' FEET BROTH. — Ingredients — Two calves' feet, 3½ qts. of water, a large teacupful of jelly, ½ glass of sweet wine, a little sugar, nutmeg, yolk of 1 egg, a piece of butter the size of a nutmeg, a piece of fresh lemon peel.

Boil the calves' feet in the water, strain and put aside ; when to be used take off the fat, put the jelly into a saucepan with the wine, sugar and nutmeg ; beat it up till it is ready to boil, then take a little of it and beat gradually to the yolk of egg, and adding the butter, stir all together, but don't let it boil. Grate the lemon peel into it.

1221. **BEEF TEA (Simplest Way of Making.)**

Cut the beef into very small pieces, and take away all the fat. Put it into a stone jar with a pint of water to each pound of beef; tie a double piece of brown paper over the top, and set the jar in a cool oven for several hours. Strain the beef tea off through a rather coarse strainer, and while it is hot take off every speck of fat with paper. If it is wanted stronger, put only half that amount of water. Should an oven be not obtainable, it will do equally well to place the jar in a large saucepan of boiling water ; but it will not do to cook it in a metal saucepan without a jar, because an invalid's palate is very sensitive, and the tea is sure to acquire an unpleasant flavor. If in the place of lean beef some beef bones are used, the tea will become a jelly when cold ; it will be less costly and less good. Any sort of flavoring may be added to it. A scrap of lemon-peel, a clove, a grate of nutmeg, a sprig of any sweet herb, or of parsley, put into the jar before cooking, will, any one of them, make a pleasant change, and a little ingenuity will soon increase the list. Such changes are grateful to a convalescent patient, and break the monotony of his life. However, a patient not decidedly convalescent needs nothing but beef and water, often not even salt. It is a lengthy process this ; and, if time is wanting to carry it out, twenty minutes is quite sufficient to set a cup of good beef tea on the table. First of all, prepare half a pint of the following

1222. **MEAT JUICE.**

Scrape with a knife, because no cutting divides it finely enough, half a pound of beef steak, and remove all the fat and skin. Put it into a basin with half a pint of tepid water, and let it stand fifteen minutes or longer. The result is what is commonly known as raw beef tea or meat-juice, every year more widely used as a restorative for infants as well as adults in cases of wasting or acute disease. Its appearance is against it, but the taste is simply that of any cold beef tea. Children generally take it without difficulty ; but adults, unless they are too weak to have an opinion on the point, have often an insurmountable objection to it. Nothing can then be done but to hide it in a colored or covered cup, or to add a little Liebig's Extract to conceal the color. The meat-juice is often prepared with hydrochloric acid, adding four drops to each pint of water; but we think the above recipe simpler, safer, and more suited for general use. Meat-juice is easier to assimilate than any form of cooked beef tea, and it is the only sort that may at all times be safely given to very young infants. It has saved many lives, especially those of rickety and wasted children and typhoid patients, and it seems right that everyone should know how to set about making it. But, to return to our

1223. QUICKLY MADE BEEF TEA.

Take the above juice and meat together, and put it on a slow fire. Let it boil for not longer than five minutes, strain it and it is ready for use. If it has been carefully scraped there will be no fat upon it, but if there should be some it can easily be removed with paper. Salt must be added to taste.

1224. Another Quick Method.

Scrape the beef as before, and remember that it is useless to put in gristle or sinew, because in none of these quick methods is there sufficient time to cook it. Set the meat over a very slow fire without water for a quarter of an hour, then add warm water and simmer for half an hour or longer.

1225. BEEF TEA CUSTARD.

This may be served alone either hot or cold, or a few small pieces can be put in a cup of beef tea, which is thus transferred into a kind of soupe royale. Beat up an egg in a cup, add a small pinch of salt, and enough strong beef tea to half fill the cup; butter a tiny mould and pour in the mixture. Steam it for twenty minutes, and turn it out in a shape.

1226. **SAVORY BEEF TEA.**—Ingredients—3 lbs. of beef chopped up finely, 3 leeks, 1 onion with 6 cloves stuck into it, 1 small carrot, a little celery seed, a small bunch of herbs, consisting of thyme, marjoram, and parsley, 1 teaspoonful of salt, half a teacupful of mushroom ketchup, and 3 pints of water.

Prepare according to the directions given in the first recipe.

1227. MUSH.

Put some water or milk into a pot and bring it to boil, then let the corn meal out of one hand gently into the milk or water, and keep stirring with the other until you have got it into a pretty stiff state; after which let it stand ten minutes or a quarter of an hour or less, or even only one minute, and then take it out, and put it into a dish or bowl. This sort of half-pudding, half-porridge, you eat either hot or cold, with a little salt or without it. It is eaten without any liquid matter, but the general way is to have a basin of milk, and taking a lump of the mush you put it into the milk, and eat the two together. Here is an excellent pudding, whether eaten with milk or without it; and where there is no milk it is an excellent substitute for bread, whether you take it hot or cold. It is neither hard nor lumpy when cold, but quite light and digestible for the most feeble stomachs.

1228. **FOWL (Stewed in barley).**—Ingredients—One chicken, ¼ lb. of pearl barley, enough milk to cover the barley, only a little salt, a bunch of sweet herbs.

Truss the chicken as for boiling; place it in a stewpan with the well-washed barley; sprinkle a little salt in and the sweet herbs; enough milk to cover the barley; put it on the fire, and let it stew *very* slowly, continue to add milk as it boils away, so that the barley may be always covered, but not the chicken, which should be dressed only by the steam from the milk. A small bird will take about three hours. When done serve with the milk and barley round it.

1229. **VEGETABLE MARROW (Stuffed).**—Ingredients—One marrow, some mince of either veal or chicken, bread crumbs, good gravy.

Take a good-sized marrow, boil until tender, halve lengthways; remove the seeds, and fill the inside with hot mince; join the two sides together, place upon a hot dish, sprinkle with grated bread crumbs; set in the oven to brown for a few minutes. Serve with a boat of good gravy.

1230. **MUTTON CUTLETS (Delicate).**—Ingredients—Two or 3 small cutlets from the best end of a neck or loin of mutton, 1 cupful of water or broth, a little salt and a few peppercorns.

Trim the cutlets very nicely, cut off all the fat, place them in a flat dish with enough water or broth to cover them, add the salt and peppercorns and allow them to stew gently for two hours, carefully skimming off every particle of fat which may rise to the top during the process. At the end of this time, provided the cutlets have not been allowed to boil fast, they will be found extremely tender. Turn them when half done.

1231. LAMBS' FRY (French).—Ingredients—Two sets of lambs' fry, 2 eggs, bread-crumbs, chopped parsley, hot lard.

Blanch the fry ten minutes in boiling water, drain them on a sieve, and when quite dry egg over with a paste brush; throw them into bread-crumbs, with which you have mixed some chopped parsley, fry them in very hot lard of a nice light brown color, dress pyramidically upon a napkin, garnish with fried parsley, and serve.

1232. RABBIT (Stewed).—Ingredients—Two nice young rabbits, 1 qt. of milk, 1 tablespoonful of flour, a blade of mace, salt and pepper.

Mix into a smooth paste the flour with half a glass of milk, then add the rest of the milk; cut the rabbits up into convenient pieces; place in a stewpan with the other ingredients and simmer gently until perfectly tender.

1233. SWEETBREADS.

These, when plainly cooked, are well adapted for the convalescent. They should be slowly boiled, and very moderately seasoned with salt and cayenne pepper.

1234. PORK JELLY (Dr. Ratcliff's Restorative).—Ingredients.—A leg of well-fed pork, 3 gals. of water, ½ oz. of mace, the same of nutmeg, salt to taste.

Take the pork just as cut up, beat it, and break the bone. Set it over a gentle fire with the water and simmer until it is reduced to one gallon. Let the mace and nutmeg stew with it. Strain through a fine sieve. When cold take off the fat. Give a large cupful the first and last thing and at noon, putting salt to taste.

1235. SHANK JELLY.—Ingredients—12 shanks of mutton, 3 blades of mace, an onion, 20 Jamaica, and 30 or 40 black peppers, a bunch of sweet herbs, a crust of bread toasted brown, and 3 qts. of water.

Soak the shanks for four hours, then brush and scour them very clean. Lay in a saucepan with all the ingredients, pouring in the water last, and set them near the stove; let them simmer as gently as possible for five hours, then strain and place in a cool place. This may have the addition of a pound of beef, if approved, for flavor. It is a remarkably good thing for persons who are weak.

1236. ARROWROOT JELLY.—½ pt. of water, a glass of sherry, a spoonful of brandy, grated nutmeg, and fine sugar, dessert spoonful of arrowroot rubbed smooth in two spoonfuls of cold water.

This is a very nourishing dish. Put into a saucepan all the

ingredients excepting the arrowroot; boil up once, then mix in by degrees the arrowroot; then return the whole into the saucepan; stir and boil it three minutes.

1237. TAPIOCA JELLY.—Ingredients—Some of largest kind of tapioca, some lemon juice, wine, and sugar.

Pour cold water on to wash it two or three times, then soak it in fresh water five or six hours, and simmer it in the same until quite clear; then add the lemon-juice, wine, and sugar. The peel should have been boiled in it. It thickens very much.

1238. MEAT JELLY.—Ingredients—Beef, isinglass, 1 teacupful of water, salt to taste.

Cut some beef into very small pieces and carefully remove all the fat. Put it in an earthen jar with alternate layers of the best isinglass (it is more digestible then gelatine) until the jar is full. Then add a teacupful of water with a little salt, cover it down closely, and cook it all day in a very slow oven. In the morning scald a jelly mould and strain the liquid into it. It will be quite clear, except at the bottom, where will be the brown sediment such as is in all beef tea, and it will turn out in a shape. It is, of course, intended to be eaten cold, and is very useful in cases where hot food is forbidden, or as a variety from the usual diet.

1239. GLOUCESTER JELLY.—Ingredients—1 oz each of rice, sago, pearl barley, hartshorn shavings, and eringo root, 3 pts. of water.

Simmer until reduced to a pint, and strain it. When cold it will be a jelly, of which give, dissolved in wine, milk, or broth, in change with other nourishment.

1240. CHICKEN PANADA.—Ingredients—a chicken, quart of water, a little salt, a grate of nutmeg, and the least piece of lemon peel.

Boil the chicken about three parts done in the water, take off the skin, cut the white meat off when cold, and pound in a mortar; pound it to a paste with a little of the water it was boiled in; season with salt, nutmeg, and lemon peel. Boil gently for a few minutes to the consistency you desire.

1241. GRAVY SIPPETS.—Ingredients—2 or 3 sippets of bread, gravy from mutton, beef or veal, salt to taste.

On an extremely hot plate put the sippets and pour over them the gravy. Sprinkle a little salt over.

1242. A GOOD RESTORATIVE (1).—Ingredients—two calves' feet, 2 pts. of water, 2 pts. of new milk.

Bake all together in a closely-covered jar for three hours and a half. When cold, remove the fat. Give a large teacupful the last and first thing. Whatever flavor is approved, give it by baking in it lemon peel, cinnamon, or mace. Add sugar after.

1243. **Another** (2).—Ingredients—6 sheep's trotters, 2 blades of mace, a little cinnamon, lemon peel, a few hartshorn shavings, a little isinglass, and 2 qts. of water.

Simmer to one quart, when cold take off the fat, and give nearly half a pint twice a day, warming with it a little new milk.

1244. **Another** (3).—Ingredients—1 oz. of isinglass shavings, 40 Jamaica peppers, a piece of brown crust of bread, 1 qt. of water.

Boil to a pint and strain. This makes a pleasant jelly to keep in the house, of which a large spoonful may be taken in wine and water, milk, tea, soup, or any way.

1245. **Another (a most pleasant Draught)**(4).—Ingredients— ¼ oz. of isinglass-shavings, 1 pt. of new milk, a little sugar.

Boil to half-pint; add for change, a bitter almond. Give this at bed-time, not too warm.

1246. **SAGO CREAM.**—Ingredients—1 pt. of boiling cream, 1 qt. of beef tea, 1 oz. of sago, ¼ pt. water, of and the yolks of 4 fresh eggs.

Boil the sago in the water till quite tender, when add the other ingredients.

1247. **CHOCOLATE.**—Ingredients—A cake of chocolate, 1 pint of water, milk, sugar.

Cut the chocolate into small pieces; put the water into a saucepan and add the chocolate; mill it off the fire until quite melted, then on a gentle fire until it boils; pour into a basin and it will keep in a cool place eight or ten days. When wanted put a spoonful or two into milk, boil it with sugar and mix well.

1248. **MILK PORRIDGE**.—Some half grits long boiled, milk, toast.

Make a gruel of the half grits; strain, and add either cold milk or warm milk as you desire. Serve with toast.

1249. **FRENCH PORRIDGE**.—Ingredients—Some oatmeal, water, milk, toast.

Stir the oatmeal and water together, let it stand to be clear, and pour off the latter; pour fresh upon it, stir it well, let it stand till next day; strain through a fine sieve, and boil the water, adding the milk while doing. The proportion of water must be small. This is much ordered, with toast, for the breakfast of weak persons, abroad.

1250. GROUND RICE MILK.—Ingredients— One spoonful of ground rice rubbed smooth in 1½ pints of milk, a piece of cinnamon, lemon peel and nutmeg.

Boil the ground rice and milk, adding the spices and flavoring. Sweeten to taste when nearly done.

1251. SAGO MILK.—Ingredients—Sago, new milk.

Cleanse the sago from the earthy taste by soaking it in cold water for an hour, pour that off and wash well, then add more, and simmer gently with the milk. It swells so much that a small quantity will be sufficient for a quart, when done reduced to about a pint. It requires no sugar or flavoring.

1252. EGGS AND TOAST.—Ingredients—2 eggs, thinly-cut slices of bread, 1 teaspoonful of vinegar, little salt, a piece of butter the size of a walnut, a few sprigs of fresh, green parsley, or some sweet geranium leaves.

Take the thinly-cut slices of bread, and toast them quickly to a light brown, without burning them. Drop an egg or two into boiling water in which the vinegar has been poured, and a little salt added to it. Pour one tablespoonful of boiling water over a piece of butter, turn it over the toast, and if it is very dry dip the whole of it into the melted butter and water, soaking the crusts completely. Skim out the eggs as soon as the whites are firmly set, and put them upon the toast. Edge the plate with a few sprigs of fresh, green parsley, or some sweet geranium leaves, and serve upon a salver covered with a white napkin, and an invalid will usually eat of it with great relish.

1253. BAKED HOMINY.—Ingredients— To a cupful of cold boiled hominy (small kind) allow 2 cups of milk, a heaping teaspoonful of white sugar, a little salt, and 3 eggs.

Beat the eggs very light, yolks and whites separately. Work the yolks into the hominy, alternately with the butter. When thoroughly mixed, put in the sugar and salt, and go on beating while you soften the batter gradually with milk. Be careful to leave no lumps in the batter. Lastly, stir in the whites and bake in a buttered pudding dish until light, firm, and delicately browned. It may be eaten as a dessert, but it is a delightful article, and the best substitute that can be devised for green-corn pudding.

1254. STRAWBERRIES—Ingredients—Fruit, white sugar, juice of 2 or 3 lemons in proportion to the fruit.

The way to make strawberries digestible to those who are

unable to eat them on account of dyspepsia or any other cause is very simple. Cover them with a very large allowance of powdered sugar and then squeeze over them the lemon juice, which brings out the strawberry flavor more than anything else, and its acidity is counteracted by the large quantity of sugar. The lemon juice should be in the same proportion as the cream would be in place of which it is used.

1255. **STRENGTHENING BLANC-MANGE.**—Ingredients— One pint of milk, ¼ oz. of isinglass, rind of ½ a small lemon, 2 oz. of sugar, yolks of 3 fresh eggs.

Dissolve the isinglass in the water, strain through muslin, put it again on the fire with the rind of the half-lemon cut very thin, and the sugar; let it simmer gently until well flavored, then take out the lemon peel, and stir the milk to the beaten yolks of the eggs; pour the mixture back into the saucepan, and hold it over the fire, keeping it stirred until it begins to thicken; put it into a deep basin and keep it moved with a spoon until it is nearly cold, then pour it into the moulds which have been laid in water, and set it in a cool place till firm. This we can recommend for invalids, as well as for the table generally.

1256. **WATER GRUEL.**—Ingredients—A large spoonful of oatmeal, water, salt, and a little piece of butter.

Rub smooth the oatmeal with two spoonfuls of water and pour it in a pint of water boiling on the fire; stir well and boil quickly. In a quarter of an hour strain it off and add the salt and butter when eaten; stir until the butter is thoroughly incorporated.

1257. **EFFERVESCING GRUEL**—Ingredients—Half a breakfast cup of thin water gruel, 1 tablespoonful of sifted white sugar, a saltspoonful of carbonate of soda, juice of a lemon.

Mix the soda and sugar well together and then put into the gruel, stirring thoroughly; have ready the lemon juice strained, throw it in and drink immediately while it is effervescing and as hot as possible.

1258. **BARLEY GRUEL.**—Ingredients—Four oz. of pearl barley, 2 qts. of water, a stick of cinnamon, ⅔ pt. of port wine, sugar to taste.

Wash the barley, boil it in the water with the cinnamon, till reduced to a quart; strain and return to the saucepan with remaining ingredients, keep on the fire about five minutes, stirring all the while. Pour into a jug and when wanted warm up again.

1259. **EGG GRUEL.**—Ingredients—Yolk of one egg, 1 tablespoonful of sugar, two-thirds of a cup of boiling water, white of the egg.

Beat the yolk of the egg with the sugar till very light; on this pour the boiling water; on the top put the white of the egg beaten to a stiff froth with a little sugar.

1260. **CUSTARDS.**—Ingredients—One qt. of milk, 1 stick of cinnamon, the rind of a lemon, a few laurel leaves, or bitter almonds, sugar to taste, the yolks of 8 eggs, the whites of 4.

Boil the milk with cinnamon, lemon rind, laurel leaves, and sugar; well whisk the yolks with the whites of four eggs, adding a little milk, then strain into a dish. When the milk boils, take it off the fire and strain it; then stir the egg into it; return the whole to the saucepan and set it on the fire again, stirring constantly; let it come to the boiling point, then take it off the fire, pour it into a large jug, and continue stirring it till it is nearly cold. It should now have the consistency of thick cream, and is ready for being poured into custard glasses; when the glasses are filled, grate a little nutmeg over them.

1261. **CAUDLE.**—Ingredients—One pt. of fine gruel, yolk of an egg beaten with sugar, a large spoonful of cold water, a glass of wine and a little nutmeg.

Put the egg beaten with sugar into the boiling gruel, and add the cold water, wine, and nutmeg. Mix by degrees. This is very nourishing.

1262. **A NICE DRINK FOR A COUGH.**—Ingredients—A fresh laid egg, ¼ pint of new milk warmed, a large spoonful of capillaire, the same of rose-water, a little grated nutmeg.

Beat the egg and mix with remaining ingredients. Do not warm it after the egg has been put in.

1263. **TOAST AND WATER.**—Ingredients—A slice of bread, jug of cold water.

Toast slowly the bread till extremely brown and hard, but not in the least black. Put into the water and cover closely for an hour before used. It should be a fine brown color before using.

1264. **A NICE DRINK.**—Ingredients—A glass of clear cold water, a tablespoonful of capillaire, a tablespoonful of some good vinegar.

Put the capillaire and vinegar into the water and it is ready.

Tamarinds, currants, fresh or in jelly, or scalded currants, or cranberries, make excellent drink; with sugar or not, according to taste.

1265. **A FEVER DRINK** (1).—Ingredients—A little tea sage, 2 sprigs of balm, a very small quantity of wood sorrel, a small lemon, 3 pints of boiling water.

Put the sage, balm and wood sorrel into a stone jug, having previously washed and dried them, peel thin the lemon, and clear from the white; slice and put a piece of the peel in; then pour on the water, sweeten and cover.

1266. **A FEVER DRINK** (2).—Ingredients—One oz. of pearl barley, 3 pints of water, 1 oz. of sweet almonds, a piece of lemon peel, a little syrup of lemons and capillaire.

Wash well the barley; sift it twice, then add the water, sweet almonds beaten fine, and the lemon peel; boil till you have a smooth liquor, then add the syrup.

1267. **APPLE WATER.** — Ingredients — Some well flavored apples, 3 or 4 cloves, a strip of lemon peel, boiling water.

Slice the apples into a large jug, they need be neither peeled nor cored. Add the cloves and lemon peel, and pour boiling water over. Let it stand a day. It will be drinkable in twelve hours or less.

1268. **CURRANT WATER.**—Ingredients—One quart of red currants, ½ pint of raspberries, 2 quarts of water, syrup—1 quart of water, about ¾ lb. of sugar.

Put the fruit with the water over a very slow fire to draw the juice, for half an hour. They must not boil. Strain through a hair sieve, add the syrup. Other fruit may be used in the same way.

1269. **BARLEY WATER.**—Ingredients—Two oz. of barley, 2 quarts of water, flavor with lemon, currant, or any juice preferred.

Wash the barley and boil in the water till it looks white and the barley grows soft; then strain and flavor.

1270. **PEPPERMINT WATER.**—Ingredients—Three quarts of water (boiling), 8 cts. worth of oil of peppermint, sugar to taste.

Boil the water and pour into a jug and let it remain till lukewarm; add the oil of peppermint; sweeten and stir till cold, then bottle.

1271. **VINEGAR WHEY (used in fevers).**—Ingredients—Half a gill of vinegar. 2 teaspoonfuls of sugar, 2 teacups of milk (boiling).

Mix the vinegar with the sugar, stir in the boiling milk; let it boil one or two minutes, cool it, and strain off the whey. Lemon juice may be used instead of vinegar, if preferred; it is then called lemon whey.

1272. **WINE WHEY.**—Ingredients—One pint of milk, 2 glasses of white wine, 2 teaspoonfuls of sugar.

Boil the milk; the moment it boils stir in the wine with the sugar; let it boil once again, stand it to cool, strain off the whey through a fine sieve or piece of muslin. The curd is indigestible.

1273. **MULLED WINE.**—Ingredients—A pint of wine, 1 pint of water, 1 egg, nutmeg and sugar.

Mix the wine with the water; boil them; beat the egg in a small pan, put it into the wine, then quickly pour the whole from one vessel to the other five or six times. Season with the nutmeg and sugar.

1274. **RICE MILK.**—Ingredients—Two tablespoonfuls of rice, 1 pint of milk, 1 tablespoonful of ground rice (if wanted thick, 2 will be required), a little cold milk.

Put the rice into the pint of milk; boil it until done, stirring to prevent it burning. Put the ground rice with little cold milk, mix smooth and stir it in; boil for about a quarter of an hour. Thick milk may be made in the same way as "rice milk," only substituting flour for rice, thickening and sweetening to taste. Five minutes boiling will do.

1275. **CHAMOMILE TEA.**—Ingredients—One oz. of dried chamomile flowers, ½ oz. of dried orange peel, 1 quart of boiling water.

Put the chamomile into a jug with the orange peel. Pour over it the boiling water, and stand on the back of the stove just close enough to the fire to keep it simmering till the strength of the peel and flower is drawn out, then strain off for use and drink a wineglass at a time.

1276. **DANDELION TEA.**—Ingredients—Six or 8 dandelion roots, according to size, 1 pint of boiling water.

Pull up the dandelion roots and cut off the leaves; well wash the roots and scrape off a little of the skin. Cut them up into small pieces and pour the boiling water on them. Let them stand all night, then strain through muslin, and the tea is ready for use. It should be quite clear, and the color of brown sherry. One wineglassful should be taken at a time. The decoction will not last good for more than two or three days, and therefore it must only be made in small quantities.

THE DOCTOR.

The following recipes are selected from eminent authorities and can be relied upon, but while in all cases it is prudent to consult a medical man as soon as possible, the information under this heading will be found invaluable where the doctor is not readily available.

1277. Fractures.

Fracture is said to be simple when there is no external wound; compound, when complicated with lesion of the surrounding soft parts; and comminuted when the bone is broken into many fragments. The symptons of fracture are pain and inability to move the limb. When there is great swelling, it is often difficult to ascertain the nature or even the existence of a fracture. The course of a simple fracture is a painful and inflamed swelling a few days after the accident, with more or less febrile reaction; these gradually subside, and with proper treatment the bone unites in from one to two months, with or without deformity according to circumstances not always under the control of the surgeon. Complicated fractures often terminate in the death of portions of bone and of the soft parts, in unhealthy abscesses and tetanus, leading perhaps to fatal results unless the limb be removed. The indications of treatment are to reduce or set the fragments and keep them at rest and in close contact so as to prevent deformity; all disturbing muscles must be relaxed, the ends of the bones extended and the parts properly supported and kept in place, the limb bandaged, and some kind of splint is applied to keep it immovable of its natural length. The variety of bandage, splints, and apparatus for the different kinds of fracture is very great, and in nothing does American surgery stand more pre-eminent than in its ingenious and effectual instruments for the treatment of broken bones. When a surgeon cannot be procured immediately the broken limb should be kept as nearly as possible in its natural position. The two portions of the bone must be pulled in opposite directions, until the limb is the same length as its fellow, then apply a splint and bind it to the part with a bandage. Of course when there is no deformity the pulling of the bones is unnecessary. Should there be much swelling a cold lotion should be used. If the patient is faint, give brandy and water, or sal-volatile and water.

1278. How to Restore a Person apparently Drowned.

Loosen everything around the neck. Turn the patient's face downward, and raise the body several inches higher than the head, and keep it in this position long enough to count five slowly. This will enable the water to escape from the mouth and nose. Place the patient on his back with the chest slightly raised (by some convenient article of clothing such as a folded coat or shawl) and the head in a straight line with the body. Then practice artificial breathing in this way:—Stand astride the patient's hips, grasp the arms, and raise them above the head until they nearly meet, which expands the chest; then pull them down and press firmly in the sides of the chest; this contracts the chest and thus forces the breath first in and then out. While this is going on let another person catch hold of the tongue with a piece of cloth and pull it out, it may be secured by fastening an elastic band over the tongue and under the chin; this opens the little air-valve covering the air-tube. While this is going on remove all wet clothing, cover the body with warm blankets, etc., and rub the body vigorously. If signs of life appear, place the patient in a warm bed in a well-ventilated room, and give hot drinks, such as milk, tea, or coffee.

1279. Scalds and Burns.

The first object is to cover the injured part with some suitable material, and this should be kept on until the cure is complete. Apply to the burn or scald a mixture of lime water and linseed oil by saturating the lint with the mixture. Do not remove when dry, but saturate by the application of fresh outer layers from time to time. If nothing better is at hand apply grated potato, flour, starch, &c.

1280. Bruises.

Excite as quickly as possible the absorption of bruised blood and apply butter, fresh raw beef, or even bathing with cold water is a very good though simple remedy.

1281. Hemorrhage

may be checked by giving strong salt and water; or by giving lemon-juice.

If an artery be cut, tie a strong string *above* the cut to prevent the escape of blood. Tighten the string if necessary by placing a ruler or stick in the string, twist this round, so as to make a knot pressing tightly on the artery. The blood from an artery is always of a very bright red and comes out in jerks or spurts.

1282. To Remove a Bee-Sting.

Remove the sting at once with a needle or the fingers; press a key tightly over the stung part, the pressure will force the poison out. Wipe the place with clean linen, suck it and then dab with the blue-bag.

1283. Bites of Snakes.

These are dangerous and require powerful remedies. The bites of the various kinds of snakes do not have the same effects, but people suffer from them in different ways. It is of the greatest importance to prevent the poison mixing with the blood and to remove the whole of it instantly from the body. Take a piece of tape or anything that is near and tie tightly around the part bitten; if it be the leg or arm, immediately above the bite and between it and the heart, the wound should be sucked several times by any person near. There is no danger to the person performing this kindness, providing his tongue or any part of the mouth has no broken skin. Having sucked the poison, immediately spit it out. A better plan is to cut out the central part bitten with a sharp instrument. This may not be a very pleasant operation for an amateur, but, as we have to act promptly in such an emergency, courage will come. After the operation bathe the wound for some time to make it bleed freely. Having done this rub the wound with a stick of lunar-caustic or, still better, a solution composed of sixty grains of lunar caustic dissolved in an ounce of water. This solution should be dropped into the wound. Of course the band tied round the wound in the first place must be kept on during the time these means are being adopted. The wound afterwards must be covered with lint dipped in cold water. There is generally great depression of strength in these cases, it is necessary therefore to give some stimulant, a glass of hot brandy and water, or twenty drops of sal-volatile. When the patient has somewhat recovered give him a little mustard in hot water to make him vomit, if on the other hand the vomiting is continuous, a large mustard poultice should be applied to the stomach and one pill given composed of a grain of solid opium. Note.—Only one of these pills must be given without medical advice.

All these remedies can be acted upon until a surgeon arrives.

1284. Bites of Dogs.

The manner of treatment is the same as for snake-bites. Many writers on the subject are in favor of the wound being kept open as long as possible. Many persons do this by placing a few beans on the wound and then putting a linseed meal poultice over the wound.

1285. Treatment of Sprains.

Immediately after the accident the part should be immersed in a bath at the heat of 100 deg., after which leeches should be applied, and then a poultice of vinegar and bran, lukewarm, or bread crumbs and camphorated spirits of wine; the following lotion, when applied in the early stage, after blood has been freely drawn by leeches, rarely fails in affording great relief:—Gourlard's extract, half an ounce; tincture of opium, two drachms; vinegar, half a pint; camphor mixture, one pint and a half. Mix for a lotion, to be applied tepid by means of folded rags. After the inflammatory action has subsided, one of the following **Liniments should be used:**

1286. (1) Soap liniment, one ounce; tincture of opium, two drachms; camphorated spirits, two drachms. Mix for a liniment, and rub in night and morning.

1287. (2) Camphorated spirits of wine, half an ounce; cajaput oil and laudanum, of each, two drachms; olive oil, half an ounce. Mix for a liniment, and apply night and morning.

1288. (3) Olive oil and spirits of turpentine, of each half an oz. Mix for a liniment, and use as above.

1289. (4) When weakness remains after a sprain, pumping cold water on the part every morning, aided by a bandage or laced stocking to support the part, will be the most effectual means of remedying it.

1290. **For Sprained Ankle.**—Bathe the ankle frequently with strong cold salt and water; sit with the foot elevated, keeping it cool. Diet, and take daily cooling drinks or medicine. Or bind on loosely, and as often as dry, first twenty-four hours, cotton batting, spread with beaten egg-whites; after that, morning and night.

1291. **To Bind a Sprained Ankle.**—Put the end of the bandage upon the instep; then take it round and bring it over the same part again, and then round the foot two or three times; finish off with a turn or two round the leg above the ankle.

1292. **Sprained Wrist.**—Begin by passing the bandage round the hand, across and across, like the figure 8; leave out the thumb, and finish with a turn or two round the wrist. Apply arnica tincture.

1293. Treatment of a Frozen Person.

Chelius, a German authority, gives the following advice for restoring a frozen person. He should be brought into a cold room, and after having been undressed, covered up with snow or with cloth in ice-cold water, or he may be laid in cold water so deeply, that his mouth and nose are only free. When the body is somewhat thawed, there is commonly a sort of icy crust formed around it; the patient must then be removed, and the body washed with cold water mixed with a little wine or brandy; when the limbs lose their stiffness, and the frozen person shows signs of life, he should be carefully dried, and put into a cold bed in a cold room; scents and remedies which excite sneezing, are to be put to his nose; air to be carefully blown into the lungs, if natural breathing do not come on; clysters of warm water with camphorated vinegar thrown up; the throat tickled with a feather, and cold water dashed upon the pit of the stomach. He must be brought by degrees into rather warmer air, and mild perspirants, as elder and balm-tea (or weak common tea) with Minderin's spirit, warm wine and the like, may be given to promote gentle perspiration.

1294. Bruises.

In slight bruises, and those that are not likely to be followed by inflammation, nothing more is usually required than to bathe the part with spirit, as Eau-de-Cologne, brandy, &c., mixed with an equal proportion of vinegar and water.

1295. In more severe cases, and where the accident is near an important part, as the eye, or any of the joints, it becomes a desirable object to prevent the approach of inflammation. For this purpose leeches must be employed, repeating them according to circumstances. If considerable fever be present, bleeding from the arm, purgatives, and low diet, may become necessary.

1296. In the last stage of a bruise, where there is merely a want of tone in the parts, and swelling from the effused blood, &c., friction should be employed, either simply, or with any common liniment. Wearing a bandage,—pumping cold water on the part, succeeded by warm friction,—a saturated solution of common salt in water, have each been found successful. The roots of briony and Solomon's seal, bruised and applied as a poultice, are highly useful in hastening the disappearance of the discoloration caused by bruises.

1297. Accidents from Edge Tools, Hard Bodies, &c.

In all recent wounds, the first consideration is to remove foreign bodies, such as pieces of glass, splinters of wood, pieces of stone, earth, or any other substance that may have been introduced by the violence of the act which caused the wound.

Where there is much loss of blood, an attempt should be made to stop it with dry lint, and compression above the part wounded, if the blood be of a florid color; and below, if of a dark color. In proportion to the importance of the part wounded, will be the degree of the discharge of blood, and the subsequent tendency to inflammation and its consequences.

1298. Substances in the Eye.

A substance getting in the eye may either lie disengaged on its surface, or, having penetrated the external coat, may there remain fixed. In the former case, it is easily removed by a camel-hair pencil, or a piece of paper rolled into the size of a crow-quill with the end softened in the mouth.

1299. Sometimes the substance sticks in the corner, when, if it cannot be removed with a probe or fine forceps, the point of a lancet should be *carefully* passed under it so as to lift it out.

1300. If the removal cannot be effected without considerable difficulty, it is better to leave it to be detached by ulceration, taking every precaution to keep off undue inflammation, by avoiding a strong light, fomenting with warm water, etc.

1301. To remove fine particles of gravel, lime, etc., the eye should be syringed with luke-warm water till free from them. Be particular not to worry the eye under the impression that the substance is still there, which the enlargement of some of the minute vessels make, the patient believe to be actually the case.

1302. Substances in the Ear.

Hard substances, such as peas, bits of slate-pencil, beads, etc., occasionally get lodged in the passage of the external ear. If the substance be within sight, and can be grasped readily with a small pair of forceps, that will be the best way to extract it; but force must not, on any account, be used.

1303. But the best and safest plan is to inject luke-warm water rather forcibly into the ear by means of a syringe, one that will hold at least two ounces. This will be found rarely to fail, the water passing beyond the substance, and being there confined by the membrane, called the *tympanum*, forces the former outwards.

1304. Should the substance have swelled, or the ear become swollen, a little sweet oil must be poured into the ear, and left there till the next day, when syringing may be used.

1305. Glass beads and similar substances, may be extracted by means of a probe, dipped into some appropriate cement, introduced into the ear, and kept in contact with the body to be removed, for a few moments till it has become set.

1306. Substances in the Throat.

A fish-bone, or pin, being lodged in the throat, may sometimes be readily got rid of by exciting vomiting by tickling the backpart of the throat.

1307. Another mode is to make the patient swallow a good mouthful of bread-crumb.

1308. Another expedient is to introduce a large goose-quill down the throat, and then twirl it round, by this means the substance may be disengaged, and so pass down into the stomach.

1309. A plentiful draught of water will sometimes be sufficient, when the substance is merely engaged in the folds of the gullet. We would, however, particularly recommend in this case the white of an egg, and, if necessary, a second.

1310. Disease of Infants.

The most frequent of these are—1, disorders of the stomach; 2, disorders of the bowels; 3, exhaustion; 4, febrile affections; 5, exanthematous diseases, or those which are attended with eruptions of the skin; 6, affections of the head; 7, diseases of the thorax, or chest; 8, affections of the abdomen, or belly.

Disorders of the stomach generally depend on improper diet; or they may be secondary, and the effects of a disordered or confined state of the bowels. They are often detected by acid or fœtid eructations and breath, or by the unusually frequent regurgitation or vomiting of food.

Disorders of the bowels can never be mistaken or overlooked by an attentive nurse, the evacuations in their number and appearance, being the perfect index to these disorders.

It must never be forgotten, that whenever the system has been exposed to sources of exhaustion, this condition may become, in its turn, the source of various morbid affections which are apt to be ascribed to other causes, and treated by improper, and therefore dangerous, measures. If the infant has had diarrhœa, or if it has been bled by leeches ; or if, without these, its cheeks are pale and cool ; and if, under these circumstances, it be taken with symptoms of affection of the head, do not fail to remember that this affection may be the result of exhaustion. This important subject seems to have been generally misunderstood.

Fever is sooner detected. In every such case it is advisable not to tamper nor delay, but to send for the medical man, and watch the little patient with redoubled care and attention.

Especially examine the skin, hour after hour, for eruptions. It may be measles or scariatina, &c. It will be especially desirable to detect these eruptio s early, and to point them out to the physician. Above all things, let not a contracted brow, an unusual state of the temper or manner, unusual drowsiness or wakefulness, or starting, and especially unusual vomiting, escape you.

Be alive to any acceleration, or labor, or shortness of the breathing, or cough, or sneezing, or appearance of inflammation about the eyes or nostrils. These symptons may portend inflammation within the chest, hooping-cough, measles. Pain of the body, with or without vomiting; or diarrhœa, with or without a morbid state of the bowels, or of the discharges, ought also to excite immediate attention. One caution should be given on this subject : some of the most alarming and fatal affections of the bowels, like some affections of the head, are unattended by *acute* pain or tenderness; their accession, on the contrary, is insidious, and it will require great attention to detect them early

Another view, and another mode of the classification of the diseases of infants, full of interest, full of admonition is—1, as they are *sudden*; or 2, as they are *insidious;* or 3, as they are, in the modes of accession, intermediate between these two extremes.

Of the sudden affections, are fits of every kind, croup, and some kinds of pain, as that of colic; of the second class are hydrocephalus, or water on the brain, and tubercles in t ,e lungs or abdomen, constituting the two kinds of consumption. Fits, again, are cerebral, and arise from diseases within the head, or from irritation in the stomach and bowels, or from exhaustion ; or they are evidence of, and depend on, some malformation or disease of the heart.

Domestic treatment should never be trusted in such terrific affections as these ; not a moment should be lost in sending for the medical man.

If anything may be done in the meantime, it is—1, in either of the two former cases to lance the gums ; 2, to evacuate the bowels by the warm water injection, made more active by the addition of Brown Sugar ; 3, and then to administer the warm bath. An important point, never to be forgotten in the hurry of these cases, is to reserve the evacuations for inspection otherwise the physicians will be deprived of a very important source of judgment.

In cases of fits arising plainly from exhaustion, there need be no hesitation in giving five drops of sal volatile in water, light nourishment may be added; the feet must be fomented and the recumbent posture preserved.

In fits arising from an affection of the heart the symptom is urgent difficulty of breathing ; the child seems as if it would lose its breath and expire. In such a case, *to do nothing* is the best course ; all self-possession must be summoned, and the infant kept perfectly quiet. Every change of posture, every effort, is attended with danger.

Sometimes the attacks assume the character of croup ; there is a crowing cough, and breathing ; or there is a difficulty of breathing, and then a crowing inspiration. The former case is generally croup ; the latter is, in reality, a fit dependent on the morbid condition of the brain or spinal marrow, although it takes the appearance of an affection of the organs of respiration.

In either case it is well to clear the bowels by means of the slow injection of from a quarter to half a pint of warm water, with or without brown sugar ; indeed this is the most generally and promptly useful of all our remedies in infantile diseases. To this the warm bath may always be added, if administered with due caution. For instance, it should not be continued so as to induce much flushing or paleness of the countenance.

1311. Measles.

Measles commences with the ordinary symptoms of fever. The attack is almost invariably attended with inflammation of the mucous membrane lining the air passages ; the eyes are red and watery ; there is defluxion from the nostrils, hoarseness, and cough. The eruption commonly appears on the fourth day, at first about the head and neck, then the trunk and arms, and finally reaching the lower extremities ; it takes two or three days to complete its course and when it reaches the feet and legs has often begun to disappear from the face. All ages are liable to it. When the eruption is fully out, the cough, at first dry and troublesome, generally becomes softer and less frequent, and at the end of six or seven from the coming out of the first papules they have disappeared. When danger occurs, it is from inflammation of the air passages. In all ordinary cases simple diet, the maintenance of an equable temperature, plenty of diluent drinks, attention should be paid to the bowels as they should be kept gently open, if a roasted apple or a little manna in the drink will not do this, give a mild saline aperient such as ipecacuanha wine and sweet spirits of nitre, 1 drachm; of tartrate of potash, 4 drachms; solution of acetate of ammonia 1 ounce; syrup of poppies, 2 drachms; cinnamon or dill water sufficient to make 4 ounces; dose, a table or dessert spoonful three or four times a day. Where there is much heat of the skin, sponging with tepid vinegar and water will commonly relieve it, and also the itching. On the third or fourth day after the subsidence of the eruption a little opening medicine should be given and care must be taken to protect the patient against change of weather, and to restore the strength by a nourishing diet. Attention should be paid to the cough, and the proper remedies given if required. Should the eruption suddenly disappear, then there is cause for alarm; the patient should be directly put into a warm bath, and have warm diluent drinks; if the pulse sinks rapidly, administer wine whey or weak brandy and water.

1312. Scarlet Fever.

This fever is distinguished from other eruptive fevers by the fact of the eruption being an exanthema, an efflorescence, or a rash, these 'terms not being strictly applicable to vesicles and pustules. The disease sometimes commences with a chill, and in most cases vomiting is a primary symptom especially in children. The fever which at once occurs is usually intense, the axiliary temperature often rising to 105°, or even higher. The surface of the body often gives to the touch a burning sensation. The rash appears in about twenty-four hours after the date of the invasion, and with few exceptions breaks out first on the face and neck. The color of the rash is scarlet, whence the name. The skin is somewhat swollen and the rash occasions a burning sensation with in some cases intense itching. Generally the eruption takes place in the throat, and the tonsils are more or less swollen. The cutaneous eruption is prolonged from four to six days. Then follows the stage of scaling, and in some instances the cuticle of the hands may be stripped off like a glove. In favorable cases the duration of this stage may be reckoned to be five or six days, when convalescence is established. In other cases it is extremely severe and may prove fatal within a few days or even hours. Scarlet fever is highly contagious and the infectious material remains for a long time in garments, etc. Children are more susceptible than adults. The treatment in mild cases is very simple. Active medication is not indicated. It suffices to diminish the animal heat by sponging the body and giving cooling drinks observing proper hygienic precautions. Smearing the surface of the limbs with fat bacon allays the itching which is often very distressing. Should the symptoms show failure of the vital powers, supporting measures of treatment (alcoholic stimulants and alimenation) are indicated. Great care must be taken to keep the patient warm right through the disease as affections of the kidneys often follow cases of scarlet fever. It is important to isolate the patient and attendant from the healthy. Remove all curtains and carpets, and clothing not actually in use from the sick chamber. On removing the patient's linen or bed clothes, throw them into water and so convey to the wash. Chloride of lime should be set about the room in plates. When the patient can be removed from the room, scrub the room with chloride of lime in the water. It is wise to keep the patient in bed for three weeks. Should the eruption be slow in appearing, sponge the body with cold vinegar and water, wrap in a blanket and keep the patient warm. Should the throat be sore, keep hot bran poultice constantly applied. If the fever runs high in the first stage, and there is great inclination to vomit (before sponging), it is a good plan to give an emetic of equal proportions of antimonial and ipecacuanha wine; dose, a teaspoonful to a tablespoonful, according to age.

1313. Hooping Cough.

This well-known disease is chiefly, but not wholly, confined to the stages of infancy, and it occurs but once in a life-time. It may be described as a spasmodic catarrh, and its severity varies greatly; sometimes being so mild as to be scarcely known from a common cough, at others, exhibiting the most distressing symptoms, and frequently causing death by its violent and exhausting paroxysms.

The first symptoms of this cough are those of an ordinary cold; there is probably restlessness and slight fever, with irritation in the bronchial passages; this goes on gradually increasing in intensity for a week or ten days, and then begins to assume the spasmodic character; at first the paroxysms are slight, and of short duration with a scarcely perceptible "hoop," but soon they become more frequent and severe; a succession of violent expulsive coughs is followed by a long-drawn inspiration, in the course of which the peculiar sound which gives a name to the disease is emitted; again come the coughs, and again the inspiration, following each other in quick succession, until the sufferer, whose starting eyes, livid face, swollen veins, and clutching hands, attest the violence of the struggle for breath, is relieved by an expectoration of phlegm resembling the white of an egg, or by vomiting. When the paroxysm is over, the child generally resumes its play, or other occupation, and frequently complains of being hungry. As the disease proceeds, the matter expectorated becomes thicker, and is more easily got rid of, and this is a sign of favorable progress: the spasmodic paroxysms become less frequent and violent, and gradually cease altogether; but the changes here indicated may extend over a month or six months, according to circumstances, the season of the year having much influence in hastening or retarding them; summer being, of course, the most favorable time. It is a common impression that, at whatever time of year an attack of Hooping Cough commences, it will not end until May; this is simply because of the change in the weather which generally takes place in or about the course of that month. With a strong, healthy child (when proper care is taken), there is little to apprehend from this disease, provided it be not complicated with others, such as inflammation of the lungs, or any head affection producing convulsions; it then proves a most dangerous malady, and is fatal to many. With children of a full habit, the fits of coughing often cause bleeding at the nose, but this should not be viewed with alarm, as it relieves the vessels of the brain, and is likely to prevent worse consequences.

To weakly children Hooping Cough is a very serious malady —to all it is frequently a very sore trial, but to them it is especially so: therefore great care should be taken not to expose them to the danger of catching it; that it is contagious there can be no doubt, and although some parents think lightly of it, and imagining their children must have it, at one time or another, deem that it matters little when, and therefore take no pains to protect them against it; yet we would impress upon all our readers, who may have the care of infants, that a heavy responsibility lies at their door. It is by no means certain that a child will have this disease; we have known many persons who have reached a good old age and never contracted it; and it is folly and wickedness needlessly to expose those placed under our care to a certain danger.

Like fever, Hooping Cough has a course to run, which no remedies, with which we are at present acquainted, will shorten; the severity of the symptoms may be somewhat mitigated, and we may, by watching the course of the disease, and by use of the proper means, often prevent those complications which render it dangerous, and this brings us to the consideration of the proper mode of

Treatment.—The first effort should be directed to check any tendency to inflammation which may show itself; to palliate urgent symptoms, and stop the spasm which is so distressing a feature of the case. To this end, the diet must be of the simplest kind, consisting for the most part of milk and farinaceous puddings; if animal food, it must not be solid, but in the form of Broth, or Beef-tea; roasted Apples are good; and, for drinks, Milk and Water, Barley-water, Weak Tea, or Whey.

Care must be taken to keep the bowels open with some gentle aperient, such as Rhubarb and Magnesia, with now and then a grain of Calomel or Compound Julep Powder if something stronger is required. An emetic should be given about twice a week, to get rid of the phlegm—it may be Ipecacuanha Wine or the Powder. To relieve the cough, the following mixture will be found effective:—Ipecacuanha Powder, 10 grains; Bicarbonate of Potash, 1 drachm; Liquor of Acetate of Ammonia, 2 ounces; Essence of Cinnamon, 8 drops; Water, 6½ ounces: Dose, a tablespoonful about every four hours. 20 drops of Laudanum, or 1 drachm of Tincture of Henbane may be added if the cough is very troublesome, but the former is objectionable if the brain is at all affected.

For night restlessness, 2 or 3 grains of Dover's Powders, taken at bed-time, is good; this is the dose for a child of three years old. Mustard poultices to the throat, the chest, and between the shoulders, are often found beneficial; so is an opiate liniment composed of Compound Camphor and Soap Liniment, of each 6 drachms, and 4 drachms of Laudanum. *Roache's Embrocation* is a favourite application, and a very good one; it is composed as follows:—Oil of Amber and of Cloves, of each ½ an ounce; Oil of Olives, 1 ounce; a little Laudanum is, perhaps, an improvement. This may be rubbed on the belly when it is sore from coughing. Difficulty of breathing may be sometimes relieved by the vapour of Ether or Turpentine diffused through the apartment. In the latter stages of the disease, tonics are generally advisable. Steel Wine, about 20 drops, with 2 grains of Sesquicarbonate of Ammonia, and 5 drops of Tincture of Conium, in a tablespoonful of Cinnamon Water, sweetened with Syrup, is a good form; but a change of air, with a return to a generous diet, are the most effectual means of restoration to health and strength.

Squinting, stupor, and convulsions are symptomatic of mischief in the brain; in this case leeches to the temples, and small and frequently repeated doses of Calomel and James's Powder should be resorted to. Fever, and great difficulty of breathing, not only during the fits of coughing, but between them, indicate inflammation in the chest, on which a blister should be put, after the application of two or three leeches. In this case, the rule must be low diet, with febrifuge medicines, such as Acetate of Ammonia, Tartarized Antimony in Camphor Mixture, and Calomel and James's Powders. Some medical practitioners have recommended the application of Lunar Caustic to the glottis in this disease, but no unprofessional person should attempt this. Others have found the Tincture of artifical Musk serviceable, beginning with 3 or 4 minim doses at the outset, and going up to 10 or 12 minims, in Barley Water, two or three times a day. Diluted Nitric Acid we have frequently administered both to children and adults, with decidedly beneficial results; from 5 to 10 drops in plain or Cinnamon Water, sweetened; it may be given very frequently; a little Ipecacuanha Wine, and Tincture of Henbane or Hemlock, about 5 drops, may be added to each dose. Cochineal and Salts of Tartar is the old popular remedy, and it is, no doubt, sometimes useful, but we would rather not depend on it.

Dr. Golding Bird recommends the following mixture:—Alum, 25 grains; Extract of Henbane, 12 grains, Syrup of Poppies, 2 drachms; Dill Water, sufficient to make 3 ounces: give a dessertspoonful every six hours.—*The Family Doctor.*

1314. Diarrhœa—(Greek *reo*, to flow).

Looseness of the bowels, sometimes called *Flux*. This is a very commom disorder, arising from a variety of *causes*, foremost among which may be mentioned suppressed perspiration, a sudden chill or cold applied to the body, acid fruits, or any indigestible food, oily or putrid substances, deficiency of bile, increased secretion of mucus, worms, strong purgative medicines, gout or rheumatism turned inwards, &c. Hence diarrhœa may be distinguished as *bilious, mucous, lienitery* (where the food passes unchanged), *cœliac* (where it passes oft in a white liquid state, like chyle), and *verminose,* produced by worms.

The *symptoms* are frequent and copious discharges of feculent matter, accompanied usually with griping and flatulency, there is weight and uneasiness in the lower belly which is relieved for a time on the discharge taking place; there is nausea, often vomiting; a pale countenance, sometimes sallow; a bitter taste in the mouth, with thirst and dryness of the throat; the tongue is furred and yellow, indicating bile in the alimentary canal; the skin is dry and harsh, and if the disease is not checked great emaciation ensues.

The *treatment* must depend in some degree on the cause; the removal of the exciting matter, by means of an emetic, or aperient medicines, will, however, be a safe proceeding at first; if the Diarrhœa be caused by obstructed perspiration or exposure to cold, nauseating doses of Antimonial, or Ipecacuanha Wine, may be given every three or four hours, the feet put into a warm bath, and the patient be well covered up in bed. When the case is obstinate, resort may be had to the vapour bath, making a free use of diluents and demulcents. Where there is acidity of the stomach, denoted by griping pains and flatulency, take Chalk Mixture, with Aromatic Confection, and other anti-acid absorbents or alkalies, such as Carbonate of Potash, with Spirits of Ammonia, and Tincture of Opium, or some other anodyne; if from putrid or otherwise unwholesome food, the proper course, after the removal of the offending matter, is to give absorbents, in combination with Opium, or if these fail, acid and an anodyne; the following is an efficacious formula: Diluted Sulphuric Acid, 2 drachms; Tincture of Opium, ½ a drachm; Water, 6 ounces; take a tablespoonful every two hours. When the looseness proceeds from acrid or poisonous substances, warm diluent drinks should be freely administered, to keep up vomiting, previously excited by an emetic; for this purpose thin fat broth answers well; a purge of Castor Oil should also be given, and after its operation, small doses of Morphine, or some other preparation of Opium. When repelled gout or rhumatism is the cause, warm fomentations, cataplasms, blisters to the extremities, and stimulant purges such as Tincture of Rhubarb, to be followed by absorbents with anodynes; if worms are the exciting cause, their removal must be first attempted, but drastic purgatives, often given for the purpose, are dangerous; in this case, Turpentine and Castor Oil, 1 drachm of the first and 6 of the last, may be recommended. The Diarrhœa which often occurs in childhood during the teething, should not be suddenly checked, nor at all, unless it prevails to a hurtful extent; if necessary to stop it, give first a dose of Mercury and Chalk, from 2 to 4 or 6 grains, according to age, and then powder of Prepared Chalk, Cinnamon, and Rhubarb, about 2 grains of each every four hours. Diarrhœa sometimes attacks pregnant women, and, in this case, its progress ought to be arrested as quickly as possible. In all cases of looseness of the bowels it is best to avoid hot thin drinks, unless given for a specific purpose; the food, too, should be simple and easy of digestion; Milk with Cinnamon boiled in it, thickened with Rice or Arrowroot, is good; vegetables, salt meat, suet puddings and pies are not; if there is much exhaustion, a little cool Brandy and Water may be now and then taken. When Dirrhœa is stopped, astringent tonics, with aromatics, should be given to restore the tone of the stomach.

This disease may be distinguished from *Dysentery*, by being unattended by either inflammation, fever, contagion, or that constant inclination to go to stool without a discharge, which is common in the latter disease, in which the matter voided is sanguineous and putrid, while that in Diarrhœa is simply feculent and alimentary.—*The Family Doctor*.

1315. Diphtheria.

In diphtheria the false membrane accompanying inflammation appears almost invariably in the fauces or throat, and in many cases it is limited to this situation. It may extend more or less over the mucus surface within the mouth and nostrils. It is not infrequently produced within the windpipe, giving rise to all the symptoms of true croup, and generally proving fatal. The disease rarely occurs except as an epidemic. Persons between three and twelve years of age are most apt to be affected with it, but no period of life is exempt from a liability to it. Frequent vomiting, diarrhœa, hemorrhage from the nostrils or elsewhere, convulsions, delirium, and coma are symptoms which denote great danger. The chief objects in the treatment are to palliate symptoms and support the powers of life by the judicious employment of tonic remedies conjoined with alimentation and alcoholic stimulants. The latter are in some cases given in large quantity without inducing their excitant effects, and there is reason to believe that they are sometimes the means of saving life. The following treatment has been tried in our own family, and has been most successful:

1316. *The Sulphur Treatment of Diphtheria*.—An eminent physician is said to have worked great wonders in treating diphtheria with sulphur during the recent prevalence of an epidemic. A person who accompanied him says: "He put a teaspoonful of flour of brimstone into a wine-glass of water, and stirred it with his finger instead of a spoon, as sulphur does not readily amalgamate with water. When the sulphur was well mixed he gave it as a gargle, and in ten minutes the patient was out of danger. Instead of spitting out the gargle, he recommended the swallowing of it. In extreme cases in which he had been called just in the nick of time, when the fungus was too nearly closing to allow the gargle, he blew the sulphur through a quill into the throat, and, if the fungus had shrunk to allow of it, then the gargling. He never lost a patient from diphtheria. If a patient cannot gargle, take a live coal, put it on a shovel, and sprinkle a spoonful or two of flour of brimstone at a time upon it: let the sufferer inhale it, holding the head over it, and the fungus will die. If plentifully used, the whole room may be filled almost to suffocation, and the patient can walk about in it, inhaling the fumes, with doors and windows closed."

1317. Typhoid Fever.

This fever is called by German abdominal typhus, and by English and American writers, for the same reason, enteric fever. This characteristic, intestinal affection, is one of the essential points of distinction between typhoid and typhus fever. Typhoid fever is undoubtedly communicable, yet it is rarely communicated to those who are brought into contact with cases of it, namely, physicians, nurses, and fellow patients in hospital wards; and it occurs when it is quite impossible to attribute it to a contagion. It is more apt to prevail in the autumnal months than at other seasons. The early symptoms are chilly sensations, pain in the head, loins, and limbs, lassitude, and looseness of the bowels. During the course of the fever stupor, as in cases of typhus, is more or less marked. In the majority of cases there is a characteristic eruption, usually confined to the trunk, but sometimes extending to the limbs. The duration of the fever is longer than that of typhus, the average, dating from the time of taking to the bed, being about sixteen days in the cases which end in recovery; it is somewhat less in the fatal cases. Milk is pre-eminently the appropriate article of diet, and alcoholic stimulants are sometimes tolerated in very large quantities without any of the excitant or intoxicating effects which they would produce in health. Favourable hygienic conditions are important, such as free ventilation, a proper temperature, and cleanliness.

1318. Fits.

Fainting fits are sometimes dangerous, at other times harmless; should heart disease be the cause, the danger is great.

If from some slight cause, such as sight of blood, fright, excessive heat, &c., there is no cause for alarm. It would be superfluous to enumerate the symptoms. The treatment: First, lay the patient upon his back with his head level with the feet, loosen all garments, dash cold water over the face; sprinkle vinegar and water over the hands and about the mouth, apply smelling salts to the nose, and when the patient has recovered a little, give 20 drops of sal-volatile in water.

1319. Apoplexy.

These fits generally occur in stout, short-necked people. symptoms, sparks before the eyes, giddiness, confusion of ideas, when the patient falls down insensible; the body is paralyzed, the face and head is flushed and hot, the eyes fixed, the breathing loud. Put the patient to bed, immediately raise the head, remove everything from the neck, bleed freely from the arm, if there is no lancet at hand use a penknife, put warm mustard poultices to the soles of the feet and the insides of the thighs, the bowels should be freely opened, take two drops of castor oil and mix with eight grains of calomel, put this as far back on the tongue as possible, the warmth of the throat will cause the oil to melt quickly, and so be absorbed into the stomach. If the blood vessels about the head are much swollen put eight leeches on the temple opposite the paralyzed side. Send for surgeon at once.

1320. Epilepsy.

These fits generally attack young persons. Symptoms: Palpitations, pain in the head, but as a rule, the patient falls down suddenly without warning. The eyes are distorted, foaming at the mouth, the fingers tightly clenched and the body much agitated; when the fit is over, the patient feels drowsy and faint. Keep the patient flat on his back, slightly raise the head, loosen all garments round the neck, dash cold water upon the face, place a piece of wood between the teeth to prevent the patient hurting his tongue. After the fit give the following pills.

1321. Dr. Cullen's Treatment of Epilepsy, or Falling Fits.

Take of ammoniate of copper, twenty grains; bread crumb and mucilage of gum arabic, a sufficient quantity to form it into a mass, which is to be divided into forty pills. In the beginning one of these is to be taken three times a day, and gradually increased to two, or even three pills, thrice a day.

1322. **Hysteria.**

A nervous affection chiefly seen in females, and generally connected with uterine irregularities; it is sometimes called *Clavus* or *Globus Histericus*, and is commonly known as *Hysterics*. As this is a very common affection, amenable to domestic treatment, it is desirable that we should devote some little space to a consideration of it. First let us observe, that the age at which there is the greatest proneness to Hysteria, is from that of puberty to the fiftieth year, that is from the accession to the cessation of menstrual life; at the beginning and end of which it is more frequent and marked than at any other period. Single women, and the married who do not bear children are most subject to it, although it sometimes occurs at the early period of pregnancy and immediately after child-birth. Persons of studious and sedentary habits, and of scrofulous and weakly constitutions, are especially likely to be the subjects of Hysteria; as are indolent and plethoric persons, and those debilitated by disease, or excesses of any kind: it may be excited by excessive evacuations, suppression of the natural secretions, strong mental emotions, or sympathy with others so affected. It is a curious circumstance connected with this affection that it simulates almost every disease to which humanity is liable. A patient suffering under Hysteria may have a rough, hoarse, croupy cough, loss of voice, hiccup, pain in the left side, fluttering of the heart, running at the eyes and nose, spasmodic contractions and convulsive movements of various kinds, vomiting, copious evacuations, delirium, and all kinds of violent and unmanageable symptoms, which subside as soon as the hysterical paroxysm does. All this shows that the whole nervous system is peculiarly influenced by the affection. An attack generally comes on with a sensation of choking; it seems as if a ball were rising in the throat and threatening to stop the passage of the air; then the trunk and limbs become strongly convulsed, so much so that an apparently feeble woman will require three or four strong persons to restrain her from injuring herself; then follows the hysterical sobbing and crying, with alternate fits of laughter; generally the head is thrown back, the face flushed, the eyelids closed and tremulous; the nostrils distended, and the mouth firmly shut; there is a strong movement in the throat, which is projected forward, and a wild throwing about of the arms and hands, with sometimes a tearing of the hair, rending of the clothes, catching at the throat, and attempts to bite those who impose the necessary restraint. After awhile, the deep and irregular breathing, the obvious palpitation of the heart, with the symptoms above enumerated will cease; there will be an expulsion of wind upwards, and the patient will sink down, sobbing and sighing, to remain tranquil for a shorter or longer period, at the end of which she may again start up, and be as violent as ever; or she may go off into a calm sleep, from which she will probably awake quite recovered. A fit of Hysteria may last for a few minutes only, or for several hours, or even days; persons have died under such an infliction: it may generally be distinguished from epilepsy by the absence of foaming at the mouth, which is nearly always present in that disease, and also by the peculiar twinkling of the eyelids, which is a distinguishing symptom of great value, and a sign of safety. In epilepsy, too, there is complete insensibility, not so in Hysteria; the patient retains a partial consciousness; hence it behoves those about her to be cautious what they say; if any remedies are suggested of which she is likely to have a dread, her recovery may be greatly retarded thereby. In epilepsy there is laborious or suspended respiration, dark livid complexion, a protruding and bleeding tongue; rolling or staring and projected eyeballs, and a frightful expression of countenance. Not so in Hysteria; the cheeks are usually red, and the eyes, if not hidden by the closed eyelids, are bright and at rest; the sobbing, sighing, short cries, and laughter, too, are characteristic of the latter affection. We point out these distinctions that no unnecessary alarm may be felt during fit of Hysteria, which is seldom attended with ultimate danger either to mind or body, although the symptoms are sufficiently distressing to cause anxiety.

Treatment.—The first efforts must be directed to prevent the patient, if violent, from injuring herself; but this should not be done in a rude, rough manner. It is, perhaps, best to confine her hands, by wrapping tightly round her a sheet or blanket. The dress should be loosened, especially round the throat, and the face freely exposed to fresh air, and both that and the head well washed with cold water; if she can and will swallow, an ounce of Camphor Mixture, with a teaspoonful of Ether, Sal volatile, Tincture of Assafœtida, or Valerian, may be administered; strong Liquid Ammonia may be applied to the nostrils; and if the fit is of long duration, an Enema injected, consisting of Spirits of Turpentine, Castor Oil, and Tincture of Assafœtida, of each half an ounce, in half a pint of Gruel. What is required is a strong stimulus to the nervous system; therefore, dashing cold water on the face, and hot applications to the spine, are likely to be of service. Sir A. Carlisle recommends that a polished piece of steel, held in boiling water for a minute or two, be passed down the back over a silk handkerchief. This has been found to prevent the recurrence of the paroxysm, which has before been periodic; by which it would seem that the patient has some power of controlling the symptoms, when a sufficiently strong stimulus is applied, to enable or induce her to exercise it.

During the intermission of attacks of Hysteria, attention should be devoted to any constitutional or organic defects, from which they are likely to arise; the patient's mind should be kept as tranquil as possible, and a tendency to all irregular habits or excesses held in check; if plethoric, there should be spare diet, and perhaps leeching; if scrofulous and weakly, good nourishing food and tonic medicines, particularly some form of Iron, the shower bath, regular exercise, cheerful company; antispasmodics, and remedies which have a gently stimulating effect, will frequently relieve the sleeplessness complained of by hysterical patients better than opiates and other narcotics. In such cases Dr. Graves recommends pills composed of a Grain of Musk and two or three Grains of Assafœtida, to be taken two or three times a day. When there is headache, dry-cupping at the back of the neck, or between the shoulders, will probably be of service. A change in the mode of life, involving entering upon new cares and duties, will frequently effect a complete cure of Hysteria, which, it has been observed, seldom attacks women of a vigorous mind. It is extremely desirable that, in the education of young females, the bodily powers should be well exercised and devloped. Too little attention is paid to this generally, and the consequence is that a great many of our young women are weak and nervous, and frequently subject to hysterical affections.

1323. Quinsy.

Though called tonsillites, the inflammation is rarely confined to the tonsils, but involves the pharynx, the soft palate and the uvula and sometimes extends to the root of the tongue. It commences with a feeling of dryness and discomfort about the throat and with pain in swallowing. The mucous membrane lining the throat is reddened and the tonsils are more or less swollen. As the disease advances, the inflamed parts, at first dry, because covered with vicid mucous, and the distress of the patient is greatly enchanced by the effort which he is tempted to make to remove this secretion. In many cases suppuration occurs in one or both tonsils; when this takes places those organs are often enormously swollen, and, together with the obstruction of the inflamed palate, may render breathing difficult and painful. In such cases the febrile reaction is strongly marked, the skin being hot and the pulse full and frequent, the patient is unable to take nourishment and the voice becomes thick and characteristic of the disease. The disease though painful is attended with little danger; but the inflammation may by extension involve the larynx, and thus prove fatal. The disease requires but little treatment. Where the mucous membrane alone is involved, a stringent gargle, repeated five or six times a day, usually gives relief. The food should be liquid—(soups, beef tea, milk, etc.,) and should be swallowed in large mouthfuls, which give less pain than smaller ones. If an abscess forms in either or both tonsils the greatest relief is obtained from frequent inhalations of warm steam, which acts as a poultice to the inflamed parts. As soon as the location of the abscess can be determined, it should be opened, after which there is usually no further trouble.

1324. An Excellent Remedy for a Cold.

Take a large tea-cupful of linseed, two pennyworth of stick-liquorice, and quarter of a pound of sun raisins. Put these into two quarts of soft water, and let it simmer over a slow fire till it is reduced to one; then add to it a quarter of a pound of brown sugar-candy (pounded), a tablespoonful of old rum, and a tablespoonful of the best white-wine vinegar, or lemon-juice. Drink half a pint at going to bed, and take a little when the cough is troublesome. This receipt generally cures the worst of colds in two or three days, and if taken in time, may be said to be almost an infallible remedy. It is a most balsamic cordial for the lungs, without the opening qualities which endanger fresh colds on going out. It has been known to cure colds that have been almost settled into consumption, in less than three weeks. The rum and vinegar are best to be added only to the quantity you are going immediately to take; for, if it is put into the whole it is apt to grow flat.

1325. Cold.

The *symptoms* of a cold are familiar to most persons, for there are few who have not experienced them; as a general rule the *treatment* should be avoidance of exposure to out-of-door atmospheric influences, unless the weather be very fine and mild; warm diluent drinks and diaphoretics at night to promote perspiration, with the use of the foot bath. The saying runs, "feed a cold and starve a fever," but this is not always the safe course; if there is an absence of febrile symptons, which is rarely the case, a warm nourishing diet may be the rule, and medicines may be pretty nearly dispensed with, but if these symptons are present, the system must be reduced by low diet and aperient medicines; two grains of Calomel, with ten grains of Dover's Powder should be given at bed-time, and a Senna draught in the morning, taking, during the day, a mixture like this: Sulphate of Magnesia, two drachms; Sweet Spirits of Nitre, two drachms; Wine of Tartarized Antimony, one drachm; Liquor of Acetate of Ammonia, six ounces; take a tablespoonful every four hours. A high medical authority has recently recommended *a total abstinence from liquids*, he says:— "To those who have the resolution to bear the feelings of thirst for thirty-six or forty-eight hours, we can promise a pretty certain and complete riddance of their colds; and, what is perhaps more important, a prevention of those coughs which commonly succeed them. Nor is the suffering from thirst nearly so great as might be expected." It is Dr. C. J. Williams who writes thus:—"We have never witnessed any evil from this abstinence from liquors for the time prescribed; but it is not unlikely that it may do harm in persons with irritable stomachs; or in those liable to urinary disorders. Moderation in liquid food is one of the best preventives against the bad effects of exposure to cold. When there is a large quantity of liquid in the system there must be increased perspiration, and, therefore, greater risk from the effect of cold." We mention this new light thrown on the subject of treatment for cold, without fully recommending its adoption, having tested the opposite method and found it efficacions; it might do in some cases, but not, we apprehend, in the great majority. For directions for the treatment of cough and other concomitants of cold, see *cough*.

1326. Colds (How to prevent).

The *Popular Science Monthly* gives good advice in regard to the prevention of colds. The mistake is often made of not taking great care to put on extra wraps and coats when preparing for outdoor exercise. This is not at all necessary in robust persons. Sufficient heat to prevent all risk of chill is generated in the body by exercise. The care should be taken to retain sufficient clothing after exercise, and when at rest, to prevent the heat passing out of the body. Indeed, persons very often catch chills from throwing off extra clothing after exercise, or from sitting about in garments the material of which is not adapted to prevent the radiation of heat from the body.

1327. Cough.

A convulsive effort of the lungs to get relief of phlegm or other matter; it may be a sympton of *Bronchitis*, or *Catarrh*, or *Croup*, or *Influenza*, or *Laryngitis*, or *Phthisis*, or *Pleurisy*, or *Pneumonia*, or *Relaxed Uvula*, also *Hooping Cough*.

We can here lay down but a few general principles with regard to the treatment of simple cough without reference to the peculiar disease of which it may be symptomatic; and first let us observe, that it may be either what is properly, as well as medically, termed *dry* or *moist*. In the former case, Opium and its preparations, are advisable, in the latter they should not be used; the irritation will be best allayed by Henbane or Hemlock, either the Tincture or Extract, with demulcents, as Barley Water, Linseed tea, etc., and Liquorice, either the Root boiled, or Extract; it is well also to add from five to ten drops of Ipecacuanha Wine to each dose; inhalation also of the steam from boiling water will generally be found beneficial—and especially if some medicinal herb, such as Horehound or Coltsfoot, be infused in it. In moist coughs there should not be so much fluid taken, and the use of demulcents must be somewhat restricted. Opiates may be administered, but not too freely, either separately, or in cough mixtures; Paregoric Elixir, in which the Opium is combined with Benzoic Acid and Oil of Aniseed (expectorants), and Camphor (antispasmodic), is perhaps the best form of administration; a teaspoonful in a glass of water, generally allays the irritation, and frequent desire to cough which arises from it. In cases where there is difficulty of expectoration, some such mixture as this should be taken:— Compound Tincture of Camphor, four drachms; Ipecacuanha Wine, and Oxymel of Squills, of each two drachms; Mucilage of Acacia, one ounce; Water, four ounces, mix and take a tablespoonful when the cough is troublesome; for old people, two drachms of Tincture of Benzoin, commonly called Friar's Balsam, may be added to the above; and if there should be much fever, two drachms of Sweet Spirits of Nitre. For all kinds of cough counter irritants should be applied, such as blisters and warm plasters, rubbing in of stimulant ointments on the chest and between the shoulders: those parts also should be well protected by flannels next the skin, dressed hare skin and other contrivances of the kind. For coughs which are more particularly troublesome by night, it is best to give the Opium, Hebane, or Hemlock, as the case may be, at bedtime, in the shape of a pill; of the Extracts of either of the latter, five grains may be given; of the first, one or two grains of the Gum, or a quarter of a grain of Morphine. A long experience of their efficacy among a large number of dispensary patients enables the author to recommend with confidence the following pills; take of Compound Squill Pill, one drachm; Ipecacuanha Powder and Extract of Hyoscyamus, of each, half a drachm; mix and make into twenty-four pills, take one or two on going to rest.

Very frequently febrile symptoms accompany coughs, and then a full diet is not advisable, and stimulants must be avoided. Great relief is often afforded by the use of the warm foot bath, and warm gruel, with a ten grain Dover's Powder after the patient is in bed; then plenty of covering to encourage perspiration. Coughs should never be neglected, they are so frequently symptomatic of organic disease; if they do not yield to simple remedies, let medical advice be sought, whether the patient be old or young. See *Colds*.

1328. Headache.

Headache may arise from a variety of causes; consequently the preventive measures vary according to the nature of the attack. When it is of that kind which is dependent on rheumatism, and which affects the muscles, extending often from the forehead to the back, and sometimes involving the temples, the patient should be as much as possible in the open air, and should use the shower-bath every morning. When the form of headache is accompanied with tenderness of the scalp, and acute pain on pressure, indicating an affection of the immediate covering of the bones,—besides exercise in the open air, the head should be shaved, and washed twice a day, namely, morning and evening, with cold water, and afterwards gently rubbed with a towel for ten or fifteen minutes. The residence should be in a dry, somewhat elevated situation; and quietude of mind should be maintained. When the pain in the forehead and the back of the head is obtuse, and accompanied with a sensation of torpor and oppression; and when this occurs in weak and irritable persons, besides the necessary medical treatment, which ought not to be neglected, all mental applications should be suspended, and cheerful society cultivated; the diet should be moderate, and the utmost attention paid to the state of the bowels. Exercise and shower-baths are as essential in this as in the other varieties of the headache. Lastly, in what is usually termed *sick* headache, denoted by either acute or dull pain over the left temple, with some tenderness of the part, throbbing, and an incapacity at the time for any mental exertion, the whole arising generally from indigestion, or some error in diet previous to the occurrence of the headache, it is scarcely necessary to say that prudence in diet, both with respect to quantity and quality, should be observed. Long fasting, excess of wine or any stimulant, protracted sedentary occupations, hurry of business and anxiety, should be known to be exciting causes, and, consequently, as far as possible, avoided by those predisposed to sick headaches; in a few words, the duty of the head and the feet should be equally balanced. Proper diet and exercise, cheerfulness of mind, and agreeable sociable intercourse, will do more to regulate the stomach and bowels, in those predisposed to this form of headache, than any plan of medical treatment which can be suggested.

1329. **Cephalic Snuff.**

Lundyfoot snuff and as-abaracca leaves, of each two ounces; lavender flowers, two drachms; essence of bergamot and oil of cloves, of each four drops. Grind the lavender with the snuff and leaves to a fine powder; then add the perfume. Much recommended in headaches, dimness of sight, &c.

1330. **Bilious or Sick Headache.**

Headache is, in general, a symptom of indigestion, or deranged general health, or in consequence of a confined state of the bowels. The following alterative pill will be found a valuable medicine:—Take of calomel, ten grains; emetic tartar, two, three, or four grains; precipitated sulphuret of antimony, one scruple; guaiacum in powder, one drachm. Rub them well together in a mortar for ten minutes, then, with a little conserve of hips, make them into a mass, and divide it into twenty pills. *Dose.*—One pill is given every night, or every other night, for several weeks in succession.

1331. **Hiccough.**

This may usually be removed by the exhibition of warm carminatives, cordials, cold water, weak spirits, camphor julep, or spirits of sal volatile. A sudden fright or surprise will often produce the like effect. An instance is recorded of a delicate young lady that was troubled with hiccough for some months, and who was reduced to a state of extreme debility from the loss of sleep occasioned thereby, who was cured by a fright, after medicines and topical applications had failed. A pinch of snuff, a glass of *cold* soda-water, or an ice-cream will also frequently remove this complaint.

1332. Cramp.

When cramp occurs in the limbs, warm friction with the naked hand, or with the following stimulating liniment, will generally be found to succeed in removing it:

The Liniment.—Take of water of ammonia, or of spirit of hartshorn, one ounce; olive oil, two ounces. Shake them together till they unite.

When the stomach is affected, brandy, ether, laudanum, or tincture of ginger affords the speediest means of cure. The following draught may be taken with great advantage:— Laudanum, forty or fifty drops; tincture of ginger, two drachms; syrup of poppies, one drachm; cinnamon or mint water, one ounce. Mix for a draught. To be repeated in an hour, if necessary.

In severe cases, hot flannels, moistened with compound camphor liniment and turpentine, or a bladder nearly filled with hot water, at 100 deg. or 120 deg. Fahr., should be applied to the pit of the stomach; bathing the feet in warm water, or applying a mustard poultice to them, is frequently of great advantage.

*** The best preventives, when the cause of cramp is constitutional, are warm tonics, such as the essence of ginger and camomile, Jamaica ginger in powder, &c., avoiding fermented liquors and green vegetables, especially for supper, and wearing flannel next to the skin.

1333. Neuralgia (Greek *neuron*, a nerve, and *algos*, pain).

A painful affection of the nerves: when it occurs in those of the face, it is termed *face-ague*, or *tic-doloreux*; when it affects the great nerve of the leg, it is called *sciatica*; other parts, such as the fingers, the chest, the abdomen, &c., are also liable to this agonizing pain, one of the most severe and wearing to which the human frame is liable; the exact nature of it is not very clear, that is to say, the origin of the disease, for although its immediate seat is a nerve, or set of nerves, yet there must be some originating cause. It can frequently be traced to some decay, or diseased growth of the bone about those parts through which the nerves pass; and in some severe cases it has been found to depend upon the irritation caused by foreign bodies acting upon those highly sensitive organs. The only *symptom* of Neuralgia generally, is a violent plunging and darting pain, which comes on in paroxysms; except in very severe and protracted cases, there is no outward redness nor swelling to mark the seat of the pain, neither is there usually constitutional derangement, other than that which may be caused by want of rest, and the extreme agony of the suffering while it lasts, which may be from one to two or three hours, or even more, but it is not commonly so long. Tenderness and swelling of the part sometimes occurs, where there has been a frequent recurrence and long continuance of the pain, which leaves the patient, in most cases, as suddenly as it comes on; its periodic returns and remissions, and absence of inflammatory symptoms, are distinctive marks of the disease. Among its exciting *causes*, we may mention exposure to damp and cold, especially if combined with malaria; and to these influences a person with a debilitated constitution will be more subject than another. Anxiety of mind will sometimes bring it on, and so will a disordered state of the stomach, more particularly a state in which there is too much acid.

As for *treatment*, that, of course, must depend upon the cause; if it is a decayed tooth, which, by its exposure of the nerve to the action of the atmosphere, sets up this pain, it should be at once removed, as there will be little peace for the patient until there is; if co-existent with Neuralgia there is a disordered stomach, suspicion should at once point thereto, and efforts should be made to correct the disorder there. If the patient is living in a moist, low situation, he should at once be removed to a higher level, and a dry, gravelly soil. Tonics, such as Quinine and Iron, should be given, and a tolerably generous diet, but without excess of any kind. In facial Neuralgia, blisters behind the ears, or at the back of the neck, have been found serviceable, and, if the course of the nerve which appears to be the seat of mischief can be traced, a Belladonna plaster or a piece of rag soaked in Laudanum and laid along it, will sometimes give relief; so will hot fomentations of poppies and camomiles, or bran poultices sprinkled with turpentine. In very severe cases $\frac{1}{4}$ of a grain of Morphine may be given to deaden the nervous sensibility, and induce sleep, which the patient is often deprived of at night, the pain coming on as soon as he gets warm in bed. Sir Charles Bell's remedy for obstinate cases was 1 or 2 drops of Croton Oil, mixed with one drachm of Colocynth Pill, divided into twelve. Weakly persons, however, must not venture upon taking this powerful remedy.

An application of Chloroform on lint has sometimes proved very effectual in relieving severe Neuralgic pains, and so has an ointment composed of Lard and Veratrine, in the proportion of six grains to the ounce.

A mixture of Chloroform and Aconite has been recommended for facial Neuralgia, the form of preparation being two parts of Spirits of Wine, or Eau de Cologne, one of Chloroform, and one of Tincture of Aconite, to be applied to the gums of the side affected, by means of a finger covered with a piece of lint, or soft linen, and rubbed along them ; the danger of dropping any into the mouth being thus avoided. When the pain is connected with some organic disease, as a decayed tooth, or chronic inflammation of the gums, or of the sockets or superficial necrosis of the bone, substitute Tincture of Iodine for the Spirit in the above formula. We would caution our readers strongly against the careless inhalation of Chloroform as a remedy for Neuralgia, which appears to be growing into a general practice ; several deaths have resulted from it, the practice being to pour a little on a pocket handkerchief, without much regard to quantity, and hold it to the mouth until the required insensibility is produced. This remedy should never be administered, except under the supervision of a medical adviser. People at all liable to this painful affection should be extremely careful not to expose themselves to wet or cold: above all to avoid draughts. A very slight cause will often bring it on where there is the slightest tendency to it.

1334. Croup.

On the first appearance of croup, a teaspoonful of the following mixture :—Ipecacuanha wine, half an ounce ; tartaric emetic, one grain ; distilled water, half an ounce. Mix. Should be immediately given, and repeated every ten minutes, until it excites vomiting. After its operation the child should be put in a warm bath, for ten to fifteen minutes, and a dose of calomel and James's powder given. If relief be not obtained from these measures, the entire throat should be covered with leeches, say eight or ten, and the bowels emptied by the following injection :—Take of common turpentine two drachms, beat it up with the yolk of an egg, and add by degrees half a pint of decoction of chamomile flowers, in which an ounce of glaubar salts has been dissolved ; strain it, and divide it into two equal parts, one of which is to be administered night and morning. If the alarming symptoms are not checked in twelve hours, the warm bath is to be repeated, and calomel, in doses of from three to five grains, with three grains of James's powder in each, should be given every third hour.

If a child recover from the attack of croup, every affection of the chest or lungs should be considered as important ; it should, therefore, be carefully guarded against cold, especially in damp weather, for which purpose the child should wear a chamois leather waistcoat next the skin, made to cover the neck and great attention be paid to the stomach and bowels. *A child having been once attacked with croup is very liable to its return from any slight exposure to cold.*

1335. Treatment of Bunions.

This consists in removing all pressure from the part. The formation of a bunion may in the beginning be prevented, *but only in the beginning* ; for when actually formed, it is scarcely possible ever to get rid of it, and it remains an everlasting plague. To prevent the formation of a bunion, it is necessary whenever or wherever a boot or shoe pinches, to have it eased at once, and so long as that part of the foot pinched remains tender, not to put on the offending shoe again. When a bunion has once completely formed, if the person wish to have any peace, and not to have it increase, he must have a last made to fit his foot, and have his shoe made upon it. And whenever the bunion inflames, and is painful, it must be bathed with warm water and poulticed at night.

1336. Stye.

The stye is strictly only a little boil which projects from the edge of the eyelid. It is of a dark red color, much inflamed, and occasionally a great deal more painful than might be expected, considering its small size. It usually disappears of itself, after a little time, especially if some purgative medicine be taken.

If the stye be very painful and inflamed, a small warm poultice of linseed meal, or bread and milk, must be laid over it, and renewed every five or six hours, and the bowels freely acted upon by a purgative draught, such as the following :— Take of Epsom salts, half an ounce ; best manna, two drachms ; infusion of senna, six drachms ; tincture of senna, two drachms ; spearmint water, one ounce; distilled water, two ounces. Mix ; and take three, four, or five tablespoonfuls.

When the stye appears ripe, an opening should be made into it with the point of a large needle, and afterwards a little of the following ointment may be smeared over it once or twice a day. *Ointment.*—Take of spermaceti, six drachms ; white wax, two drachms : olive oil, three ounces. Melt them together over a slow fire, and stir them constantly until they are cold.

1337. For Inflamed or Weak Eyes (1).

Half fill a bottle with common rock salt; add the best of French brandy till all but full. Shake it, let it settle, and bathe the outside of the eye with a soft linen cloth on going to bed and occasionally through the day. This will be found a good application for pains and bruises generally.

1338. Another way (2).

Mix a few bread crumbs with the white of an egg, put it in a bag of white muslin, and apply it to the eye. It is best applied at night or when lying down. After removing the poultice bathe the eye with warm water, using a piece of soft rag, not a sponge.

1339. Deficiency of Wax in the Ear.

Deafness is sometimes the consequence of a morbidly dry state of the inner passages of the ear. In such cases, introduce a piece of cotton wool, dipped in an equal mixture of oil of turpentine and oil of almonds, or in the liniment of carbonate of ammonia.

1340. Accumulation of Wax in the Ear.

To remedy this, which is a very frequent cause of deafness, introduce a small piece of cotton wool, upon which a little oil of almonds has been dropped, into the ear, and let it remain there for a day or two. Then syringe the ear with a little warm milk and water, or a solution of soap or with a solution of common salt and water, in the proportion of two drachms of the former to half an ounce of the latter. The solution of salt is the best solvent of accumulated wax in the ear.

1341. To remove Nervous Anxiety.

Keep the bowels regular with mild purgatives, take plenty of exercise in the open air, adopt a light nutritious diet, and seek pleasant society. A teaspoonful of carbonate of soda, or of magnesia, or a few drops of laudanum taken the last thing at night, will generally have the effect of preventing watchfulness.

1342. Hysterics.

Assafœtida, one drachm; peppermint water, one ounce and a half; ammoniated tincture of valerian, two drachms; sulphuric ether, two drachms. Mix. A dose of this mixture is a tablespoonful every second hour.

1343. To Produce Perspiration.

Twelve drachms of antimonial wine and two drachms of laudanum. Of this mixture eighteen drops may be taken in water every five or six hours.

1344. Lotion to remove Freckles.

Mix two ounces of rectified spirits of wine, add two teaspoonfuls of muriatic acid, with one pound and a half of distilled water.

1345. Ointment for Chilblains.

Calomel and camphor, of each two drachms; spermaceti ointment, eight drachms; oil of turpentine, four drachms. Mix well together. Apply, by gentle friction, two or three times daily.

1346. To raise a Blister Speedily.

A piece of lint dropped into vinegar of cantharides, and immediately after its application to the skin covered over with a piece of strapping to prevent evaporation.

1347. Dyspepsia, Heartburn, and Acidity.

Pure water, five ounces; carbonate of ammonia, 2 drachms; syrup of orange peel, one ounce. Mix. For a six-ounce mixture.

1348. Warming Plaster.

Burgundy pitch, seven parts, melt and add plaster of cantharides, one part. Some add a little camphor. Used in chest complaints, local pains, etc.

1349. Rules for the Preservation of Health.

Adopt the plan of rising early, and never sit up late at night.

Wash the whole body every morning with cold water, by means of a large sponge, and rub it dry with a rough towel, or scrub the whole body for ten or fifteen minutes with flesh-brushes.

Drink waters generally, and avoid excess of spirits, wine, and fermented liquors.

Sleep in a room which has free access to the open air, and is well ventilated.

Keep the head cool by washing it with cold water when necessary, and abate feverish and inflammatory symptoms when they arise, by persevering stillness.

Symptoms of plethora and indigestion may be corrected by eating and drinking less per diem for a short time.

Never eat a hearty supper, especially of animal food; and drink wine, spirits, and beer only after dinner.

Exercise regularly adopted conduces to preserve the health and should always be taken by those who value so inestimable a blessing.

WHAT TO NAME THE BABY.

Our dear Baby, what shall we call it? Consult the following list, and select the prettiest name you can find. This dictionary has been prepared at great expense and trouble, and is made as complete as possible; but no surnames, that are sometimes used as Christian names, such as Sydney, &c., are included.

AARON,	*Hebrew*,	Inspired	ALFRED,	*Old Ger.*	Good
ABDIEL,	*Hebrew*,	The servant of God	ALGERNON,	*French*,	counselor Withwhiskers
ABEL,	*Hebrew*,	Vanity	ALLAN,	} *Slavonic*,	Harmony
ABIATHAR,	*Hebrew*,	Father of plenty	ALLEN, ALMON,	*Hebrew*,	Hidden
ABIEL,	*Hebrew*,	Father of strength	ALONZO, ALPHEUS,	*Old Ger. Hebrew*,	Willing Exchange
ABIEZER,	*Hebrew*,	Father of help	ALPHONSO,	*Old Ger.*	All ready
ABIJAH,	*Hebrew*,	To whom Jehovah is a father	ALVAH, ALVAN, ALVIN,	} *Hebrew*, } *Old Ger.*	Iniquity Beloved by all
ABNER,	*Hebrew*,	Father of light	ALWIN,		
ABRAHAM,	*Hebrew*,	Father of a multitude	AMARIAH,	*Hebrew*,	Whom Jehovah promised
ABRAM,	*Hebrew*,	Father of elevation	AMASA AMBROSE,	*Hebrew*, *Greek*,	A burden Divine
ABSALOM,	*Hebrew*,	Father of peace	AMMI,	*Hebrew*,	My people
ADAM,	*Hebrew*,	Red-earth	AMOS,	*Hebrew*,	Courageous
ADIEL,	*Hebrew*,	The ornament of God	ANDREW, ANDRONICUS,	*Greek*, *Greek*,	Manly A conqueror of men
ADIN,	*Hebrew*,	Delicate			
ADOLPH, ADOLPHUS,	*Old Ger.* *Latin*,	} Noble } hero	ANSELM, ANSEL,	} *Old Ger.*	Protection of God
ADONIRAM,	*Hebrew*,	Lord of height	ANTHONY,	} *Latin*,	Praiseworthy
ALAN,	*Slavonic*,	Harmony	ANTONY,		
ALARIC,	*Old Ger.*	Noble ruler	APOLLOS,	*Greek*,	Of Apollo
ALBERT,	*Old Ger.*	Illustrious	ARCHELAUS,	*Greek*,	Ruler of the People
ALBION,	*Celt*,	Mountainous land	ARCHIBALD,	*German*,	Holy prince
ALEXANDER,	*Ger.*	A defender of men	ARIEL,	*Hebrew*,	Valiant for God

ARISTARCHUS, *Greek*, A good prince
ARNOLD, *Old Ger.* Strong as an eagle
ARTEMAS, *Greek*, Gift of Artemis
ARTHUR, *Celt*, Noble,
ASA, *Hebrew*, Physician
ASAHEL, *Hebrew*, Made of God
ASAPH, *Hebrew*, A collector
ASARELAH, *Hebrew*, Upright to God
ASHBEL, *Hebrew*, Fire of Bel
ASHER, *Hebrew*, Happy
ASHUR, *Hebrew*, Blackness
ATHANASIUS, *Greek*, Immortal
ATHELSTAN, *Ang-Sax.* Noble stone
AUBREY, *Old Ger.* Ruler of spirits
AUGUSTIN,
AUGUSTINE, } *Latin*, Belonging to Augustus
AUSTIN,
AUGUSTUS, *Latin*, Exalted
AURELIUS, *Latin*, Golden
AZARIAH, *Hebrew*, Helped of the Lord

BALDWIN, *Old Ger.* Bold
BAPTIST, *Greek*, Purifier
BARACHIAS, *Heb.* Whom Jehovah has blessed
BARDOLPH, } *Old Ger.* A dis-
BARDULPH, } tinguished helper
BARNABAS, } *French*, Son of cor-
BARNABY, } ruption
BARTHOLOMEW, *Heb.* A warlike son
BARZILLAI, *Hebrew*, True
BASIL, *Greek*, Royal
BENEDICT, *Latin*, Blessed
BENJAMIN, *Hebrew*, Son of the right hand
BENONI, *Hebrew*, Son of grief or trouble
BERIAH, *Hebrew*, In calamity
BERNARD, } *Old Ger.* Bold as a
BARNARD, } bear
BERTRAM, *Old Ger* Bright raven
BETHUEL, *Hebrew*, Man of God
BEZALEEL, *Hebrew*, In the shadow of God
BONIFACE, *Latin*, A benefactor

BRIAN, *Celt*, Strong
BRUNO, *Old Ger.* Brown
CADWALLADER, *British*, Battle arranger
CÆSAR, *Latin*, Blue-eyed
CALEB, *Hebrew*, A dog
CALVIN, *Latin*, Bald
CECIL, *Latin*, Dim-sighted
CEPHAS, *Aram*, A stone
CHARLES, *Old Ger.* Manly
CHRISTIAN, *Latin*, Belonging to Christ
CHRISTOPHER, *Greek*, Bearing Christ
CLARENCE, *Latin*, Illustrious
CLAUDIUS, } *Latin*, Lame
CLAUDE, }
CLEMENT, *Latin*, Merciful
CONRAD, *Old Ger.* Resolute
CONSTANT, *Latin*, Faithful
CONSTANTINE, *Latin*, Resolute
CORNELIUS, *Latin* (Uncertain)
CRISPUS,
CRISPIN, } *Latin*, Having curly hair
CRISPIAN,
CUTHBERT, *Ang-Sax.* Noted splendor
CYPRIAN, *Greek*, Of Cyprus
CYRIL, *Greek*, Lordly
CYRUS, *Persian*, The Sun

DAN, *Hebrew*, A judge
DANIEL, *Hebrew*, A divine judge
DARIUS, *Persian*, Preserver
DAVID, *Hebrew*, Beloved
DEMETRIUS, *Greek*, Belonging to Ceres
DENIS, } *Greek*, The god of
DENNIS, } wine
DERRICK, *Old Ger.* See Theodoric
DEXTER, *Latin*, Fortunate
DIONYSIUS, *Greek*, The God of wine
DONALD, *Celt*, Proud chief
DUNCAN, *Celt*, Brown chief

EBEN, *Hebrew*, A stone
EBENEZER, *Hebrew*, The stone of help

WHAT TO NAME THE BABY.

EDGAR,	Ang-Sax.	A protector of property
EDMUND,	Ang-Sax.	Defender of property
EDWARD,	Ang-Sax.	Guardian of property
EDWIN,	Ang-Sax.	Gainer of property
EGBERT,	Old Ger.	Famous with the sword
ELBERT,	Old Ger.	Illustrious
ELDRED,	Ang-Sax.	terrible
ELEAZER,	Hebrew,	To whom God is a help
ELI,	Hebrew,	A foster son
ELIAB	Hebrew,	God is his father
ELIAKIM,	Hebrew,	Whom God sets up
ELIAS,	Hebrew,	Jehovah is my God
ELIHU,	Hebrew,	God the Lord
ELIJAH,	Hebrew,	Jehovah is my God
ELIPHALET,	Hebrew,	God of Salvation
ELISHA,	Hebrew,	God of my Salvation
ELIZUR,	Hebrew,	God is my rock
ELLIS,	Hebrew,	A variation of Elisha
ELMER,	Ang-Sax.	Noble
ELNATHAN,	Hebrew,	God gave
EMMANUEL,	Hebrew,	God with us
EMERY, EMMERY, EMORY,	} Ang-Sax.	Rich
ENEAS,	Greek,	Praised
ENOCH,	Hebrew,	Dedicated
ENOS,	Hebrew,	Man
EPHRAIM,	Hebrew,	Very fruitful
ERASMUS,	Greek,	Amiable
ERASTUS,	Greek,	Lovely
ERIC,	Ang-Sax.	Rich
ERNEST, ERNESTUS,	} German,	Earnest
ESAU,	Hebrew,	Covered with hair
ETHAN,	Hebrew,	Firmness
EUGENE,	Greek,	Noble
EUSEBIUS,	Greek,	Pious
EUSTACE,	Greek,	Healthy
EVAN,	British,	The gracious gift of God
EVERARD,	Old Ger.	Strong as a wild boar
EZEKIEL,	Hebrew,	Strength of God
EZRA,	Hebrew,	Help
FELIX,	Latin,	Happy
FERDINAND,	Old Ger.	Brave
FERNANDO,	Old Ger.	Valiant
FESTUS,	Latin,	Joyful
FRANCIS, FRANK, FRANKLIN,	} French,	Free
FREDERIC, FREDERICK,	} Old Ger.	Peaceful ruler
GABRIEL,	Hebrew,	Man of God
GAIUS,	Latin,	Rejoiced
GAMALIEL,	Hebrew,	Recompense of God
GARRET,	Old Ger.	Strong with the spear
GERMAN, GERMAINE,	} Latin,	German
GEOFFREY,	Old Ger.	At peace with God
GEORGE,	Greek,	A landholder
GERALD, GERARD,	} Old Ger.	Strong with the spear
GERSHOM,	Hebrew,	An exile
GIDEON,	Hebrew,	A destroyer
GILBERT,	Old Ger.	Famous
GILES,	Greek,	A kid
GIVEN,	English,	Gift of God
GODDARD,	Old Ger.	Virtuous
GODFREY,	Old Ger.	At peace with God
GODWIN,	Ang-Sax.	Good in war
GREGORY,	German,	Watchful
GRIFFITH,	British,	Having great faith
GUSTAVUS,	Swedish,	A warrior
GUY,	French,	A leader

HANNIBAL, *Punic*, Grace of Baal
HAROLD, *Ang-Sax.* A champion
HEMAN, *Hebrew*, Faithful
HENRY, *Old Ger.* The head or chief of a house
HERBERT, *Ang-Sax.* Glory of the army
HERCULES, *Greek*, Lordly fame
HERMAN, *Old Ger.* A warrior
HEZEKIAH, *Hebrew*, Strength of the Lord
HILARY, *Latin*, Merry
HILLEL, *Hebrew*, Praise
HIRAM, *Hebrew*, Most noble
HOMER, *Greek*, Security
HORACE, } *Greek*, (uncertain)
HORATIO,
HOSEA, *Hebrew*, Salvation
HOWELL, *British*, Whole
HERBERT, *Old Ger.* Bright in spirit
HUGH, } *Dutch*, Spirit
HUGO,
HUMPHREY, *Ang. Sax.* Protector of the home
ICHABOD, *Hebrew*, The glory has departed
IGNATIUS, *Greek*, Ardent
IMMANUEL, *Hebrew*, God with us
INCREASE, *English*, Increase of faith
INGRAM, *Teutonic*, Raven,
INIGO, *Greek*, Ardent
IRA, *Hebrew*, Watchful
ISAAC, *Hebrew*, Laughter
ISAIAH, *Hebrew*, Salvation of the Lord
ISRAEL, *Hebrew*, A soldier of God
ITHIEL, *Hebrew*, God is with me
IVAN, *British*, The gracious gift of God
IVORY, *English*, The gracious gift of God
JABEZ, *Hebrew*, He will cause pain
JACOB, *Hebrew*, A supplanter
JAIRUS, *Hebrew*, He will enlighten
JAMES, *Hebrew*, A supplanter
JAPHETH, *Hebrew*, Enlargement
JARED, *Hebrew*, Descent
JASON, *Greek*, A healer
JASPER, *Persian*, (uncertain)
JAVAN, *Hebrew*, Clay
JEDEDIAH, *Hebrew*, Beloved of the Lord
JEFFREY, *Old Ger.* At peace with God
JEREMIAH, }
JEREMIAS, } *Hebrew*, Exalted of the Lord
JEREMY,
JEROME, *Greek*, Holy name
JESSE, *Hebrew*, Wealth
JOAB, *Hebrew*, Jehovah is his father
JOB, *Hebrew*, Afflicted
JOEL, *Hebrew*, The Lord is God
JOHN, *Hebrew*, The gracious gift of God
JONAH, } *Hebrew*, A dove
JONAS,
JONATHAN, *Hebrew*, Gift of Jehovah
JOSEPH, *Hebrew*, He shall add
JOSHUA, *Hebrew*, God of salvation
JOSIAH, } *Hebrew*, Given of the Lord
JOSIAS,
JOTHAM, *Hebrew*, The Lord is upright
JUDAH, *Hebrew*, Praised
JULIAN, *Latin*, Sprung from
JULIUS, *Greek*, Soft-haired
JUSTIN, *Latin*, Just
JUSTUS, *Latin*, Just
KENELM, *Ang.-Sax.* A defendor of his kindred
KENNETH, *Gaelic*, Commander
LABAN, *Hebrew*, White
LAMBERT, *Old Ger.* Illustrious with landed possessions

LANCELOT, *Italian*, A little angel
LAURENCE, } *Latin*, Crowned
LAWRENCE, } with laurel
LAZARUS, *Hebrew*, God will help
LEANDER, *Greek*, Lion-man
LEBBEUS, *Hebrew*, Praise
LEMUEL, *Hebrew*, Created by God
LEONARD, *German*, Strong as a lion
LEONIDAS, *Greek*, Lion like
LEOPOLD, *Old Ger.* Bold for the people
LEVI, *Hebrew*, Adhesion
LEWIS, *Old Ger.* Bold warrior
LINUS, *Greek*, Flaxen-haired
LIONEL, *Latin*, Young lion
LLEWELLYN, *Celt*, Lightning
LOAMMI, *Hebrew*, Not my people
LODOWICK, *Old Ger.* Bold warrior
LORENZO, *Latin*, Crowned with laurel
LOT, *Hebrew*, A veil
LOUIS, *Old Ger.* Bold warrior
LUBIN, *Ang-Sax.* Beloved friend
LUCIAN, *Latin*, Belonging to Lucius
LUCIUS, *Latin*, Born at break of day
LUDOVIC, *Old Ger.* Bold warrior
LUKE, *Latin*,
LUTHER, *German*, Illustrious warrior
LYCURGUS, *Greek*, Wolf-driver
MADOC, *Welsh*, Good
MALACHI, *Hebrew*, Messenger of the Lord
MANASSEH, *Hebrew*, Forgetfulness
MARCELLUS, *Latin*,
MARCIUS, }
MARCUS, } *Latin*, **A hammer**
MARK, }
MARMADUKE, *Ang-Sax.* A mighty noble
MARTIN, *Latin*, Warlike
MATTHEW, *Hebrew*, Gift of Jehovah

MATTHIAS, *Hebrew*, Gift of the Lord
MAURICE, *Latin*, Moorish
MAXIMILIAN, *Latin*, The greatest .Emilianus
MEREDITH, *Celt*, Sea protector
MICAH, *Hebrew*, Who is like the Lord
MICHAEL, *Hebrew*, Who is like God
MILES, *Latin*, A soldier
MORGAN, *British*, A seaman
MOSES, *Egyptian*, Drawn out of the water
NAAMAN, *Hebrew*, Pleasantness
NAHUM, *Hebrew*, Consolation
NAPOLEON, *Greek*, Lion of the forest dell
NATHAN, *Hebrew*, Given
NATHANAEL, } *Heb.* The gift of
NATHANIEL, } God
NEAL, }
NEIL, } *Latin*, Dark
NEHEMIAH, *Heb.* Comfort of the Lord
NICHOLAS, } *Greek*, Victory of the
NICOLAS, } people
NOAH, *Hebrew*, Comfort
NOEL, *Latin*, Born on Christmas day
NORMAN, *German*, A native of Normandy
OBADIAH, *Hebrew*, Servant of the Lord
OBED, *Hebrew*, Serving God
OCTAVIUS, } *Latin*, The eighth
OCTAVUS, } born
OLIVER, *Latin*, An olive-tree
ORESTES, *Greek*, A mountaineer
ORLANDO, *Teutonic*, Fame of the land
OSCAR, *Celt*, Bounding warrior
OSMOND, } *Old Ger.* Protection of
OSMUND, } God
OSWALD, } *Old Ger.* Power of God
OSWOLD, }
OWEN, *Celt*, Lamb

Name	Origin	Meaning
OZIAS,	Hebrew,	Strength of the Lord
PATRICK,	Latin,	Noble
PAUL, PAULUS, PAULINUS,	Latin,	Little
PELEG,	Hebrew,	Division
PEREGRINE,	Latin,	A stranger
PETER,	Greek,	A rock
PHILANDER,	Greek,	A lover of men
PHILEMON,	Greek,	loving
PHILIP,	Greek,	A lover of horses
PHINEAS, PHINEHAS,	Hebrew,	Mouth of brass
PIUS,	Latin,	Dutiful
PLINY,	Latin,	(uncertain)
PRESERVED,	English,	Redeemed
PTOLEMY,	Greek,	Mighty in war
QUINTIN,	Latin,	The fifth
RALPH,	Old Ger.	Famous wolf
RANDAL,	An.-Sax	House wolf
RAPHAEL,	Hebrew,	The healing of God
RAYMOND, RAYMUND	Old Ger.	Wise protection.
REGINALD,	Old Ger.	Strong ruler
REUBEN,	Hebrew,	Behold, a son
REUEL,	Hebrew,	A friend of God
REYNOLD,	Old Ger.	Strong Ruler
RICHARD,	Old Ger.	Rich hearted
ROBERT,	Old Ger.	Bright in fame
RODERIC, RODERICK,	Old Ger.	Rich in fame
RODOLPH, RODOLPHUS	Old Ger.	Fam. wolf
ROGER,	Old Ger.	Famous with the spear.
ROLAND,	Old Ger.	Fame of the land
ROWLAND,	Old Ger.	Fame of the land
RUDOLPH, RUDOLPHUS	Old Ger.	Hero
RUFUS,	Latin,	Red
RUPERT,	Old Ger.	Bright in fame
SALMON,	Hebrew,	Shady
SAMSON, SAMPSON,	Hebrew,	Splendid sun
SAMUEL,	Hebrew,	Heard of God
SAUL,	Hebrew,	Asked for
SEBA,	Hebrew,	Eminent
SEBASTIAN,	Greek,	Reverend
SERONO, SERENUS,	Greek,	Peaceful
SETH,	Hebrew,	Appointed
SHADRACH,	Hebrew,	Rejoicing in the way
SIGISMUND	Old Ger	Conquering protection
SILAS, SILVANUS,	Latin,	Living in a wood
SYLVESTER, SILVESTER,	Latin,	Bred in the country
SIMEON, SIMON,	Hebrew	Hearing with acceptance
SOLOMON,	Hebrew,	Peaceable
STEPHEN,	Greek,	A crown
SWITHIN,	An.-Sax	Strong friend
SYLVAN, SYLVANUS,	Latin,	Living in a wood
THADDEUS,	Syriac,	The wise
THEOBALD,	Old Ger.	Bold for the people
THEODORE,	Greek,	The gift of God
THEODORIC	An.-Sax.	Powerful among the people
THEOPHILUS	Greek,	A lover of God
THERON,	Greek,	A hunter
THOMAS,	Hebrew,	A twin
TIMOTHY,	Greek,	Fearing God
TITUS,	Greek,	(Uncertain)
TOBIAH, TOBIAS,	Hebrew,	Distinguished of the Lord
TRISTAM, TRISTRAM	Latin,	Grave
TYBALT,	Old Ger.	A contraction of Theobald
ULYSSES,	Greek,	A hater
URBAN,	Latin,	Of the town
URIAH,	Hebrew,	Light of the Lord
URIAN,	Danish,	A husbandman
URIEL,	Hebrew,	Light of God

VALENTINE, *Latin*, Strong
VICTOR, *Latin*, A conqueror
VINCENT, *Latin*, Conquering
VIVIAN, *Latin*, Lively
WALTER, *Old Ger.* Ruling the host
WILLIAM, *Old Ger.* Resolute helmet
WINFRED, *An Sax.* Win peace
ZABDIEL, *Hebrew*, Gift of God
ZACCHEUS, *Hebrew*, Innocent
ZACHARIAH } *Hebrew*, Remembered of the Lord
ZACHARY, }
ZADOK, *Hebrew*, Just
ZEBADIAH } *Hebrew* Gift of the Lord
ZEBEDEE, }
ZEBINA, *Hebrew*, Bought
ZECHARIAH *Hebrew*, Remembered of the Lord
ZEDEKIAH, *Hebrew*, Justice of the Lord
ZELOTES, *Greek*, A zealot
ZENAS, *Greek*, Gift of Jupiter
ZEPHANIAH, *Hebrew*, Hid of the Lord

ABIGAIL, *Hebrew*. My father's joy
ACHSA, *Hebrew*, Anklet
ADA, *Old Ger.* Happiness
ADALINE,
ADELA,
ADELAIDE, } *Old Ger.* Of noble birth
ADELIA,
ADELINA,
ADELINE,
AGATHA, *Greek*, Kind
AGNES, *Greek*. Pure
ALBERTA, *Old Ger.* Feminine of Albert
ALETHEA, *Greek*, Truth
ALEXANDRA. } *Greek*, Feminine of Alexander
ALEXANDRINA, }
ALICE, } *Old Ger.* Of noble birth
ALICIA, }
ALMIRA, *Arabic*, Lofty
ALTHEA, *Greek*, A healer
AMABEL, *Latin*, Lovable
AMANDA, *Latin*, Worthy to be loved
AMELIA, *Old Ger.* Busy
AMY, *Latin*, Beloved
ANGELICA, } *Greek*, Lovely
ANGELINA, }
ANN,
ANNA, } *Hebrew*, Grace
ANNE,
ANNETTE,
ANTOINETTE, *Greek*,
ANTONIA, *Latin*, } Inestimable
ANTONINA, *Latin*,
ARABELLA, *Latin*, A fair altar
AUGUSTA, *Latin*, Feminine of Augustus
AURELIA, *Latin*, Feminine of Aurelius
AURORA, *Latin*, Brilliant
AZUBAH, *Hebrew*, Deserted
BARBARA, *Greek*, Strange
BEATRICE, } *Latin*, Making happy
BEATRIX, }
BELINDA. (Uncertain)
BENEDICTA, *Latin*, Feminine of Benedictus
BERTHA, *Old Ger.* Beautiful
BLANCH, } *Teutonic*, White
BLANCHE, }
BONA, *Latin*, Good
BRIDGET, *Celt*, Strength
CAMILIA, *Latin*, Attendant at a sacrifice
CAROLINE, *Old Ger.* Feminine of Carolus
CASSANDRA, *Greek*, She who inflames with love
CATHARINA,
CATHARINE, } *Greek*, Pure
CATHERINE,

WHAT TO NAME THE BABY.

Name	Origin	Meaning
CECILIA, CECILY,	Latin,	Feminine of Cecil
CELESTINE,	Latin,	Heavenly
CELIA,	Latin,	Feminine of Coelius
CHARITY,	English,	
CHARLOTTE,	Old Ger.	Feminine of Charles
CHLOE,	Greek,	Blooming
CHRISTIANA, CHRISTINA,	Greek,	Feminine of Christianus
CICELY,	Latin,	
CLARA, CLARICE, CLARISSA,	Latin,	Illustrious
CLAUDIA,	Latin,	Feminine of Claudius
CLEMENTINA, CLEMENTINE,	Latin,	Mild
CONSTANCE,	Latin,	Firm
CORA,	Greek,	Maiden
CORDELIA,	Latin,	Warm-hearted
CORINNA,	Greek,	Maiden
CORNELIA,	Latin,	Feminine of Cornelius
CYNTHIA,	Greek,	Belonging to Mt. Cynthus
DEBORAH,	Hebrew,	A bee
DELIA,	Greek,	Of Delc
DIANA,	Latin,	Goddess
DIANTHA,	Greek,	A pink
DINAH,	Hebrew,	Judged
DORA,	Greek,	A contraction of Dorothea
DORCAS,	Greek,	A gazelle
DORINDA,	Greek,	The gift of God
DOROTHEA, DOROTHY,	Greek,	The gift of God
DRUSILLA,		(Uncertain)
EDITH,	Old Ger.	Happiness
EDNA,	Hebrew,	Pleasure
ELEANOR, ELINOR,	Greek,	Light
ELISABETH, ELIZABETH, ELIZA,	Hebrew,	Worshipper of God
ELLA, ELLEN,	Greek,	A contraction of Eleanor
ELVIRA,	Latin,	White
EMELINE, EMMELINE,	Old Ger.	Industrious
EMILY,	Old Ger.	Industrious
EMMA,	Old Ger.	Industrious
ERNESTINE,	Ger.	Fem. and dim. of Ernest
ESTHER,	Persian,	A star
ETHELIND, ETHELINDA,	Teutonic,	Noble snake
EUDORA,	Greek,	Good gift
EUGENIA, EUGENIE,	Greek,	Feminine of Eugene
EULALIA,	Greek,	Fair speech
EUNICE,	Greek,	Happy victory
EUPHEMIA,	Greek,	Of good report
EVA,	Hebrew,	Life
EVANGELINE,	Greek,	Bringing glad news
EVE, EVELINA, EVELINE,	Hebrew,	Life
FAITH,	English,	
FANNY,	German,	Free
FAUSTINA,	Latin,	Lucky
FELICIA,	Latin,	Happiness
FIDELIA,	Latin,	Faithful
FLORA,	Latin,	Flowers
FLORENCE,	Latin,	Blooming
FRANCES,	German,	Feminine of Francis
FREDERICA,	Old Ger.	Feminine of Frederick
GEORGIANA, GEORGINA,	Greek,	Feminine of George
GERALDINE,	Old Ger.	Feminine of Gerald
GERTRUDE,	Old Ger.	Spear-maiden
GRACE, GRATIA,	Latin,	Grace
GRISELDA,	Teutonic,	Snow-heroine
HANNAH,	Hebrew,	Grace
HARRIET, HARRIET,	Old Ger.	Fem. dim. of Henry

HELEN, HELENA,	Greek, Light	KETURAH,	Hebrew, Incense
		KEZIAH,	Hebrew, Cassia
HENRIETTA,	Old Ger. Fem. & dim. of Henry		
HEPHZIBAH,	Hebrew, My delight is in her	LAURA, LAURINDA,	Latin, A laurel
		LAVINIA,	Latin, Of Latium
HESTER, HESTHER,	Persian, A star	LEONORA,	Greek, Light
		LETITIA, LETTICE,	Latin, Happiness
HILARIA,	Latin, Feminine of Hilary	LILIAN, LILLY,	Latin, Lily
HONORA, HONORIA,	Latin, Honorable	LOIS,	Greek, Good
HOPE,	English,	LORINDA,	Latin, A laurel
HORTENSIA,	Latin, A lady gardener	LOUISA, LOUISE,	Old Ger. Feminine of Louis
HULDAH,	Hebrew, A weasel	LUCIA, LUCINDA,	Latin, Feminine of Lucius
IDA,	Old Ger. God-like	LUCRECE, LUCRETIA.	Latin, Gain
INEZ,	Greek, Pure		
IRENE,	Greek, Peaceful	LUCY,	Latin, Feminine of Lucius
ISABEL, ISABELLA,	Hebrew, Worshipper of God	LYDIA,	Greek, A native of Lydia
JANE, JANET,	Hebrew, Feminine of John		
		MABEL,	Latin, Lovable
JAQUELINE,	Hebrew, Feminine of James	MADELINE, MAGDALENE	Hebrew, Belonging to Magdala
JEAN, JEANNE, JEANNETTE,	Hebrew, Feminine of John	MARCELLA,	Latin, Feminine of Marcellus
		MARCIA,	Latin, Feminine of Marcius
JEMIMA,	Hebrew, A dove		
JERUSHA,	Hebrew, Married	MARGARET,	Greek, A pearl
JOAN, JOANNA, JOHANNA,	Hebrew, Feminine of John	MARIA,	Hebrew, Bitter
		MARIANNE,	Hebrew, Compound of Mary and Ann
JOSEPHA, JOSEPHINE,	Hebrew, Feminine of Joseph	MARION,	Hebrew, a French form of Mary
JOYCE,	Latin, Sportive	MARTHA,	Hebrew, The ruler of the house
JUDITH,	Hebrew, Praised		
JULIA,	Latin, Feminine of Julius	MARY,	Hebrew, Bitter
JULIANA,	Latin, Feminine of Julian	MATHILDA, MATILDA, MAUD,	Old Ger. Mighty battle-maid
JULIET,	Latin, Feminine of Julius	MAY,	The month of May
JUSTINA,	Latin, Feminine of Justin	MEHETABEL, MEHITABLE,	Hebrew, benefited
		MELICENT,	Latin, Sweet singer
KATHARINE, KATHERINE,	Greek, Pure	MELISSA,	Greek, A bee

Name	Origin	Meaning
MERCY,	English,	
MILDRED,	Ger.	Mild threatener
MIRANDA,	Latin,	Admirable
MIRIAM,	Hebrew,	Bitter
MYRA,	Greek,	She who weeps or laments
NANCY		A familiar form of Anne
NORA,		A contraction of Honora and Leonora
OCTAVIA,	Latin,	Feminine of Octavius
OLIVE, OLIVA,	Latin,	An olive
OPHELIA,	Greek,	Serpent
OLYMPIA,	Greek,	Heavenly
PATIENCE,	English,	
PAULA,	Latin,	Fem. of Paulus
PAULINA, PAULINE,	Latin,	Feminine of Paulinus
PENELOPE,	Greek,	A weaver
PERSIS,	Greek,	A Persian woman
PHEBE,	Greek,	Pure
PHILIPPA,	Greek,	Feminine of Philip
PHILLIS,	Greek,	A green bough
PHŒBE,	Greek,	Pure
PHYLLIS,	Greek,	A green bough
PRISCILLA,	Latin,	Somewhat old
PRUDENCE,	English,	
RACHEL,	Hebrew,	A ewe
REBECCA, REBEKAH,	Hebrew,	Of enchanting beauty
RHODA,	Greek,	A rose
ROSA,	Latin,	A rose
ROSABEL, ROSABELLA,	Latin,	A fair rose
ROSALIA, ROSALAE,	Latin,	Little and blooming rose
ROSALIND,	Latin,	Beautiful as a rose
ROSAMOND,	Teutonic,	Horse protection
ROXANA,	Persian,	Dawn of day
RUTH,	Hebrew,	Beauty
SABINA,	Latin,	A Sabine woman
SABRINA,	Latin,	The river Severn
SALOME,	Hebrew,	Peaceful
SALVA,	Latin,	Safe
SARA, SARAH,	Hebrew,	A princess
SELINA,	Greek,	Parsley
SERENA,	Latin,	Feminine of Sereno
SIBYL, SIBYLLA,	Greek,	A prophetess
SOPHIA,	Greek,	Wisdom
SOPHRONIA,	Greek,	Of a sound mind
STELLA,	Latin,	A star
STEPHANA,	Greek,	Feminine of Stephen
SUSAN, SUSANNA, SUSANNAH,	Hebrew,	A lily
TABITHA,	Syriac,	A gazelle
TEMPERANCE,	English	
THEODORA,	Greek,	Feminine of Theodore
THEODOSIA,	Greek,	The gift of God
THERESA,	Greek,	Carrying ears of corn
THOMAS, THOMASINE,	Hebrew,	Feminine of Thomas
TRYPHENA,	Greek,	Delicate
TRYPHOSA,	Greek,	Dainty
ULRICA,	Old Ger.	Rich
URANIA,	Greek,	Heavenly
URSULA,	Latin,	She-bear

VALERIA,	*Latin*,	Feminine of Valerius
VICTORIA,	*Latin*,	Victoria
VIDA,	*Erse*,	Feminine of David
VIOLA,	*Latin*,	A violet
VIRGINIA,	*Latin*,	Pure
VIVIAN,	*Latin*,	Lively
WILHELMINA,	*OldGer*.	Feminine of Wilhelm
WINIFRED,	*Teutonic*,	A lover of peace
ZENOBIA,	*Greek*,	Having life from Jupiter

INDEX.

	RECEIPT
A German dish	138
A good restorative (1)	1242
" (2)	1243
" (3)	1244
" A pleasant drink	1245
Accidents from edge tools, &c.	1297
" " substances in the eye (1)	1298
" " " (2)	1299
" " " (3)	1300
" " " (4)	1301
" " substances in the ear (1)	1302
" " " (2)	1303
" " " (3)	1304
" " " (4)	1305
" " substances in the throat (1)	1306
" " " (2)	1307
" " " (3)	1308
" " " (4)	1309
Ale or beer, to recover flat	1136
Mulled	1137
Almonds & raisins for dessert.	910
Annisette	1140
Apoplexy	1319
Apples, dessert of	913
" and rice, stewed	901
" " spiced	902
Artichokes, with white sauce	446
Au gratin	452
Fried	450
Mashed	449
Stewed	451
With cream	447
With gravy	448
Asparagus	442
" and eggs	444
" in ambush	443
" pudding	445

	RECEIPT
Beans, Haricot (1)	410
" " (2)	411
" French	414
" " to preserve	415
" Lima	412
" " and butter	413
Beef, fillets of, with olives	161
A la mode	166
Braized	178
Cake (cold meat cookery)	168
Collops	171
Corned	167
(Cold meat cookery)	169
Fillets of, a la Chateaubriand	164
Grenadins of	162
Hunter's	180
Olives	175
Omelet	177
Sausages	172
Spiced	159
Stewed (1)	165
" (2)	179
Tea, quickly made (1)	1223
" (2)	1224
" savory	1226
Tongue	184
Beefsteak pudding	160
" pie	163
" bruized	182
" stuffed	176
Beer, hop	1138
Nettle	1139
Bee sting, to remove	1282
Beet roots	382
Beets, to pickle	485
Bifsteck, saute	183
Biscuits, seed	622
Cocoanut	692
Graham	588

	RECEIPT		RECEIPT
Biscuits (continued)—		Bread (continued)—	
Hard	697	Rice	579
Lemon	591	" and wheat	567
Milk	590	Rye	576
Oatmeal	689	Soda	581
Of fruit	698	White	564
Orange	688	Yeast	565
Plain, and very crisp	697	Broth, Scotch mutton	7
Rice	694	A splendid, for weakness	1218
Rock	690	Beef	1215
Soda	695	Beef, simple way of making	1221
"	589	" mutton and veal	1219
Biscuit baking powder	591	Calves' feet	1220
" " for babies	693	Chicken	1211
Bites of snakes	1283	Eel	1213
Of dogs	1284	Egg	1212
Blanc-mange, isinglass	885	Hasty	1217
Almond	892	Scotch	1216
Chocolate	890	Veal	1210
Clear	886	Bruises	1280
Corn-flour	888	Bunions, treatment of	1335
Ribbon	889	Bubble and squeak (cold meat	
Rice	887	cookery)	176
Strengthening	1255	Bullock's heart, roast	173
Blister, to raise a, speedily	1346	Buns	603
Bloater toast	87	Easter	604
Brandy, caraway	1209	Spanish	602
Cherry, excellent (1)	1207	Buttermilk	1086
" " (2)	1208	Butter, preserving	1083
Lemon	1206	Apple	1090
Orange	1205	A pretty dish of	1095
Bread & cake, observations p.	164	Curled	1092
Bread, American corn	582	Daisy	1093
Brown (1)	569	Maitre d'Hotel	1088
" (2)	570	Melted	1094
" (3)	571	To serve as a little dish	1091
" (4)	572	Water cress	1089
" (5)	573	Cabbage, boiled	363
" steamed	574	A la cauliflower	364
" Boston, delicious		A la creme	367
and genuine	575	En ragout	366
Corn, steamed, (Canadian)	577	Farce, or stuffed	365
" " baked	578	Red, to pickle	478
French	568	" to stew	370
Home-made (1)	562	Cake, a rich plum	629
" (2)	563	Almond	638
Omelet	580	" icing for	621
Plain	566	Apple	654

	RECEIPT		RECEIPT
Cake (continued)—		Cake (continued)—	
Buckwheat	609	Short, Scotch	666
Buttermilk	607	" Spanish	664
Charlotte, a la Polonaise	675	Shrewsbury	683
Chocolate (1)	668	Silver	676
" (2)	669	Soda	625
Cocoanut	677	Spice	642
Corn starch	685	Sponge	658
Cream and chocolate	639	Sponge jelly	612
Drop ginger	648	" rolled	614
Economical fruit	626	Squash	662
Ginger cup	643	Strawberry, short	663
" nuts (1)	644	Tipsy	651
" " (2)	645	" sauce	652
" bread	646	Washington	665
Hickory nut	660	White bride	681
Indian meal, breakfast	617	Without eggs	673
" loaf	637	Calf's head, collared	218
Italian sponge	659	Hashed (1)	225
Jelly rolls	613	" (2)	226
Johnny	616	" a la poulette	222
Lemon	671	Canned fruits, cherries	1040
Malaga	674	Peaches (1)	1027
Marble spice	684	" (2)	1028
Metropolitan	656	" (3)	1029
Milk and butter	611	" (4)	1041
Mush	608	Pears (1)	1030
New York plum	627	" (2)	1037
Plain Fruit (1)	623	Pineapples	1031
" " (2)	624	Plums (1)	1032
Plain luncheon	682	" (2)	1038
Plum	628	Strawberries	1039
Potato	686	Capers, to pickle	481
Queen's (1)	640	Caper sauce, an excellent	
" (2)	641	substitute for	536
Rice (1)	633	Carrots, to boil	420
" (2)	635	Stewed	421
Rich rice	634	Carottes, glacees	422
" bride	680	Cassis	1151
Rose jelly	615	Caudle	1261
Rye batter	610	Cauliflower, boiled	433
Scotch snow	678	Fried	434
" oat	679	Scalloped	435
Seed	630	Celery, puree of	234
" good	631	Champagne cup	1152
Short blackberry	665	Rhubarb	1194
" Raspberry or Huckleberry	667	Charlotte Russe (1)	895
		" (2)	896

INDEX.

	RECEIPT
Charlotte Russe (3)	897
Apple	903
Cherries, canned	1036
Cherokee	539
Chestnuts, to keep for winter use	1025
Cheese cakes, curd	864
Curd for	1115
Lemon	863
Cheese, a cheap and nutritious dish of	1116
Apple	1105
Cream (1)	1098
" (2)	1099
" (3)	1100
" (4)	1101
" (5)	1102
" (6)	1103
Dish	1111
Muscle plum	1109
Parmesan fondue	1113
Potted (1)	1107
" (2)	1118
Roast	1108
Sago	1104
Stewed	1114
Straws (1)	1106
" (2)	1120
Toast (1)	1110
" (2)	1112
To make	1096
To preserve sound	1057
Chicken patties	118
A la jardinière	122
Braided, with mushrooms	131
Croquettes	126
Cutlets, with rice	121
Jellied	124
Rissoles	123
To pull (1)	127
" (2)	128
Chilblains, ointment for	1345
Chocolate icing for cakes, simple	622
To prepare	1128
" for sick room	1247
Chou rouge, en quartiers	368
Aux pommes	369

	RECEIPT
Chou rouge (continued)—	
Marine	371
Chutnee, green gooseberry	540
Himalaya	543
My mother's	542
Claret cup	1160
Cocoa, to make	1127
Cod's head and shoulders, boiled (1)	45
" (2)	46
Cod, salt	47
Balls	53
Crimped, and oyster sauce	51
Curry of	48
Fish cakes	50
Roes	49
Stakes, with mock oyster sauce	52
Coffee, how to refine	1124
Another method of making	1126
Milk	1129
Cold	1325
An excellent remedy for a	1324
Cold, how to prevent	1326
Colorings for confectionary p. 253	
Pink	924
Red	925
Cherry red	926
Blue	927
Yellow	928
Green	929
Brown	930
For soups or gravies	297
Cordial, a strong	1172
White currant	1171
Corn, boiled	429
Green, stewed	428
Roasted	430
Cough	1327
A nice drink for a	1262
Hooping	1313
Crab, hot	70
Boiled	71
Mock, dressed	72
Soft	73
Cracknels	687
Cramp	1332
Cranberry drink	1130

INDEX.

	RECEIPT
Cream, almond	964
Brandy	956
Burnt (1)	945
" (2)	946
Caramel	950
Chocolate	960
" ice	932
Clouted	1084
Coffee	961
" ice	931
Crystal palace	958
Dutch	949
French rice	957
Ginger	968
Ice (1)	933
" (2)	935
" from milk	937
Italian ice	934
Lemon	962
" solid	963
" made without cream	952
Orange	954
Parisienne,	947
Pine apple	948
Raspberry	955
Ratafia	953
Soda	1167
Strawberry	951
Substitute for	944
Tapioca	969
Tea	965
To manage for whey butter	1087
Velvet	959
Whipped	966
" for a trifle	967
Cream of tartar whey	1162
Croup	1334
Cucumbers, to dress	403
A la maitre d'hotel	406
A la poulette	408
Fircis	407
Fried	405
Frits	409
Pickled	482
Stewed	404
Currants, frosted	911
Curries, observations on, page	93

	RECEIPT
Curry	281
A Turkish dish	277
A dry Malay	274
Boiled rice for	278
Dry	287
Indian	271
Mutton	273
Potato (1)	283
" (2)	284
" (3)	285
" (4)	286
Powder	270
Curried beef	280
Eggs	279
Lobster	275
Rabbit	272
Tripe	282
Custard	986
Almond	983
" boiled	982
Apple	989
Baked	987
Beef tea	1225
Boiled	981
Caramel	992
Chocolate	990
For cake	998
" sick room	1260
French	991
Frozen, with fruit	985
Orange	984
Snow	993
Dessert, observations on fruit, etc.	248
Impromptu	912
Devonshire junket	908
Diarrhœa	1314
Diptheria	1315
Sulphur treatment of	1316
Diseases of infants	1310
Doughnuts	606
Draughts, effervescing saline	1174
Drink, a nice	1264
A fever (1)	1265
" (2)	1266
Drowned, how to restore a person apparently	1278

INDEX.

	RECEIPT
Dumplings, apple, boiled	702
Currant	703
Lemon	705
Norfolk	704
Oxford	738
Dyspepsia, heartburn and acidity	1346
Ear, deficiency of wax in the	1338
Accumulation of wax in the	1339
Eel pie	109
Eels, to boil	110
Egg plant, baked	424
Eggs, observations on...page	147
A la soubise	494
A la maitre d'hotel	495
Au gratin	491
Buttered	498
Fried (1)	499
" (2)	500
" with black butter	501
Fried, with tomatoes	502
" " bacon	503
" " ham	504
In cases	497
Pickled	484
Poached, on toast	486
" on ham toast	487
" and spinach	488
" and minced chicken	489
" on a puree of game	490
Scrambled, with asparagus	506
" " tomatoes	507
" " onions	508
" " fish	509
" " ham	510
" " cheese	511
" " on toast	512
Stewed	493
Stuffed	492
To keep fresh for several weeks	525
With sorrel	496
Egg tea toast	1252
Epilepsy,	1319
" Dr. Cullen's treatment of	1320

	RECEIPT
Eyes, for weak, or inflamed (1)	1337
" (2)	1338
Fever, typhoid	1317
" scarlet	1312
Figs, dish of	914
Fish, observations on ...page	31
Croquettes	113
Pate	69
Fits	1317
Flavors, bisque	940
Chocolate ice cream	941
Fruit ice cream	942
" ices	943
Lemon	939
Vanilla	938
Floating island	906
Flummery (1)	881
" (2)	882
Dutch	884
Rice	883
Forcemeats, observations on p.	161
Forcemeat, to force fowls or meat	549
Balls for mock turtle	554
" for soup	555
Common, for veal or hare	551
For cold savory pie	550
" pulled turkey	151
" fish soups	552
Oyster, for roast or boiled turkey	556
Very fine balls, for fish soups, or stewed fish	553
Fowl, to boil	119
Braized, with macaroni	130
Galatine of	129
Stewed in barley	1228
To roast	120
Fractures	1277
Freckles, lotion to remove	1343
Fritters, apple	848
Cheese	851
Cream	846
Custard	850
Orange (1)	843
" (2)	844

INDEX.

	RECEIPT
Fritters (continued)—	
Plain	849
Raspberry	853
Rice	847
Spanish	845
Frothing, excellent for cakes	620
Froth, for	907
Fruits, mixed dish of	920
Canned	page 279
Compote of	921
To bottle	1038
Stone, to bottle	1040
Game, chaufroid	149
Espec	150
Puree of	132
Garlic vinegar	546
Gateau de Savoie, French sponge cake	657
Genoise, chocolate	826
Almond	827
Giblets, to stew	130
Ginger, apple	919
Biscuits	649
Snaps	650
Gingerbread, honeycomb	647
Gingerette, Spanish	1149
Ginger beer (1)	1146
" (2)	1147
" powders	1144
Cordial	1148
Liqueur	1145
Pop	1150
Gooseberry fool	898
Gooseberries, green, to bottle	1039
Grapes, in brandy	1024
Gravy, for pulled turkey	152
A good beef, for poultry or game	288
For roast meat	290
" venison	291
" hashes	294
" a fowl, when there is no meat to make it from	295
Savory, thick	289
Sippets	1241

	RECEIPT
Gravy (continued)—	
Strong fish	292
Veal	296
Gravies, general directions respecting	page 99
Coloring for soups or	297
Gruel, water	1256
Effervescing	1257
Barley	1258
Egg	1259
Haddock, with tomatoes	112
Halibut, baked	115
Boiled	114
Stake	116
Ham, baked	201
How to boil to give it an excellent flavor	199
Potted	200
To glaze a	202
Haricot beans, puree of	233
Headache	1327
Bilious, or sick	1329
Health, rules for the preservation of	1348
Hemorrhage	1281
Herbs, to dry	533
Herb powder, for winter use	544
Herrings, red, to dress	85
Baked, or sprats	86
Hiccough	1331
Hominy (1)	973
" (2)	974
" and cheese	1117
Baked	1253
Hooping Cough	1313
Hysteria	1321
Hysterics	1341
Iceland Moss	1067
Ices and creams	page 255
Icing for cakes (1)	618
" " (2)	619
Jam, apple	1009
Apricot, or plum	1004
Blackberry	1003

	RECEIPT		RECEIPT
Jam (continued)—		Jelly (cont...ned)—	
Black currant	996	Quince (1)	1050
Cherry	1007	" (2)	1062
Damson	999	" and apple	1063
Gooseberry	998	Raspberry	1069
Green grape	1002	Red currant	1052
Mulberry	1000	Red gooseberry	1059
Plum	994	Sago	1077
Quince	1008	Shank	1235
Raspberry	997	Sweet wine	1075
Red currant	995	Tapioca	1237
Rhubarb	1001	White currant	1054
Strawberry	1005	Jumbo pickle	477
" or barberry	1006	Jumbles	636
Jannemange	891		
Jellies, observations on	page 284	Ketchups, observations on,	page 156
Jelly, a nice	1071	Ketchup, a useful	547
A tasty	1082	Lemon	527
Apple (1)	1064	Mushroom	526
" (2)	1076	Oyster, without the liquor	548
Arrowroot	1236	Tomato (1)	528
Aspic	1079	" (2)	529
Barberry	1056	Walnut	530
Black currant	1053		
Blackberry	1055	Lady fingers	661
Cherry	1051	Lamb, epigrammes of	251
Claret	1080	Chops	255
Crab apple	1049	Fry, French	1231
Cranberry and rice	1081	Stewed	254
Fruit	1046	Tails of	256
Gloucester	1239	Lard, to make	253
Green gooseberry	1058	Leaves, to frost	923
Hartshorn	1072	Lemon kali	1143
Ivory	1073	Lemons, to pickle	480
Lemon	1069	Lemonade (1)	1132
Macedoine de fruits a la gelles	1078	" (2)	1133
		Milk	1134
Meat	1238	Liquors, to refine	1180
Medlar	1057	Lobster croquets	67
Milk	1068	" "	68
Mixed fruit	1061	Potted	64
Mulled	1048	" as at Queen's hotel	65
Orange	1070	To boil	63
Peach	1066	To dress	66
Pineapple	1047		
Pork	1234	Macaroni	1122
Punch	1074	A la runi	1123

	RECEIPT		RECEIPT
Maccaroons	672	Mutton (continued)—	
Mackerel	92	Kidneys, grilled	265
Pickled, called caveade	93	" with macaroni	266
Scalloped	94	Kidney toast	267
Maids of honor	865	" a l'Indienne	268
Marma'ade, apple	1018	Pudding	250
Orange	1017	Shoulder of, boiled with	
Quince	1016	oysters	257
Measles	1311		
Meats, observations on, page	61	Nasturtium for capers	537
Meat juice	1222	Nervous anxiety, to remove	1341
Milk, butter and cheese, ob-		Neuralgia	1333
servations on page	294	Nougats, small	653
Milk rice	1274	Noyeau	1165
Mincemeat, without meat	743	"	1166
With meat	744	Nuts, dish of	915
Mouton cornettes de	247		
A l'Italienne	248	Oatmeal, drink	1131
Muffins, breakfast	593	Omelet, cheese	517
Graham	594	Fish	522
Oatmeal	596	Ham, or bacon	516
Rice	595	Kidney	524
Mullet, baked	95	Mushroom	521
Red, called the sea wood-		Oyster	523
cock	96	Plain	514
With tomatoes	97	Savory	515
Mush	1227	Tomato (1)	518
Mushrooms	389	" (2)	519
A la creme	393	" (3)	520
Baked	392	Onions, boiled	383
Broiled	391	" pickled (1)	474
Essence of	395	" " (2)	475
Pickled	479	Spanish, a la Grecque	384
Powder	396	" baked	385
Ragout of	394	" stewed	386
Stewed	390	Stuffed	388
Mustard, French	541	Oranges, chartreuse of	1065
To make	531	Compote of	893
" for immediate use	532	Orange chips	904
Mutton, boned leg stuffed	253	Fool	894
Cutlets	229	For dessert	909
" delicate	1230	Souffle	905
Chartreuse of	245	Orangeade	1135
Croquettes of	246	Ox tougue, baked	181
Haricot	249	Oysters, stewed (1)	74
Kidneys a la brochette	263	" " (2)	79
" fried	264	Angels on horseback	81

	RECEIPT
Oysters (continued)—	
Boiled	75
Broiled	77
Cream on the half she'l	82
Fried, to garnish boiled fish	78
Patties	83
Sausages	80
Scalloped	76
Panada, chicken	1240
Pancakes, English	815
French (1)	811
" (2)	812
Irish	814
Rice	813
Parsley, to keep for winter use	545
Parsnips	397
American fashion	398
Buttered	399
Fried	401
Fricassed	402
Mashed	400
Paste, for mince pies	831
Light, for tarts	823
Potato	839
Puff	833
Pyramid	830
Pastry and puddings, observations on	page 198
Pastry, almond (1)	828
" " (2)	829
For sweet sandwiches	832
Genoise (1)	824
" (2)	825
To ice or glaze	821
Venison	785
Peaches	1037
In brandy	1022
Canned (1)	1027
" (2)	1028
" (3)	1029
" (4)	1037
Pears, canned	1033
For dessert	1041
Moulded dish of	918

	RECEIPT
Peas, puree of, to serve with epigrammes of lamb	252
A la Francaise	439
Au sucre	440
En puree	441
Green, to keep	436
" as practised in the Emperor of Russia's kitchen	437
Stewed	438
Perch and tench	88
And trout, to boil	91
Perspiration, to produce	1343
Petit choux, a la creme	866
Picalilli, to pickle	483
Pickles, observations on	143
Pickle, sweet tomato	1020
Sweet peach	1021
Pie, apple	816
"	817
Beefsteak and oysters	791
Black currant	804
Chicken	789
Cocoanut	805
Cottage	779
Damson	802
Eel (1)	781
" (2)	782
Giblet	790
Gooseberry	801
Hare	786
Lemon (1)	796
" (1)	797
" (3)	798
Macaroni	788
Marlborough	810
Mutton	795
Orange and apple	818
Oyster	792
Peach	799
Pigeon	783
Pudding	806
Pumpkin (1)	807
" (2)	808
" (3)	809
Raised beefsteak	784
" French	787

	RECEIPT		RECEIPT
Pie (continued)—		Potatoes (continued)—	
Red currant and raspberry	803	To mash	349
Rhubarb	800	" roast	347
Veal	793	Poultry and game, observa-	
" chicken and parsley	794	tions on	page 49
York	780	Powders, seidlitz	1173
Pickles, observations on,	page 143	Preserves, observations on	p. 268
Pig, sucking, roast	195	Preserve, citron	1012
Pig's pettitoes	196	Green fig	1010
Fry	191	Melon	1011
Pigeons	146	Orange	1015
To boil	141	Pumpkin	1013
To roast	142	Quince, whole	1014
Pineapples	1031	Pudding, a good baked	754
Plaster, warming	1347	Almond	699
Plums	1032	Amber	700
Canned	1034	Apple, boiled	701
Polish dish	174	" baked	706
Pop-overs	605	Bakewell	707
Pork cheese	197	Butter	708
Cutlets	194	Bread	709
Hashed	193	Brown bread	710
Leg of, to roast	185	Cabinet	735
" to boil	186	Caramel	711
Loin and neck of	187	Carrot (1)	712
Neck of, rolled	189	Carrot (2)	713
Pickled	192	Charlotte	716
Pie	190	Christmas	747
Shoulders and breast of	188	College	736
Porridge, milk	1248	Company	732
French	1249	Cream tapioca	762
Potato balls	356	Currant, boiled	717
Cake	359	" bun	718
Chips	358	Custard	771
Potatoes, Bermuda, fried	353	Favorite	727
Escalloped	357	" Florentine	767
Lyonnaise	351	French tapioca	764
Saratoga	352	Fruit	741
Sautees au beurre	354	Ginger	720
Stewed	355	Gingerbread	719
Sweet, roast	360	Graham	778
" boiled	361	Ground rice	761
" fried	362	Holiday	733
" Stuffed	350	Ice	749
To boil	345	Indian corn flour	773
" broil	346	Layer	742
" fry	348	Lemon (1)	725

INDEX.

	RECEIPT
Puddings (continued)—	
Lemon (2)	726
Macaroni	770
Marrow (1)	739
" (2)	740
Martha's	714
Marmalade (1)	728
" (2)	729
" sauce for	730
Newcastle	757
Oatmeal	772
Orange (1)	721
" (2)	722
" (3)	723
Peas	715
Plain rice	758
Plum	745
" an excellent	746
" a tetotaller's	747
Raspberry	752
Red currant	751
Rice and raisin	755
" and apple	760
" custard	759
Roly poly jam	750
Seminole	768
Sir Watkin Wynne's	756
Shropshire	724
Sponge cake	731
Steamed	737
Steak	777
Sunday	774
Sweet potato	753
" macaroni	769
Swiss	748
Tapioca	763
Tea cake	731
Velvet	765
" sauce for	766
Yorkshire (1)	775
" (2)	776
Puffs, almond	854
Chocolate	862
Cream	858
For dessert	855
Graham	860
Lemon	861

	RECEIPT
Puffs (continued)—	
Orange	859
Plain	856
Spanish	857
Puffetts, apple	875
Pumpkins, stewed	453
Baked	454
Quail pie	134
Roasted, with ham	135
Quinces, brandied	1023
Quinsy	1323
Rabbit pie	136
Stewed	137
" for sick room	1232
Raspberry, drink	1161
Acid	1159
Ratafias	670
Quince	1141
Rennet, to prepare	1085
Rice milk, ground	1250
Ricotta	1121
Rolls, breakfast	687
Butter	584
Swiss	586
Vienna	585
Roux, brown, a thickening for soups and gravies	327
White, for thickening white sauces	328
Rusks	583
Sage and onion stuffing for pork, ducks, geese, &c.	557
Sago cream	1246
Milk	1251
Salads, observations on, page 137	
Salad	455
Anchovy	463
Beet root	468
Celery	469
Dressing, Rev. Sydney Smith's receipt for	471
Egg	466
Game	464
Lettuce	456

INDEX. 399

Salad (continued)—	RECEIPT
Lobster	461
Oyster	472
Potato (1)	457
" (2)	458
" (3)	459
" (4)	460
Red cabbage	470
Russian	467
Sardine	462
Sally lunn	592
Salmon, dressed, Italian sauce	60
Dried	58
Fresh, to boil	61
Fried, with anchovy sauce	59
Salt, to souse	54
To broil	55
To pot	56
To dry	57
Salsify, boiled	423
Sarsaparilla, simple decoction	1177
Compound decoction of	1178
Sauces, observations on, page	102
Sauce, a cheap brown	322
Anchovy	315
Bread, for poultry or game	334
Brown, Genevoise	321
Caper	336
Cauliflower	309
Chesnut (1)	235
" (2)	236
" for roast duck	153
Cranberry	323
Dutch	311
Egg	307
Fennel	303
Governor's, a Canadian recipe	308
Grill	314
Hollandais	329
Horse radish	318
Italian (1)	237
" (2)	238
Liver	302
Mango Chutnee, Bengal recipe	306

Sauce (continued)—	RECEIPT
Mayonnaise	319
Mint	315
Mushroom (1)	239
" (2)	240
" (3)	310
Onion, brown	326
Oyster	332
Peach	324
Piquante, without eggs	312
Plum pudding	325
Poor man's	320
Remoulade	317
Shrimp	304
Soubise (1)	231
" (2)	232
Sweet	316
" for venison	335
Tartare	331
Tomato (1)	330
" (2)	241
" (3)	242
" (4)	243
" (5)	244
Wine	305
White	298
" Allemande	301
" Supreme	300
" Velante	299
Worcester	333
Sausages	198
Scalds and burns	1279
Scarlet fever	1312
Shad and herrings, to pot	84
Sherbet powder	1163
Persian	1164
Sippets, fried	513
Smelts, to fry	108
Snuff, cephalic	1328
Soles (1)	98
" (2)	99
" (3)	101
Au gratin	102
Fillets of, a l'Indienne	100
Souffle, apple	976
A la Viceroy, hot	980
Chocolate (1)	977

	RECEIPT
Souffle (continued)—	
Chocolate (2)	978
Egg	971
Of bread and walnuts	972
Rice	975
Small cheese	979
Soups, observations on, page.	17
Soup a la Dauphine	25
Almond (1)	31
" (2)	41
Apple	24
Asparagus	45
Barley, creme d'orge	32
Beef gravy	17
Brown chicken	16
Calf's head	13
Celery	21
Crowdie, or Scotch	1
Eel	42
French	10
Giblet	12
Good gravy	6
Greek	11
Green pea	20
Hare	35
Julienne	26
Lobster, bisque	33
Macaroni	2
Made from bones	34
Milk	3
" with vermicelli	19
Mock turtle (1)	38
" (2)	39
Mullagatawney (1)	14
" (2)	27
Onion	40
Oyster, a la reine	15
Oxtail clear	36
" thick	37
Rice flour	18
Roast beef and boiled turkey	8
Spanish (1)	28
" (2)	29
" (3)	30
Tapioca	4

	RECEIPT
Soup (continued)..	
Tomato (1)	22
" (2)	43
Veal and lamb	9
White	23
Spinach	343
Sprains, treatment of	1285
Squashes, summer	431
" winter	432
Stocks, observations on, page	112
Common	337
Fish	341
Gravy	338
Veal	339
White	340
Strawberries, dish of	916
And cream	922
Canned	1035
Sick room cookery	1254
Stuffing for pickle, haddock and small cod	117
Sturgeon, fresh	104
To roast	103
Stye	1335
Summer drink	1142
Sweet dishes, observations on page	240
Sweetbreads	258
" Sick room	1233
Lambs	262
Larded	261
Ragout	260
Roasted	269
Syllabub, lemon	877
Solid	880
Whipped (1)	878
" (2)	879
Syrups for canned fruit (1)	1042
" " (2)	1043
" " (3)	1044
" " (4)	1045
Currant and raspberry	1176
Tart, almond	867
Apple (1)	819
" (2)	872
" (3)	873
" (4)	874

	RECEIPT		RECEIPT
Tart (continued)—		Veal (continued)—	
Cherries	870	Cutlets	220
Greengage	868	Fricandeau of	216
Tartlets, apple	871	Gelantine	228
" Raspberry and currant	869	Haricot of	221
Rice paste for	820	Mashed	213
Tea, or coffee, with eggs	1125	Minced	223
Camomile	1275	Pudding	210
Dandelion	1276	Quenelles of	215
Toast and water	1263	Roast, stuffed	207
Tomato pie	377	Rolled	217
Fritters	379	Sausages	219
Tomatoes, au gratin	378	Stewed	208
Baked	373	Trimballs of	227
Broiled	380	Vegetables, observations on p.	114
Raw	381	Vegetable marrow, fried	426
Stewed	372	Roasted	430
Stuffed	374	Stuffed	1229
With macaroni (1)	375	To boil or stew (1)	342
" " (2)	376	" " (2)	427
Trifle, a very fine	899	With ginger	1019
Gooseberry or apple	900	Venison, breast of stewed	155
Tripe, to dress	204	Hashed,	156
Fried	205	Roast haunch of	154
Stewed	206	Vinegar, Chili	538
Trout and grayling, to fry	89	Currant	1157
A la Genevoise	90	Horse-radish	535
Truffle and chesnut stuffing	146	Mint	534
Sauce	147	Primrose	1156
Turbot, au Mayonnaise	105	Plant (1)	1153
Au gratin, a nice dish for		" (2)	1154
luncheon	107	Raspberry	1158
Fillet of, with Dutch sauce	106	Sugar	1155
Turkey, braized	145		
Pulled	148	Waffles	599
To roast (1)	143	Rice	600
" (2)	144	without yeast	601
Turnips, a la creme	418	Walnuts, pickled	476
A la de maitre	419	To keep fresh	1026
Boiled	416	Water, distilled	1169
German recipe for cooking	417	Apple	1267
Turnovers, apple	876	Barley	1269
		Currant	1268
Veal, braized loin of	224	Gooseberry, currant, rasp-	
And ham pie	209	berry and strawberry	1169
Veal cake (1)	211	Peppermint	1270
" " (2(	212	Rhubarb	1170

INDEX.

	RECEIPT
Whey, vinegar, used in fevers	1271
Wine	1272
White bait	111
Whitings, fried	62
Wild duck, roast	133
Stewed	157
Wines and brandies, page	318
Wine, bottling of	1179
Apricot	1187
Blackberry	1195
Black currant	1202
Cherry	1192
Damson	1188
Elder, black or white	1198
Falsified	1181
Family, excellent	1197
Ginger	1191
Gooseberry (1)	1189
" (2)	1190

	RECEIPT
Wine (continued)—	
Grape (1)	1185
" (2)	1186
Lemon	1184
Malt	1204
Mulled	1273
Orange	1203
Raisin	1196
Raspberry (1)	1199
" (2)	1200
" and currant	1201
Rhubarb, Stone's patent	1193
To mull (1)	1182
" (2)	1183
Woodcock	158
Yeast (1)	558
" (2)	559
Compressed	560
Potato	561

www.ingramcontent.com/pod-product-compliance
Lightning Source LLC
Chambersburg PA
CBHW020106010526
44115CB00008B/712